WOMEN
A PSYCHOLOGICAL PERSPECTIVE

ELAINE DONELSON
MICHIGAN STATE UNIVERSITY

JEANNE E. GULLAHORN
MICHIGAN STATE UNIVERSITY

JOHN WILEY & SONS
NEW YORK
SANTA BARBARA
LONDON
SYDNEY
TORONTO

Cover photo by Tom Heyman.

Copyright © 1977, by John Wiley & Sons, Inc.

Library of Congress Cataloging in Publication Data:
Main entry under title:

Women : a psychological perspective.

  Bibliography: p.
  Includes index.
  1. Women—Psychology. 2. Women—United States.
I. Donelson, Elaine. II. Gullahorn, Jeanne E.
HQ1206.W8   155.6'33   76-54924
ISBN 0-471-21779-4
ISBN 0-471-21781-6 pbk.

Printed in the United States of America

10 9 8 7 6 5 4 3 2 1

LOVINGLY DEDICATED TO
LITTLE BAREFOOT, PETER, AND TIMOTHY
AND TO
LAURIE, LESLIE, GREG, AND JOHN GULLAHORN

PREFACE

The recent women's movement has generated determined optimism and enthusiastic persistence in striving to liberate all people from the constraints of traditional sex roles. It also has generated an entrenchment behind defenses of the status quo. Most people of either persuasion feel that they are being open, fair-minded, and factual in developing and defending their position. Yet, other people often feel confused and in conflict after hearing polarized presentations.

Part of the problem people encounter in drawing conclusions and sharing their views with others is lack of accurate information. In this book we shall not be pronouncing "correct opinion" about issues that often extend beyond the domain of psychology. We shall discuss what is currently known about women's psychological functioning and the nature and consequences of sex differences. Firm and simple conclusions are seldom appropriate because of the complexities so far revealed by available research.

Although the book is intended primarily for undergraduates in psychology or women's studies courses, it can provide a sound foundation also for graduate students and laypersons not in formal courses. This is a well-documented, solid psychology book; but it is not an exhaustive, encyclopedic collection of technical facts and research controversies. We aimed for a balance between scholarly thoroughness and meaningfulness to the general audience, encouraging authors to synthesize as much as they felt appropriate.

Similarly, we attempted to provide continuity to unite the perspectives of individual authors and their content areas. Given the current state of knowledge, these syntheses are preliminary; they are intended as heuristic prods for the reader's own thinking and observation and for continuing professional research. We do believe, though, that our attempted integration will falter less under scientific scrutiny than the attempts of many previous psychologists to perpetuate popular but unfounded negative stereotypes about women. Nevertheless, some readers of earlier manuscripts have expressed discomfort because our presentations indicate that many preconceptions about women are *mis*conceptions without empirical support.

In contrast, other readers have criticized our failure to consistently praise women and to censure "male oppressors." We did not consider such a position appropriate. Some also have questioned our including four male psychologists among the nine contributors to the book. We selected authors on the basis of their professional expertise and their earlier supportive contribution to the psychology of women course that we developed at Michigan State University. Many people automatically undervalue works of women, as documented in this volume; we did not wish to repeat this genetic fallacy of discounting a product on the basis of the sex of its author.

Furthermore, the work on this book has been a truly consciousness raising experience for all of us. We were able to share the similarities and differences in our views that have resulted from our experiences as women and men, as well as professionals in diverse fields. Our increased knowledge and sensitivity have had benefits for our work as colleagues, teachers, and researchers. We hope our readers will experience similar benefits from sharing and cooperative discussion about the issues raised.

Many people have contributed emotional support and helpful suggestions as we worked on this volume. We appreciate the contributions of our families, friends, undergraduate and graduate students, colleagues, and our editor, Jack Burton. We hope we offer through this book some support to many other women and men who are trying to understand what it means to be developing toward personhood.

ELAINE DONELSON
JEANNE GULLAHORN

East Lansing, Michigan

CONTENTS

WOMEN
A PSYCHOLOGICAL PERSPECTIVE

PART ONE
GENERAL ORIENTATION

CHAPTER
1
UNDERSTANDING THE PSYCHOLOGY OF WOMEN

Every woman is like all other women, like some other women, and like no other women. Every woman is like all men, like some men, and like no men.

In short, every person is like all other persons, like some other persons, and like no other persons (Kluckhohn & Murray, 1964).

(The social scientists who originally published this observation used the terms *men* and *man* instead of *person(s)*. We ask their understanding for our change of words.)

When, and in what ways, are women like each other and when are they different? When, and in what ways are women and men like each other, and when are they different? To a large extent, the psychology of women is formed of such questions. This book presents some of the answers that are currently available.

WHY A BOOK ON WOMEN?

Why not a book about the psychology of *persons* rather than the psychology of *women?* Or why not, at least, a book on sex differences rather than on women per se? Is not attention to women specifically an example of sexual discrimination? In limited perspective, yes; in broad perspective, no. There has been a neglect and misrepresentation of women that must be corrected before we can hope to have a psychology of persons. This correction is better made by concentrating on women rather than focusing only on sex differences, though the topic of sex differences is an important part of this endeavor.

Just as folklore among laypersons contains many assumptions about women that are considered "just obvious" and not needing examination, so too there are many unexamined—and often sexist—assumptions held by psychologists. For example, a professional expert on aggression wrote in a prominent book,

. . . it is highly probable that the *undoubted* superiority of the male sex in intellectual and creative achievement is related to their greater endowment of aggression. . . . The hypothesis that women, if only given the opportunity and encouragement, would equal or surpass the creative

achievements of men is hardly defensible . . . (Storr, 1968, p. 62, italics added).

The author not only makes demeaning statements about women, he also rejects an hypothesis that has not been tested, and ignores evidence of women's achievements that suggests it might have validity.

RESEARCH NEGLECT
Psychologists have not been studying women as much as men. As reflected by the populations investigated, the psychology that claims to be a science of human behavior is in reality the science of the college sophomore, and, more specifically, the science of the male college sophomore. Males are used as subjects twice as often as females in studies reported in personality and social psychology journals (Carlson, 1971a; Holmes & Jorgensen, 1971).

Why the Neglect? Several implicit biases among the preponderantly male investigators may account for the relative neglect of women in psychological research. Perhaps the researchers are guided in selecting individuals to study by feelings of greater empathy with persons of their own sex, by "paternalistic" concern about imposing upon "fragile" females, and possibly by unacknowledged biases that males are more important anyway. Sometimes, too, investigators seem to view women subjects as unnecessary, since they treat their findings from males as indicative of people in general. For example, in a recent study regarding how much "individuals" facilitate desirable outcomes for another person, the researchers compared "samples of individuals from widely different cultures—India and the United States" (L'Armand & Pepitone, 1975, p. 189). The "individuals" sampled were all males, though the researchers' theorizing and generalizing seemed intended to encompass "all people" within each culture.

"Forget the Women." Even when data are available for both female and male subjects, many researchers do not analyze their data for sex differences; and among those who do, some then do

not further explore the differences they find. For example, in almost 900 pages reviewing research on achievement motivation, women are discussed in a *footnote:*

Perhaps the most persistent unresolved problem in research on *n* Achievement (need for achievement) concerns the observed sex differences. . . . The average *n* Achievement score of American college women . . . (is) already as high under relaxed conditions as it is for men or women under aroused conditions (Atkinson, 1958, p. 77).

In subsequent research and discussions of achievement, the quandary expressed in the footnote has been forgotten. What has been emphasized is the finding that the research procedures that increased achievement concerns in men were not effective for women (whose scores were high already, without special instructions). This finding was "popularized" in the conclusion that women are *deficient* in achievement motivation—the prevailing view until very recently among "informed" psychologists. Thus the misrepresentation of early findings led to a vastly erroneous view of women's achievement orientations (Chapter 11). Furthermore, since women were viewed as "deviants" because they typically did not respond in the way men did, the bulk of achievement research has involved only male subjects.

If researchers themselves do not ignore intriguing findings regarding sex differences, some textbook authors are not so conscientious. For example, the findings from one study are summarized in a recent textbook: ". . . the students who were more effective academically were more self-accepting and were more accepted by both their mothers and their fathers than were the least effective students" (Byrne, 1974, p. 283). However, the analyses reported in the original publication showed sex differences the researcher thought worthy of comment: "That the relationship of self-acceptance to academic effectiveness did not reach significance among females suggests that additional factors should be taken into account when considering the sources of academic effectiveness in females. . . . It may be

noteworthy that maternal acceptance was related positively to academic effectiveness among males but not among females" (Wyer, 1965, p. 315). Curiously, the textbook author had to go to some trouble to obtain the statistical calculations he reported that hide the sex differences obvious in the table that the researcher originally presented.

Obviously, neglect and bias must be overcome in order to have a psychology of persons that includes females as well as males. This book is part of a larger effort toward that goal.

TIMELINESS
We live in an era of equalization. During the past decade a revitalized women's movement has been pressing for women's rights to realize their potential and to be accepted as persons equal to men.

Professional Support. As part of this movement, professional and academic women have formed caucuses and organizations within larger professional associations (Chapter 16). Both the Association of Women Psychologists and the American Psychological Association's Division 35, on the Psychology of Women, are designed to help end psychology's role in perpetuating unscientific assumptions about the supposed "natures" of women and men, and to promote research on women whose results can be integrated into psychological knowledge and applied within the larger society.

Psychology of Men. In view of the professional support and increasing research and courses about women, some people (mainly men) ask, "Why not a Psychology of Men?" As noted already, the main body of the psychology that we now have actually is about men rather than about people—women and men. Nevertheless, concern about women and about sex roles has provided fresh perspectives, for example, regarding the psychological impact of role-based socialization practices on men, as well as on women. Such perspectives stimulated by the psychology of women will contribute to a viable psychology of persons.

The Pace of Social Change. In view of the activity about women both in the society at large and within professional disciplines, it is easy for some people to *over*estimate the actual changes that have occurred, and for others to *under*estimate their importance and long-range implications. While many people are questioning traditional attitudes about women and about sex differences, many social practices have not changed sufficiently to alter markedly the "average" picture. Particularly among students in liberal college environments, there is a tendency to dismiss findings from all but very recent studies as no longer applicable. Yet, college students' depictions of sex roles and their own statements about themselves and others with respect to the roles show remarkable similarity when one compares studies done in the 1950s with those of the late 1960s and early 1970s (Chapter 8). Similarly, the author of a recent study of parent–child interaction concludes: "Despite the fact that these families were picked from a young student population that is most likely to have been affected by the feminist movement, the majority of the parents did not differ greatly, either in the home observations or in the questionnaire from the mothers studied by Sears et al. in 1957" (Fagot, 1974, pp. 557–558).

Thus, although on some topics data gathered longer ago than yesterday may not be trusted as applicable to today, on others, the findings of 20 years ago may still hold. Assessing constancies and changes is part of the ongoing research concern and challenge in the psychology of women.

THINKING ABOUT SEX DIFFERENCES

"Vive la difference!" is a popular rallying cry in conversations about sex differences. Usually this statement elicits chuckles, after which the topic generally is dropped, possibly because of its strong emotional undercurrents. Part of the reason for defensiveness about sex differences is the importance of sex roles as ideals in our culture.

SEX ROLES

Most cultures assign different **roles** to women and men. Although there is tremendous variation, as we shall see, many cultures elaborate roles around women's childbearing functions and men's greater average physical size and strength. Aside from expecting each sex to perform different tasks, many societies expect females and males to differ also in psychological characteristics. **Sex roles** thus involve all of the shared cultural beliefs about the different behaviors and characteristics that people think should be associated with members of each sex. The term gender role also is sometimes used interchangeably with sex role.

In our society, the traits dominant in the roles prescribed for females primarily relate to and facilitate social concerns and interpersonal warmth; for males, the traits are basically related to personal competence and achievement (see Broverman, et al., 1972; Rosenkrantz, et al., 1968). Women are expected to be gentle, sensitive to others' feelings, and emotional; men are expected to be self-confident, independent, and ambitious (Table 1-1). Of particular relevance in the psychology of women is the fact that the role assigned females includes more unfavorable and fewer favorable traits than does the male sex role (Chapters 8, 9, 15, and 16). Furthermore, not only are members of each sex expected to display "appropriate" traits, but they also are expected *not* to have the traits considered definitive of the other sex. Thus, roles demand mutual exclusiveness in the relevant psychological traits. Women are supposed to be "feminine" and men are supposed to be "masculine" in the ways each sex role prescribes. Future chapters will challenge the assumption that roles are an accurate depiction of the way people are. Here we emphasize some of the broad fallacies usually associated with thinking in terms of roles and the related concepts of femininity and masculinity.

ERRONEOUS ASSUMPTIONS

The misleading assumptions prevalent in thinking about sex differences and illustrated by what is known as masculinity-femininity (M–F) research, can be grouped into three general categories. According to the assumption of **unidimensionality,** there is some one basic way in which females and males differ; though there may be many manifestations of the dimension, they all "go together."

TABLE 1-1.
Valued Traits in the Female and Male Roles *

Female Role	
Does not use harsh language	Interested in own appearance
Talkative	Neat in habits
Tactful	Quiet
Gentle	Strong need for security
Aware of feelings of others	Appreciates art and literature
Religious	Expresses tender feelings

Male Role	
Aggressive	Feelings not easily hurt
Independent	Adventurous
Unemotional	Makes decisions easily
Hides emotions	Never cries
Objective	Acts as a leader
Not easily influenced	Self-confident
Dominant	Not uncomfortable about being aggressive
Likes math and science	Ambitious
Not excitable in a minor crisis	Able to separate feelings from ideas
Active	Not dependent
Competitive	Not conceited about appearance
Logical	Thinks men are superior to women
Worldly	Talks freely about sex with men
Skilled in business	Knows the way of the world
Direct	

* *Source.* Reproduced from Rosenkrantz, Vogel, Bee, Broverman, & Broverman, 1968, p. 291. Copyright by American Psychological Association and reproduced by permission.

In everyday judgments, we ask only one question rather than many, and make one judgment rather than many. "Am I feminine?" "He's not very masculine." Our thinking is crude and global. Similarly, in research, one score rather than many is often used to reflect a person's position on an hypothesized dimension of M–F. The assumption of **bipolarity** is also prevalent: Masculinity and femininity are assumed to be opposites; for example, a woman is supposed to be dependent and a man independent. Typically, high masculinity means low femininity, or, the opposite of a masculine response is presumed indicative of femininity (even if females have not answered in that way!).

In addition, the assumption of **biopsychological equivalence** is also pervasive, namely that M–F is virtually the same thing as physical maleness and femaleness. In this view, sex roles are justified by a physical substrata. As discussed later (Chapter 4), physical femaleness–maleness is itself not one dimension nor a matter of a distinct contrast of opposition between females and males as physical beings. Thus, biopsychological equivalence can hardly be a strong assumption that justifies assumptions of unidimensionality or bipolarity (Donelson, 1975). Nonetheless, it is often assumed so.

Typical M–F Research. That these assumptions are not warranted is also suggested by the relative failures of research approaches based on them (Constantinople, 1973). Conventional self-report M–F (masculinity–femininity) inventories typically consist of items that females and males answered differently. (They assume biopsychological equivalence.) The tests typically use only one score, with a high score typically meaning high M and low F. About the only success of such tests has been in demonstrating an average difference between groups of males and females. The findings that different M–F tests have little in common and generally are weaker for females than males challenge the assumptions of unidimensionality and bipolarity.

Masculinity and Femininity. Other approaches have given more interesting and meaningful results, especially about within-sex variation. For example, comparison of **projective** measures, supposedly tapping unconscious views of self, and self-report measures, supposedly tapping conscious views of self, show that men may be M in one way and F in another, with different behavioral consequences (Lipsitt & Strodtbeck, 1967). The same may be true of females as well, but they have not been as well studied as males. Even on self-reports alone, F or M attributes are not mutually exclusive. For example, over the four college years, the women in one study became more "masculine" in reporting less conventional and passive behavior; however, they also became more "feminine" in indicating greater awareness of their inner life (Webster, 1956). In fact, recent research indicates that college students are as likely to be equally F *and* M as they are to be very M *or* F; that is, they are as likely to be **androgynous** as they are to be strongly **sex-typed** (Chapter 8). Much will be said in future chapters about the increasingly discussed value of androgyny, implying the combination of attributes from both sex roles.

Recognizing explicit or implicit use of erroneous assumptions will facilitate evaluating available findings about women and sex differences, as will some appreciation of considerations in psychological research.

RESEARCH CONSIDERATIONS

Group Differences. Females and males often differ from each other—as groups. For many of the behaviors and characteristics considered in subsequent chapters, the average female and the average male are not alike. Although such information is valuable, there are limitations to keep in mind when considering averages, or the statistical **mean.**

Nature of the Sample. The average person is not the same at all ages. While this is relatively obvious, it is often overlooked in generalizing about research evidence. What is true about girls may not be true about women; furthermore, women and men may not differ in the same ways that girls and boys do. The limited specificity of some sex differences is illustrated by studies of perceptual judgments as measurements of **field dependence,** where sex differences do not appear until about age 8, are at their maximum during late adolescence, and then virtually disappear by age 24 (Kogan, 1973). In much of the psychological literature, however, the age specificity of the sex difference has been overlooked in generalizations that women are more dependent on external environmental cues for perceptual judgments than are men.

Generalizing to people with different characteristics from those of the individuals studied is particularly problematic in view of the previously noted tendency for researchers to investigate convenient samples of college students. Students may differ in systematic ways from people in the general population—for example, in race (blacks are underrepresented in most colleges and in most psychological research), socioeconomic level, and age range, as well as in other, less obvious characteristics. Thus, observed differences between college women and men may not apply to younger students, to noncollege people of the same age, or to older persons, whether or not they are college graduates. In assessing group differences, therefore, we should note the characteristics of the individuals who actually have been studied and regard generalizations to nonsimilar people as hypotheses requiring additional investigation.

Relativity of Differences. Any difference between two or more groups, say females and males, or college and high school females, should be interpreted as relative differences. To say that men are not as sensitive as women is not the same as saying that men are insensitive; it simply means that men are less sensitive—on the average. Seldom, if ever, do psychologists have the absolute scales that would be necessary to claim that women are 100 percent sensitive and men are 0 percent sensitive, were that the case.

Variability around the Mean. The averages of two or more groups may differ significantly according to relevant statistical criteria. However, there may still be large individual differences within each group. In addition to variation *between* the means of groups, there also is variation *around* the mean of any one group. That is, there is **between-group variation** and **within-group variation.** Height is an easy example. Men in general are taller than women in general; the average height for a group of men is greater than the average height for a group of women. Yet, women differ considerably in their height, as do men. Some women are taller than the average man; some men are shorter than the average woman.

Individual differences within a group make it likely that there will be overlap in the scores of different groups. Percentage overlap refers to the percentage of one group that is at or beyond the mean of the other group. For example, although the averages are different, about 20 to 25 percent of females are better than the average male on tests of spatial abilities. Unfortunately, researchers seldom provide clear statements of percentage overlap. As indicated in Figure 1-1, overlap can be so great that statements about average differences are not particularly informative. Thus, some psychologists prefer to study within-sex variation rather than between-sex variation.

Within-Sex Differences. Discovering differences between groups is only a first step that provides a **descriptive statement** of the content of group differences. Sometimes, however, people assume that a descriptive statement also is a **prescriptive statement** of the way things ought to be or must be. The jump from description to prescription often is made because of the biopsychological assumptions. As we shall note in our introduction to Part II of this book, prescriptions often beg the

question by asserting that an observed difference occurs because "it's only natural." Thus, since women in this culture seem to display greater social responsiveness than men, some people erroneously conclude that women are "naturally" that way.

A more adequate approach to understanding observed sex differences involves an attempt to understand the reasons for variation *within* each sex. How do the more socially responsive women differ from the less responsive? Do certain factors within each sex influence the behavior in the same way? With such an approach one can better understand findings about group sex differences. Often, average differences occur because many members of one sex and only a few of the other sex have been exposed to conditions facilitating a certain behavior.

Nature and Nurture. As just noted, some people assume that any sex differences that are found are "just natural," so that deviations from the average are "unnatural," indicating that something is wrong with the deviant person. Just as extreme and simpleminded is the declaration that sex differences are all "just due to socialization" and thus presumably amenable to any kind of change through environmental manipulation. These polarized statements are not *explanations;* rather they are assumptions or hypotheses about reasons for sex differences that require testing.

Furthermore, polarizing hypotheses about women and men into such extremes of "biology versus environment" or "nature versus nurture" is a recurring variety of fallacious either–or thinking. The task of understanding sex differences is not one of deciding in favor of biology or environment, but rather one of understanding human beings, who are **psychobiological** organisms developing and having experiences in a social setting. When distinctions are made between sex roles and gender roles, it is often on the basis that the attributes of gender roles are only culturally induced, while those of sex roles are biological necessities. In view of the fact that biological persons live in social environments, the distinction becomes somewhat meaningless. Human behav-

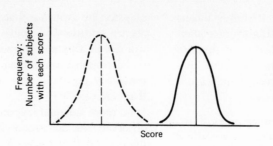

Example A

There is small within–group variation for each group, and no overlap between groups. The distributions are "tight" and widely separated.

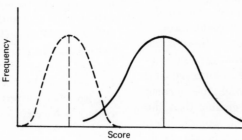

Example B

The average for each group is the same as in A. However, there is more within–group variation than in A, and overlap. Also, there is more within–group variation for one group than for the other.

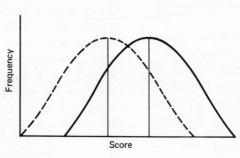

Example C

There is a great deal of within–group variation for each group, and the amount of variation is about the same for the two groups. The means for the two groups are different (perhaps significant by statistical criteria), but the implications of the group difference are much different than in A and B. In this case, the distributions are neither "tight" nor widely separated. There is much overlap.

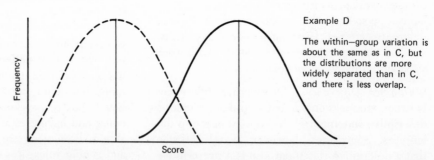

Example D

The within–group variation is about the same as in C, but the distributions are more widely separated than in C, and there is less overlap.

Figure 1-1.
Selected examples of possible relations between frequency distributions for two groups of subjects.

ior is a function of a complex interplay of biological and environmental factors, though at some times and for some behaviors one of these factors makes a more obvious contribution than the other. Some of the intricacies of the interplay of biological factors and experience will be exemplified shortly.

IMPLICATIONS
OF SEX DIFFERENCES

If a sex difference exists, so what? What difference *does* it make in the lives of individuals? What difference *must* it make? Sex differences often are made to have implications in the lives of people that are not necessitated by the nature of females and males as psychobiological organisms. An obvious example is that, for biological reasons, women can bear children and men cannot. However, this fact is irrelevant to many women, and could be relatively irrelevant over large portions of the life spans of those women who do have children. For example, the average mother in this culture spends almost two-thirds of her life alone or with a husband but with no children under 18 years of age living with her (Rossi, 1971). She is pregnant or breast-feeding during a very small part of her total life (Figure 1-2). Nonetheless, over a broad range of cultures, including our own, the social consequences of the biological potential of motherhood is that women are defined largely in terms of their reproductive functions.

Humans obviously have a vast capacity to interpret the implications of their biological constitutions and to regulate their behavior through language and culture. Human activities and feelings are organized by the interaction of biological predispositions with culture-specific expectations. Some of the cultural expectations linked with biological facts seem rather far-fetched. For example, among the Mundugumor people of New Guinea, being born with the umbilical cord around one's neck is considered indicative of artistic talent. The belief is so strong that ". . . only those who are so born can paint good pictures, while the man born without a strangulating cord labours humble and unarrogant, and never attains any virtuosity" (Mead, 1935/1963, p. 12). Perhaps many of the sex differences considered "just natural" in our own and other societies have no more immediate relationship to the biological facts of sex than does the ability to paint have to manner of birth. But, "believing can make it so."

BEHAVIORAL VARIATION

People live in environments. The prevailing cultural attitudes and practices as well as the requirements of the physical environment influence what women are like and, more broadly, the extent and specific content of particular sex differences. Cultural variation in sex-role content is one illustration of the weakness of assumptions about biopsychological equivalence—"it's just natural"—as well as those of unidimensionality and bipolarity. Women are complex persons, and understanding women and sex differences requires sensitivity to the variety of influences leading to marked behavioral variation. The same points are

Figure 1-2.
An average woman's life span (based on 1970 averages).

Over half of the life span remains

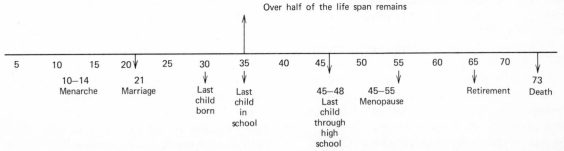

5	10	15	20	25	30	35	40	45	50	55	60	65	70	
	10–14 Menarche		21 Marriage		Last child born	Last child in school		45–48 Last child through high school	45–55 Menopause			Retirement		73 Death

also well illustrated by considering individual development, even within one culture.

CROSS-CULTURAL VARIATION

Many of the social and psychological characteristics that we might assume to be natural and prescriptive consequences of biological sex actually are neither necessary, natural, nor universal. The extraordinary cultural diversity in interpretations of biological femaleness and maleness is well illustrated by Margaret Mead's descriptions of three primitive New Guinea tribes (1935/1963). Mead initially assumed that there is a "natural sex temperament." She hoped to discover in the primitive, simple social organizations the range in deviations from the normal so she could distill the essentials of biologially sex-based psychological traits from the cultural accessories and elaborations. However, Mead found that in one tribe, women and men had markedly different sex temperaments but the traits reflected a *reversal* of the sex attitudes of our culture. In two other tribes, females and males had relatively homogeneous temperaments, but a different constellation of traits was emphasized in each.

Among the "gentle Arapesh," a farming tribe living in mountainous country, both women and men were cooperative, unaggressive, contented, responsive to others' needs, "maternal" in their attitudes toward children, and unaware of a powerful sex drive in either sex. Arapesh women and men alike displayed passivity, responsiveness, and willingness to cherish children—temperamental characteristics traditionally ascribed only to women in our culture. Among the head-hunting Mundugumor, however, this "feminine" temperament was actually "outlawed." Women as well as men were ruthlessly aggressive, suspicious, jealous, and minimally involved in child-care responsibilities.

In contrast to these tribes that presented only one standardized pattern for *all* its members without distinctions as to rank, age, or sex, the Tchambuli elaborated different traits for each sex. Women were impersonal in outlook, definite in their plans, dominating in their management of the food supply and production of trade articles,

and active in initiating sex relations. The men, on the other hand, were delicate and socially responsive, emotionally dependent, playful and unpractical, and flirtatious but rather timid in sexual relations—much like the stereotype of Victorian women. Much of the men's time was spent dressing in elaborate ceremonial costumes and curling their hair. When the women allowed them to go to the trade market, the men could not spend the profits without their wives' consent, which was given usually only after the men's languishing looks and soft words had "softened" the women.

Limits to Variation. Observing the Tchambuli reversal of our sex-typed traits and finding that traditional "feminine" traits can be instilled among men (as well as women) in one tribe and outlawed for women (as well as men) in another, Mead concluded there was no necessary biological basis for regarding temperamental traits as sex-linked. Thus she rejected the assumption of biopsychological equivalence. While other anthropologists have confirmed the cultural variability in traits displayed by females and males, they have noted also the relative preponderance across cultures of sex-typing comparable to that in our culture. There is cultural variation, for example, in the extent to which children display egoistic behavior (e.g., seeking attention, dominating, and demanding help) or altruistic behavior (e.g., offering help, giving support, and providing responsible suggestions). Despite the differences in overall cultural emphasis, however, sex differences begin to appear at about ages 7 to 11 with girls behaving more altrusitically and boys behaving more egoistically (Chodorow, 1972). While girls and boys in our country show the same sex differences, the girls have higher egoistic behavior scores than do the boys in some other parts of the world. Thus, although there is some cross-cultural consistency in the sex difference, the levels of the scores vary considerably from culture to culture.

Some cultural variation in roles is associated with variations in the environment and related methods of obtaining food. This was illustrated by a study of childhood socialization practices in 110 mainly primitive cultures. In agricultural or herding societies that rely on accumulating resources, *all* children are trained to be compliantly responsible and obedient. In such contexts, "irresponsible" behavior could ruin a crop or lose a herd, thus diminishing the group's food supply for a long period. In hunting or fishing societies, where daring behavior might pay off and does not pose a long-term threat to food supply if it does not, children of both sexes are trained to be more assertively independent, self-reliant, and achievement-oriented. Again, despite the tremendous cultural variations in the levels of compliance or assertiveness encouraged in both sexes, girls nevertheless generally are trained to be more compliant than boys, whereas boys are encouraged to be more assertive than girls (Barry, Child, & Bacon, 1959).

THEORIZING ABOUT BIOSOCIAL INFLUENCES

Despite the dramatic exceptions exemplified in Mead's studies, the overall preponderance of sex-role differentiation favoring altruism and compliance in girls and egoism and assertiveness in boys has led some social scientists to argue that there is a universal pattern of interdependence within the family, with the males focusing on "task specialization" and the females on "social-emotional" support. This assumed universal social pattern is "explained" by biological factors related to women's reproductive functions and men's physical strength—hence the theorizing is biosocial.

Evolutionary cultural theorists, for example, argue that human social existence originated in the cooperative task-oriented activities of early *men*, who were hunters. The biosocial argument is that hunting large animals demanded the coordinated efforts of several individuals; males were selected because the hunt often involved danger and extensive travel that was unfeasible for women because they were constrained by nursing and other child-care responsibilities. In emphasizing the role of "Man the Hunter" in social evolution, many theorists have neglected the contribution of female food gathering in early social life.

Women have been "invisible" in anthropology as well as in other fields of study.

Actually, a recent systematic investigation of women's roles in the subsistence economy of their societies showed that, on a worldwide basis, women contributed 44 percent of the food. Even in the cultural area where women's food contribution was the lowest of all studied, women produced about a third of the food for their society (Aronoff & Crano, 1975). These findings regarding women's activities provide no support for the theoretical position that there is universal task segregation and sex-role differentiation of male "breadwinners" versus female "homemakers" in the family. Bipolar either–or thinking is no more appropriate for characterizing the division of labor than it is for other aspects of sex roles. In addition, with reference to the overdrawn implications of the social cooperation and "male bonding" demanded by hunting (Tiger, 1969), it is important to note that women's activities of food gathering and socializing children required cooperative and communicative skills as complex as those involved in hunting: The traits adaptive for women's activities could have had an impact on the creation of early social patterns of comparable importance to those of men (Linton, 1973).

Biosocial Impact of Life-Style Changes. Obviously, in attempting to reconstruct the past or to explain the present, there is danger of overinterpreting obvious biological sex differences and making them seem to have implications they do not or need not have. The complexities of the interactions of biological functioning, social practices, and trait development are well illustrated by the case of the South African !Kung. (The exclamation point in *!Kung* represents a clicking sound made in pronouncing the name.) In the span of a generation or so, the !Kung have changed from hunter–gatherers to farmer–herdspeople—a transition comparable to that during the Neolithic Revolution, when people forsook lives of hunting and gathering and began to farm and herd domestic animals. For the !Kung this life-style change has been accompanied by a rise in population, a reduction in women's status, and a change in aggressiveness among the children (Kolata, 1974).

Diet and Birthrate. Since the !Kung have settled down, there has been a decrease in the age of menarche (first menstruation) as well as a decrease in the average time between births. !Kung women marry at puberty; therefore the earlier menarche provides an earlier start to reproductive life, inasmuch as the !Kung do not practice contraception or abortion. According to recent evidence (Frisch & McArthur, 1974), body fat must reach a minimum level for menarche and for the maintenance of the menstrual cycle. Although the nomadic !Kung were well-nourished (and in fact did not suffer from degenerative diseases characteristic of more "civilized" populations), their diets lacked the milk and grains that they now consume; thus they were thinner than they are currently. Change in diet thus could account for the earlier onset of menarche, and it also is related to the decrease in time between births. The nomadic !Kung women had no soft food to give their babies; therefore they nursed them for four or five years, and this prolonged lactation had a contraceptive effect. Lactating women need about 1000 extra calories a day; thus the nursing !Kung woman probably had too little body fat for ovulation to occur. The sedentary !Kung wean their babies sooner with grain and cow's milk, and they reproduce more frequently.

Status and Childrearing. In the nomadic !Kung society, women gathered half the food consumed by their group. They freely left camp to find food, just as men left to hunt; and whichever women or men were left in the camp shared the job of caring for the children. Now, however, women are less mobile than men and stay in the village to prepare food and mind the children while the men go work in the fields or care for the cattle of their Bantu neighbors. The men learn the Bantu language and also observe the male-dominated Bantu society firsthand. All of these changes have diminished !Kung women's status.

The sedentary life also accentuates sex-role differences among children. When the nomadic

!Kung lived in small bands, there were only a few children; therefore children of both sexes and a wide age range played together. This group composition made competitive games unfeasible and discouraged the development of different games and different roles for girls and boys. Now in the villages, girls and boys play separately in narrow age groups, and they have become more aggressive toward one another. In the nomadic bands, there was little aggression among children or adults. When adults were in conflict, one or the other families generally would leave and join another !Kung band. Being tied to their land now restricts the !Kungs so they cannot so easily move away from trouble. Thus the elaborated social and biological consequences of life-style changes can have profound effects on the personalities and destinies of individual women and men.

DEVELOPMENTAL PERSPECTIVE

Cultural views about behavior and life-styles within a given physical environment affect people's characteristic behavior patterns. Within any one societal group and environment, there is developmental variation as well, because of changes in the growing individual's capacities and needs and changes in others' specific expectations. Therefore, what is adaptive or useful for a person is age-dependent. There are both similarities and differences between the sexes in terms both of attributes of the growing children themselves and the expectations held for them. Some dimensions of assumed appropriateness vary with age; some are similar between the sexes; some are different between the sexes.

Ratings of Femininity and Masculinity. Although sex roles tend to be mutually exclusive ideals that are held for people of all ages, the roles are not consistently translated into specific expectations. For example, in judgments of adults and preschoolers, people used similar traits to describe both the most "feminine" women and girls and also the most "masculine" men and boys (Vroegh, 1971). There are some indications that whatever is considered appropriate for a person of a given age is considered "feminine" if the person is a female and "masculine" if the person is a male.

Some aspects of assumed appropriateness vary with age. In one study teachers and peers rated the degree to which children acted in the way a girl or boy is expected to act; and these ratings were compared with the children's self-reported personality traits (Vroegh, 1971). In Grades 4 to 6, attributes relevant to intellectual and personal competence (e.g., being outgoing rather than reserved, confident rather than apprehensive) were related to judged femininity *and* masculinity; femininity was also related to being patient and naive. For boys, the same traits were related to judgments of masculinity in Grades 1 to 3; but in Grades 7 to 8, assertiveness, group dependence, and venturesomeness were the correlates of masculinity ratings. These and other findings about preschoolers may indicate that perceived masculinity is related to self-development and achieving personal competence in early years. However, in the junior high school years, perceived masculinity is correlated with developing competencies in social relationships, particularly with peers. For females, the relative lack of clear relationships between self-rated traits and others' perceptions of femininity, and the lack of a developmental pattern may be associated with less early pressure on girls for sex-typed behavior (Chapter 8). Or, it may be that what people mean by femininity and expect of girls is more ambiguous and ill-defined than what they expect of boys.

It is noteworthy that attributes related to perceived femininity and masculinity differ more around Grades 7 to 8 than in younger years or than in adulthood. During early adolescence, "Boys and girls seem to make special efforts to distinguish themselves from the other sex" (Vroegh, 1971, p. 200). Of course, even what appears to be the same sort of behavior in females and males may have different origins and different implications (Tyler, 1965). For example, other research suggests that intellectual competence may not have the same effects in girls' and boys' personality organization and overall devel-

opment (Chapters 8 and 11). And, some intellectual accomplishments are achieved by the use of different abilities.

Sex Differences in Ability Development.

Physical, intellectual, and social developments generally are more rapid, even, and stable for girls than for boys. On the average, girls excel in verbal abilities, whereas boys are superior in non-verbal abilities, with potentially important implications for the development of each (Chapter 6). For example, linguistic skills appear more strongly related to girls' than to boys' general intellectual development and school performance. Girls' verbal skills may also support their increasing social orientation, given the role that words play in social interaction. In a social system that emphasizes verbal skills, boys therefore are at a relative disadvantage, which they are pressed to overcome. More young boys than girls have school problems. On the other hand, boys' lesser facility with words may encourage a reliance on shared activity (e.g., sports, and playing with objects) as the content of their interaction with others.

An asset may also function as a liability. A girl's verbal success may discourage her from developing nonverbal abilities, while a boy's lag in developing verbal skills may encourage an overreliance on dealing with the environment via his more rapidly developing nonverbal skills. Expectations by teachers and the children themselves about what girls and boys "should be good at" probably reinforce a relatively one-sided development to the detriment of both females and males. Thus, in abilities as well as in other traits, each sex tends to have different underdeveloped areas.

The Total Person.

At least in this culture, there seems to be a general patterning in sex differences so that some differences are maximum in adolescence and early adulthood—the time when producing offspring has become physically possible. Perhaps some sex-typing helps to promote mating and thus species survival in ways that are not yet well understood. (See discussion of **sexual**

dimorphism, Chapter 3.) However, many sex-typed expectations seem to extend far beyond necessity. Moreover, other cultures have managed to perpetuate themselves without our sex-role system. Thus we suggest that whatever sex differences are initially necessary for species perpetuation become irrelevant or detrimental for growth into maturity.

Life is more than mating for the continuation of the species. While the issue of what is "basic human nature" is subject to much discussion (Chapter 2), it may be much the same for females and males. Androgyny, rather than strong sex differentiation, becomes necessary for self-development and a meaningful community life in a psychological sense. Rigid and extreme sex-role expectations lead us astray in our development as mature human beings and mask the underlying similarities between females and males.

Often, members of the two sexes want or need the same thing, but differ in the kinds of expressions they are allowed in a social environment concerned with role appropriateness. Some people are comfortable with the behaviors allowed them; others wish more latitude. We can understand members of the other sex (or our own) better if we can see from their own perspective of themselves and the alternatives they think they have for doing and being. We are often similar in our differences. The similarities may be as important for understanding each other, and humanness, as are the differences.

SUMMARY

Partly as a result of erroneous, unchallenged assumptions and unwarranted value judgments, women have been neglected in psychological theory and research. Understanding women and human beings—both men and women—has been impeded by assumptions that femininity and masculinity are unidimensional or bipolar attributes. Often, too, biopsychological equivalence is assumed in claims that sex differences in traits and behavior are "natural" and inevitable consequences of physical sex differences. Such reasoning leads some people to convert descriptive statements about observed sex differences into prescriptive statements that such differences *must* exist. Some of these prescriptions are incorporated in idealized sex roles that emphasize acquiescence and social concern in women and competition and personal achievement in men.

In spite of some cross-cultural consistency in the general nature of sex-typed socialization, there is marked variation as well, indicating the tremendous influence of the physical and social environment. And within any one culture, there are individual differences between people of the same age and sex as well as developmental differences within individuals. Some sex differences are obvious at one age period, but minimal or nonexistent at others. In working toward a psychology of persons, we must attend not only to the average similarities and differences between women and men but also to the variations within each sex and seek the causes of these variations.

The following chapters explore different sources of variations. As we shall see, there are many deficiencies in the current state of knowledge, and much research yet to be undertaken. But even the available information, for example, regarding the impact of sex-role socialization on both women and men, can help readers to explore alternatives that may better contribute to the enrichment of their lives. By increasing understanding of themselves and others, people are better able to assume responsibility for their own choices and personal development.

CHAPTER
2
CONTRIBUTIONS FROM PERSONALITY THEORY

THEORIZING ABOUT PERSONALITY
IMPLICIT PERSONALITY THEORY
SOME BASIC ASSUMPTIONS

REACTIVE AND PROACTIVE MODELS: PAWN OR ORIGIN?
OTHER RELEVANT THEORIES
AGENCY AND COMMUNION

SIGMUND FREUD
SOME BASICS: A REACTIVE MODEL
THE PHALLIC STAGE
FEMALE DEVELOPMENT
MALE DEVELOPMENT

PAST THE PHALLIC
IDENTIFICATIONS
SUPEREGO
THE GENITAL STAGE

COMMENTARY

TOWARD THE SELF
CARL JUNG
OVERVIEW: REACTIVE AND PROACTIVE
INNER AND OUTER CHARACTERS—MASK AND SOUL
Animus and Anima
Relations with Others
LOGOS AND EROS
SELFHOOD
COMMENTARY

CARL ROGERS
ACTUALIZATION
INCONGRUENCE
FULLY FUNCTIONING PERSON
COMMENTARY

SUMMARY

Considering the increasingly recognized need for *facts* to replace stereotyped assumptions about women, one may well ask what is the value of discussing personality *theory*. The truth is that we are all personality theorists. And, we *must* be to live comfortably in a public world of people and in the private world of ourselves. We can, however, become better theorists and more effective persons. Thus, this chapter will focus on selected personality theorists to help increase an awareness of some issues in personality theory and research and to help improve the depth and accuracy of our individual theorizing, and perhaps our lives.

THEORIZING ABOUT PERSONALITY

IMPLICIT PERSONALITY THEORY

The theories that people use in making sense out of their world are called **implicit personality theories.** Usually, we are largely unaware of our theory; thus, it is implicit rather than explicit. It includes a set of assumptions about human beings, and dimensions or concepts (constructs) used in thinking about people, just as do formal theories. Although it is implicit, it shapes our perceptions and gives us a feeling of relative stability, predictability, and order in the world. Life would be chaotic without such a structuring theory. We would feel helpless in trying to understand ourselves and others and, in fact, we would be helpless. However, implicit personality theories also cause trouble because they so often are implicit, incomplete, and inaccurate. We tend to see what we expect to see and have difficulty seeing outside of the dimensions and assumptions of the theory. Deviations from what we expect can be disturbing and lead to defensiveness, distortions, and derogations of the people who are not as the theory predicts they "should" be.

Many assumptions of implicit personality theories are based on sex. The emotionality likely in conversations about sex differences suggests that the assumptions are very important in views about how people "should be." A person who is fond of asserting, "Women should be seen and not heard" would be likely to have difficulty accepting a woman participant in an intelligent conversation. This kind of person very well may hold the assumption that "beauty, womanness, and lack of intelligence are associated." Within this theoretical perspective, a remark made by a man may be seen as helpful, astute, and intelligent; the same remark by a woman may be seen as distracting, silly, or "uppity." If forced to accept and acknowledge the intelligence of the woman's comments, our hypothetical theorist might be inclined to consider her as "manly," or at least not attractive as a woman. The reader can easily imagine more specific and vivid comments likely to be made about the woman in such a case. The implicit assumption causing the problem is not an accurate one, but it has a strong influence nonetheless. Some people can persist remarkably long in clinging to their assumptions in spite of contrary evidence. Some people, when their assumptions are threatened, become angry, depressed, or defensive, without knowing why.

Are there accurate assumptions about sex differences that people *could* use? Research discussed in later chapters provides some answers. The point right now is that people *do* use assumptions, often unexamined ones. Even people who are participants or supporters of movements toward sexual equality are likely to have lingering assumptions about women and men. Habits of thinking developed over a lifetime are not easily overcome. No matter how subtle or blatant, the assumptions influence interactions with other people, one's own views of self, and one's own growth.

Some Basic Assumptions. Formal theorists do not typically make the erroneous assumptions about sex differences discussed in the preceding chapter (unidimensionality, bipolarity, and biopsychological equivalence). However, they do continually deal with the issues involved. Most theorists acknowledge both biological and cultural contributors to personality development, though they differ in assessments of the relative impact of these factors (cf. Hall and Lindzey, 1970). Does biology set limits on us that cannot be overcome?

Does the social context have more control over who we are than we do ourselves? Do early experiences, which we did not control, continually influence our lives? Can we choose what we want to be? If a woman is not comfortable with herself, need she stay that way? Your answers to such questions are likely to reflect whether you are essentially a proactive or a reactive personality theorist. Whatever your position, you have some company among formal theorists.

REACTIVE AND PROACTIVE MODELS: PAWN OR ORIGIN?

In the **reactive model** of human beings, people are Pawns in the chess game of life (Allport, 1955, 1961; de Charms, 1968). People simply react to basic "givens" of their lives, much as a computer reacts to the input and produces an output response that is dictated by the current and previous input. In the **proactive model,** people initiate action; they are Origins of their behavior, and of themselves, rather than Pawns.

According to the reactive model, we behave as we do because the environment provides stimuli and reinforcers. We react to the environment as a function of what we have been previously reinforced for doing, and we are not necessarily aware of why we behave as we do. We are particularly likely to perform responses that are effective in attaining relatively basic rewards (like food and approval) and avoiding anxiety, conflict, and tension. In contrast, according to the proactive model, we decide what we will do, and our decisions are conscious ones, based on our values, goals, and intentions for the future. We recognize that biological and social factors, both past and current, may pose some limitations, but we *use* those factors rather than *being used* by them. We create with them rather than being molded by them. We act to change an unsatisfactory environment rather than "giving in" to it and reacting to it in an attempt to adjust. If we do not like ourselves, we can become a person who is more consistent with the values we hold. We are free to originate. The use of this freedom is not necessarily easy, but the freedom is ours nonetheless.

Which is the correct view of human beings?

The question is difficult, perhaps impossible to answer empirically. There is evidence consistent with each view. Quite likely, any one person may sometimes be more of a Pawn than an Origin. Quite likely, some of us are more Pawns than we need to be. One important theorist, Gordon Allport (1955, 1961), has suggested that becoming psychologically mature is a matter of changing from reactive functioning (characteristic of children, the mentally ill, and immature adults) to proactive functioning. Implicit assumptions that the reactive model is "correct" probably retard movement toward proactive functioning.

Freud will be discussed as a prime example of a reactive theorist, Carl Rogers as an example of a proactive theorist. Carl Jung combines proactive and reactive themes.

OTHER RELEVANT THEORIES

Although they are not personality theories by conventional definitions, both behavioristic theory and cognitive development theory must be mentioned for their importance in contemporary American psychology and their relevance to proactive and reactive models of behavior. Behaviorism differs radically from Freudian positions in a number of respects, but shares a highly reactive perspective on human behavior. The behavioristic position typically assumes that human behavior is to be described by empirical laws stating relationships between observable events, namely stimuli and responses. Internal events such as thoughts, feelings, and anxieties are not considered. Behavior is a function of environmental events. The particular ways in which an organism responds is affected by previous experiences. A response that was previously rewarded is likely to be repeated in similar circumstances; a response that was previously punished is likely to have a very low probability of recurring in similar circumstances. Issues about human choice, feelings, and values—or even implicit theories!—are assumed to be irrelevant to the goal of predicting behavior.

In relative contrast, cognitive developmental theorists, such as Piaget and Kohlberg, have a strong proactive orientation. The capacities of the human being to select and structure information from the environment are emphasized. Environmental stimuli, including rewards and punishments, are not disregarded, but they are not "in control" of behavior as typical in reactive models. Similarly, both past and current environmental experiences affect the rate of cognitive development and the content of the cognitive structures that are developed. However, the emphasis is upon the inherent capacities of the person to organize information from the environment in terms of existing and developing cognitive structures and to make decisions for action accordingly.

Much research data discussed in coming chapters was collected within a behavioristic framework, though it need not be interpreted within that model. Cognitive theory, with a "dash" of behaviorism, is used in a later chapter (Chapter 8) to describe the development of children's concepts about sex roles and their resulting behavior. Actually, many theories can be combined in any one person's attempt to understand human beings, and many theories hold similar positions on some basic issues, although their terminology differs.

AGENCY AND COMMUNION

A recurring theme among formal theorists, whether they use a reactive or a proactive model, is that a complete, ideal, mature person blends many kinds of diverse characteristics. Many of the traits discussed by theorists seem to reflect what David Bakan (1966) calls an agentic orientation, often assumed typical of men, and a communal orientation, often assumed typical of women. Bakan postulates that all human beings, and perhaps all life forms, have these two fundamental orientations to the world that should be developed and used. **Agency** is concerned with the organism as an individual and is shown in self-protection, self-assertion, and self-expansion. **Communion** describes the individual organism as it exists in a community of others, and shows itself in the sense of being at-one-with other organisms. Unmitigated (extreme and uncontrolled) agency (for example, exploitation and unre-

strained technological expansion) represents evil. The viability of both the individual and of society depends on the successful integration of agency with communion. In the mature organism, the two are balanced and integrated. "Masculinity" is tempered with "femininity"; "femininity" with "masculinity." Bakan suggests that human beings, as a species, are currently in a phase of adolescent agency. However, agency is more emphasized for males, and communion inhibited; communion is emphasized for females, and agency inhibited.

The basic theme of agency and communion and the value of their interaction recurs in different personality theories, and in recent empirical research (such as Chapters 8, 9, 11, and 16), though under many different labels. The mature individual develops **androgynously** rather than in a one-sided way. We shall consider this theme in the following discussion of selected dominant personality theories.

SIGMUND FREUD

Freud is widely acknowledged as one of the most influential psychologists, yet he has been repeatedly criticized for his theory about women. However, his theory is often misunderstood and misused, and his views about women specifically taken out of the context of his total theory. Many criticisms are more appropriately directed toward Freud*ians* than toward Freud himself, and toward popularized careless presentations and comments. Freud was apologetic about the "unfriendly" view of women he evolved, and voiced an uncertainty and recurring dissatisfaction with his theory of women that is an amazingly refreshing contrast to the confidence and finality with which many contemporary psychologists state their analysis of such a complicated area.

The unfair malignment of Freud is recognized by some leaders of the women's movement, and his concepts about principles of personality development are used by them (e.g., Juliet Mitchell, 1973, 1975; Shulamith Firestone, 1971). This is not to say that Freud's theory of women is consistently valid. His explanation of the typical woman includes some details not supported by research, as discussed later. However, he did point to important phenomena of personality development in our culture and to the impact of role-based expectations. In other words, it is useful to many to distinguish between Freud's *description* of women and of personality generally, and his *explanations*, a specific version of the descriptive-prescriptive distinction discussed previously (Chapter 1). The details of Freud's explanations may not have wide applicability, but his theory seems to have some validity in descriptions of some of the impact that early experience and continuing role pressures in interpersonal interaction have on many women. Perhaps the women for whom his views are descriptive, and those for whom his explanations are reasonably valid, are reactive rather than proactive. Perhaps considering the Freudian perspective can help increase awareness of the reactive functioning that other theorists maintain is not necessary with maturity. To benefit from Freud's theory, one must take is seriously and consider it openmindedly.

SOME BASICS: A REACTIVE MODEL

Freud attempted to explain all human behavior, the irrational and the sublime, from an assumed biological base (Freud, 1940/1963, 1933/1965, 1925/1972a, 1931/1972b). All human activities require instinctual, psychic energy. The goal of *all* our activities is instinctual satisfaction, with death as the final goal. Until death, we are in continual conflict with ourselves and with society, which attempts to inhibit instinctual gratification, particularly sexual and aggressive. Because of biological similarity, we are relatively similar in our basic desires. However, it is through experience that we learn specific ways to use (channel) energy in attempts to obtain pleasure and avoid pain. In part because of different social experiences, we become different from each other. Freud's theory of personality dynamics and development deals with how energy is distributed.

The patterns of energy distribution, of seeking satisfaction and avoiding punishment, are essentially set by about age 6 (with the end of the phallic stage, discussed below). Later development serves to "fill in" some specifics within the core structure. Thus, early experiences have tre-

mendous importance throughout the life of the adult. Many of these experiences are associated with punishment and anxiety. Therefore, we use defenses such as repression, which involves keeping from consciousness some painful facts about ourselves. But our desires do not go away just because we do not recognize them. Much of our behavior is unconsciously motivated, as we seek gratification in disguised ways. Angry denials or ridicule of a Freudian interpretation of our underlying motives may be evidence of the validity of the interpretation and our anxiety and defensiveness when confronted with the truth we are trying to repress.

In sum, Freudian theory is highly reactive. What we are as adults is determined by past experiences; we function to avoid anxiety and maximize instinctual pleasure; much of our motivation is unconscious, as we defend against what is unpleasant about ourselves.

Notice that although Freud is a strong determinist, he is *not* the pure *biological* determinist he is often said to be. In fact, for his day, he was a rather sophisticated **psychobiologist** who recognized the necessity of understanding personality within a social context (Mitchell, 1973). Of particular concern to Freud were the life experiences occurring in intimate interpersonal relationships, typically within a family. Freud did not recognize the variety of social contexts that people throughout the world experience. His view was limited to that of a **nuclear,** father-dominated (patriarchal) family, a perspective also assumed by many contemporary psychologists, even though they have anthropological data not available to Freud. Most psychologists today acknowledge the importance of early interpersonal relationships within the family and agree with Freud also that even in early years, many facets of interpersonal relationships are different for girls and boys.

THE PHALLIC STAGE

In Freud's theory, the sex differences in interpersonal experiences are most prominent and crucial during what he termed the **phallic** stage, occurring around ages 4 to 6. The male-centeredness of much of Freud's theorizing is illustrated by his characterization of this period as "phallic," referring to a distinctly male organ. Females thus are defined by male standards as being nonmale. During this time, a child who was bisexual initially—that is, capable of developing traits considered masculine or feminine—begins to develop into a girl or a boy. Freud did not hypothesize innate femininity in females *versus* innate masculinity in males, nor innate attraction to a person of the other sex. Like many other theorists after him, he rejected such notions and considered basic human trends to be bisexual (in modern terminology, androgynous). However, personality develops with the interplay between biological givens and the environmental possibilities for gratification. Thus, personality development is sex differentiated. Actually, the differential treatment of girls and boys begins much earlier (Chapter 7), as Freud realized.

Female Development. The first hypothesized critical event of the phallic stage involves children's discovery that, contrary to their assumed previous belief, some people have a penis and others do not. A high valuation of the penis, and of the people who possess it, supposedly appear spontaneously in both sexes so that people without a penis are considered inferior. According to Freud, the little girl is *ashamed* to discover that her clitoris is not a penis, as she formerly thought. Her feeling of *inferiority* for her deficiency extends to her whole self. Mother, too, is devalued because of her own lack and because she has not given the girl a penis. (The fact that it is the male's sperm and not the female's egg that determines the sex of a child is irrelevant to the child and, therefore, to theories about children's thoughts and feelings.)

Freud claims that the girl gives up her active, "masculine," clitoral masturbation because it reminds her of her own shame and of the superiority of males. "She is wounded in her self-love by the unfavorable comparison with the boy who is so much better equipped and therefore . . . repudiates her love toward her mother and at the same time often represses a good deal of her sexual impulses in general" (Freud, 1933/1965, p.

126). With the abandonment of clitoral masturbation, some activity is renounced, and there is then "a wave of *passivity* . . . which opens the way to the turn towards femininity" (Freud, 1933/1965, p. 130). The normal Oedipal situation for the girl becomes established only when the wish for a penis is replaced by a wish for a baby. The father can satisfy this wish. Freudian theory does not require that the girl know the mechanisms of intercourse, nor desire it. She simply wants a baby with father; the details that are so important to adults are irrelevant to the child. It takes little psychological sophistication to observe young girls saying, "I'm going to marry Daddy and we'll have lots of babies." In sum, for the girl, the castration complex ("I've been castrated") leads to the **Oedipal complex** ("I want Daddy as my lover"), or as some psychoanalysts term it, the **Electra Complex.** The reverse is true for the boy.

Male Development. The young boy has been forming a close attachment with mother, so that with the increased genital interest of the phallic stage, he turns to her for genital satisfaction. Freudian theory does not require that the boy know the mechanics of sexual intercourse. Mother has fed him, caressed him, and bathed him, "By her care of the child's body she becomes his first seducer" (Freud, 1940/1963, p. 90). This is the Oedipal situation for the boy.

Mother is likely to reject the boy's sexual overtures, while accepting those of father. Meanwhile, the father is pressuring the boy to become a "little man" instead of "mama's boy." The boy, in fear of his rival, experiences castration anxiety, lest he lose his penis, as he has previously lost other valued objects (e.g., mother's breasts). Although ridiculous to adult ears, the fear is reasonable to the child; he thinks the penis is the source of the problem, so it seems reasonable that father might remove it. And, the boy now knows that some people do not have a penis. In rare cases of "perfect" development, the castration anxiety is so intense that the son's repression of his longing for mother and hostility toward father entirely destroys the Oedipal complex. In sum, Freud hypothesized that for the boy, the Oedipal situation leads to intense castration anxiety triggering the repression that destroys the Oedipal complex.

PAST THE PHALLIC

Identifications. For both girls and boys, the phallic stage ends when the child represses desire for the other sex parent and identifies with the same sex parent. **Identification** involves assuming characteristics of another person and is a widely used concept even among psychologists who are not Freudian (Chapter 9). For both sexes, Freud claimed that the identification is based on fear of retaliation from the same sex parent, as a powerful rival (**defensive identification,** or, identification with the aggressor) and on fear of losing the love of that parent, as a benevolent loved one (**anaclitic, or dependent, identification**). Actually, identification occurs with *both* parents. The Oedipal situation is actually a *fourfold* one: Both girls and boys have both affection and hostility toward the other sex parent as well as toward the parent of the same sex. Freud suggested that this double identification reflects physical bisexuality (only the sperm and the ovum are unambiguously one or the other). He also noted that girls often tend to "bring masculinity into prominence" and identify with father more than does the boy with mother. This, he speculated, was possibly because girls have an "active" ("malelike") clitoris, whereas boys lack a "passive" ("femalelike") structure corresponding to the vagina.

Superego. Because her hypothesized anxiety has been less than that of the boy (she has already lost what he fears losing), the girl's repression of the Oedipal situation is less complete than the boy's. Therefore, according to this reasoning, she will have a weaker superego and a less clear-cut and consistent identity as "feminine" than the boy will have as "masculine." The **superego** is an internalization of the child's perceptions of parental standards of what is appropriate and inappropriate; it rewards with feelings of pride and self-worth for appropriate behavior and punishes with guilt and self-devaluation for violation of standards. It is formed with the energy formerly used

in sexual and aggressive feelings toward the parents. The girl's weaker repression of the Oedipal situation frees less energy for superego development. With an impoverished superego, the girl is more externally defined and evaluated, dependent upon the approval or disapproval of other people more than on her own evaluations of herself. Freud also predicted that her moral judgments will be more dependent upon concrete aspects of a specific situation and, for example, on her compassion for the others involved rather than on abstract principles.

An important part of the superego standards are those regulating societally defined feminine or masculine thoughts, feelings, and actions. Thus, with a weaker superego the girl, and later the woman, presumably shows recurring signs of the masculinity she has not completely renounced and of her penis envy. Her inherent bisexuality has more free expressions than a man's. In Freudian theory, women who engage in masculine activities and deprecate themselves and other women have unresolved Oedipal feelings. According to Freud, a woman's femininity is mature and she is fully satisfied when she compensates for her penis envy and feelings of inferiority by having a child, especially a son. The desire for a son may also influence her relations with her husband, "Even a marriage is not made secure until the wife has succeeded in making her husband her child as well and in acting as a mother to him" (Freud, 1933/1965, pp. 133–134).

The Genital Stage. The genital stage, during adolescence, is in many ways a reliving of the phallic stage, though the person at this later age is more mature and capable of tenderness than was true at earlier ages. Remnants of the phallic stage may be seen in the choice of partners for romantic attachment, as the girl's favorite suitor turns out to be much like her father, and the boy searches for "a girl just like the girl who married dear old dad." However, the girl's choice is different if she is free of the Oedipus complex: "Where the choice is able to show itself freely, it is often made in accordance with the narcissistic ideal of the man whom the girl had wished to become" (Freud, 1933/1965, pp. 132–133). More generally, a man may search for a wife who is more caregiver and mother than a wife, and he may not be able to enjoy sex with the woman he loves, just as he was not allowed to enjoy sex with mother. The woman may want a man with the dominance she perceived in her father, while also being envious and hostile about his dominance. For Freud, maturity is associated with orgasm in heterosexual intercourse. He claimed that women's problems in achieving a mature orgasm are complicated by the necessity to shift from the "active clitoris" to the "passive vagina." (Modern research does not support Freud's distinction between vaginal and clitoral orgasms; see Chapter 12).

Although Freud emphasized passivity in women and activity in men, he was clear that activity–passivity in particular, and masculinity–femininity in general, are *not* simple either–or matters. "The reactions of human individuals of both sexes are of course made up of masculine and feminine traits" (Freud, 1925/1972a, p. 190). He discussed the appropriateness and necessity of tremendous activity in the pursuit of goals he labeled passive, mentioning particularly the active nature of childbirth.

COMMENTARY

Global theories like Freud's are difficult to test, and available findings are mixed. Generally, there is minimal research support for the explanatory mechanisms postulated (e.g., castration anxiety, penis envy), for either masculine or feminine development (Sherman, 1971). For example, young children do not seem to have the accurate body concepts implied by Freudian theory and do not seem particularly upset about the genitals of either sex. There is little evidence of castration anxiety in women or of widespread anatomical envy. In fact, some research suggests that girls' lack of a penis may be more upsetting to boys than to girls. It seems unlikely that penis envy plays the role in the psychology of women that Freud assigned to it.

However, some of Freud's broad descriptions of the consequences of social experiences do have

confirmation from research, such as that discussed in several later chapters (especially 8, 9, 10, 11, and 12). As Freud observed, both women and men report higher evaluation of males than of females. Fewer desirable traits are used in describing women than men; the work of women is recognized and praised less than that of men, even when it is the same work. Girls are less rigidly and thoroughly feminine than boys are masculine (by role criteria). Many women let or encourage a man to be the active leader in their relationship and get their way by subtle manipulation (activity under the cloak of passivity). Many women do feel useless and depressed if they are not actively involved in having children.

If not by penis envy, how does all this come about? Much of the research of psychology of women is an attempt to find the answers. Perpetuating a *literal* concept of penis envy as broadly explanatory of women generally does not seem helpful. Perhaps if Freud had had more information about the human body, he might have diminished his emphasis on the penis and discussed other biological factors (see Chapters 3, 4, 6, and 7). Yet, his emphasis on the penis had some merit. Young children are aware of different attributes and valuation of males and females; thus they might try to understand the differences on the basis of an obvious physical difference. Boys do eagerly compare penis length. Impotence is more feared by many adult men than loss of an arm or leg. Adult women who are angry with a man often express their feelings with derogatory statements about his genitals.

In some species, penile erection is a power display that subdues or repels attackers; in some human cultures, actual or portrayed penile erection is thought by the people involved to repel both natural enemies and evil spirits (Wickler, 1969/1972). Thus, Freud might have had some wisdom in choosing the penis as a symbol of power. Some recent Freudians emphasize that it is the *power* symbolized that is important rather than the penis itself as an object (e.g., Clara Thompson, 1964/1971; Maria Torok, 1970).

However, we may still ask why Freud did not give equal attention to the comparable deficiency of men: Men do not have a vagina and cannot carry a fetus within their womb, nor nurture an infant at their breast. Some psychoanalysts have tried to correct Freud's masculine bias. Karen Horney (1926) hypothesized that the femininity complex of men is more severe than the masculinity complex in women; Bruno Bettelheim (1962) concluded that womb envy has been underestimated and penis envy overestimated. Can men be less well explained in terms of womb envy than women in terms of penis envy? If so, perhaps it is our cultural values that we should criticize. Freud did not cause the problems he tried to depict and explain, and he recognized the imperfections of men as well as women in meeting the ideals he himself postulated.

. . . we shall, of course, willingly agree that the majority of men are also far behind the masculine ideal and that *all human individuals,* as a result of their bisexual disposition and of cross inheritance, *combine* in themselves *both* masculine and feminine characteristics, so that pure masculinity and femininity remain *theoretical constructions* of *uncertain content''* (Freud, 1925/1972a, p. 193, italics added).

For this statement, at least, Freud has much modern empirical support (see Constantinople, 1974; Donelson, 1975).

TOWARD THE SELF

Whatever the merits or demerits of Freud's theory, other theorists have done more to develop concepts regarding the self and to emphasize that personality growth continues throughout life. With a more proactive view, they emphasize that humans are capable of assuming responsibility for the conscious direction of their own lives in spite of societal pressures. Carl Jung and Carl Rogers are discussed here to illustrate such theorists.

CARL JUNG

Overview: Reactive and Proactive. Life is creative. It is a continuing movement toward the ideal of self-**actualization.** However, one must courageously assume personal responsibility for creative development into selfhood. According to Jung, each of us has *all* human qualities, by virtue of our common human heritage; personality development requires recognizing and dealing with all aspects of our personality. We are all introvert and extrovert, masculine and feminine, poet and scientist; we all have tendencies to approach the world with logic and reason and with feelings of personal like or dislike. We differ in the responsibility we assume for our own development and, of course, we differ in life experiences. Nevertheless, some experiences are relatively pervasive. Most of us prefer to recognize our own good and to deny the existence of our own evil nature. What we do not accept as our own and do not deal with as a fact of ourselves is nonetheless present in the unconscious, or in our inner character, and influences our behavior.

In short, we have as givens all human qualities and our overt expression of these is a function of early and continuing social experiences. Thus, Jung is a reactive theorist. He is also proactive. We are to assume responsibility for our development throughout life. We have a past but also a future, and we can direct our life toward the ideal of selfhood (see Jung, 1943, 1945/1956; Campbell, 1971; Jacobi, 1942/1968).

Inner and Outer Characters—Mask and Soul. Some traits and principles of functioning are considered masculine and some are considered feminine. Jung suggested that females may have a genetic tilt favoring the stronger development of their feminine relative to their masculine potential, whereas males may have a tilt favoring the reverse pattern. However, Jung agrees with Freud about the inherent bisexuality of human beings and views everyone as both feminine and masculine. Full development requires recognition of this fact. The problem is that social experiences are likely to encourage the development of only one set of characteristics and discourage the development of the other. We are thus often led to "forget who we really are."

More accurately, we often never know who we are. We are encouraged to think of ourselves only in terms of what we consciously develop and show to the world as our outer character—the mask that Jung calls the **persona** (Latin for *theater mask*). The persona is feminine or masculine, and whatever qualities are lacking in this outer character are present in the inner character, or the soul. The unrecognized, inner characteristics may influence our behavior in unusual ways.

Animus and Anima. For Jung, the masculine aspect of a woman's total being is the **animus** (Latin, for *spirit*, masculine). Her soul is masculine. The feminine soul of a man, which complements his outer character, is the **anima** (Latin for *spirit*, feminine). His soul is feminine. Because of reciprocal development of inner and outer traits, the most feminine women outwardly are the most masculine inwardly; the most masculine men outwardly are the most feminine inwardly. Recognizing one's masculinity *and* femininity is necessary for effective interpersonal relations as well as for progress toward selfhood.

Relations with Others. To the extent that people accept and develop their own animus or anima, they may appreciate each other. Because of her own masculinity, a woman may understand a man; because of his own femininity, a man may understand a woman. If we have not accepted all of our own characteristics, we distort our perceptions of others, particularly by projection. That is, we try to see in them what we do not acknowledge in ourselves. We see what we need to see to complete our view of self. The man who does not accept his own femininity may therefore prefer extremely feminine-acting women and have difficulty accepting women who clearly violate his ideal. Conversely, a woman who insists on extreme masculinity in her male acquaintances may be denying her own masculinity and projecting it onto men, rejecting those for whom the projection is not easy. We see and love (or hate) in others what we are ourselves but cannot see and love (or hate) in ourselves.

Specifically, according to Jung, the woman who sees her lover as the Conquering Hero is herself that. The mother who sees her daughter as a Temptress and the man who sees that daughter as the Young Innocent are themselves what

they see in that woman. To react strongly to the Witch in another woman may indicate lack of acceptance of the Witch in ourselves. Vehement denunciation of "castrating women" may be but a sign of an unrecognized desire to act as they seem to be acting. Few women, if any, come close to being a perfect embodiment of femininity, in either its positive or negative aspects; few men, if any, are perfectly masculine in either positive or negative ways. We do ill by others, and by ourselves, if we try to make them into what we need them to be to complete ourselves.

Conversely, relationships with others affect the development of our inner character. If we have good relationships with members of the other sex, we are more likely to be able to deal with the qualities of the other sex that we ourselves have. If a man does not establish good relations with the real women he encounters, femininity will dominate his inner life and cause further problems with women. One outcome may be an overly masculine outward adaptation, particularly when there are extreme pressures from others to "be a man." Or, his femininity may erupt and take over his life. If a woman does not establish good relations with the men in her life, she may attempt to deny her own masculinity. She may then relapse into an infantile helplessness, or perhaps an all-absorbing motherhood that engulfs her children and perhaps her husband as well. Her unrecognized animus may erupt in excessive demands for obedience and prestige in the home; instructions to children and husbands are given with the stern vehemence of, "Now hear this . . ." Opinionated stubborness may also express a woman's uncontrolled masculinity.

Logos and Eros. Jung seemed to identify Logos as the masculine principle of personality. **Logos,** often equated with light, is the principle that forms and differentiates, brings order out of chaos and strives for mastery and competence. The feminine principle is **Eros,** often equated with darkness: the principle of relatedness and receptivity, a tendency to love and nurture life potentialities. The typical developmental trend for males is in the direction of Logos (an agentic orienta-

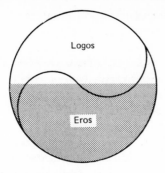

Figure 2-1.
Symbol denoting Logos and Eros in complete personality.

Jung uses the conventional symbolic imagery in which light stands for masculinity and dark for femininity. Light is also used to represent consciousness, while dark represents unconsciousness. Thus, the usual symbols of this kind do not depict the typical woman hypothesized very well, in whom femininity, or Eros, is conscious and Logos, or masculinity, is more unconscious. This problem is not specific to Jung.

For Jung, the complete person, of either sex, is both light and dark, just as the complete day is both light and dark. With movement toward actualization, we develop and differentiate more and more of what was previously unconscious.

Actualized personality for Jung is a complete totality, symbolized by the circle, or mandala, which is considered a perfect figure.

tion); and, for females, toward Eros (a communal orientation). As with other aspects of personality, what is denied in self is sought in others. However, the complete person operates by *both* Logos and Eros, just as the complete day is both light and dark. Completeness is frequently symbolized as a circle, denoting the fullness of selfhood (Figure 2-1).

Selfhood. Self is both a potential that directs our growth toward wholeness and is the ideal result of the growth. As an outcome, it is a perfect whole, which includes and integrates all aspects of personality. Self is a point of unity that gives stability among one's diverse human characteristics. Given the complexity of the human being, it takes time to develop our humanity fully. Thus, the self and its movement toward development and integration is not usually clearly evident until middle age. Even then it is not complete, but remains a motivating ideal. We may expedite our growth, even in younger years, if we accept the responsibility of freedom for our own growth: "Personality can never develop itself unless the individual chooses his own way consciously and with conscious, moral decision" (Jung, 1939, p. 287).

Commentary. Some modern readers may like Jung's conclusions about the wholeness of development, but resist his general division of many human traits into feminine or masculine, and the equation of Logos with light and Eros with dark. Jung does seem to assume the association of femininity with femaleness and masculinity with maleness (biopsychological equivalence). However, the kinds of personality attributes he assumes to be feminine or masculine do match well with contemporary role stereotypes. Perhaps more important, his views about the necessity of development of both kinds of characteristics are supported by research and modern conceptions of androgyny, which means having characteristics of both sexes (Donelson, 1975). For example, androgyny is related to cognitive development and to creativity. In other chapters we shall further consider the value of self-fulfillment and of androgyny specifically. Jung seems the first to explicitly develop such a modern theme as an integral part of a theory of personality.

CARL ROGERS

Although they approach their work as personality theorists from vastly different backgrounds, both Carl Rogers and Carl Jung see life as a creative growth process. Rogers did not discuss sex similarities and differences in the detail of Freud or Jung, but his theory still is relevant to our concerns. Like Jung, Rogers notes that restrictive social experiences interfere with growth by inhibiting the recognition of one's potentialities. But Rogers differs somewhat from Jung in viewing the unfolding of life potential as a more natural, spontaneous, and effortless process (1959, 1961, 1963).

Actualization. Rogers assumes that all life forms, human and nonhuman, have an inherent *actualizing tendency:* a biological pressure to grow and behave consistently with something like a genetic blueprint. This actualizing tendency is selective, constructive, and directive. We strive to maintain and enhance our life; so we do not develop *all* potentials, such as the potential for inflicting pain on ourselves. Anyone who has seen the persistent quiver of growth in a tiny flower shoot emerging from its seed or the insistence of a bean sprout moving the earth clods around it can appreciate the inherent power and health of this growth tendency. The growth of a human being is no less miraculous and no less detectable to the observer who cares to look. Rogers further suggests that humans would be better off if we, like the flower, could trust that life force and not interfere with it by being as self-aware and as dominated by our conscious intellect as many of us are. We are wiser than our intellect, but do not trust that wisdom. We try to actualize what we think we are (self) rather than what we really are in our totality (organism).

The *self-actualizing tendency* is a distinctly psychological offshoot of the actualizing tendency: a pressure to behave, develop, and experience in a way consistent with our *conscious* views of who we are. Self or **self-concept** consists of the perceptions available to awareness of I or me, and the perceptions of the relationships of I or me to other people and aspects of life. In early life, we begin developing a self-concept from the perceived approval or disapproval of others. Because the experience of self is associated with satisfaction or frustration of the need to be loved, the growing child comes to have a need to approve of self, to have a sense of self-worth. The standards one uses for self-evaluation are those that others are perceived as using. Thus, the views of others are internalized, much as for Freud's concept of

the superego, and we try to behave consistently with those views.

Incongruence. Unfortunately, many of our socialization experiences, with parents for example, foster an incongruence between the self-actualization tendency and the actualization tendency. Rogers calls this incongruence the "basic estrangement." The estrangement occurs because people have held *conditional positive regard* for the individual. That is, standards of behavior are laid down, and the individual is accepted, loved, and respected *only* on the condition that those standards are met. The person is not accepted when the standards are violated. Because of others' conditional regard, we come to hold **conditions of worth** for self: We accept ourselves *only* upon conditions. To engage in behavior inconsistent with the conditions of worth, or even to recognize our desires to do so, leads to self-disapproval, guilt, and feelings of unworthiness. Therefore we use defenses that deny or distort part of our total experience in order to prevent violations of the conditions of worth and an incongruence among conscious perceptions of ourselves. Although the defenses enable us to keep our self-perceptions consistent and feel that we are meeting our conditions of worth, they restrict our actualization tendency (Figure 2-2). By trying

Figure 2-2.
Schematic diagram of Rogers' theory about growth and defensiveness.

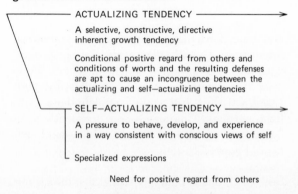

ACTUALIZING TENDENCY

A selective, constructive, directive inherent growth tendency

Conditional positive regard from others and conditions of worth and the resulting defenses are apt to cause an incongruence between the actualizing and self–actualizing tendencies

SELF–ACTUALIZING TENDENCY

A pressure to behave, develop, and experience in a way consistent with conscious views of self

Specialized expressions

Need for positive regard from others

Need for self–regard

to be what we think we should be, we do not do a good job of being what we are. We interfere with our own nature.

Fully Functioning Person. Rogers believes that the basic estrangement may be avoided, or minimized, if we receive *unconditional positive regard;* others accept us without conditions. We can then develop *unconditional* self-regard. Although parents and others may establish and enforce some rules for a child, their *acceptance* of the child is not contingent upon her or his behavior. A child may be punished for violating a standard, but still feel accepted, valued, and loved. A friend may complain about our behavior without making us feel like a worthless person. The message is to "hate the sin, love the sinner." With unconditional positive regard, there are no conditions of worth, and no need for defenses that interfere with the actualization tendency. We can allow all of what we feel and are and want into our awareness. We can choose to refrain from aggressive behavior, for example, but we need not feel ashamed of our aggressive feelings nor deny them. There is congruence between self-concept and our total being (organism). We can be open to the experience of all that we are, and all that other people are as well. We can be a congruent, genuine, fully functioning person: We can (1) be creative, (2) be open to experience, (3) live in the reality of the moment rather than trying to twist it to fit our preconceptions and defensive needsn (4) trust ourselves to make correct and constructive decisions, and (5) experience ourselves as choosing freely.

Unless we are very unusual, we are not functioning fully because we have some conditions of worth. Are we doomed to continue a life of defensiveness, fearing discovery of who we really are? No! And we need not go to a professional therapist to grow. Changes from a defensive toward an open style of living may occur any time one congruent, genuine, fully functioning person has an impact upon another person. The greater the genuineness and congruence in one person, the greater the likelihood of growth in the other, because a genuine person is free to accept others

unconditionally, without the constrictive need to try to force them to be as one's own defenses need them to be. The others can become more free to express, respect, and value themselves. Friends, lovers, teachers, students—all may provide such a therapeutic experience. The possibilities for personality development and growth in adulthood are limitless. So, too, are the possibilities for the perpetuation of defensiveness in meeting our conditions of worth and holding conditional regard for others. Our lives are highly intertwined. As we grow toward the freedom of knowing and valuing who we are, we become more able to know and value others and to assist them in their own growth.

Commentary. Rogers' theory has a reasonable amount of research support on several counts (Donelson, 1973). For example, self-acceptance and acceptance of others tend to be related. Children with high esteem come from homes in which they were clearly valued and respected as persons and were expected to abide by few but reasonable and firmly enforced rules. In general, college students' views of themselves are related to their views of how their parents perceive them.

Although Rogers has not explicitly developed a psychology of women or of sex differences, as other theorists have, it is obvious that **role** expectations are dominant sources of conditional positive regard and of conditions of worth. Too often, people disparage a woman who behaves as they expect a man to behave or a man who shows behavior they consider feminine. In Rogers' terms, they are holding conditional positive regard for others, perhaps because of their own conditions of worth. Some people who consider themselves enlightened, tolerant, and liberal, react to role-inconsistent behavior with the presumed acceptance of, "Well, you can be a little nutty if you want to be." They have missed the point. They are still devaluing and censuring another human being.

Aside from others' censure, we may limit ourselves because of our *internal* conditions of worth. Thus a woman student may "explain away" her fascination with physics that would lead to what she considers a "masculine" career by attributing it to a crush on the physics instructor. The mother who wants to return to school or start a private business may feel guilty that motherhood is not enough for her and squelch what she feels are inappropriate desires. Similarly the man who wants to quit his executive job to become a writer may decide against his dream for fear that he could not then live up to his own image as a financially successful provider for his family. In such cases, it is possible that the other people im-

mediately involved do make their acceptance conditional upon role-consistent behavior. However, it is also true that because of our own rigid conditions of worth, we may be slow to realize that we *are* accepted and loved for what we are. When we cannot let go and be what we are, we miss the chance to discover that our friends and loved ones will accept us still, even if our behavior changes. We may have difficulty accepting ourselves because of strong conditions of worth that are not relevant to important others. We fear.

SUMMARY

From their diverse perspectives, personality theorists have some common themes that can help us examine and develop our own implicit personality theories as well as improve our own lives. Some formal theories, like complete implicit personality theories, are reactive; some are proactive. However, they all agree on the common human problem that people develop defenses as a result of unpleasant experiences, mainly in interactions with other people. The defenses prevent self-knowledge, inhibit the expression of some of our potential, and distort perceptions of other people. For Freud, some defensiveness is necessary for civilized society to curb our aggression and sexuality. For Jung and Rogers, defenses prevent self-awareness. They note that in order to grow we need to recognize all of our potentials, even those we do not want to act upon.

Many of the potentials that we are not aware of, or do not feel free to act upon, involve expectations based on conceptions of "femininity" or "masculinity." The traits males are led to accept

in themselves are essentially agentic ones (e.g., activity and Logos). The traits females are led to accept in themselves are essentially communal ones (e.g., passivity and Eros). With defensiveness, we do not accept all of ourselves and, thus, cannot fully accept other people as what they are, just as they do not fully accept us for the persons we are.

What if other people are not willing or able to help us to be what we really are? Within a purely proactive model, we can choose, perhaps with what Jung called a moral decision, to help ourselves. We will be in a better position to help ourselves if we have more knowledge about specific ways in which biological and socialization factors have shaped our development. Other chapters in this book will offer some of the currently available information about how women become what they are, some of the problems they have, and some of the ways in which some women have chosen to seek alternatives to the traditional life-style expected of them.

PART TWO

PSYCHOBIOLOGICAL FOUNDATIONS OF SEX-TYPED BEHAVIOR

INTERPRETING NATURE'S LESSONS

The chapters in this section deal with biological sex differences in humans and in other species and also with the behavioral implications of these differences. Because arguments about the appropriateness or desirability of human sex roles often are buttressed by the assertion, "But it's only natural!" it is important to know *what* is natural. With this issue, as with many in the Psychology of Women, there is much selective misinformation and fuzzy thinking. Some people consider as "just natural" what species other than humans do. This kind of argument has many fallacies. What is natural for other species is not necessarily natural for humans. Even among human species, there is considerable variability, and many complexities of interaction between individuals and their environment.

For example, as a "natural" defense of a traditional division of labor between human females and males, some people cite the case of selected species—such as baboons—where the females concentrate on care of the young while the males focus their energies on looking out for predators and defending the group. This argument extrapolates from a limited sample of information, assumes a biological explanation, and fails to examine other variables that might account for the baboon social structure. Actually, the baboon's division of labor between the sexes is common also among other monkeys *when* the group is in an environmental situation where foraging for food is problematic and complicated by the presence of many predators. However, this social structure is *not* common among monkeys in different habitats where food is more plentiful and predators less of a menace. Thus factors in the physical and social environment affect social behavior, so that a workable arrangement between the sexes in one setting may not occur in another.

NATURAL "PURPOSE"?

A further extrapolation from the "laws of nature" occurs when people claim their principles for moral conduct are based on biological universals. For example, in their prescriptions regarding human sexual behavior, some people assert that the "natural purpose" of copulation is procreation. Although selected examples from some nonhuman species support this assertion, there are many additional instances that do not. The genitalia of some animals are used for functions in addition to copulation. Male monkeys often display their penises as a threat or indication of group boundaries; and many mammals deposit scents from their genitalia to indicate travel routes or to mark territories. Furthermore, sexual behavior between two members of a species is not always exclusively procreational. There are many instances of sexual encounters between same-sex members of a species, where clearly procreation will not result. In addition, in some primates copulation between a male and female is not only for procreation but also serves to maintain the bond between the mated pair (Wickler, 1972). Thus, the asserted natural law basis for moral statements against contraception or homosexuality is not supported by the facts discovered by direct observation of nature.

What is Natural? Ratner's chapter on a comparative view further documents the tremendous variability of female and male behaviors in different species and within a species, depending on various biological and environmental conditions. Even the division of a species into two distinct sexes does not occur throughout the natural world. Furthermore, where there are two sexes, the behavior of an organism cannot be predicted only from knowledge of its sex. A female is an individual who produces an egg; a male is one who produces a sperm. Beyond that, specific behaviors relevant to sexual behavior and care of the young vary across species, with the female's responses predominating in some, the male's responses in others, and both in still other species. So the most accurate answer to the question, "*What* is natural?" is, "Everything!"

With reference to the human situation, Ratner notes the utility of several findings from comparative studies of species, particularly the plasticity of behavior among domesticated species (which humans certainly are) and the impact of early life experiences in shaping behavior. What, then, can we safely conclude about consistent natural laws? In view of the natural diversity in behaviors of females and males, only two human occupations should have specific sex qualifications: The job of *sperm donor* and the job of *wet nurse* (a lactating female who supplies milk for infants).

SEX AND GENDER

Although there is within-sex variation in physical characteristics and in behavior among humans, as well as other species, people tend to oversimplify sex and gender into two mutually exclusive classes. Sex refers to the biological male-female division; gender to divisions partly based on distinguishable characteristics such as sex, but including also relatively arbitrary characteristics. In Chapter 4, Hatton dismisses the prevalent unidimensional and bipolar conceptualization of

women and men (Chapter 1): he notes that gender designations of femininity and masculinity are based on multidimensional criteria involving structural appearance, biological functioning, and overt behavior.

Even the "structure of sex" is much more complex than a simple female–male distinction based on external genitalia. Judgments about whether a person is biologically female or male depend upon the criterion used in the evaluation—one may be female by one criterion and male by another. Sex definition includes the following components: (1) *chromosomal* sex; (2) *gonadal* sex, such as ovaries and testes; (3) *hormonal* sex, including the fetus' production of and sensitivity to hormones; secondary sex characteristics that become prominent at puberty; (4) internal accessory organs, such as the uterus and fallopian tubes or the prostate gland; and (5) external genital organs, such as the clitoris or penis. Different combinations of these criteria can occur, so that the "biological basis" of sex can be very ambiguous. **Hermaphrodites,** for example, may possess the internal organs of one sex and the external organs of the other sex. Furthermore, their external organs may not correspond to their chromosomal sex.

HORMONAL CONTRIBUTIONS

Thus sex, like gender, is complex and multidimensional. Even the so-called sex hormones are not the exclusive property of one sex. Progesterone is considered a female hormone and androgen a male hormone, but physically normal females and males have both. The difference is not all-or-none, but rather a matter of degree. Androgen is associated with sexual desire in both females and males, although it is not the exclusive determinant of desire in either sex. Furthermore, as Hatton elaborates, androgen also plays a crucial role in the differentiation of male genitalia in a developing fetus. Genetic males with *androgen insensitivity* can develop a sufficiently feminine outward appearance to qualify for a career in fashion modeling. *Androgenized females* possibly are more "tomboyish" than other girls, including their siblings; otherwise they are fairly typical achieving females.

TRANSEXUALS

Much has been learned about hormonal influences on sex through animal experimentation and clinical studies of humans with various hormonal anomalies. However, transexuals remain a mystery. Transexuals typically are physiologically "normal" members of their sex according to standard criteria. They appear normal and are capable of reproductive activity. Yet, in spite of the evidence of their sexual normality, transexuals firmly believe they are trapped in the wrong body—that they "really" are members of the other sex. Psychotherapy is notoriously ineffective in modifying their self-definition; the only effective treatment seems to be a surgical and hormonal sex change. Interestingly, there are more male than female transexuals.

CONSEQUENCES
OF SEX DIFFERENCES

Physical sex differences occasion different dilemmas, decisions, and satisfactions that vary with the environment and with the individual. For example, a host of day-to-day decisions are associated with beard growth. Menstrual cycles may have a more profound impact on women's lives in some cultures than in others. As Landers discusses, cultures very in the content of their often emotion-laden responses to menstruation. In some cases, menstrual myths enhance a woman's status because of the presumed magical qualities of menstrual blood. More often, however, such myths result in a restriction of a woman's freedom and social devaluation of her "unclean" nature. Even within a single culture, there is much within-sex variation. The topic of menstruation illustrates an important point: the uniqueness of a common experience. All physically normal women menstruate, but the implications of the process are as varied as are their individual personalities. For women in general, there is an increase in "symptoms" premenstrually and menstrually. However, within that general trend, women differ in exactly what physical or psycho-

logical indices are associated with their cycle, and when they occur. Some women have increased *positive* feelings premenstrually. Others are more anxious during the middle of their cycle than around the time of menstruation. More generally, menstruation is one of many research areas in which past researchers have been misled by conventional but erroneous preconceptions. Women do not inevitably become "witches" at "that time of the month."

COGNITIVE ABILITIES

Global assertions about which sex is more intelligent are misleading and oversimplified because of the many abilities relevant to intelligence measurement. Generally females score higher than males on measures of some types of verbal abilities, perceptual speed, rote memory, and manual dexterity. Males typically score higher than females on measures of spatial ability, numerical reasoning, and scientific knowledge. The broad classes of verbal and spatial abilities have been particularly well studied, and Harris discusses some of the pervasive sex differences in these measures (Chapter 6).

VERBAL AND
SPATIAL ABILITIES

Girls generally progress faster than boys in various aspects of language development, including amount of vocalization, age of first word spoken, verbal fluency, articulation, and comprehensibility of speech. Conversely, more males than females exhibit reading disabilities and expressive speech disorders, such as stuttering and stammering. Some of the sex differences appear during the first year of life, with the beginning of articulate speech, and continue into adulthood. The average male never quite catches up to the average female in articulation and fluency, though there is overlap as usual. Evidence is conflicting about the existence and direction of sex differences in vocabulary size and in verbal comprehension and reasoning beyond early school years.

In contrast, males generally perform better than females on spatial tasks, although about 20 to 25 percent of females reach or exceed the male average. Spatial abilities involve the effective perception and processing of information about objects and their spatial relationships. Such abilities may be manifest in activities like aiming at a target, arranging objects in a given pattern, imagining how an object would appear if rotated, or having a good sense of direction.

EXPLANATIONS OF SEX DIFFERENCES

Generally sex differences in spatial and verbal abilities are not disputed, but there is continuing debate about *why* they occur and their implications in the lives of individuals. Preschool boys tend to prefer—and are encouraged to prefer—games emphasizing movement, strength, body contact, and throwing—activities that might facilitate development of spatial ability. But a purely environmentalistic explanation of male superiority in spatial ability is weakened by the fact that once sex differences for many indices of spatial ability appear in children, the differences are of approximately the same magnitude as differences among adults. If the differences were due *only* to sex-dif-

ferentiated experience, they should increase with age, as more sex-typed experiences are encountered. With reference to biological contributors, a reasonable—though not conclusive—case has been made that spatial ability is associated with a genetic sex-linked factor that is more likely to be expressed in males than in females (Harris, 1975).

For verbal abilities, Harris presents a careful overview of the evidence regarding possible brain hemispheric differences as well as evidence regarding environmental influences. The interplay of these factors is complex and the research still is very much in the "in progress" stage.

The chapters in this section thus present a foundation for a **psychobiological** perspective on females and males, in which biological predispositions have implications varying with individuals and their environments. In the coming sections we shall discuss some effects of environmental experiences on the developing individual. Already we have been forewarned that much about the sexes that is considered "just obvious" or "just natural" is considerably more complex.

CHAPTER 3
GENDER THROUGH THE ANIMAL WORLD: THE COMPARATIVE VIEW *

PERSPECTIVE AND BACKGROUND
REPRODUCTION
SEXUAL DIMORPHISM
GENERALITY AND QUALITY OF SEXUAL DIMORPHISM
REASONS FOR SEXUAL DIMORPHISM
MODES OF SEXUAL REPRODUCTION

ANALYSIS OF BEHAVIORS OF FEMALES AND MALES
RESEARCH ON ANIMAL BEHAVIOR
NATURALISTIC OBSERVATION
EXPERIMENTAL CONTROL AND MANIPULATION
Varying Hormonal Adjustments
Changing Learning Experiences
BEHAVIOR ANALYSIS OF REPRODUCTION
APPETITIVE SEXUAL BEHAVIOR COMPONENT
CONSUMMATORY SEXUAL COMPONENT
POSTCONSUMMATORY SEXUAL COMPONENT
NESTING AND CARE OF EGGS AND YOUNG
Constructing a Nest
Finding a Ready-Made Nest

CHARACTERISTICS OF SPECIES AND SEX SPECIFIC BEHAVIORS
THE FUNCTION OF DISPLAYS
DECREASING DISTANCE
COMMUNICATING NONVERBALLY
DYNAMIC PROPERTIES
TEMPORARY BEHAVIOR MODIFICATIONS
PERMANENT CHANGES
Effects of Domestication

SUMMARY

* Dr. Stanley Ratner died in December, 1975. The editors wish to acknowledge the contributions of Dr. Eileen Van Tassell of the Department of Natural Science at Michigan State University. Dr. Van Tassell assisted in general revisions of Dr. Ratner's earlier version of this chapter, and she also expanded the evolutionary perspective on reproduction.

Comparative psychology deals with the behaviors of all species of animals, including humans, and emphasizes the diversities of behaviors (Denny & Ratner, 1970; Ford & Beach, 1951, 1970). By exposing the tremendous variety and complexity of behaviors shown by females and males of different species, the comparative view provides a *perspective* for considering the psychology of women, as well as a *vocabulary* for describing behavior. Because of their importance and their relevance to sex differences, this chapter will focus on behaviors associated with reproduction, including sexual behavior, nesting, and care of the young.

PERSPECTIVE AND BACKGROUND

REPRODUCTION

Understanding reproduction is so important that early in most biologists' training, they learn that the chicken and egg question has a somewhat humorous answer: "A chicken is an egg's way of producing another egg." The evolutionary goal of every individual is to pass its genes on to greater numbers of offspring than its competitors. The environment interacts with the genes in very complex ways, often referred to as natural selection, and this interaction determines the effectiveness of every individual in producing viable offspring. Some reproductive behaviors that initially seem unnecessarily elaborate and complicated have in reality enabled organisms to reproduce with competitive success.

Eggs and sperm, and even male and female forms of an organism, are actually secondary features in sexual reproduction. The major feature of sexual reproduction is the combination of genes from two diffrent organisms and the consequent "shuffling of the deck" to produce offspring somewhat different from either parent. Through sexual reproduction a large range of genetic combinations are "tried out" on the environment. In evolutionary perspective, the environment itself is constantly changing so that "trial models" may be successful in a new environment, whereas they would not succeed in the old one. Thus some combination of the parents' genes survive. This process has been compared to a game in which the object is not to "win" but to play again. The number and variety of mechanisms for accomplishing this recombination are astounding, and only a brief account can be given in this chapter.

Sexual reproduction occurs in all species of vertebrates (animals with backbones, including humans) and most species of invertebrates, such as insects and worms. However, litrally thousands of species of invertebrates reproduce by asexual means; that is, by reproduction involving only one parent with no special reproductive structures. Some of these reproduce by division; some by growing buds that then break off as independent individuals. Some species reproduce by asexual or by sexual means, depending on conditions of their age, health, and the environment. Almost every possible strategy for reproduction occurs in one or more species of invertebrates.

SEXUAL DIMORPHISM

The occurrence within a species of two forms or two types of individuals for purposes of reproduction is called sexual **dimorphism**. Dimorphism includes differences between females and males in bodily structure, physiology, and behavior. Actually, sexual dimorphism is but one example of **polymorphism** that occurs for many species of animals. Polymorphism is the occurrence of individuals of a species in more than one form; it is one way for the species to get a number of vital functions performed. For example, feeding, defense, and reproduction are accomplished by different individuals in different forms in one species of jellyfish.

In contrast, some species are unimorphic, meaning that the individual members have only one form. If the species has asexual reproduction, the unimorph reproduces itself exactly and endlessly, for instance by budding. If the species has sexual reproduction, each individual must carry sexual products of both sexes and fertilize itself or, more commonly, provide its own eggs (or sperm) to receive the sperm (or eggs) of another individual. The individuals of a unimorph species that reproduces sexually are called **hermaphrodites**—each individual has both female and male structures, processes, and behaviors. Such hermaphrodites include earthworms and snails. Among some protozoans, an individual may behave as a female to one organism and as a male to the next. Interestingly, among certain vertebrate fishes, a single individual may spend part of its life as a male and part as a female.

Generality and Quality of Sexual Dimorphism. In some species, such as humans, the differences between female and male individuals are usually noticeable throughout the adult lives of the animals. In other species, the differences are very subtle and appear and recede at various stages of the reproductive cycle. For example, inquisitive humans can distinguish the female and male of some species of oysters and sea anemones only by microscopic examination of reproductive tissue. Even among some mammals like the spotted hyena, males and females are so similar that close inspection of external genitalia is necessary to positively distinguish a "he" from a "she" (Wickler, 1969/1972). On the other hand, humans and some other mammals and birds are notable for conspicuous, permanent differences between adult females and males. Even the casual observer can discriminate the female from the male robin or the female from the male lion.

Differences between adult females and males in some butterflies and beetles include chemical secretions, **pheromones,** from the female that mix with the air and are detected by the male. Minute quantities of the pheromone in the air enable the male to move upwind until the stimulus is sufficient to provide a directional orientation to the female. Possibly pheromones are involved with some human behavior relevant to reproduction (Chapter 4). However, the sex differences most obvious to humans include shape, voice pitch, and quantity and distribution of body hair—secondary sex characteristics that become pronounced during puberty.

These few examples of sexual dimorphism illustrate the range of differences that appear between females and males of a species. No single index of dimorphism allows us to distinguish the female from the male for all species. That is, females neither have higher voices nor lower voices than males for all species. Similarly, females are neither always larger nor always smaller than males for all species. Thus, there is a wide range of differences between the sexes: Some species show conspicuous differences, some muted differences, some temporary and subtle differences, and others show almost no differences. Furthermore, the differences that do appear can go in any direction. In addition to the variation between females and males of a species, there also are individual differences within each sex of a species (within-sex variation) in numbers and extent of typical dimorphic characteristics. Among humans, there is no single measurement that always defines every individual as either female or male—not even childbearing since some women cannot biologically do so.

Reasons for Sexual Dimorphism. Sexual reproduction that involves the combination of genetic materials from two or more individuals of the species requires that the individuals of the species get their genetic materials together. Once again, almost every conceivable strategy has evolved. The females and males of some species that live in water merely shed eggs and sperm materials that drift together. The oyster and sea anemone, animals that show almost no sexual dimorphism, reproduce in this manner. However, individuals of species that move and reproduce sexually must get together in order to share genetic materials. If the sexes look different from each other, then problems associated with finding the appropriate mate are reduced.

However, the need to find a mate often must be counterbalanced by the need to avoid predators. Many species, therefore, develop dimorphic mechanisms other than conspicuous visual differences. For example, "look-alike" sexes may evolve song or sound patterns, dances, flight patterns, or touch sequences by which to recognize members of the other sex. Thus the principle function of different types of sexual dimorphism seems to be to facilitate sexual reproduction in one or more of its phases.

MODES OF
SEXUAL REPRODUCTION

The dimorphic differences between behaviors of females and males within a species usually are most obvious in reproductive activities. Again, there is extraordinary variety. Humans have been remarkably creative in developing a range of reproductive behaviors. However, the performances of the rest of the animal world reveal diversity of even greater magnitude, as described by a number of nature writers (e.g., Bolsche, 1931; Fabre, 1914; Lorenz, 1952; Wendt, 1965). The variety is expected, considering both the range of structural differences between females and males of different species and the necessity of reproduction in the evolution and maintenance of the species. Because most people are relatively familiar with reproduction among mammals, we will enlarge appreciation of diversity by considering forms of reproduction in other animals.

Individuals of one species of worms that live in relatively deep water swarm toward the surface at spawning time, the time for reproduction. When the numbers of females and males reach a critical density at the surface, the females attack the males, bite off and swallow the tails. The males return to their deep, rocky crevices and regenerate tails, while the females digest the tails that contain the testes and spermatozoa of the males. The spermatozoa penetrate the gut of the female, enter the body cavity, and fertilize the eggs in the cavity.

Males of other species pay with their lives for copulation. Fabre (1914), the great French naturalist reports that the female preying mantis, with her muzzle turned over her shoulder, gnaws at her "gentle swain," while the "masculine stump, holding on firmly, goes on with the business" (p. 84).

The female of some arthropods (e.g., lobsters, crabs, insects, and spiders) is both larger and better equipped for fighting than the male, and concludes reproductive activites by killing and eating her mate. However, not all male spiders pay for mating with their lives. In some spiders the females manufacture a powerful poison and the males have a pair of appendages, palps, near their front legs. The male spins a web into which it deposits a drop of semen containing sperm. The male dips one palp into the drop of semen and fills an injecting organ. Then, while holding the poisonous female at bay with several legs, the male inserts the specialized palp into the genital orifice of the female, injects the semen, and retreats quickly. In other spider species the male gives the female a prey wrapped in a ball of silk to distract her until thier union is completed.

ANALYSIS OF
BEHAVIORS OF FEMALES
AND MALES

So far, our descriptions of the diverse behaviors of females and males have been rather general and described in everyday vocabulary. Now we shall discuss the kinds of research that provide examples used in our discussions as well as the technical vocabulary used by comparative psychologists and other investigators.

RESEARCH ON
ANIMAL BEHAVIOR

Naturalistic Observation. At one level the research is almost anthropological, or what psychologists call naturalistic observation studies. The investigator goes to where the animals live and observes and records behavioral sequences with minimal intrusion into the lives of the animals. In describing the courting of monogamous jackdaws (birds), Lorenz (1952) easily invests human qualities to the process:

The betrothed pair (or birds) form a heartfelt mutual defense league, each of the partners courting the other most loyally . . . constantly in an attitude of maximum self display, and hardly ever separated by more than a yard, they make their way through life. . . . It is really touching to see how really affectionate these two wild creatures are to each other. Every delicacy the male can find is given to his bride and she accepts it with plaintive begging gestures and notes, otherwise typical of baby talk. . . . For minutes on end, and this is a long time for such a quick silvery creature, she preens her husband's beautiful, long, silken, neck feathers, and he, with sensuous expression and half-shut eyes, stretches his neck toward her (p. 157).

These preliminaries last for approximately one year before the jackdaw couple copulates for the first time. And it is reported that the courting is repeated year after year for the several decades of the adult life of the mating pair.

The result of naturalistic investigation is an **ethogram** that includes a detailed specification of the animals' behavior. Usually the behaviors are described in terms of **sign stimuli** and **fixed responses.** For example, in the description of jackdaw courting, the female's opening her beak provides a sign stimulus for the male's response. The male places food in the beak, a fixed response that at the same time is the sign stimulus for the female to take the food and tilt her head. The response of the female then is the sign stimulus for the male to extend his neck, which in turn is the sign stimulus for the female to preen his neck feathers, and so on, during the months of courting. The first frame in Figure 3-1 summarizes this sequence. Other interesting examples of naturalistic investigation include the reports of Tinbergen on the gull (1953), Schaller on the mountain gorilla (1965), and Mowatt on the wolf (1963). Sexual behavior, nesting, and care of the young are behavioral classes that investigators almost always include in such research.

Experimental Control and Manipulation.

The ethogram can provide strong and valid hints about stimulus-response sequences. But other levels of research are ordinarily used to verify these observations. Investigators may move the animals to the laboratory or otherwise create a situation in the field where specific aspects of the

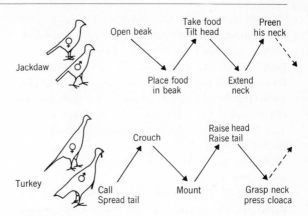

Figure 3-1.
Stimulus and response elements in the appetitive, courting, component of sexual behaviors of jackdaws and turkeys. The arrows from the response of one individual to the response of the other indicate the flow of stimulus and response elements in these courting sequences.

stimulus situation can be controlled and aspects of the responses can be carefully measured. At the highest level of experimental control and analysis, investigators might systematically reduce a stimulus complex to determine the specific element or sign stimulus that is related to a fixed response. For example, in the courting sequence of turkeys, diagrammed in the bottom half of Figure 3-1, the female raises her head after the male mounts. To investigate the possible significance of the female's head raising, an investigator may present models of parts of a female turkey to a male to determine whether the head in fact serves as a sign stimulus for the male's next response. Such research has shown that male turkeys become quite disoriented when the head of a female model is not raised (DeRopp, 1969). In other experimental manipulations, bird and insect sounds are recorded and played to other members of the species to determine if the sounds in the absence of the animal serve as sign stimuli. For some species of insects presenting the sounds of the male elicits fixed mating responses from the female.

Varying Hormonal Adjustments. Other experiments on species specific behavior involve manipulating hormonal adjustments. In general the impact of such manipulations is greater the earlier they occur in the life of the animal. For example, removing the sex glands (gonads) of a male animal shortly after birth changes the development of specific behaviors, including in the case of dogs, modification of the way the animal urinates. A similar surgical procedure after adolescence has only moderate effects.

Figure 3-2 illustrates the effects of the sex gland hormones on some of the secondary sex characteristics of chickens. When hormonal adjustments are experimentally modified by removing the sex glands (castrating the male by removal of the testes, and ovariectomizing the female by removal of the ovaries), the secondary sex characteristics diminish so that both birds soon look

Figure 3-2.
Effect of transplantation of testes or ovaries on secondary sex characteristics of fowl. (From S. P. Grossman. *A textbook of physiological psychology.* New York: Wiley, 1967, p. 487. Copyright by John Wiley & Sons and reproduced by permission.)

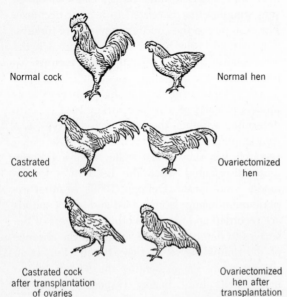

Normal cock

Normal hen

Castrated cock

Ovariectomized hen

Castrated cock after transplantation of ovaries

Ovariectomized hen after transplantation of testes

quite alike. Final evidence of the importance of the gonadal hormones on secondary sex characteristics is illustrated in the bottom frames of Figure 3-2 showing the cock after ovaries were implanted and the hen after testes were implanted. The cock looks even more like a hen than it did after castration, and the hen looks increasingly like a cock. The hen has a large comb and wattles that are bright red, she has long neck feathers that are usually multicolored, she has a long and luxurious tail and, although not shown, she has spurs on her legs as well as the piercing voice of a rooster.

Changing Learning Experiences. As in the case of hormonal modifications, learning experiences early in the life of the animal have stronger effects than similar experiences introduced later. As noted in studies of **imprinting,** early experiences involve the establishment of stimuli as sign stimuli for later behaviors (Eibl-Eibesfeldt, 1970). Accidental early learning can produce imprinting, as in DeRopp's report (1969) of the "male peacock in the zoo in Vienna who, to save it from perishing of cold, had been raised in the reptile house. For the rest of its life the beautiful bird totally ignored the prettiest peahens and made advances only to the giant tortoises" (p. 68). Birds will make courting responses to people, boxes, or even shoes, if these stimuli are presented early in their lives, in the absence of adults of their own species.

In these examples the main effect of early learning is to *change* the stimulus to which fixed responses are directed. Under other conditions the effects of early learning, especially if they involve early failures to learn, result in *blocking* the occurrences of fixed responses. This is the type of effect that Harlow (1959) reports for monkeys that were raised with little or no mothering or with little or no interactions with peers. These monkeys failed to respond to sign stimuli associated with sexual behavior and to sign stimuli associated with care of their young. Thus some animals, including humans, are highly dependent on the environment and on learning to fully develop and express their genetic potential (see Money & Ehrhardt, 1972).

TABLE 3-1.
Language for the Analysis of Species Specific Behaviors

Unit of Analysis	Concept	Example
Behavioral class	Consummatory sequence	Sexual behavior
Components of each class		
First component	Appetitive or preconsummatory	Courting
Second component	Consummatory	Copulating
Third component	Postconsummatory	Self-grooming
Elements of components		
Stimulus element	Sign or releasing stimulus	Mating song
Response element	Fixed or innate response	Approach mate

BEHAVIOR ANALYSIS OF REPRODUCTION

Several systems of behavior are prominent in the reproduction of many species. The discussion of these activities, assumed vital for the maintenance of the species, illustrates **species specific behavior,** which involves sequences of responses that are influenced in large measure by genetic factors. Some relevant terms used in describing species or sex specific behavior are shown in Table 3-1, with examples involved in species reproduction. Any behavior class, such as sexual behavior, involves a consummatory sequence composed of three components; each component involves both stimulus and response elements.

Appetitive Sexual Behavior Component. The **appetitive** or **preconsummatory behavioral component** includes the behaviors that get the animal into the state and position necessary for the next component. Courting is an example of the preconsummatory component of sexual behavior. As noted previously, jackdaw courting involves a year of moderately fixed responses to stimuli associated with the movements of the intended mates. Among bower birds the male builds an elaborate hut, or bower, as the first element in courting. Decorating the bower with clay, pebbles, flowers, and bits of paper takes him about a month. Then he begins the second stage of courting by repeating calls until a female approaches the bower. The bower and songs thus act as sign stimuli for the first elements of the courting re-

sponses of the female. Her responses include moving toward the bower and making seductive postural responses.

During the rut, the time of courting for deer and related species, the male urinates and defecates in a small clearing and works these products together into an odorous mix. He then retires and waits for a female to respond to this sign stimulus by approaching the clearing. This stimulus reduces the distance between the two animals; and after the animals are close to each other, the next elements of courting occur, including mutual rubbing and licking.

Consummatory Sexual Component. Courting reduces the distance between the female and the male. Copulation, which is the sexual consummatory behavioral component, requires continued closeness. Once the individuals are close together, they must coordinate their responses so that their genetic materials meet in an environment that protects the fertilized egg. Almost every arrangement occurs. Some species mate quickly and "on the go." The male and female of one freshwater fish

. . . lie side by side at the surface of the water and jump repeatedly from this position onto the under side of an emergent leaf where the spawn is deposited during brief periods of adhesion to the leaf (1–4 seconds). Then the male splashes the eggs repeatedly with its tail until they hatch and the fry fall into the water. (Krekorian & Dunham, 1972, p. 356).

Whales, too, copulate during the several moments they are out of water while leaping belly to belly. The timing of the leaps is established and coordinated as the two animals swim together during courting. Similarly, the female and male of a species of antelope copulate while continuing to move at a slow trot. Birds (excluding the ostrich where the male has a rudimentary penis) may mate by bringing their reproductive openings (cloacas) together during flight. Or, the male bird may stand on the female's back, holding her neck feathers in his beak.

Among some species the males have strong and prolonged grasping responses that are elicited when the female comes between the forelegs of the male. The males of some species of frogs and toads embrace the female continuously for more than one or two days during copulation. Dogs, bears, and minks copulate with a locking mechanism, whereby the penis of the male becomes enlarged and mechanically fastened into the female for periods up to several hours after ejaculation.

Postconsummatory Sexual Component. The **postconsummatory behavioral component** of sexual behavior is less frequently described than the other components. It involves "let down" or disengaging behaviors that are moderately fixed and conclude the consummatory sequence. Among several species of birds, especially water birds, females make repeated dives under the water after copulation, while the males groom themselves. No postconsummatory sequences are reported for female rats immediately after copulation, but males repeatedly groom their genitals. When the male is prevented from doing this by putting a collar around its neck, the penis remains erect and moves with rapid reflexes. The female cat often strikes with a forepaw at the male and drives him away. She then drags her genital region across the ground. Some female spiders succeed in stinging and killing the male after copulation and then place the male among the eggs to become the young's first meal when they hatch. Obviously, there is variety of form in post-

consummatory as well as in the other components.

Nesting and Care of Eggs and Young. The behaviors involved in nesting and care of the eggs also reveal sexual dimorphism and great variations. For some species, males build the nest and care for the eggs; for others the roles are reversed, and for others the roles are shared. There is tremendous variation even within closely related species. Among the cuckoos who build their own nests, in some species either the female or the male builds the nest, but both defend it; in another species of cuckoo both mates build the nest; and in other cuckoo species large groups of females and males build community nests and defend the communal area.

Constructing a Nest. The nest construction of many species involves a long sequence of responses to a variety of stimuli associated with the location of the nest and with the building materials. These stimulus and response elements comprise species or sex specific behaviors that result in a nest that is relatively unique for the species. The social insects such as ants, termites, and bees build complex structures using natural products and secretions from their bodies. The building may require months and continue after the major structure is completed, so that the adults and young have a permanent home that is used for years. Birds that build nests build them primarily as containers for the eggs and their young (Orcutt, 1971). Thus, the structures are used for only part of the year and then abandoned either permanently or until the next reproductive cycle begins.

Like a number of other small fish, males of the blue gourami species build a foam or bubble nest at the surface of the water; and the mating pair spawn at the nest so that the fertilized eggs are caught in the foam. Nests of other fish consist of pits they dig by picking up sand or gravel in their mouths. Many mammals also dig pits and dens for nesting. For example, the female rabbit expertly excavates a hole and then lines it with fur that she pulls from an abundant supply beneath her chin.

Finding a Ready-Made Nest. Instead of building it themselves, some animals find ready-made nests. The female octopus in the Mediterranean Sea finds a pit, moves rocks around its entrance, and then enters the hole to care for the thousands of fertilized eggs she attaches to the top and sides of the hole. Among some cuckoos, the female lays her eggs in nests of other birds that already contain eggs. The host then incubates the eggs and

Figure 3-3.
The female bitterling fish uses a mussel as a ready-made nest. She makes a sequence of responses to the stimulus of the mussel: (*a*) head-down posture; (*b*) head-down posture with erection of the base of the ovipositor, the structure used to deposit eggs; (*c*) touching the mussel; (*d*) pressing the eggs through the ovipositor, and (*e*) leaving the mussel where the ovipositor is being removed from the syphon of the mussel. (Adapted from: P. R. Weipkema. An ethological analysis of the reproductive behaviour of the bitterling [Rhodeus Amarus Bloch], *Archiv Neerlandaises de Zoologie*, 1961, *14*, 103–199, p. 121. Reproduced by permission, E. J. Brill, publishers.)

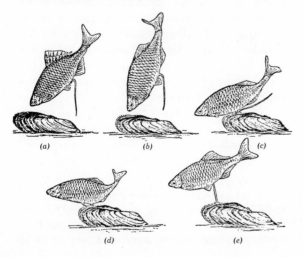

(*a*) (*b*) (*c*)

(*d*) (*e*)

later cares for the young cuckoos. Figure 3-3 shows a female bitterling (a much studied fresh water fish) placing her eggs into the syphon of a fresh water mussel. The male searches for and defends a mussel that is partly exposed and partly open. Then he leads the female to the "correct nest," skims over it, and may eject semen both before and after the female lays her eggs (spawns).

Another variation of nesting involves using *the parent as a nest.* Sometimes the female provides the nest, as exemplified by marsupial animals such as the opossum and kangaroo; sometimes the male provides it. The female sea horse deposits her eggs via a long genital organ into the pouch of the male. The male then swims away carrying the fertilized eggs in his brood pouch, where they develop until the infant sea horses are delivered. The male of the so-called midwife toad draws strings of eggs from the body of the female, fertilizes them, and then wraps the strings around his legs where he keeps them until the young hatch. The male of the marsupial frog spreads the fertilized eggs from the female over the back of the female where the young develop in a number of brood pouches on her back. Cooperation in nesting occurs with even greater partnership in species of penguins; the female and the male take turns holding and keeping the eggs warm in a brood patch. While the female is brooding the eggs, the male is away feeding himself. When the male returns, he takes the eggs and the female departs for her week of feeding.

CHARACTERISTICS OF SPECIES AND SEX SPECIFIC BEHAVIORS

Reproduction illustrates the fact that species and sex specific behaviors involve the animal in *sequences of responses to stimuli.* Another feature of these behaviors is their *variety* and *diversity,* both within species and between species. Neither all the females nor all the males of a species behave alike. Variation of behaviors in the relations between the sexes is also strong. For some species the responses of the female predominate through the consummatory behavior; for other species, the responses of the male predominate; and for still others, the responses of both combine almost equally as the female and male move through the behavioral components (as in the examples of Figure 3-1). The variety and diversity are apparent in sexual behavior, nesting, and care of the fertile eggs. They also appear for some species in components of feeding and of fighting. Among adult lions, for example, the appetitive component of feeding for the female involves stalking the game, running it, hitting it, and finally bringing it down. The appetitive component for the male, on the other hand, typically involves moving to the game that the female has pursued and killed.

THE FUNCTION OF DISPLAYS

Many sign stimuli are associated with individual species members' appearance and movements, which are also features of the animal that reveal sexual dimorphism. The male spider reacts to the posture and color of the female; the male turkey reacts to the posture of the hen, while the hen reacts to the colors of the male and its tail feathers. These dimorphic sign stimuli are called displays. Displays are particularly important for consummatory sequences like sexual behavior and care of the young that involve two or more members of the same species. A display that is a fixed response for one individual may at the same time be a sign stimulus for the next response of the other individual (Figure 3-1). In other words, many displays are responses for one individual and stimuli for the other, and so on, in a sequence of coordinated behavior.

A number of different kinds of displays have been identified. For example, the male turkey's preconsummatory courting displays include a waltzing display, tail display, strut display, and so on. In some species a female's chemical display, or pheromone, functions as a sign stimulus for a male's touching response. Many humans also use natural or artificial odors, dancing, music, and vocal displays in courting.

Decreasing Distance. According to the **ethologist,** Tinbergen (1953), many courting displays have *distance decreasing functions.* Copulation requires that two individuals be very close together, yet this situation is unusual for individuals of most natural species that reproduce sexually. Sexually dimorphic displays help individuals of the species detect each other and get together. Care of the young also requires individuals to be very close together and special displays are used, especially displays by the young that lead the adult to approach. Many displays or sign stimuli that are used by the young members of the species to bring the parent close are similar to displays used by adults in courting. Examples of these include postural displays, such as tipping the head while opening the mouth, and vocal displays (baby talk) such as Lorenz described for the female jackdaw.

Communicating Nonverbally. The "movement language" or nonverbal communication of humans can be described as postural displays that act as sign stimuli for other humans. Smiling is a good example, especially for babies; and most adults respond to this display. Interestingly, both deaf and blind children show these facial expressions from a very early age (Eibl-Eibesfeldt, 1970). In addition to mutual smiles, vocal and postural displays are common in the interactions of human parents and their young. Both the parent and the young human make soft sounds to each other and also touch each other.

Since children have had less cultural experience than adults, their behavior may provide better examples of genetically organized responses to common stimuli. One ethological study of nursery school children presents the following analysis of the possible functions of responses such as the "shoulder hug":

. . . it may function as contact comfort, stimulated by the reactor's prior indications of distress, for example, accidental fall, or loss of toy. It also occurs in dramatic or "rough and tumble" contact play. This shoulder hugging is more likely to occur among age-peers and to be of shorter duration (than in contact comfort). It seems to be a sign of mutual affection and/or a means of directing another child's attention or movements. Adults commonly perform shoulder hugging towards children, and posters and illustrations use it to signify friendship and guidance. It is also a preliminary boy-to-girl stage of the Western adolescent courtship ritual (McGrew, 1972, p. 103).

DYNAMIC PROPERTIES

Temporary Behavior Modification. Experimental manipulation can produce temporary or permanent changes in an animal's sexual and nesting sequences. One condition leading to a temporary change involves the use of a *supernormal sign stimulus*. When experimenters replace a normal goose egg with a very large replica of an egg, the goose chooses the superegg over the normal egg and cares for the superegg more energetically and persistently than it cares for a normal egg. The superegg is a supernormal sign stimulus that exaggerates the features of a sign stimulus and leads to exaggerated responding. Among humans, sex symbols seem to incorporate features of supernormal sign stimuli, as in displays of large breasts in advertisements. Eye makeup to exaggerate the apparent size of the eyes as an approach stimulus may be another example, as were the bustles used to exaggerate the hips sign stimuli in olden times, and the shoulder padding in men's jackets.

Another condition that temporarily changes response elements in consummatory sequences involves *blocking the sequence* by removing a sign stimulus or by preventing a response to a sign stimulus. These conditions lead to *displacement,* a reaction that Lorenz (1952) considers a "sparking over" of motivational energy. For example, if a female goose fails to make appropriate display responses as courting progresses, the male displaces his responses from sexual behavior to other consummatory sequences such as nest-building responses. Other studies show that a blocked animal makes feeding responses, grooming responses, or even fighting responses when an ongoing sequence is blocked. Displacement also occurs among humans when their consummatory sequences are blocked. For example, frustrated people often kick things, cry, or eat when their ongoing behavior is blocked.

Permanent Changes. Previously we noted animals' susceptibility to early experience. Literally hundreds of experiments with animals ranging from insects to monkeys have shown that early life experiences can markedly and even permanently change features of consummatory sequences. Humans seem especially influenced by their early experiences, and the variety of their behaviors reflects the diversity of early cultural experiences. For humans and other species, however, one of the limiting conditions of some changes induced by early experience is that the substituted stimulus must be presented during the **critical period** for the development of the behaviors in question. In addition, for some species some stimulus elements seem to be unchangeable. That is, these animals seem to be preprogrammed to particular stimuli and they are not susceptible to modification even during early experience.

Effects of Domestication. Relatively permanent changes in consummatory sequences also result from *domestication of a species*. Domestication does not mean merely taming an individual of a species; rather it means controlling the environment and mating of the species so that the new domesticated species is different from the original natural species. Domestication changes animals' appearance, physiological processes, and behaviors. The extent of these changes depends on the number of generations of domestication and the degree to which domestication has controlled the environment and the mating of the animals. Laboratory rats are domesticated species. They look, function, and behave in different ways from their natural relatives. The same things are true for dogs that are domesticated from wolves and African canines, and for chickens that were domesticated from jungle birds.

In general the effects of domestication involve an increase in the *plasticity* of stimuli and responses that the domesticated animal uses as compared with the natural species. In other words, a wider range of stimuli serve as adequate sign stimuli and the stimuli elicit a wider range of responses for domesticated as compared with natural species. In some cases very minimal stimuli or muted responses are necessary for portions of consummatory components. For example, **artificial insemination** can be used in place of sexual behavior for some domesticated species; minimal materials can be used for nesting; and the young of different species can be cared for by some domesticated parents.

Humans are a domesticated species so that plasticity occurs in our consummatory behaviors. We are not so predictable as jackdaws or bitterling fish in terms of the specificity of stimuli that elicit our responses, nor in specificity of responses. Reviews of human behaviors reveal large variations both within and between societies. The variations occur for virtually every class of behaviors including sexual behavior, care of the young, feeding, fighting, and nesting. Despite the variations, however, available data suggest that each human consummatory behavior has an appetitive, a consummatory, and a postconsummatory component. Further research is needed to identify stimulus and response elements as well as dynamic properties that increase the range of human species and sex specific behaviors. At the present time comparative psychological research is only at the threshold of the study of human behavior, but the comparative view prepares us to look for regularities and to expect diversities.

SUMMARY

Using the perspective and vocabulary of comparative psychology, this chapter has explored the diversity of species and sex specific behaviors of females and males. Differences between females and males are related to the mode of reproduction of the species—sexual or asexual reproduction. Among species that reproduce sexually, sexual dimorphism—the distinctiveness of the female and the male—assists partners in finding each other to share genetic materials that are carried in the egg and the sperm. With the exceptions of producing eggs and producing sperm, no other aspect of the behavior of the female or the male is entirely predictable across species.

Species and sex specific behaviors involve a sequence of appetitive, consummatory, and postconsummatory components. Each component consists of a relatively stereotyped sequence of fixed responses to sign stimuli. To illustrate the diversity among species, we have described the components and the stimulus and response elements of sexual behavior, nesting, and care of the fertile eggs. In some species the responses of the female predominate in reproductive behavior components; in others the responses of the male predominate; and in others the responses of both the female and the male combine almost equally.

Consummatory sequences have dynamic properties and can be changed. Short-term changes occur if supernormal sign stimuli are used or if the elements in the components are blocked so that displacement occurs. Long-term changes in the components occur as a result of early experience and domestication.

Some similarities exist between the species and sex specific behaviors of humans and those of other species. Although dynamic features predominate in the behaviors of humans, the concepts of sign stimuli and fixed responses apply to some extent to behavioral components in courting, care of the young, and other sequences. In future research on human behavior, the comparative view prepares us to look for regularities and to expect diversity.

CHAPTER 4
BIOLOGY AND GENDER: STRUCTURE, SEX, AND CYCLES*

* This chapter was prepared while G. I. Hatton held a Career Development Award, 1K04 GM22, 680, from the National Institute of General Medical Sciences, U.S. Public Health Service. Also acknowledged is support from N.I.H. Grant NS09140, National Institute of Neurological Diseases and Stroke.

For centuries, human societies have perpetrated the myth that all (or nearly all) of the differences between men and women were of "natural" origin, meaning by this, of biological origin. The term biological was not always used, of course; "God given" or "by nature" were expressive of the same notion. The strong implication of labeling such differences as natural was that they had best not be tampered with, lest some disaster befall. Thus, when men tagged women with being "basically emotional and feeling creatures rather than reasoning or logical ones," it was not open to question whether or not these traits were culturally determined. There was flat denial that these were behaviors that societies instilled in girls as being appropriate to their sex. It only remained for society to prize reasoning and logic, and to disdain emotionality, and the doctrine of feminine inferiority seemingly was airtight. Actually, there is no evidence, whatsoever, that there are biologically based differences between the sexes in logic or emotionality. Yet, as a nineteenth-century **misogynist** proclaimed in a philosophical treatise:

The nobler and more perfect a thing is, the later it is in arriving at maturity. A man reaches the maturity of his reasoning powers and mental faculties hardly before the age of twenty-eight, a woman at eighteen (Schopenhauer, 1851/1951, p. 53).

Obviously, there are biologically based differences between the sexes. The human species is sexually **dimorphic** (Chapter 3). The problem is to distinguish those traits that are biologically based from those that are not. This chapter will present evidence regarding some of the biological factors that do profoundly influence the expression of physical sexual characteristics in both females and males. We also shall point out some of the ways in which structural sex differences dictate markedly different functioning.

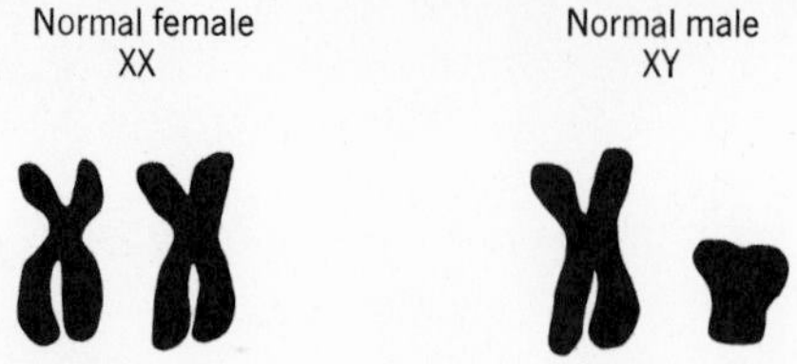

THE STRUCTURE OF SEX

GENETIC INFLUENCES

The sex of an individual is determined, in large part, by the type of chromosomal material re-

Normal female
XX

Normal male
XY

Figure 4-1.
Representation of human sex chromosomes.

ceived at conception. In humans, there are normally 23 pairs of **chromosomes** that are found in most cells of the body. One of these pairs is called the sex chromosomes because they exert control over the development of many structures (and their functions) related to femaleness or maleness. These chromosomes continue their influential role in sex-related functions after physical development to maturity is complete, that is, in the adult. As shown in Figure 4-1, the normal female pattern for these sex chromosomes is XX (a pair of similar structures), whereas XY (a nonsimilar pair) is normal for males (Burns, 1972; Carter, 1962). Occasionally anomalies occur so that some individuals have an extra sex chromosome—such as XXX, XXY, or XYY—or some are missing a sex chromosome—such as individuals with Turner's syndrome, XO (Money & Ehrhardt, 1972).

A person's genetic or chromosomal structure constitutes a **genotype.** The **phenotype** is the overt expression of the genotype that develops in the environment. Because of variations in environmental conditions, before or after birth, the genotype may or may not be easily detectable on the basis of the phenotype. Thus, as we shall discuss later, individuals with the same genotype may look and behave very differently. Sometimes genetic females or males may have phenotypes with attributes that are not typical of their genotypic sex.

Genital Development. A major activity of the sex chromosome is to direct the differentiation of a developing embryo into a fetus of one sex or the other. The external genitalia develop from the *same* set of tissues in the two sexes. In humans, differentiation of the external genitalia begins around the eighth week of fetal life; before that time the initial structures that will become the external genitalia are identical in the two sexes (Figure 4-2). Not only are they alike, but these structures also have the capacity to differentiate as either female or male organs, depending upon the influence of androgens. Androgens are hormones (chemical substances) that are secreted by the testes of a male and also by the adrenal glands in both sexes. The undifferentiated *genital tubercle* (see Figure 4-2) will become a clitoris if androgens are absent; if androgens are present at a critical time, it will enlarge to form a penis. Without these hormones, the *urethral folds* remain separated to be the inner labial folds on either side of the vaginal opening. The presence of androgens causes the folds to fuse and form the urethral tube of the penis. Similarly, other tissues

Figure 4-2.
External genital differentiation in the human fetus. Three stages in the differentiation of the external genital organs. The male and the female organs have the same beginnings and are homologous with one another. (Reprinted from J. Money & A. A. Ehrhardt. *Man & woman, boy & girl.* Baltimore: Johns Hopkins Press, 1972, p. 44. Copyright by the Johns Hopkins Press and reproduced by permission.

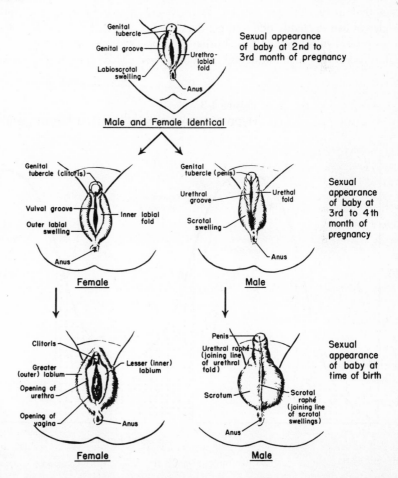

remain separated and become the outer labia of a female or form the scrotum of a male by fusing (Money & Ehrhardt, 1972). If androgens are excessively present in the uterine environment of an XX fetus, male genitalia may develop.

Thus unless additional androgens are added, normally from the fetus itself, female external genitalia result, even if the fetus is genetically male (XY). From this fact, some people conclude that nature's "first impulse" is to produce a female. Others counter that maleness represents a new "complexity" added to the basic plan. The *neutral* truth is that this arrangement probably has evolved as an efficient method of accomplishing sex differentiation.

FEMININITY AND MASCULINITY

One can make a case for considering femininity and masculinity as near-extremes on a continuum rather than as two distinct entities. In this view, the idea of two distinctly different genders is simply an artifact of a **bimodal distribution** of structural (physical and anatomical) and functional (be-

havioral and physiological) attributes (Figure 4-3). When we see someone with full breasts and buttocks, narrow waist, and clear facial skin with little or no facial hair, we say that the person looks like a woman. We might note that this person's appearance is *very* womanly, which implies that there are others who also appear female, but less so. If we also observe that this individual has a high-pitched voice, broadened hip structure, and slender ankles, then this person is classified as having an extremely feminine physical *appearance*.

Before deciding that this individual is "truly feminine," however, we consider other important dimensions. We need to know something about the behavior and attitudes, of a person in a variety of situations, because much of what has traditionally been called femininity or masculinity is learned behavior, such as playing with dolls and helping mother rather than playing with trucks and helping dad. Gender classifications therefore cannot accurately be made on the basis of a single dimension like biological sex, or even on a small

Figure 4-3.

Hypothetical bimodal distribution of gender characteristics.

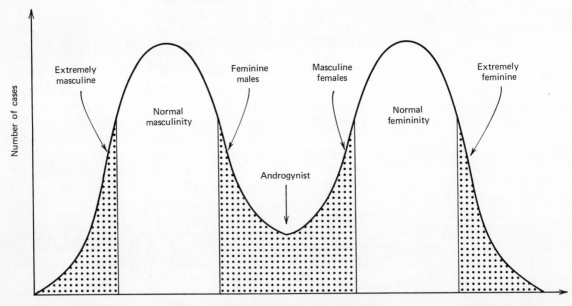

number of dimensions. Our judgments of femininity and masculinity are not necessarily equivalent to femaleness or maleness.

In other words, our estimates of a person's degree of femininity or masculinity are based on a rather large combination of physical characteristics, behaviors, and attitudes that lie on separate, perhaps independent, continua or scales. When individuals are at or near one of the extremes of many or all of these scales, we tend to classify them as very feminine or very masculine (Figure 4-3). Most people cluster around a mode (the most frequent case). That is, they are in the unshaded areas of the gender scale and are typically considered "normal" feminine or masculine individuals. This fact, along with society's reluctance to tolerate deviance, has created the myth of two distinct and mutually exclusive gender classes—an idea that is diminishing under the pressure of accumulating modern knowledge. Some individuals present a mixture of attributes. They display behavior, attitudes, and mannerisms that do not conform to expectations for only one gender class. These people are represented in the shaded area in the middle of the distribution. They can be referred to as **androgynous,** meaning that some of their characteristics are traditionally male (*andro*) and others are traditionally female (*gyne*). Androgynists may stand out, mainly because they do not fit stereotypes based on the modal woman or man.

FEMALENESS AND MALENESS

Even the underlying biological expression of femaleness and maleness can be placed on a similar type of continuum. Individuals who possess XX chromosome patterns *and* who fully express the typical physical traits of XX genotypes (the actual genetic material carried) show the modal female phenotype (the overt expression of the genotype in a given environment). That is, they have ovaries, a uterus, a vagina, a clitoris, labia, etc., all of normal size and function. Another modal type occurs almost as frequently, namely, individuals with XY genotypes along with the male phenotype involving the testes, penis, scrotum, and other glands of normal size and function.

These two modal types could be represented by unshaded areas in a continuum like that in Figure 4-3. However, the more we learn about the expression of genotypes, the more understandable becomes the rather sizable number of *atypical* phenotypes who represent a gray area between "the two sexes."

Hermaphroditism. There are many well-documented cases of **hermaphroditism**—the possession of both female and male genital structures (Brewer & DeCosta, 1967; Carter, 1962). Sometimes the external genitalia are male and the internal genitalia are female. Sometimes the reverse is the case. Usually accompanying this internal-external incongruity is some modification of the typical structures that are present. The penis may be very undersized or the clitoris enlarged; the gonads (testes or ovaries) may be undeveloped or simply not functional. Secondary sex characteristics, such as breast development, hair growth, and fat deposits may correspond to the internal or the external genitalia present, or to both in a mixed fashion. Virtually all combinations seem possible. Families of hermaphrodites usually treat them from birth onward as either boys *or* girls. Often the incongruity is not recognized until puberty, when the secondary sex characteristics of the other sex develop. Since gender identity is so well instilled by puberty, hermaphrodites generally seek hormone and possibly surgical treatment so that their physical bodies correspond more completely to their assigned sex (Money, 1969).

Practical problems occur in sports activities because of ambiguous gender. Some competitors in women's Olympic events have been suspected to be hermaphrodites. The suspicion was based on observations of outward physical appearances and behaviors. Some people went so far as to accuse certain nations of deliberately entering men disguised as women. The accusations were never completely refuted for some athletes, because they retired rather than submit to sex tests, which became mandatory in 1967.

The sex testing that is now required for participating in the Olympic Games involves only one criterion for sex definition—the genetic chromosome pattern. The test is usually done without inconvenience by sampling easily obtainable cells, such as hair cells or cells of the lining of the mouth, and counting the chromosomes in them. The chromosome count involves pairing chromosomes of like size and shape. Females normally have 23 like pairs; males have 22 like pairs and one nonsimilar pair, the XY couplet. There still is a great deal of variability in body structure possible within the XX genotype (also, of course, within the XY genotype). Thus, such tests will not eliminate women who appear "masculine" but are genetically XX individuals.

The structure of sex, therefore, involves a biological continuum that has typical femaleness and maleness at the extremes and hermaphroditism in the middle. Since the largest number of cases are in the extreme portions of this continuous scale, it is a bimodal distribution similar to the one depicted in Figure 4-3. This fact has led us, in our human passion to divide the world into two mutually exclusive categories, to believe that there are two "opposite" sexes with little in common save an interest in each other.

Chemical Influences. The body's chemical environment is important in determining variations in outward appearances represented on the previously described continuum of sex characteristics. Idiosyncratic chemical conditions are influential, in one way or another, from the earliest developmental stages through puberty and perhaps longer in some cases. They determine the *extent* to which genetically determined structures, such as the clitoris or the penis, develop. Some of the contributors to this chemical environment *in utero* are: the mother's blood chemistry (e.g., hormonal balance, alcohol, and other drug levels), the fetus' own hormonal and metabolic variations, and interfetus interactions in the case of twins, triplets, etc. Incidentally, it is likely that such interfetus exchanges will differ greatly depending upon whether or not the fetuses are of the same sex. Interactions with the mother's chemistry also complicate the exchanges that occur between womb mates. Thus, possibly an astonishing amount of the variability in the

people we observe (that is, in phenotypes) is due to environmental events that occur subsequent to the fertilization of the egg. Phenotypes, therefore, can display traits in such variety that, as in the extreme case of hermaphrodites, the either–or nature of their genetic (XX or XY) constitution is completely obscured.

Androgen Effects. One extremely important influence in the uterine environment and, thus, on the developing fetus, is androgen. As noted before, androgen is necessary for the development of male genitalia in an XY fetus, and if excessively present it also can lead to the development of male genitalia in an XX fetus. There is a great deal of evidence that the administration of androgens to a pregnant mother, directly to the fetus, or to the newborn results in masculinized genitalia in otherwise female (XX) animals (Money & Ehrhardt, 1972). There seems to be a **critical period** during which the levels of androgen in the bloodstream affect the individual's appearance.

Research with Other Species. Androgen also seems to influence cortical functions. Some years ago, researchers discovered that in a variety of animals there is a critical period during development when the brain becomes "programmed" for later sex-typical behaviors (Young et al., 1965). If androgen is present during this brief period following genital development, the brain is "masculinized"; if not, the brain remains unaltered, that is, "feminine." In the ideal development of masculinization, it is the male fetus' own testicular hormone that is the effective agent; and, similarly, ideal feminization is lack of such an agent during this critical period. Occasionally, insufficient levels of fetal male hormone at this sensitive period leave a genetic and genital male with a female brain. Conversely, masculinization of the brain can occur in genetic and genital females.

Both of these effects have been experimentally produced in a wide variety of animals, including rats and rhesus monkeys. The laboratory animal turns out looking like an individual of one sex but displaying behaviors more typical of the other sex, such as in postures, movements, and consummatory patterns, especially in mating sequences (Chapter 3). The dramatic effects are accomplished by modifying the normal hormonal conditions. The male fetus, or the male newborn in some species, is functionally castrated (chemically or surgically), which removes testosterone. Later, as an adolescent and as an adult, the animal will display female sexual postures and behaviors. Similarly, if the pregnant mother or the female fetus is dosed with androgen during this period, the genetic female animal will display male sexual responses at puberty.

Variations in Humans. In ignorance of these mechanisms, physicians have sometimes performed comparable "experiments" on humans. In some cases, the progestin treatment used to prevent spontaneous abortion caused inadvertent masculinization of the external genitalia of the female offspring (Ehrhardt & Money, 1967). Fetal hyperadrenalism, a condition in which the androgens are secreted by the overactive adrenal glands of the fetus itself, also can produce essentially the same masculinizing effects (Money, 1969). Since any sex-specific sexual behaviors that occur in humans are more plastic than those observed in other animals, the later behavioral consequences of the androgenization are not so obviously dramatic as for laboratory animals. Human females who have experienced early androgenization generally turn out to be more physically active than their nonandrogenized female siblings, and their families identify them as "tomboys," a label they also apply to themselves (Ehrhardt & Baker, 1974).

It should be noted, however, that from 51 to 87 percent of American college and noncollege women report they were tomboys (Hyde & Rosenberg, 1974). The normal childhood experience for females—and males—may be the activity many in this culture believe to be characteristic only of males. Hence the label, tomboy. In addition, one cannot assume that hormones alone account for apparent differences in androgenized females. Particularly in cases where the human female infant underwent surgery to correct masculinized genitalia, the experience may have affected the parents' image of their little girl, resulting in subtle modifications of their

expectations for her. Insofar as later sexual behavior is concerned, androgenized females typically have a heterosexual orientation.

Since the early androgen effects can occur through the mother's circulation, and since the adrenal glands of both males and females secrete androgens (Turner & Bagnara, 1971), it is entirely possible that androgenization of female fetuses could occur naturally in mothers with very high internal secretions of the hormone. Therefore much of what we know as the physical components of sex and even some of what we call gender can be influenced by events that occur after the fertilization of the egg, though that is the moment of genetic combination, and long before the process of socialization begins.

In sum, we can point to three distinct types of biological sex determination that occur *in utero* for mammals. First, there is genetic endowment; second, gonadal development; and third, the determination of the "sex of the brain" or, more accurately, determination of *future* sexual behavior potential. With appropriate hormonal interventions, sex researchers report that they can produce an animal with almost any desired combination of attributes—for example, an XY individual with a penis who shows all the female sexual responses expected of typical untreated females of that species (Coniglio, Paup, & Clemens, 1973).

The "structure of sex," therefore, is somewhat more shaky and unstable than conventional notions of it might lead us to believe. The discussions that follow, however, will lend at least some support to the validity of a distinction between sexes. We must, however, be judicious in what we choose to call sex differences. As noted at the beginning of this chapter, the age-old "War of the Sexes" is fraught with arguments based on erroneous assumptions of differences between females and males; and it has usually been fought without facts as prime weapons.

SEX DIFFERENCES

Great arguments can be stirred up and bitter battles waged over such matters as whether or not men are more creative than women. One side notes that no outstanding composer of music has been a woman, and that few females number in the ranks of the "master" painters. The other side counters with arguments about prevailing social inhibitions, the dominance of the homemaker role, male chauvinism, and so on. Such arguments about "inherent" differences in creativity remain at the level of verbal duels mainly because we lack evidence from controlled investigations. We do know, however, that creative women and men tend to be androgynous in personality traits and thus do not conform to conventional sex-role expectations (Chapter 8). Unlike creativity, a number of attributes on which there is good evidence about biologically based sex differences do exist, and we shall consider several of these.

PHYSICAL DIFFERENCES

As noted in Chapter 1, there is a great deal of overlap on virtually all scales on which women and men can be measured. Thus, although women's average scores are higher than men's on some of the measures we shall discuss, some men nevertheless score higher than the low-scoring women.

Longevity. Perhaps the most well-known difference between women and men is the disparity of life expectancies. We are all familiar with the simple fact that women live longer than men do (Table 4-1). What many people do not realize is that this fact cannot be explained as due to the "hard life" men have in our society or the "easy life" women are claimed to have. A difference of two to eight years occurs in virtually all countries (including many not listed in Table 4-1). The one exception is Venezuela. Why women typically live longer is not known. One suggestion is that women have a lower basal metabolic rate, which slows down the inevitable ultimate heat death of their body's cells. Another suggestion is that because of both genetic factors and *in utero* environmental factors, they are better equipped for life in the first place. This argument receives strong support from the following facts: There are more males conceived, but the chance of miscarriage is 25 percent higher for male than for female fetuses; there are 6 percent more male births but

TABLE 4-1.
Life Expectancy at Birth (In Years) *

Country	Women	Men
United States	73	67
Canada	73	68
Sweden	75	72
USSR	73	65
Japan	71	66
Congo	40	38
Turkey	50	46
India	47	45
Venezuela	60−	60+

* *Source.* Data from Nourse, 1968.

more male infant deaths, so that by about age 20, females outnumber males.

Anatomical Measures. Selected measures with consistent average differences between American women and men are given in Table 4-2. Most of the measures simply reflect the larger size of men; and, of course, there is much overlap between the sexes on these measures. The one rather striking inversion of direction of the sex difference (fat) is discussed later. There are some additional physical sex differences, some of which appear even prior to puberty. In many cases we can only guess at their possible functional significance. For example, we do not know what purpose is served by the fact that the first finger of most human females is longer than their ring finger, while the reverse is true for most males. This index finger length difference is a sex-influenced trait—dominant in females and recessive in males.

For other structural differences, particularly those appearing around puberty, the functional significance is easier to discern. The broader shoulders that men develop during and after puberty may be related to the strength that was relevant for survival in the wild. In women, the broadening of the pelvis under the influence of hormonal changes in puberty is in preparation for childbearing. The pelvic changes have the added consequence of altering slightly the hip joint orientation, so that the walking gait of postpubertal

TABLE 4-2.
Selected Physical Measures for Normal Women and Men in the U.S.A.*

Measure	Women	Men
Weight of brain	45 oz	49 oz
Weight of heart	8 oz	10 oz
Blood volume	3.5 qt	4.5 qt
Body surface	1.93 sq yd	2.21 sq yd
Water (as % body weight)	51–54%	60–61%
Muscle (as % body weight)	36%	42%
Bone (as % body weight)	18%	18%
Fat (as % body weight)	28%	18%
Length of vertebral column	24 in.	28 in.
Total lung capacity	4.4 qt	6.8 qt
Blood count (red blood cells/cu mm)	4.2–5.4 million	4.6–6.2 million

* *Source.* Data from Nourse, 1968.

women is modified. The degree of modification is small enough, however, that men and women can mimic one another with a little practice, as we have all seen from time to time. In cultures that elaborate on this **dimorphism,** women adopt a noticeably swinging gait.

Fat Distribution. The time during and after puberty is also when sex differences in subcutaneous (under the skin) fat occur. The most striking differences are the accumulations of subcutaneous fat of the hips and the triceps (at the back of the upper arm). The accumulations can be sizable in women and usually are not in men (Table 4-2). This average percentage difference is likely to be less in cultures where women engage in more physical activity than is generally true in the United States. Since fat is a relatively low density tissue compared to muscle, women float more easily in water than men do. This buoyancy and added insulation from the cold probably has contributed to the fact that women hold the records for swimming the English Channel and that the daring food divers off the coasts of Korea and Japan are predominantly women.

For a woman, the fat changes in puberty, along with breast and pubic hair development, are major secondary sex characteristics. These give her the "womanly curves," which may have had an important reproductive function in providing sexual stimulation and attraction to males.

Secondary sex characteristics, especially in Caucasian men, include the beard, lowered voice, and body hair. These characteristics are quite different in type from women's, though they have likely served a similar attracting function. Maximizing sexual dimorphism in this way in humans seems to be nature's game plan (Chapter 3).

Energy Consumption. Many of the anatomical differences between women and men are accompanied by sizable functional differences. For example, the greater size of men presumably is associated with their greater energy expenditure in a variety of conditions (Table 4-3). It is not surprising, therefore, that men need more calories per day in their diets than do women. The energy consumption differential is attended by differences in the volume of air taken in per breath

TABLE 4-3.
Energy Consumed in Calories per Minute *

Activity	Women	Men
Lying at rest	0.98	1.19
Standing	1.11	1.25
Peeling potatoes	1.29	2.7
Washing dishes	1.53	3.3
Walking	2.9	5.1
Making beds	5.4	7.0

* *Source.* Data from Nourse, 1968.

(women: 0.36 quarts; men: 0.79 quarts). The disparity is even more pronounced with imposed workloads.

THE MENSTRUAL CYCLE

One obvious difference between women and men is the presence in women of menstrual cycles. Since discussions below and in the next chapter deal with menstrual cycles, we should review the major physiological events that take place.

The average length of the menstrual cycle in humans is 28 days, though considerable variability exists. Since there is constant hormonal feedback in menstrual cycles, it really is arbitrary which phase of a cycle is considered the beginning. Because the menstrual (bleeding) phase of each cycle is easiest to recognize, it generally is regarded as the beginning of that cycle. Menstruation could just as well be considered the terminal event. The bleeding is the sloughing off of the lining of the uterus that has been building up since the last menstruation in preparation for a fertilized egg.

Figure 4-4 presents a summary of the four commonly distinguished phases of the menstrual cycle: the menstrual, follicular, ovulatory, and progestational phases. The menstrual cycle is dated from the first day of menstruation, not the last day. Near the end of the menstrual phase, the follicular phase begins: Blood estrogen begins to condition the uterine wall, increasing its vascularization (blood supply). At the same time, the ovaries are being acted upon by a pituitary hormone, the follicle-stimulating hormone (FSH), to produce a mature follicle (a small saclike structure) containing an ovum. FSH is, in turn, controlled by hormones released directly from the hypothalamus, the part of the brain closest to the pituitary gland.

Late in the follicular phase when blood estrogen levels are high, but not increasing, blood progesterone begins to rise. At about the middle of the cycle, these two hormones reach appropriate relative concentrations and ovulation results, partly because of the release under these conditions of another pituitary hormone, luteinizing hormone (LH). This hormone is a major factor in causing ovulation, the time at which conception can occur if a sperm is present. The follicular cells in the ovary from which the ovum is extruded become a "yellow body," the corpus luteum, and begin to secrete progesterone with small amounts of estrogen.

For the next 14 days, the uterine wall grows

Figure 4-4.
Summary of phases of the menstrual cycle.

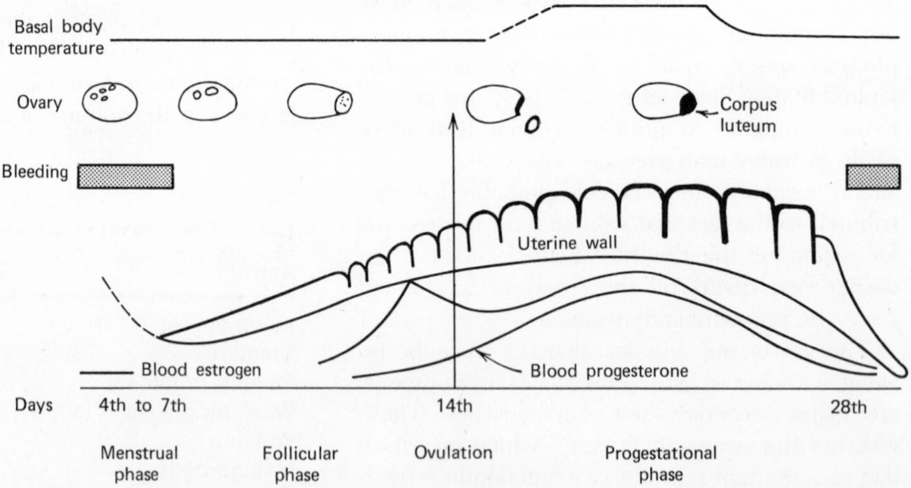

and differentiates into a structure suitable to maintain an embryo if the egg gets fertilized. Preparation of the uterus occurs under the influence of relatively high blood levels of both estrogen and progesterone. If implantation of a fertilized egg does not occur, this progestational phase ends with the decline of the corpus luteum and, with it, reduced progesterone levels. Since the wall of the uterus needs progesterone for maintenance, the breakdown and sloughing process begins, issuing in the menstrual phase once again. If implantation of a fertilized egg does occur, then the developing embryo produces a hormone that keeps the corpus luteum secreting progesterone until the placenta is formed. The high progesterone levels are maintained and menstruation does not occur.

As shown in Figure 4-4, basal body temperature also changes during the phases of the menstrual cycle. On the average a woman's temperature is relatively lower during the first half of the cycle. There are fluctuations at the time of ovulation, followed by a rise in temperature during the progestational phase.

There is a delicate balance among the hormonal concentrations and the timing of their rises and declines that is necessary for the events of the menstrual cycle to run off smoothly. Maintaining relatively high estrogen levels throughout the cycle can inhibit ovulation. Some birth control pills work this way by providing additional doses of estrogen.

SOME BEHAVIORAL CONSEQUENCES OF SEX CHARACTERISTICS

At this point we can safely conclude that there are well-documented, substantial sex differences in basic biological structures and functions that affect behavior. As we move on to examine more complex physiological and behavioral relationships, we find it increasingly necessary to infer, speculate, and even guess, because of the paucity of published data. Many simple sex-associated characteristics produce complex implications for everyday life.

DECISIONS REQUIRED BY SECONDARY SEX CHARACTERISTICS

Culturally Determined Effects. Many decisions are required because of sex characteristics, and the difficulty of the decisions as well as their content and implications vary with cultural standards. Some groups of men, including some North American tribes and some orientals, do not experience beard growth. But among a majority of Caucasian men in this culture, postpubertal beard growth creates a chain of circumstances, some of which continue throughout life. From the time the first fuzz appears at the corners of the mouth, the maturing boy is conscious of approaching manhood. He may be teased by family and friends about this new sign, and, depending on his response to these social stimuli, he may decide to let it grow or to shave it off. In either case, he has to *decide*. He has passed a point of no return; every day for the rest of his life the potential decision is there: "Should I shave it off or let it grow"? In addition, cultural views often fluctuate. At one time, having a beard is "manly"; at another, it is "rebellious." Such inconsistencies in social definitions only add to the day-to-day difficulties of making decisions, even about only one secondary sex characteristic.

Obviously, to let facial hair grow is the simpler and easier path that is less cluttered with trivial activities, but for whatever the reason (comfort, vanity, or conformity), a large proportion of men continue to choose shaving. This decision is followed by others, like what kind of shaver and what kind of shaving lotion to use. Those who decide on beards have other decisions about which style of beard to grow—full, Van Dyke, just a moustache, and so forth. The point here is that all of these behaviors, attitudes, and decisions are only necessary, indeed only possible, for some men; furthermore, they stem from only *one* secondary sex characteristic—beard growth. Some women, however, do have more facial "fuzz" than others, and because they do not meet dichotomized cultural expectations that women should not have facial hair, they often feel very concerned about their "abnormality." Perhaps such women would not feel so uncomfortable if people's expectations were more in accord with the facts of natural variation.

Physically modal women also have many decisions to make because of their typical secondary sex characteristics. In cultures where women cover their breasts, whether or not to wear a bra and what type of bra to consider are decisions for women only. Often, too, these decisions embroil women with other people's different views. Should the prepubertal girl wear a "training bra"? She and her mother may well disagree. Mature women, too, have continual decisions to make. If a woman is comfortable at home without a bra, should she be seen in public without one? And so on. Men do not have these kinds of decisions, though men who have larger breasts than usual also experience concern.

Generally, therefore, women and men have different concerns and different decisions stemming not only from differences in sex characteristics, but also from cultural reactions to different possible behaviors associated with these characteristics. Appreciation and understanding of members of the other sex are enhanced by an awareness of these more or less subtle but profoundly influential differences. The implications of the menstrual cycle in women are even more far-reaching.

IMPLICATIONS OF MENSTRUATION

A complex set of behaviors in women, with no obvious counterpart in men, are those behaviors associated with particular phases of the menstrual cycle. Physiological bases for some of these behaviors are known, while for others they are at best obscure. Lack of information is lamentable. We shall discuss some findings about behavioral and physiological correlates of menstrual cycles, and the next chapter will deal with other facets of the experience. Here we shall consider menstruation within the theoretical framework that behavior can be, and often is, influenced subtly or profoundly by the state or change in state of the body's internal environment (i.e., body chemis-

try). These chemical changes can be in the form of fluid exchanges, nutritional states, or hormonal shifts, and usually they involve many or all of these to varying degrees. Similarly, overt behaviors, perceptions, and attitudes can influence many of these internal events, so that we have a reciprocal "two-way street" that can vary in function from a fine system of checks and balances to a vicious cycle.

Like other aspects of physical maturity, menstrual cycles evoke cultural reactions, as discussed in the next chapter. Menstruation also requires a set of decisions that men cannot experience firsthand. Women must anticipate when the flow will begin as well as when it is likely to be heavy or light. Some may decide to modify their activities on the basis of these predictions. In addition, women have decisions in choosing from the available range of types and sizes of sanitary napkins and tampons. All of these decisions and consequences emanate from just one aspect of women's biological functioning.

PREMENSTRUAL SYMPTOMS

Several physiological and behavioral events occur during the phase of the menstrual cycle between ovulation and menstruation. As described before, blood estrogen is high, progesterone levels are rising, and the deciduous wall of the uterus is thickening. This thickening is due, in part, to a local edema, or accumulation of water in the tissues of the uterine lining. Water retention results from increased estrogen, and is measurable as a regular premenstrual weight gain in many women. In addition, women frequently report greater thirst and water intake than at other times during the month. Sometimes they also prefer salty foods. Taking in salt promotes the accumulation of interstitial water (water in the spaces between the cells).

In many women, this phase passes without significant untoward effects, but in some others this is a time of tension, depression, anxiety, hostility, and physical discomforts, such as migraine headaches, backaches, and swelling of hands and feet (Chapter 5). Severe premenstrual syndromes like these are often relieved, or at least improved, by a low salt diet and small doses of ammonium chloride, a compound that causes excretion of sodium and, with it, water. Some women have reported (without prior knowledge of why I was asking) that in the late stages of water retention (shortly before the onset of menstruation), they experience cravings for various foods or drinks. Most frequently reported are cravings for chocolate, tea, and alcoholic beverages, *all* of which are diuretics and can aid in ridding the body of excess water stores. To the extent that premenstrual discomforts are due to water retention, acting on such cravings has therapeutic value. Unfortunately such physiological foundations are not well known; thus many women and their associates dismiss such cravings as simply "just one more" peculiarity of premenstrual women.

Olfactory Acuity. Another concomitant of high levels of circulating estrogens is a sharpening of the olfactory sense, or sense of smell. Thus, for example, some women report being more sensitive to cigar smoke at certain times in their cycles than at others. Olfactory acuity is generally greater between menstrual periods and seems to vary directly with estrogen levels. There is some evidence that women generally have a more acute sense of smell than men, and it is this already acute sense that is sharpened with increases in estrogen. However, both men and women apparently have diurnal (daily) rhythms in olfactory acuity, being more acute in the morning and less so in the late evening (Stone, 1970). Thus, women have cycles within cycles. Their daily cycles are superimposed on the variations occurring with the menstrual cycle estrogen fluctuations. Men do not experience changes of such magnitude in odor sensation.

Sexual Desire. Periods of peak sexual desire also tend to coincide with the elevated estrogen levels that occur prior to menstruation and are associated with the changes in tension and sensory thresholds just described. Sexual receptivity of many lower animals occurs at times physiologically equivalent to the premenstrual phase in hu-

mans, and these animals can be induced into sexual receptivity by injections of estrogen (with a bit of progesterone, also). Thus, it is tempting to ascribe a sexual "priming" function to estrogen in humans. There is, however, an often reported second time of peak sexual desire in women that occurs shortly after menstruation. This is a time when both estrogen and progesterone are at low levels and are unlikely to be causative factors in the desire. At present there does not seem to be any obvious physiological correlate of this second peak. Some have suggested that the peak is a rebound from the relative sexual deprivation some women experience during the menstrual period. With this second peak we might find physiological events that are more similar to states of alertness and general well-being than to states associated with the premenstrual peak. It is also possible that elevated androgen levels following menstruation account for some of the increased eroticism of the postmenstrual phase. Androgenic hormones appear to be related to sexual desires, attendant imagery, sensations, and actions in both women and men—at least in those studied in sex clinics (Money, 1961).

Amenorrhea. At present there are many curious and puzzling facts concerning the interactions of psychological factors with menstrual cycling. Perhaps the best known and least mysterious is amenorrhea—the cessation of the entire cycle by various stressors, psychological or otherwise. Typical causative or at least precipitating factors include excessive anxiety over approaching events, emotional trauma, and illness. All of these can produce increases in the release of adrenal hormones, some of which alter estrogen levels and thus interfere with the normal menstrual stages. This can produce a vicious cycle in which a woman fails to menstruate because she is worried about whether or not she is pregnant; her lack of menstruation increases her worry; and so on.

Thus, there are important psychological implications of the menstrual cycle. A woman's cycle phase can influence her interactions and her day-to-day decisions. In addition, her ongoing experiences and interactions may also influence her cycle, as suggested by the findings we shall now consider.

SOCIAL RELATIONS AND MENSTRUAL CYCLES

One of the most fascinating findings to come to light recently is that cycles of closely interacting women tend to become synchronized and that cycles can be lengthened by the absence of male contacts. These findings were reported by Martha McClintock (1971) who studied dormitory residents in a suburban women's college. She collected data about the duration of menstrual cycles and the number of times per week the women were in the company of males. She also determined "closest friends," that is, pairings of two women who indicated that they saw each other most often. Closest friends were not necessarily roommates.

Synchronization. McClintock found that over a six-month time span, starting at the beginning of the school year, the difference between the day of onset of menstruation decreased markedly for roommates and for closest friends. There was a trend toward more synchrony between women who were both roommates *and* closest friends. No tendency toward synchronization was noted in groups living at the same end of the hall, nor between randomly chosen pairs. Interestingly, most of the synchrony developed within the first four months of the academic year, and had stabilized by January.

Cycle Length. Another interesting result in this study was the effect of contact with males on the length of the menstrual cycle. Women who were in male company from zero to two times per week were compared with those who spent time with males on three or more occasions during a week. The latter group experienced cycles of approximately 28 days, which corresponds with national norms. Those who spent less time with males experienced significantly longer times between menstrual periods. The duration of menstruation itself did not differ between the two groups, however. Also, upperclass women and underclass women were equivalent in cycle length, indicating that maturational factors do not account for the cycle length and the dating frequency.

McClintock examined the possibility that the time spent with males might be the *effect* rather than the cause of longer cycles—that is, that women with longer cycles might be less likely to spend time with males. But she found evidence to the contrary. Many of her subjects spontaneously mentioned that they had become more regular and had shorter cycles when they dated more often. One subject, for example, went from a six-month cycle to one of 4.5 weeks after she began to see males more frequently. Then, when she stopped seeing males as often, her cycle lengthened again.

Pheromones. Two phenomena have been described in mice that seem to parallel some of the results of McClintock's study. One of these is the Van der Lee-Boot (1955, 1956) effect: female mice grouped together without males become anestrous or pseudopregnant. For present purposes, this simply means that hormonal balance is upset in such a way that the normal estrous cycle no longer occurs, and one stage of the cycle is constantly present. The other phenomenon was described by Whitten (1956, 1968), in which the suppression of estrous cycling (found in the Van der Lee-Boot effect) can be released by introducing the *odor* of a male. Such potent and specific odors are usually called **pheromones** or airborne hormones.

Whether or not the results of McClintock's study reflect the operation of pheromones in humans remains an open question at this time. But in the context of these findings it is interesting to recall the previous discussion concerning olfactory acuity in women and its fluctuations with the menstrual cycle. Remember that the sense of smell is at its sharpest when estrogen levels are highest, between the time of ovulation and menstruation. This would be the biologically critical time for a male to appear on the scene. Just how the absence of the pheromone would operate to elongate the cycle or cause up to six-month delays in menstruation is not at all obvious, though it is not implausible. In any case,

McClintock's study suggests that some interpersonal physiological process may affect the menstrual cycle. Of course, we must await replication of these findings. Since McClintock included in her study women who were taking contraceptive pills (and hence had regular, monthly periods), we do not know what impact these women had on the overall findings. Clearly more research with better controls is needed to explore this area.

CYCLES IN MEN?

Are there also periodic fluctuations of body chemistry, and hence of behavioral expression, in men? Once it was thought that men are invariant, completely stable over time, and that only females have cycles of any kind. Now and then, some slightly eccentric psychologist would suggest that men show what could be called "ups and downs" in behavior patterns or moods, but no one took these insinuations too seriously—not even other psychologists! With the scientific attention given since the 1950s to the phenomenon of **circadian rhythms** (cycles of about 24 hours), a belief in the absence of cycles in men is no longer tenable. The clear demonstration of daily rhythms in many bodily functions, in all sorts of animals of either sex, dispels the myth of male invariance. Only the establishment of cycles longer than 24 hours in men remains to be documented thoroughly. Evidence is accumulating that there are such cycles in men.

There is little doubt that men experience fluctuations in mood, productivity, sensuality, and so on, over periods of days or even weeks. In her book on biological rhythms, Luce (1971) reviews a study done in an industrial setting, showing mood and productivity cycles in normal male factory workers. Luce also alludes to the fact that periodic, rhythmic illnesses such as manic-depressive psychosis, epilepsy, and migraine strike women and men alike, suggesting underlying rhythmic pathology of some sort. Bouts of such illness can appear in cycles much longer than a day.

Arguments are likely to arise, however, over whether these cyclic changes are inherent in the male organism or are "purely" environmental in nature. Whether or not men have the extended cyclic variations in hormone levels that women have is not yet known. It would not be terribly surprising if this were the case. Adolescent boys seem to have "sieges" of nocturnal emissions that apparently come and go at more or less regularly spaced intervals. This build-up-to-a-release, release, then subsequent build-up kind of cycle may be detectable in the adult male, if the appropriate studies can be done to determine such relationships. Since all of the sex hormones are present in both men and women, perhaps measures of men's fluctuations in estrogen and progesterone, as well as in testosterone levels, might provide relevant data.

At least, it is fair to say that no longer should we dismiss the notion of cyclicities in men, which are not altogether unlike those recognized, indeed gloated over, in women since antiquity. Clear demonstration of extended cycles in men would necessitate men having to forgo whatever pride or comfort they obtain from claiming stability and predictability. However, there might be advantages of greater import. For example, women who have premenstrual symptoms such as nervousness or depression can at least know that there may be a clear physiological foundation for their feelings rather than fearing that they are "about to go to pieces" or that their entire psychological health is in jeopardy (see Chapter 5). Men who have such feelings are currently left with self-doubts in the absence of evidence that the feelings may be comparably associated with a physiological cycle. Thus, they cannot say, "It's just normal," when, perhaps, it is.

SUMMARY

In this chapter we have considered the genetic and environmental factors that determine the development of sexual structure, function, and behavior. Although the genetic endowment of the individual is fixed at the moment of conception, hormonal influences can affect the nature and extent of expression of sexual characteristics. Genitals can be masculinized or feminized by abnormalities in the chemical environment of the developing organism. The hormonal upsets can also alter later behavior of animals, including monkeys and to some extent humans as well. Partly because of this modulation by events occurring after conception, neither femaleness and maleness nor femininity and masculinity can be seen as distinct, separate, concepts. Rather, the concepts are better considered in terms of a continuum with virtually all types and degrees of overlap.

There are many biological differences between females and males. Some, like longevity, have rather clear implications for one's life plans. Others, such as broader shoulders in the male, seem to have less relevance, especially for modern living. Some differences between the sexes, such as facial hair in men and menstruation in women, unavoidably have behavioral implications in terms of the decisions and planning they require. The implications cannot be fully appreciated by members of the other sex. Our bodies make a difference in our everyday lives.

Similarly, our everyday lives affect the functioning of our bodies. One study reports that the menstrual cycles of young women who are close friends become synchronized. Furthermore, young women in this study who had frequent contact with males experienced cycles of average length, while those with infrequent contact with males reported longer cycles. This variation might be due to pheromones. While cycles in women are better understood (though data are still incomplete) than cycles in men, there is accumulating evidence of cycles in men. The myth of the invariant male is questionable.

Appeal is often made in popular arguments to biological explanations for differences between women and men. Although the attempts at biological explanations are often vastly misused in light of evidence, it is nonetheless true that humans are a sexually dimorphic species. Women and men have different bodies. The nature and functioning and implications of female and male bodies must be understood if women and men are to be understood.

CHAPTER 5

THE MENSTRUAL EXPERIENCE *

* The author wishes to express appreciation to Dr. Antoinette Krupski, Graduate School of Education, U.C.L.A. for her consultation on the section on physiological concomitants of the menstrual cycle and to acknowledge her participation in collecting physiological data in the Landers (1972) study.

Until fairly recently, the topic of menstruation generated more fiction and fantasy than fact. Still today, many people are ill-informed and show at least the remnants of various myths in their thinking about the topic. Perhaps the prevalence of erroneous assumptions about menstruation would not have occurred were it a process shared by women and men alike. In any case, it is one of the few ways in which physically normal women and men are distinctly different, and one that has evoked varying degrees and combinations of awe, fear, nurturance, and deprecation of women.

Women do show cyclic changes in behavior. However, the extent of the changes and their negative qualities have been overestimated by researchers of the past and in cultural folklore. What is more striking than the changes that can and do occur cyclically is the fact that women are really quite consistent, with minor cyclic changes occurring within rather stable behavior patterns. Furthermore, the kinds of changes that occur vary from woman to woman. Although physiological changes of the menstrual cycle may provide a biological predisposition for the exaggeration of some attributes, they do not radically alter a woman.

FICTION AND FACT

MENSTRUAL MYTHS

"Unique" best describes the condition and status attributed to the menstruating woman. While the word *unique* is relatively neutral, characterizations of menstruating women have been anything but neutral, ranging from highly positive to highly negative. Speculations and beliefs about menstruating women are many and various. The striking thing, however, is that most all societies do, indeed, have some set of beliefs about the menstruating woman's "uniqueness." These beliefs seem to fall into three basic categories, emphasizing either weakness, evil power, or capacity for doing good.

Varieties of Myths *"Protect Her."* In old world Italy, menstruating women are considered vul-

nerable to psychological and physical disturbances and must be protected. They are forbidden to go out in the cold, take cold baths, wash their hair, or do heavy housework. They must avoid sour foods and consume wine to restore blood. Menstrual blood must run freely out of the body: If it doesn't, it may go elsewhere, such as to the head and cause insanity. Infrequent changing of sanitary napkins is recommended, because clean ones are believed to stop the blood while stained ones keep it flowing (Abel & Joffe, 1950). Many primitive societies have similar anxieties about the menstruating woman's vulnerability to illness and suffering. Some recommend that she avoid certain foods or use medicines and charms for protection (Ford, 1945).

"Protect Us from Her." Despite such concerns about her welfare, statements concerning the contaminating properties of the menstruating woman seem to occur more frequently than any other kind. Menstruation is viewed as dirty and dangerous—something from which things, animals, and people must be protected. Italian folk wisdom suggests that a menstruating woman is a community danger. She must avoid anything related to food preparation. Bread she bakes won't rise; her tomato sauce won't turn out well. Her gaze is thought to dull mirrors, blunt knives, and cause abortions in pregnant animals. Her touch withers flowers; her presence blights crops; her urine kills laurel trees (Abel & Joffe, 1950).

Religious sanctions in the Talmud and the Old Testament (Leviticus, Chapter XV) regulate the behavior of the menstruating Orthodox Jewish woman, who is believed capable of contaminating others, especially by touching them. The special fear of the husband's contamination through sexual intercourse with his menstruating wife is handled by restricting her contact with him and by weakening her attractiveness to him. For example, she is forbidden to wear rouge at this time. Furthermore it is alleged that children conceived during menstruation will be diseased, deformed, or monsters. If, in spite of all the prohibitions, a persistent husband forces a wife to engage in sexual intercourse during menstruation, this act provides grounds for divorce (Abel & Joffe, 1950).

Where fire is sacred, household fires must be protected from the menstruating woman. When an Ojibwa woman menstruates, her family removes the fire and ashes from the wigwam and constructs new fires, believing that if they failed to do this, sickness would result (Briffault, 1972).

Similar taboos are prevalent in diverse primitive cultures (Ford, 1945). One society warns that intercourse with a menstruating woman leads to worms attaching themselves to the feet and possibly an acute case of gonorrhea. Another society simply threatens to kill anyone having sexual relations with "an unclean woman." Among the 64 societies reviewed, nearly one-third had taboos forbidding menstruating women to prepare food for men. Over one-fifth isolated the menstruating women in some sort of special shelter. For example, the primitive Arapesh in New Guinea believe that the menstrual blood would endanger their village: "Around each village the ground falls away into these bad places, which are used for pigs and for latrines, and on which are built the huts used by menstruating women. . . ." It is said that even the "marsalai," a supernatural creature, dislikes menstruating women (Mead, 1935/1963).

"There's Power in the Blood." More positive things seem attributed to the menstrual flow within the German cultural tradition than within others (Abel & Joffe, 1950). Though menstruation is viewed as dirty and dangerous, it is also believed that the menstrual blood has healing powers and can keep dangers away. It can be used to treat eczema. Eating bread soaked in the blood of a first menstrual flow can help another woman whose menstrual periods are slow in coming. Weapons, to be successful, are forged with the aid of a virgin's menstrual flow. Menstrual blood is used in sorcery. Adding the first day's menstrual blood to a lover's coffee is thought to make him more passionate.

Among some Italians, the blood of a girl men-

struating for the first time may be used to heal warts or cure malaria. A baby girl may be cuddled in her mother's stained linen to insure the child's later fertility. To improve a mature woman's fertility, her clothes are washed with the clothes of a woman who has a heavy menstrual flow (Abel & Joffe, 1950).

Belief in a supernatural power of the menstruating woman is also seen among the Arapesh (Mead, 1935/1963). A man who feels he has been subjected to sorcery can go to a menstruating woman for help. She will pound on his chest and drive out the harmful, magical force.

Here and Now. Thus, the menstruating woman may be regarded as a hindrance or a help; and she may be avoided, isolated, or sought out, depending upon custom and need. The American "melting pot" has, to a great degree, dissolved the idiosyncratic beliefs of peoples of distinct cultural backgrounds. In the United States today, ideas of menstruation as a danger and a threat to the community are rare. One hears few references to a menstruating woman's contaminating powers. The suggestion that menstrual taboos are less severe among societies that have efficient methods of collecting the menstrual flow seems reasonable (Ford, 1945), although it has not gone unchallenged (Stevens, 1961). However, the idea of the menstruating woman as vulnerable has not entirely dissipated and has received some empirical support, which will be discussed later. We still have our own versions of menstrual myths.

Origins of Menstrual Myths. Why do menstrual myths develop? One suggestion is that unpleasant psychological symptoms experienced by menstruating women are the basis for myths (Chadwick, 1932). Another suggestion, based on the belief that women experience an unusually high sexual appetite while menstruating, is that menstrual taboos arise to safeguard community stability (Weiss & English, 1957). Thus, in part myths may develop from a desire to protect people from the "once-a-month witch" or even the "once-a-month nymphomaniac." But a more neutral conclusion is that menstrual myths, like others, are generated to explain something that is not well understood.

Myths develop about the mysterious, not the familiar. While menstruation is a regularly occurring physiological process, its mechanisms often are not well understood by the general public. The significance of blood as a life force also fosters the development of myths (Hays, 1971). Given the uncertainty and awe regarding the flow of blood, any "unusual" behaviors associated with menstruation are likely to be incorporated into a society's folklore. Systematic investigation of behavioral accompaniments of the menstrual cycle is of relatively recent origin.

BEHAVIORS ASSOCIATED WITH THE MENSTRUAL CYCLE

During the early 1900s, investigators began conducting a great many studies relating a wide variety of behaviors to phases of the menstrual cycle. These studies are correlational, indicating only the extent to which changes in moods or behaviors occur at the same time as certain phases of the menstrual cycle. Such data must be interpreted with the understanding that correlation does not imply causality. That is, a correlational study allows a statement that two variables tend to vary together, but from such information alone, we cannot conclude that changes in one (e.g., menstrual cycle phase) *cause* changes in the other. Also, it is relevant to keep in mind that if a behavior were occurring randomly throughout a 28-day cycle, about 14 percent of the behavior would be expected to occur in *any* given *four*-day phase, and about 28 percent in any two phases combined.

Of female industrial employees who reported sick, 45 percent did so during the four premenstrual and the four menstrual days of their cycle (Dalton, 1964). It has been estimated that the monthly absenteeism of women causes industry in the United States an annual loss of five billion dollars (Parker, 1960, cited by Dalton, 1964). However, this widely publicized statement may be misleading. A recent Public Health Service

study revealed only a slight sex difference, less than half a day, in the yearly absentee rate: 5.2 days for men; 5.6 days for women (U.S. Department of Labor, 1974).

A variety of indices have shown that health problems occur more often during the four premenstrual days and the four menstrual days of the cycle: 52 percent of accident admissions to hospital emergency wards, 49 percent of acute medical and surgical admissions, and 46 percent of hospital admissions for acute psychiatric problems (Dalton, 1964). Others report that 47 percent of the women who seek psychiatric help as emergencies or as walk-ins to clinics do so during these eight days (Jacobs & Charles, 1970). Of children brought to clinics with minor coughs or colds, 54 percent are brought during the premenstrual or menstrual phase of their mother's cycle (Dalton, 1966). Perhaps the irritable or sick child is most troublesome or irritating to the mother at that time.

Among women who commit or attempt suicide, 22 to 36 percent are estimated to do so during menstruation (Gregory, 1957a, 1957b). Dalton (1964) reports that 53 percent of women's attempted suicides occur during the four premenstrual or the four menstrual days.

Estimates of the percentage of women criminals who commit their crimes in the premenstrual or menstrual phase range from 49 to 85 percent (Cooke, 1945; Dalton, 1964; Morton et al., 1953). However, it may be that women who commit crimes throughout the month are just getting careless and getting caught at this time; the data would be the same.

The percentages above exceed the 14 percent or 28 percent base rate expected with random occurrence. Nonetheless, attention might not be drawn to the association of these behaviors with the menstrual cycle if only a small number of women were involved. Thus, the next issue becomes, how many women are "suffering"?

PREVALENCE OF MENSTRUAL CYCLE SYMPTOMATOLOGY

Data from surveys dealing with the incidence of menstrual cycle symptoms further attest to the importance of the menstrual experience. A recent cross-cultural study of American, Japanese, Nigerian, Apache, Turkish, and Greek women suggests that variation of behavior with the menstrual cycle is a universal phenomenon; however, severity and type of symptomatology differ from culture to culture (Janiger, Riffenburgh, & Kersh, 1972). Similarly, within this culture, distress and its correlates vary among religious groups (Paige, 1973). Although estimates of the proportion of women within this country who report distress vary, it is clear that a large number of women have symptoms of some kind (Table 5-1). Exactly how many women have exactly what experiences is open to debate. Why they have the experiences they do is even more uncertain. Much of the relevant research has flaws that ought to be considered in its evaluation. Though research is generally regarded as providing fact rather than fiction, data that are carelessly gathered or inappropriately interpreted hardly provide a basis for truth. Thus, we must consider some facets of menstrual research.

TABLE 5-1.
Incidence of Menstrual Cycle Symptoms

Investigator	Subjects	Percent	Symptoms
Altmann, Knowles, & Bull, 1941	10 women; 8 single, 2 married; ages 22–36; associated with a College of Home Economics	61.5 80	Premenstrual depression Premenstrual tension
Freed, 1945	60 patients from private practice; 6 referred specifically for treatment of premenstrual tension	40	Distress affects their intimate social contacts, leads to inefficiency, and decrease in ability to concentrate
Israel, 1938	10 women who had reported premenstrual tension	40	Symptoms included: fatigue, irritability, lack of concentration, backache, and a vague sensation of pelvic discomfort
Pennington, 1957	1000 housewives, business women, attendants, and high school and college girls	95	One or more of the following: dysmenorrhea, irritability, nervousness, back pains, headaches, nausea, general aches, painful breasts, insomnia, acne, abdominal enlargement, anorexia, difficulty in concentrating, dizziness, weakness, edema, frequency of urination, and water retention
Shainess, 1961	103 women in high economic and educational levels; most were married	85 15	Premenstrual tension Severe, disabling tension
Suarez-Murias, 1953 (Sutherland and Stewart, 1965)	107 student nurses, all considered in good health	85.1	One or more of the following premenstrual symptoms, either "frequently," "occasionally," or "at some time": tension, irritability, depression
Sweeney, 1934	42 normal, healthy young nurses	30	Weight gain of 3 or more pounds premenstrually or menstrually

METHODOLOGICAL CONSIDERATIONS

The lack of caution of researchers studying the menstrual experience is apparent in a number of methodological weaknesses of most of the research on this subject. The relevant methodological considerations are probably important for research on cycles in men as well (Chapter 4). Also, they are general enough to be of interest to any reader who observes and tries to understand behavior.

The Women Studied. There is wide variation in what kinds of women are studied, as is evident in Table 5-1. Research samples that include subjects of a wide range of ages often report a lower incidence of symptomatology because premenstrual complaints are more frequent among older women, aged 30 to 45 years (Koeske, 1973). Incidence of complaints also varies with religious affiliation (Paige, 1973).

How the women are selected for the research is also important. Researchers frequently study women who are easily available and seeking medical or physiological treatment for various complaints related to reproduction.—It is not surprising that patients report more distress related to menstruation than do healthy women!— Generalizations about a high incidence of problems from such samples are inappropriate.

Subject Expectations. Regardless of the composition of the sample, subjects typically know that they are in a study about menstrual cycles and may, knowingly or unknowingly, alter their reports. That is, they are responding to *demand characteristics*, the features of a research situation that influence a subject's response by communicating the investigator's expectancies. It has been demonstrated repeatedly that subjects' awareness of the purpose of an investigation can influence their performance (Orne, 1962). Yet, the vast majority of menstrual cycle researchers have failed to take this into account. If women are asked to complete a "Menstrual Distress Questionnaire" or requested to report to a study when they begin menstruating, they are likely to realize that they are participating in menstrual research

and may be likely to be "set" to focus attention on complaints. With widespread *mis*information about the influences of the menstrual cycle, it is especially important that investigators make every attempt to avoid biased results by disguising the purpose of their research. More important, the menstrual experiences of individual women— even when they are not participating in research— may be affected by their expectations of what is "supposed to happen" to them, as we shall see later; research participation only exaggerates this problem.

The Symptoms Studied. There is wide variation also in the particular correlates of menstrual cycles which are selected for investigation.

More attention has been focused upon negative than positive ones, and an inappropriately narrow focus is likely to intensify expectations of menstrual misery. In the same vein, it is certainly not surprising that reports of experiencing premenstrual symptoms "at some time" are more frequent than reports of "severe, disabling tension" (Table 5-1).

Perhaps a greater problem for understanding menstrual cycle fluctuations is the fact that all women do not show cyclic concomitants in the same way or at the same time of their cycles. Although most women do seem to exhibit some changes associated with the menstrual cycle, they do not seem to be affected in equal degrees by menstrual cycle influences. Also, for each individual woman, some variables are more sensitive to the influence of the cycle than others. The variables sensitive to phasic differences for one woman, or group of women, may not be the same for another woman or another group. Thus, the usual procedure of reporting only on the "average symptom" of "the average woman" can be very misleading.

Time Within the Cycle. Behavior changes associated with the menstrual cycle do not always occur in the premenstrual or menstrual phase of the cycle. At least as often as not, intermenstrual and/or ovulatory scores on "symptom-type" behavior variables are as high or higher than scores during menstruation or premenstrually. Observing women only at selected times, such as at premenstruation, may give a biased view, because it is a view obtained without a context baseline. Baselines must be established before evaluating change (Parlee, 1973). For example, if leg movement as a manifestation of tension were the only variable studied in subjects observed only premenstrually and at ovulation, one could find twice as much "anxiety" premenstrually. However, the truth might be that the behavior is more frequent at times other than the premenstrual days, though low at ovulation. Without information throughout the cycle, the sign of "tension" premenstrually might appear unduly dramatic.

Locating Phases. A critical aspect of all menstrual cycle research involves locating menstrual cycle phases. Determining the days of menstruation involves no guesswork. Defining a premenstrual phase is also a fairly straightforward matter after menstruation begins. However, fixing the point, day, or phase of ovulation is no small accomplishment. Of course, if one has funds and facilities available for the analysis of **vaginal smears,** locating ovulation is relatively easy. Alternatively, there is a "fertility tape," which changes color (like litmus paper) when pressed against the area around the cervix. The tape reacts to the presence of glucose, which normally appears a few days before and after ovulation. However, for the less fortunate, who must rely upon intuition or basal body temperature recordings (which improve upon intuition only slightly), the following discussion may be of interest.

There is little consistency in the methods researchers have used to locate ovulation or the ovulatory phase. Many criteria have been used: two weeks prior to the onset of menstruation, two weeks after the onset of menstruation, the drop before the rise in basal body temperature, three consecutive days on the ascending arm of the basal body temperature curve, the middle of the cycle. Rarely do all these criteria coincide.

Rhythm Method. Body temperature fluctuations have important implications for the use of the **rhythm method** of birth control. The rhythm method is based on the fact that a woman usually releases only one egg during each menstrual cycle. The egg has an active life of about 12 hours, sperm for about four to five days. Thus, there typically are about five to six days each month when sexual intercourse can lead to pregnancy: four to five days *before* ovulation and about half a day *after.* Obviously, *predicting* the precise time of ovulation is critical to the success of the rhythm method of avoiding intercourse when the time is not "safe." There are various recommendations for ascertaining the safe period, some involving calculations based on basal body temperature recordings over a year. However, variability is so great that people who rely on the rhythm method of birth control can wind up with rather large families! Overall, about 20 percent of the pregnancies of women who use this method of birth control are unplanned ones.

COMPONENTS OF CYCLIC VARIATIONS

What precisely are the particular components of menstrual cycle symptomatology? In what specific ways are women "suffering"? Since all that is necessary to contend that a behavior is related to the menstrual cycle is for the behavior to occur in repeated association with any one phase of the menstrual cycle, early investigators began their inquiries by searching for relationships between phases of the menstrual cycle and what, in retrospect, looks like anything and everything that might possibly vary with the biological rhythm of the menstrual cycle. For example, women have been asked to report on fatigue, abdominal pain, headache, backache, breast changes, sexual feelings, depression, elation, tendency to cry, irritability, intellectual capacity, tension, physical activity, worries, changes in appetite, diarrhea, constipation, facial acne, dry scalp and hair, oily scalp and hair, body swelling, aching in varicose veins, hypersomnia, and insomnia (McCance, Luff, & Widdowson, 1937; Altman, Knowles, & Bull, 1941; Sutherland & Stewart, 1965). Data from studies using this approach do provide some evidence for physical and psychological periodicity associated with menstrual cycle phases.

Yet, recent investigators have begun to ask more sophisticated questions and have tried to develop integrated formulations of the physiological and clinical concomitants of the cyclical changes that define the menstrual cycle. Theories about changes associated with the menstrual cycle seem to fall into two groups. The first group is concerned with the "why" of the changes. These efforts to explain the basis of mood or behavior changes tend to be primarily, but not exclusively, physiologically oriented. The second and larger group of theories is concerned with the "what" of the changes. These efforts describe the nature of the changes in women at different phases of their cycle, and they tend to be more psychologically oriented, characterized more by the parlance of the clinician and the personality theorist than the physiologist.

PHYSIOLOGICAL CONCOMITANTS

The autonomic nervous system regulates activity generally considered involuntary. In view of the well-documented, intimate relationship between it and the endocrine system (which includes the ovaries), attempts to measure and relate phases of the menstrual cycle to changes in autonomic responsivity are extremely relevant. Some of the very few studies that have been reported indicate that significant relationships exist and warrant further exploration.

For example, a rise in blood pressure has been found to accompany the premenstrual phase. The high level was sustained for the first two days of the menstrual phase and followed by an abrupt drop during the last two days. After menstruation, the blood pressure regained its normal level, but became elevated again at ovulation (Eagleson, 1927). Skin potential responses (a measure of body electrical activity) and sublingual temperature readings have also shown significant changes across cycle phases (Altman, Knowles & Bull, 1941; Wineman, 1971).

However, other researchers have failed to find a clear relationship between phases of the menstrual cycle and respiration, galvanic skin response, or "muscle thickening" (Seward & Seward, 1934). The more one reads (e.g., Montagu,

1963; Kimmel & Kimmel, 1965), the more true seems the rather trite conclusion that the relationship between the endocrine system and the autonomic nervous system is far from simple (Wineman, 1971).

Similarly, the currently popular hypothesis that menstrual symptoms are due to endocrine sensitivity requires much additional research to determine which hormonal effects and which system changes are related to premenstrual symptoms (e.g., see Koeske, 1973).

EMOTIONAL CONCOMITANTS

In their pioneer investigation of the menstrual cycle, Benedek and Rubenstein (1939a, 1939b) asked if phases of the cycle were reflected in the psychological processes that were observed in psychoanalysis. Solely on the basis of the content of the dream material produced by her patients in analysis, Benedek made predictions about the phase of the menstrual cycle that the patients were experiencing. Rubenstein, having access only to the patients' vaginal smears, determined menstrual cycle phases. The two kinds of records corresponded nearly perfectly, supporting the conclusion that emotional states were correlated with hormonal states. Researchers have continuously tried to specify such a relationship.

Neuroticism. The possibility of a relationship between menstrual cycle symptomatology and neuroticism has received a fair amount of consideration. The assumption is often made that the body changes preparatory to or accompanying menstruation revive conflicts and fantasies about reproductive themes that women who are neurotic have not resolved. Several researchers claim that those women who suffer from premenstrual tension are more neurotic than others. In one study, 500 patients of general practitioners completed a questionnaire about several menstrual cycle phase symptoms and another that measured neuroticism and extraversion. The investigators concluded that premenstrual symptoms are an exacerbation of personality traits related to neuroticism (Coppen & Kessel, 1963).

However, it has also been noted that while a

premenstrual syndrome occurs more often in neurotics than in normals, there is no simple relationship between neuroticism and the syndrome: Many severely neurotic women are completely free from premenstrual symptoms and, conversely, severe suffering can exist in women who show little or no sign of neurosis, maladjustment, or instability (Rees, 1953). Furthermore, the finding that injections of progesterone have relieved some sufferers of the premenstrual syndrome casts additional doubt upon the idea of a simple symptom–neuroticism relationship (Greene & Dalton, 1953).

Anxiety. Nonetheless, both anxiety (the chief characteristic of neuroses) and hostility have been found to vary with phases of the menstrual cycle. The Verbal Anxiety Scale (Gottschalk et al., 1962), which involves a **content analysis** of speech samples, was designed specifically to measure fluctuations in these emotional states. The investigators hypothesized that anxiety and hostility would vary with the phases of the menstrual cycle in a consistent fashion. They also predicted that the quality and quantity of the changes in these affects would depend upon the meaning of the different phases of the cycle to the *individual* woman; therefore there would not necessarily be *group* patterns of anxiety and hostility. Of five women studied, three (two observed through three cycles and one observed through two cycles) showed significant rhythmical patterns of anxiety and hostility levels, as predicted. The other two women (one observed for two cycles; one observed for only one cycle) did not. There was no uniformity among all five women in patterns of change in the emotional variables.

This study is important for two reasons. First, it predicted and found *individual consistency* in the experience of the menstrual cycle but *no group pattern*. Second, it suggests that to minimize the effects of extraneous factors and to observe the effects of the cycle clearly, one must make frequent observations during each phase, over several cycles.

Other investigators have reported sizable individual variation within group trends. Ivey and Bardwick (1968) used the Verbal Anxiety Scale to examine differences in anxiety level of 26 women during two menstrual cycles. Verbal speech samples were recorded at ovulation and premenstrually. For the subjects *as a group*, premenstrual anxiety scores were higher than anxiety scores at ovulation. However, for five subjects—nearly 20 percent—anxiety level at *ovulation* was consistently higher than in the premenstrual phase.

Symptom Groups. The work of Moos (1968a, 1968b, 1969a, 1969b; Moos et al., 1969) attempts to integrate previous research findings which indicate that the cyclical changes associated with the menstrual cycle resist explanation in terms of a single, collective group pattern. Moos developed a short Menstrual Distress Questionnaire and asked over 800 women to rate their experiences of a variety of symptoms. He analyzed the responses for the premenstrual, menstrual, and intermenstrual phases of the women's most recent cycle and for their worst cycle ever. Eight symptom groups resulted (see Table 5-2). Notice in Table 5-2 that Moos' research contains an interesting, heretofore neglected bit of information. The existence of the "Arousal" category acknowledges that *good* changes can be associated with the menstrual cycle!

Moos found that women report consistent symptoms from one cycle to another: for example, they do not experience physical pain one month and a negative affect the next. Furthermore, women who reported specific premenstrual and menstrual symptoms reported experiencing the same symptoms to some extent intermenstrually too. However, according to Moos, the data also indicate several groups of women; women within a group are similar to each other but differentiated from women of other groups in terms of their particular symptom areas.

SYMPTOM SUBTYPES AND EXACERBATION THEORY

The literature just reviewed suggests that menstrual cycle symptomatology consists of more than a single menstrual cycle syndrome. There seem

TABLE 5-2.
The Eight Symptom Groups *

1. Pain	5. Water Retention
Muscle stiffness	Weight gain
Headache	Skin disorders
Cramps	Painful breasts
Backache	Swelling
Fatigue	6. Negative Affect
General aches and pains	Crying
2. Concentration	Loneliness
Insomnia	Anxiety
Forgetfulness	Restlessness
Confusion	Irritability
Lowered judgment	Mood swings
Difficulty concentrating	Depression
Distractible	Tension
Accidents	7. Arousal
Lowered motor coordination	Affectionate
3. Behavioral Change	Orderliness
Lowered school or work	Excitement
performance	Feelings of well-being
Take naps, stay in bed	Bursts of energy, activity
Stay at home	8. Control
Avoid social activities	Feelings of suffocation
Decreased efficiency	Chest pains
4. Autonomic Reactions	Ringing in the ears
Dizziness, faintness	Heart pounding
Cold sweats	Numbness, tingling
Nausea, vomiting	Blind spots, fuzzy vision
Hot flashes	

* *Source.* Reproduced from Moos, 1969a, p. 390–402. Copyright by The C. V. Mosby Co. and reproduced by permission.

to be groups of women with different types of symptoms. Even the general timing of symptoms may not be the same: Some women may experience most symptoms premenstrually and menstrually; others may experience most symptoms in just one phase, and so on. It is possible that the two subjects who did not show significant changes in the previously mentioned study of anxiety and hostility (Gottschalk et al., 1962) were not what Moos might have labeled the "negative affect type." If, for example, they experienced symptoms in the "Concentration" or "Water Retention" categories, their lack of variation in anxiety and hostility would be easily understood. Similarly, it is possible that the five subjects who did not adhere to the modal pattern of cyclical

changes in anxiety (Ivey & Bardwick, 1968) were not the "negative affect type" either.

Furthermore, it appears that the symptoms that occur in the premenstrual and/or menstrual phases are exaggerations or exacerbations of symptoms that occur to a lesser extent throughout the cycle. For example, it has been suggested that premenstrual symptoms represent an exacerbation of personality traits related to neuroticism (Coppen & Kessel, 1963).

An **exacerbation theory** implies continuity: The woman does not take on any radically new and different characteristics during any one phase of her menstrual cycle; rather, existing characteristics appear more prominently at one time than at others. Testing such a theory requires observations during each phase of the menstrual cycle over several cycles. Such a **longitudinal study** was undertaken by Landers (1972).

A Test of Exacerbation Theory. Landers (1972) expected to find evidence for both symptom subtypes and for an exacerbation explanation of the specific groups of symptoms. To support the existence of symptom subtypes, her study had to reveal differences among women in their specific symptoms. To support exacerbation theory, the study had to demonstrate (1) that changes do occur in association with menstrual cycle phases, but (2) that these changes are subsumed within the broader framework of a general consistency of behavior within each individual woman. Thus, behaviors that are generally characteristic of a woman were expected to remain so, despite any fluctuations that might occur in conjunction with the menstrual cycle phases. Likewise, behaviors that are not generally characteristic of a woman were not anticipated during particular phases of the menstrual cycle. In essence, exacerbation demands variation, but variation within a larger, consistent pattern of behavior.

Research Design. Landers studied six young college women over four complete menstrual cycles. The rather grandiose title of the project, "Human Female Psychological Research Project," was intended to communicate to the subjects a general interest of the researchers in the human female rather than a concern with the menstrual cycle specifically, since, as noted earlier, results can be confounded if subjects know the focus is

on the menstrual cycle, as discussed previously. Five days each week, at the same time each day, the subjects reported to the project and participated in clinical and physiological phases of data collection. For the clinical portion, they completed a questionnaire composed primarily of items from the Menstrual Distress Questionnaire (Moos, 1969b) and the Mood Adjective Check List (Nowlis, 1965). Next, subjects talked by themselves for about five minutes, communicating what events, of importance to them, had happened since they had last come to the study. The speech sample was videotaped and scored for both content (following the Gottschalk et al., 1962 procedure) and nonverbal behavior. Five four-day cycle phases (Menstrual Phase, Intermenstrual Phase I, Ovulatory Phase, Intermenstrual Phase II, and Premenstrual Phase) were determined by daily basal body temperature recordings and the women's reports of days of menstruation. For the sake of brevity, only the data for nonverbal behavior will be discussed. However, every conclusion based upon these data applies to the questionnaire and content data as well. Behavioral data, as opposed to self-report data, is assumed to be of greater importance and there is less relevant information available about it (Parlee, 1973). Nonverbal behavior is of special interest because it can reflect feelings and emotional states without the conscious or nonconscious distortion often present in verbal reports.

Some Base Rate Data. Individual women differ in their nonverbal behavior. As depicted in Table 5-3, the 11 nonverbal behaviors studied were not

TABLE 5-3.
Mean Proportion of Each Subject's Total Nonverbal Behaviors Falling into Each Behavioral Category

	Smiling	Squinting	Brow/ forehead	Head hanging down	Shrug shoulders	Leg/foot movement	Arm/hand movement	Scratching	Change position	Play with hair	Long pause
S_1	.22	.00	.16	.16	.03	.19	.19	.02	.00	.02	.00
S_2	.06	.00	.31	.06	.06	.01	.34	.11	.02	.04	.00
S_3	.04	.00	.36	.45	.01	.04	.10	.00	.00	.00	.00
S_4	.06	.00	.35	.22	.01	.00	.31	.02	.00	.02	.00
S_5	.03	.00	.05	.04	.03	.25	.47	.09	.02	.01	.00
S_6	.14	.11	.27	.07	.01	.05	.22	.08	.01	.02	.04

equally characteristic of each of the subjects. For example, S_1 produced more smiling than any other nonverbal behavior; in fact, smiling accounted for over one-fifth of her nonverbal behavior. For S_3, head hanging down and brow and forehead movement accounted for over four-fifths of her nonverbal behavior. Still, if every woman were completely different from every other woman, the subtype notion would be inappropriate: A subtype implies a grouping. Thus, it is important that some of the subjects do appear similar. For example, S_3 and S_4 are primarily brow and forehead wrinklers, who move their arms and hands a lot, while hanging their head down. Such similarities seem to indicate symptom subtypes.

Individual Consistency. Exacerbation theory demands consistency of behavior across menstrual cycle phases. Each subject's nonverbal behavior did remain highly consistent as she moved from one phase of her menstrual cycle to another. Behavior did not change radically during certain phases of the menstrual cycle. Behaviors with a low frequency of occurrence at ovulation did not suddenly appear prominently premenstrually; rather, they retained their low frequency. Likewise, the behaviors characteristic of an individual remained characteristic of her, regardless of menstrual cycle phase.

Figure 5.1 illustrates, for one subject, the kind of consistency across phases that was characteristic of *all* the subjects in the study. Notice that

Figure 5-1.

Nonverbal behavior of one subject during each phase of the menstrual cycle.

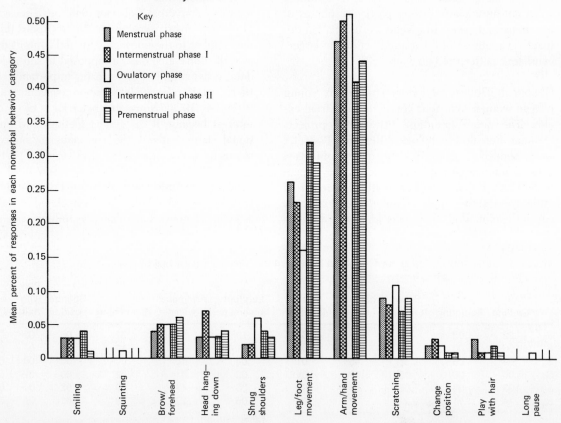

arm and hand movement is more characteristic of S_5 than the other behaviors. Despite phasic fluctuations in the amount of arm and hand movement, it is *always* more characteristic of S_5 than any other behavior. Even when the behavior is at its lowest frequency (in Intermenstrual Phase II), there is still more of it than anything else. Similarly, leg and foot movement and scratching are the two next most frequent behaviors and always retain their position as S_5's second and third most characteristic nonverbal behaviors, in spite of phasic variations. Conversely, S_5 rarely squinted or paused. For each woman in the study, the consistency across phases was more striking than the variation.

The evidence of changes *within* variables coupled with a consistent relationship *among* variables supports the exacerbation position. Thus, *women do show changes associated with the menstrual cycle, but they are changes that occur within a consistent individual pattern of behavior.* Such overall consistency in a woman's behavior is really not surprising. The idea of a general behavioral consistency, as opposed to radical change, is compatible with most psychological theory. Women, most clearly, do not become radically different at "that time of the month"— they simply become more or less of what they have been all month long. And they may become more or less at *any* time of the month.

In sum, the exacerbation position is supported only if interpreted broadly. The interpretation must allow for exacerbation at ovulation *or* intermenstrually, since not all women experience symptoms or behavioral changes premenstrually or menstrually. Thus, for some women, the premenstrual phase, for example, might be accompanied by a reduction in "symptoms" and a rise in positive feelings and behaviors.

Such an interpretation also tempts one to do away with the traditional menstrual cycle vocabulary. *Exacerbation* implies a worsening; *symptom* implies an ailment. To speak of smiling becoming "exacerbated" illustrates the point. Words like *exaggerated* and *trait*, aside from being more neutral than *exacerbated* and *symptom*, seem more accurate as well. Using language with negative connotations to describe the menstrual experience unnecessarily perpetuates a view of women as the more infirm and generally less competent sex. Indeed, one would have difficulty debating the suggestion that, "If men menstruated, they would probably find a way to brag about it" (Broyard, 1976).

EXPECTATIONS AND "EXPLANATIONS"

Almost without exception, expectations surrounding the experience of menstruation have been negative ones. In many settings, uttering the 12-letter word, menstruation, is viewed with three times the alarm generated by the verbalizations of so-called "four-letter words." Care is often taken to store sanitary napkins in places far less conspicuous than those reserved for deodorants or toothpastes. Special holders are available to disguise tampons carried in one's own handbag. Even hormonal problems prove more palatable topics for discussion when a thyroid gland, rather than an ovary, is the "culprit."

It has been convincingly demonstrated (Schacter & Singer, 1962) that expectations about effects of a physiological state of arousal influence the experience of that state. In fact, virtually opposite moods and actions have been "induced" by merely manipulating expectations about how a physiological arousal state "should" make one feel and behave. Coupling this with the findings that a heightened state of arousal is associated with the premenstrual phase (Wineman, 1971) sets the stage for the heavy impact of expectation upon the menstrual experience.

Bad Mood? Don't Blame Biology! The menstrual cycle is beginning to look like an innocent victim of cultural expectations. Koeske and Koeske (1975) report that both college women and men expect women to experience premenstrual irritability and depression, and they interpret bad moods and emotional behavior during this phase as a result of biology. On the other hand, premenstrual good moods and rational behavior are *not* seen as explainable by biology. The familiar argument, "you can't have it both ways," seems appropriate here.

People encounter varying degrees of stress all the time. Thus, it would be most unusual if women never encountered stressful situations during the premenstrual phase of their menstrual cycle. To attribute situationally appropriate tension to biology rather than to a problem situation, simply because the problem arises premenstrually, makes no sense at all. Only when premenstrual problems are recognized as problems occurring *at* the premenstrual phase, not *because* of it, can women begin to take their most effective actions to solve them.

SUMMARY

Current knowledge suggests that the influence of the menstrual cycle has been overestimated. Until only recently, researchers had generally examined just a few, usually somewhat "pathological" behaviors, and concluded that the menstrual cycle exerts a dramatic effect upon them. There was really no perspective or baseline against which to evaluate the magnitude of the changes. With a baseline, however, overall behavioral consistency emerges in a striking, undeniable way. Behaviors are, indeed, changing in association with the biological rhythm, but the changes are not so dramatic as previous research and superstition have led many people to believe. People do not present one picture of themselves one day and a markedly different picture the next. Actually, it is somewhat remarkable that the belief that women become weird and completely different at "that time of the month" has endured for so long.

Yet, the statistics regarding the relationship of the menstrual cycle to suicide and requests for medical treatment, for example, are impressive and cannot be ignored. The suggested integrative conclusion is that the menstrual cycle exerts its influence by providing a biological predisposition. Environmental factors and possibly other internal factors exert more influence than the cycle itself in determining the behavior that a woman finally exhibits. However, the menstrual cycle takes on added importance in extreme cases, such as women who are chronically depressed or characteristically impulsive. In such instances, the menstrual cycle might act as a "last straw." An exacerbated depression might take the form of suicide; an exacerbated impulsivity, the form of crime. Investigations of "extreme" populations such as women psychiatric patients or women prisoners seem like a logical next step.

For now though, the position consistent with the facts rather than the fiction is that the "once-a-month witches" must be pretty spooky all month long!

CHAPTER
6
SEX DIFFERENCES
IN THE GROWTH AND
USE OF LANGUAGE

I am not so lost in lexicography as to forget that *words are the daughters of earth, and that things are the sons of heaven.*

Samuel Johnson,
Dictionary (1755), Preface

We have medicine to make women speak; we have none to make them keep silence.

Anatole France, *The Man Who Married a Dumb Wife*, Act II, sc. iv

The pleasure of talking is the inextinguishable passion of a woman, coeval with the act of breathing.

Alain René Le Sage,
Gil Blas, bk. VII, Ch. 7

A squaw's tongue runs faster than the wind's legs.

American Indian Proverb

All of these "slanders" express stereotypes about women—that they talk more than men, and that their talking often serves psychological purposes different from men's. Is there a germ of truth in these stereotypes? The simple, most general answer is, Yes. Psychological research has disclosed sex differences in these and other aspects of language. We shall begin by reviewing representative psychological studies so that we can learn something of the size and consistency of the differences and of the various dimensions of language in which they appear. We then shall consider neurological and environmental, or "social-learning," explanations of these differences. Finally, we shall consider possible links between sex differences in language ability and sex differences in other cognitive skills.

SEX DIFFERENCES IN MASTERY OF LANGUAGE MECHANISMS

MEASURES OF LANGUAGE DEVELOPMENT

Table 6-1 lists several measures of language development for which sex differences have been found. It must be emphasized that with language, as with other measures of human attributes and

behaviors (Chapters 1 and 4), there often are large differences among individual children so that there nearly always will be some boys ahead of some girls. But on the average—when the language scores for groups of boys and girls as a whole are considered—the girls usually are ahead.

Rate of Acquisition of Phonemes. One early measure of language development is the rate with which the child makes the basic speech sounds out of which mature language is built. There are about 35 such **phonemes** in adult English and there is some evidence that girls make the full variety of these sounds sooner than boys. In one study, transcriptions of samples of the spontaneous vocalizations of 95 infants one month to 30 months of age disclosed different rates of acquisition for boys and girls, so that by 30 months, girls had achieved a higher number of phonemes (Irwin & Chen, 1946). Still, the average difference was small—just over 1.5 phonemes—and the authors understandably were reluctant to conclude that a genuine sex difference existed. The results, however, were corroborated in an investigation of eighty 16- to 29-month-old children (Harms & Spiker, 1959). At all ages, girls were ahead of boys.

Age of First Words. Another early measure of language development is the age when the child begins to make meaningful one-word utterances like "Up!" "No!" "Ball," and the like. Most children begin to speak these first words sometime toward the end of their first year, and girls do so a bit sooner than boys. These are among the earliest studies in the developmental literature. For instance, Mead, in 1913, found an average "first word" score for girls to be 15.5 months, for boys, 16.5 months. Morley (1957) reported scores of 11.4 months for girls, 12 months for boys. The same or even larger margin of difference has been found in "special" populations of children, for example, children with behavior problems (Abt et al., 1929), children with high I.Q.s (Terman and associates, 1925), and retarded children (addi-

TABLE 6-1.
Sex Differences in Language Mastery

Language Measure	Observed Difference and Age of Subjects Studied
Acquisition of phonemes	Girls faster than boys 6–30 months of age
Age of first words	Girls slightly younger than boys 11–12 months of age
Vocabulary size in early childhood	Girls ahead of boys 2–3 years of age
Articulation	Girls clearer than boys 3–8 years; mixed findings beyond 8 years of age
Comprehensibility	Girls' speech more understandable than boys' 18 months–10 years of age
Loquacity	
Infants	Conflicting reports, but where sex differences found, girls do more prelinguistic vocalizing than boys
Preschoolers and kindergarteners	Girls more talkative than boys
Older children and adults	No data available
Word fluency	Girls get higher scores than boys 8–18 years of age
Reading skill	Girls read better than boys (primary grade children)

tional sample in Mead, 1913), though the rate of speech development may be faster or slower.

Vocabulary Size and Complexity of Speech in Early Childhood. Other measures of language growth include vocabulary size and complexity of speech. By age two, most children understand and can use more than 300 different words; by age three, more than 1000. But the girls' vocabulary grows somewhat faster than the boys'. Again, the psychological research spans many years: In one very early report (Doran, 1907), boys at two years of age were credited with knowing an average of 367 words, girls, 573. For two-and-a-half-year-olds, the average scores were 838 for boys, 1109 for girls. Nearly 70 years later, Katherine Nelson (1973) charted vocabulary growth between the first and second year of life and found that girls, on the average, acquired their first 50 words by 18 months, boys by 22.1

months. While there were individual differences among the girls and the boys, nearly all of the boys were slower than the slowest girl. Girls' speech also tends to be more complex. Among 24- to 50-month-olds, girls were more likely than boys to use "mature" construction, including the passive voice, reflexives, conjunctions, and subordinate clauses (Horgan, 1976).

Articulation. To speak—to vocally articulate the sounds of a language—requires extremely fine, precise, and coordinated movements of the jaw, tongue, lips, palate, and larynx. In spontaneous speech, where the child talks freely or is asked to repeat invididual words or phrases or identify pictures of familiar objects, boys' and girls' articulation skills seem to develop at the same rate—until about three to eight years when girls start to improve faster than boys (Matheny, 1973; Poole, 1934; Templin, 1953, 1957).

Beyond eight years, reports disagree as to whether the girls' lead in articulation is maintained; some indicate that it is not (e.g., Templin, 1957), others that it is (e.g., Saylor, 1949). In the latter report, 2000 children between grades 7 and 12 each read aloud a list of simple sentences. At all grades except the 12th, the boys on average made more articulation errors than the girls.

None of the children in Saylor's (1949) investigation had received speech training or correction, and none were known to have any "problem" in speaking, so the sex differences found were in children whose articulation skill was within normal range. A small number of children, as well as adults, however, have articulation problems serious and persistent enough to warrant clinical treatment, and among these individuals, the sex difference is far larger. The ratio of male to female stutterers, for example, ranges from 2:1 to as much as 10:1 (Schnell, 1946, 1947; Bentzen, 1963; Yedinack, 1949). Speech disorders, where they exist, also may be less severe and more correctable in girls (Sommer, 1932).

Comprehensibility. If girls articulate better than boys, girls' speech ought to be easier to understand. Evidence here is slim, but at least three studies have been made: One investigator found that among 18- and 24-month-olds, the percentage of comprehensible verbalizations was substantially higher for girls than boys; by 36 months, 99 percent of girls' speech was comprehensible, a level reached by boys only a year later (McCarthy, 1930). The two other investigations revealed comparable sex differences in 2½- to 5½-year-olds (Young, 1941) and 8- to 10-year-olds (Eisenberg et al., 1968).

Loquacity. It is not the female's superior articulation, comprehensibility, or faster acquisition of speech that occasioned the witticisms quoted at the beginning of this chapter. The inspiration instead is the female's loquacity—her supposed passion for talking. Do females talk more than males? And if they do, how soon do they begin?

Several investigators have looked for differences as early as the first six months of life.

One of the first reports involved 72 newborn boys and girls (Gatewood & Weiss, 1930). While the babies lay in their hospital cribs, the investigators recorded all vocalizations, excluding such "nonlinguistic" vocalizations as hiccoughs, coughs, crying, and sneezing sounds. The sex difference was pronounced: the girls vocalized substantially more than the boys. More recently, Moss (1967) observed three-week-old infants with their mothers and found that the girls vocalized more than the boys. By three months, vocalization rate in both boys and girls had increased, but the boys' rate increased more than the girls', so that the sex difference found at three weeks was now gone. A later study of infants at three weeks and again at three months of age failed to find sex differences in amount of vocalization at either age (Jones & Moss, 1971). Other observations of three-month-olds (Lewis, 1972) and six-month-olds (Kagan & Lewis, 1965) similarly disclosed no differences.

In somewhat older infants, the sex difference appears more reliably. In one study, psychologists watched 13-month-old girls while they played, one at a time, in a room containing simple toys. The mother stayed with her child but was told to react passively if the baby tried to engage her attention. During a 15-minute period, the girls vocalized to their mothers an average of 170 seconds, the boys only 107 seconds (Goldberg & Lewis, 1969).

These investigations have dealt with the prelinguistic vocalizations of infants. What about the more mature language of older children? Among preschool-age children, some psychologists (e.g., Goodenough, 1930; Fisher, 1934) have found no differences. Others have. For example, 2½-year-old girls were noted to talk more than boys of the same age while the children stacked blocks, strung beads, and did other tasks under the mother's supervision (Halverson & Waldrop, 1970). And in the study of the speech comprehensibility of 2½- to 5-year-olds, described earlier (Young, 1941), the girls also reportedly talked more than the boys. One measure was the percentage of one-word word responses the children made to an adult's questions. At all ages the boys were more "succinct." In still another case, Olson and Koetzle (1936) counted the words spoken by four- to six-year-old nursery and kindergarten children in their classrooms. On average, boys talked less. Furthermore, the difference increased with age—the girls being more talkative than boys by a greater margin in kindergarten than in nursery school.

So there is mixed scientific evidence on the question, "Do females talk more than males?" Some investigators have found sex differences, others not, though where differences appear, it generally is the female who talks more. Our review, however, covers only infants and children; though if differences exist early, it increases the likelihood that they will be found later on. Talkativeness appears to be a consistent trait, at least through early childhood. Shirley (1933) observed 25 babies at regular intervals during the first four and a half years and found that the talkative babies became talkative children while the nontalkative babies tended to become nontalkative children.

Content of Conversation. Not only is it said that females talk more than males, but that what they talk about is different. Smith and Connolly (1972) recorded all vocalizations by 40 two- to four-year-olds during play. This time there was no sex difference in total number of vocalizations, but there was a striking difference when the kind of vocalization was taken into account. Girls' vocalizations were predominantly "talk," that is, recognizable words spoken with other children; boys' vocalizations, particularly younger boys', were more evenly distributed between talk and noises made in play like "brr-brr" and "bang." These differences are in accord with an earlier study of preschoolers in which girls tended to talk about other people more than boys did, while boys talked about things (objects) more than girls did (Fisher, 1934). Similar differences in the content of conversations have been noted among adults (Carlson, Cook, & Stromberg, 1936; Landis & Burtt, 1924; Stoke & West, 1931). These are old studies, but chances are that things have not changed that much.

Other Language Measures. As noted in Table 6-1, there are sex differences on still other measures of language development and skill. Among 8- to 18-year-olds, girls outscore boys on "word fluency" tests, requiring the subject to write, as rapidly as possible, words containing a certain letter, or the names of things belonging to a given class (e.g., "fruits that are red"), or four-word sentences, each word to begin with a given letter (e.g., "G . . . w . . . t . . . v . . ."; Give women the vote; Go wash those vases) (Havighurst & Breese, 1947; Herzberg & Lapkin, 1954). Whether the same difference exists after 18 years is uncertain since most research on this subject stops at this age.

In reading achievement, spelling, and grammar, girls generally are superior to boys in the grade school years (Bennett, Seashore, & Wesman, 1959, 1966; Gates, 1961; Stanford Research Institute, 1972). And, as in the case of stuttering, when we consider reading ability poor enough to be considered "reading disability," males far outnumber females by a margin of as much as four or six to one (Bennett, 1938; Bentzen, 1963; Critchley, 1964; Eisenberg, 1966; Miller et al., 1957).

VERBAL COMPREHENSION AND REASONING

If it can be agreed that girls are superior to boys in the sheer mechanics of vocal language, it is less certain that girls also are better in the use of language in thinking as measured by tests of verbal comprehension and reasoning. Such tests include, for example, questions about written or spoken passages; meaning of proverbs; identification of antonyms or synonyms; verbal analogies of the form "___ is to night as breakfast is to___," where the subject must choose from alternative pairs of words; and "digit symbol"—a kind of code-substitution test requiring translation of numbers into symbols according to a translation key.

Evidence is mixed. One investigation of sex differences on different cognitive tests found females to be superior on most of those tests which chiefly involved verbal ability, including measures of verbal reasoning or comprehension like those described above (Guilford, 1967). And among college students, women have been found to be slightly better than men on an "artificial language test." Given a short vocabulary of "nonsense" words and a few simple grammatical rules, the subject must "translate" a short English passage into this artificial language (Canady, 1938; Livesay, 1937).

On the other side, standardized tests of 13- and 17-year-olds have disclosed no sex differences in verbal reasoning, though the girls, as usual, outperformed the boys in spelling and grammar (Bennett, Seashore, & Wesman, 1959, 1966). In another study of 13-year-olds, girls were superior on word fluency but no different from boys in vocabulary, antonyms and synonyms, sentence completion, and reading comprehension (Havighurst & Breese, 1947). Finally, in a test of 16- to 18-year-olds on the same measures, girls were better than boys on word fluency at all ages, but were better on the comprehension tests only at age 17 (Herzberg & Lapkin, 1954).

On certain measures of verbal comprehension, differences frequently *favor* males. For example, in the studies by Canady (1938) and Livesay (1937) mentioned above, college men, though poorer than women on the artificial language test, were better on tests of sentence completion and use of analogies. On balance, then, there do not appear to be reliable sex differences in verbal comprehension or in the *ability* to use language in thinking.

EXPLANATIONS OF SEX DIFFERENCES IN LANGUAGE SKILLS

Many explanations have been offered for the sex differences reviewed here. One kind that recently has attracted attention is suggested by evidence from **neuropsychology**—a field that joins the disciplines of psychology and neurology. To understand this evidence, we first must review some basic facts of human **neuroanatomy**.

NEUROANATOMY AND HEMISPHERIC SPECIALIZATION

The human brain, when mature, weighs about three pounds and occupies the entire cavity enclosed by the skull. Our interest here is with the part of the brain called the cerebrum, for this part is generally believed to be critical for "higher mental processes" such as thinking and problem solving. Figure 6-1 shows a side view. As befits its role, the human cerebrum is very large, constituting about half the weight of the entire nervous system. Indeed, it is so large and cramped into the skull that it shows a great number of ridges and surface folds, or "invaginations." This design greatly increases the amount of its covering, or "cortex," which is composed of nerve cells ("gray matter").

The cerebrum has several remarkable features. First, there is not one cerebrum but two. The cerebrum is divided into two halves, or "hemispheres," by a deep longitudinal groove that runs along its midline. Figure 6-1 therefore shows the left hemisphere. The two hemispheres are linked to the body primarily in a "contralateral" (opposite side) rather than "ipsilateral" (same side) fashion, so that the left side of the body is controlled mainly by the right hemisphere, the right side of the body by the left hemisphere. In the

Figure 6-1.
The left hemisphere of the human brain.

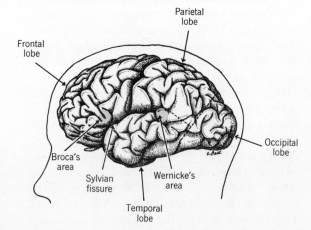

case of the hands, this means that each hand is better neurally "projected" in the sensorimotor region of the opposite cerebral hemisphere. Consequently, when a pencil is felt with, say, the left hand, the tactual sensory information specifying its shape and texture travels primarily to the right brain. This information is not confined there but travels to the left brain through a thick bundle of nerve fibers, called the **corpus callosum**, which links the hemispheres and, in a very real sense, lets them communicate with one another.

The cerebrum's most remarkable feature, however, is that its two hemispheres are important for very different mental processes. In nearly all right-handed persons the left hemisphere is specialized for language functions, the right hemisphere for spatial-perceptual functions. (The same is true for about two-thirds of left-handers, although the degree of lateralization is usually less.) Thus, if you close your eyes and feel a pencil with your left hand, you can *say* what the object is because the sensory information projected to your right "spatial" hemisphere travels across to the left hemisphere where it can be described in language.

EVIDENCE FOR HEMISPHERIC SPECIALIZATION

Studies of Brain-Injured Persons. The best known evidence for specialization of the cerebral hemispheres is from analysis of the psychological deficits caused by a **lesion**, or injury, of the brain, such as might result from a "stroke" resulting in the obstruction or rupturing of blood vessels in the brain, or from a spontaneous growth (tumor), or from an injury like that produced by a bullet wound. Injury to the left side of the brain is associated with a variety of language disorders known as **aphasias**. Injury to the right side of the brain generally has negligible effects on language skills but significantly impairs nonlanguage spatial skills, such as sense of direction, the ability to locate objects in space, or even the ability to dress oneself, which requires subtle spatial discriminations (see Harris, 1975, in press).

The kind of language disturbance resulting from left-hemisphere injury is related to the part of the hemisphere affected. Each hemisphere is composed of lobes or divisions, the most important of which for language are the "frontal lobe" in the area behind the forehead, and the "temporal lobe" just below and behind it. Within the frontal lobe is an area called "Broca's area" after its discoverer Paul Broca (1861), a French anthropologist and surgeon. This area is just in front of that part of the cortex that controls the muscles critical for the production of speech—the jaw, tongue, lips, palate, and larynx. Earlier, we noted that speaking requires very fine, precise, coordinated movements of these parts. After damage to Broca's area, this coordination is disrupted, though the organs of speech themselves are not paralyzed. The victim's speech is typically slow, the articulation poor, with many words and parts of words omitted. The ability to *understand* language, however, typically is unimpaired. This condition is called "Broca's," or "motor," aphasia. A different kind of disturbance is associated with damage to an area within the *temporal* lobe called "Wernicke's area" after its discoverer Carl Wernicke (1874). The victim's articulation is quite normal, but the content is confused, and, unlike Broca's aphasic, language comprehension is often disturbed. This condition is known as "sensory," or "Wernicke's," aphasia.

Dichotic Listening. Left-hemisphere specialization can be assessed in healthy as well as in brain-injured persons. One procedure is called **dichotic listening**. The subject wears earphones that permit a different signal to be played to each ear at the same time. To one ear, the signal might be a sequence of spoken digits, for example, "one, four, two, nine," while different digits are presented to the other ear. In reporting what they have heard, subjects usually make a more accurate report of the signal played to the *right* ear. Since the left and right ears have the same basic capacities to detect sound, this right-ear superiority has been interpreted (Kimura, 1961) as reflecting the fact that the auditory system, like the hand-motor system, has more contralateral than ipsilateral connections. One might say that the left hemisphere "understands," or "processes," speech better through the right ear. The "right ear effect" thus reflects the known specialization of the left hemisphere for speech perception.

Electrical Activity of the Brain. Another way to measure hemispheric specialization is to place an electrode on the scalp and record "evoked (electrical) potentials"—fairly crude measures of activity of nerve fibers in the cortex underlying the skull. When the subject hears language sounds, a recording from the left side yields evidence of greater neural activity than a recording from the right side. With this procedure, the question of the origin of the left hemisphere's special role in language functions has been addressed. In a recent study with 10 infants one week to 10 months old, recordings were made from areas of the scalp over Wernicke's area and from a corresponding area in the right hemisphere while various sounds were played. The sounds were the spoken words "boy" and "dog" and the syllables /ba/ and /dac/. All 10 infants responded with greater left-hemisphere activity to the speech syllables, and nearly all also showed greater left-hemisphere activity to the words as well (Molfese, 1973). Thus left-hemisphere specialization exists from the very beginning of life. Of course, the infants did not really "understand" what they heard. The results mean instead that the left hemisphere is genetically programmed to be sensitive to certain *structural* features of speech sounds, such as the consonant sound, well before their meanings, or *semantic* features, are learned.

IMPLICATIONS OF NEUROPSYCHOLOGICAL EVIDENCE

We now can consider some neuroanatomical and neuropsychological studies that offer a few hints as to the course and nature of sex differences in language development. Since the left cerebral hemisphere is specialized for language functioning, one possibility is that known sex differences in language skill will be reflected at the neurological level and therefore measurable in terms of

sex differences in left-hemisphere functioning. Evidence for such a difference is unclear. Since the sex difference in some aspects of language development first appears in infancy, one might expect that hemisphere differences in auditory evoked responses to speech sounds would be stronger and more reliable in girls than boys. There is no evidence of this (Molfese, 1973).

Sex differences have been found, though, in older children with the dichotic listening procedure. A test of five- to eight-year-olds revealed large right-ear effects in all groups *except* the five-year-old boys (Kimura, 1967). Another test with five- to ten-year-olds disclosed a weaker lateralization effect for the younger children and for boys (Pizzamiglia & Cecchini, 1971). Still another test of 6- to 14-year-olds showed a clear laterality effect for the girls by age 10, with the boys lagging considerably behind (Bryden, Allard, & Scarpino, 1973). Even these findings have not been well supported, however, since in several other dichotic-listening studies with children, the right-ear advantage has been found but not sex differences (Geffner & Hochberg, 1971; Satz et al., 1975).

We do not yet understand why one technique—measurement of electrical activity of the brain—discloses hemispheric specialization for language in infants, but not sex differences, while for older children, with another technique—dichotic listening—the predicted sex difference appears, albeit inconsistently. It may be the difference in methods of measurement, though variations of a dichotic listening procedure with infants also have failed to show sex differences but have shown a right-ear advantage (Best & Glanville, 1976; Entus, 1975). More likely, as the child moves beyond the simple vocalization skills of infancy to the later, more complex speech skills (when the sex differences, too, are more reliable), the sex differences begin to be reflected in the functioning of those cortical structures that underlie language functions. To put this idea somewhat differently, the left hemisphere, despite its disposition to subserve language functions even at birth, nevertheless may become still more specialized through the first several years of life, and this further specialization may proceed more rapidly in girls than in boys.

Maturation Hypothesis. This "explanation" sounds like a neurological expression of a "maturation" hypothesis. Since girls reach puberty more than a year earlier than boys on the average (Nicolson & Hanley, 1953), and maintain their lead through adolescence (Bayley, 1956; Flory, 1935; Pyle et al., 1961; Stuart et al., 1962; Tuddenham & Snyder, 1954), girls' faster language development in infancy and early childhood simply may reflect their greater maturational age. If so, girls should maintain this lead at least as long as the physical maturational lag exists—that is, through adolescence. But as we have seen, for some measures of language development—vocabulary and verbal comprehension—boys reach and sometimes even surpass girls as early as at five or six years of age—while in other measures—articulation and fluency—some studies suggest that males continue to lag behind. As for serious stuttering and other speech disfluencies, males far outnumber females well into adulthood—long past the stage when differences in maturational rate could be involved. The sex differences in language development and language use therefore are probably not mere correlates of sex differences in the rate of physical and neurological maturation. Perhaps other neurological factors are involved, so that at the cerebral level, the sex difference is not simply in the speed with which the left hemisphere becomes specialized beyond the level existing at birth, but in the extent—even at maturity—of its specialization.

Sex Differences in Hemispheric Structures. There are two questions here. The first is, are there *structural* asymmetries between the hemispheres that can explain the *functional* hemispheric differences known to exist in both sexes? And if there are, the second is, are there further structural asymmetries *between* the sexes that could account for the behavioral differences between males and females? To take the first question first: dissections of the brains of adults, infants, and even fetuses who have died of causes other than brain disease have revealed an interesting asymmetry: the "temporal plane," a part of the temporal cortex that has folded inward (invaginated), is about one-third larger on the left than on the right side in most brains (Geschwind & Levitsky, 1970; Wada et al., 1975; Witelson & Pallie, 1973). A comparable asymmetry also exists in the speech area of the frontal lobe (Wada et al., 1975). If the frontal and temporal areas are larger on the left than the right, this means that proportionately more cortical surface of the left hemisphere than of the right is taken up with language functions, leaving relatively less room in the left hemisphere, but more room in the right hemisphere for occipital cortex, or visual-spatial functions. So there is some evidence that an anatomical basis for the language specialization of the left hemisphere lies within the frontal and temporal cortical areas.

With respect to our second question, therefore, if there is an anatomical basis for sex differences in language development and language skill, it could lie within either the frontal or temporal speech areas. The evidence for this possibility is weak at best. Witelson and Pallie mention that in the brain specimens of the youngest infants—those who had died within a few days after birth—the hemisphere difference in planum size looked more marked in the female than in the male brains. And Wada et al. (1975) noted slightly more asymmetry for female infant brains in the frontal area. These results may be related to the sex differences in age of development of language skills in early childhood. But comparable sex differences in the adult brains studied in these two investigations were not found, though as we have noted, several of the *behavioral* differences between the sexes persist beyond childhood. The critical difference, however, well might be in very fine neuroanatomical structure and organization rather than in gross measures such as amount of cortical surface. For instance, even a minute difference in the structural organization of the left frontal area—the motor speech area—could underlie the female's finer expressive, or mechanical, language skills.

On balance, then, if the available anatomical

evidence begins to explain left hemisphere specialization for language, it falls short of explaining sex differences in language skill. A neurological explanation cannot be rejected definitively, though, since so few investigations have been conducted. Time—and more research—will tell.

ENVIRONMENTAL FACTORS

So far we have been discussing sex differences in language as though they were spontaneous and inevitable. But research suggests that these differences are also stimulated by the environment. One indication is that in some cultures, for some skills related to language, the sex difference has been reported to be diminished or even reversed. For example, Johnson (1973, 1974) evaluated the reading skills of second-, fourth-, and sixth-graders in Canada, the United States, England, and Nigeria—all English-speaking nations. Generally, girls scored higher than boys in Canada and the United States, while boys were superior in England and Nigeria. One wonders about the teacher's role: In Nigeria, for example, the teachers said they *expected* the boys to read better. But let us not overgeneralize this example. While one's expectation that a child will and should succeed (or fail) perhaps can influence performance sufficiently to reverse the girl's usual advantage in reading, it is not likely that all the kinds of sex differences in language discussed so far can be explained in this way. For instance, in one of the studies cited earlier, the subjects were girl–boy twins who presumably shared more similar learning experiences than nonrelated children (Matheny, 1973). Yet, the girl twins' articulation scores were consistently higher than the boys'.

Social Class Influences. Another indication of the role of the environment is that various measures of language development are related to the social class of the child's parents. For example, recall that infant girls were found to vocalize to their mothers more often than the boys did (Goldberg & Lewis, 1969). The parents in this study had middle-class occupational and educational histories. Later, with subjects from a lower socioeconomic class, the same sex difference was

found, but the total amount of vocalization was less (Messer & Lewis, 1972). The combined average for the middle-class boys and girls (Goldberg & Lewis, 1969) was 139 seconds of vocalization in a possible 900-second period. The score for the lower socioeconomic-class infants (Messer & Lewis, 1972) was only 54 seconds. It is not that the infants of lower-class parents were less interested in their mothers, for they spent just as much time as the "middle-class" infants in visual and physical contact with their mothers. They simply vocalized much less.

Social class also plays a role in dichotic listening studies. The sex difference has been reported to be weaker or absent altogether in children from high socioeconomic backgrounds, and both girls and boys show the right-ear advantage (reflecting left-hemisphere language specialization) earlier than do children from lower-class families (Geffner & Hochberg, 1971; Kimura, 1963; Pizzamiglio & Cecchini, 1971).

These results are consistent with results of standardized tests of linguistic ability. Generally, overall linguistic development is slower, with sex differences more pronounced in children of poorer, less well-educated parents than in children from middle-class backgrounds (McCarthy & Kirk, 1963; Shipman, 1971; Stanford Research Institute, 1972; Young, 1941).

Certain features of the middle-class environment may speed the child's acquisition of linguistic skills, and at a more nearly equal pace for boys and girls. One often mentioned possibility is that highly educated parents talk more to their children, and discriminate less in their treatment of boys and girls, than less well-educated parents do. Whatever the reason in the dichotic listening task, the earlier appearance of a right-ear advantage in middle-class children probably does not mean, as has been suggested, that "for low socioeconomic children the process of cerebral lateralization is slower and less complete, and consequently, auditory asymmetry delayed" (Geffner & Hochberg, 1971, p. 200). A more likely explanation is that because the lower-class child's overall linguistic development is slower, the dichotic task is relatively more difficult, thus imposing a "floor" on performance that artifactually diminishes the ear difference (Satz et al., 1975).

Parental Influences. It is certainly possible that certain dimensions of the child's language are affected by other persons. An adult can increase an infant's rate of vocalization by smiling and otherwise rewarding the infant when it emits sounds (Rheingold, Gewirtz, & Ross, 1959). Even certain kinds of sounds can be strengthened rather than others. In one such demonstration, some infants were reinforced only for "consonant" sounds, others only for "vowel" sounds. Both groups increased their production of consonants and vowels, but the babies in each group showed a greater relative increase in those sounds for which they were reinforced (Routh, 1969).

The question thus arises whether, in ordinary life, girls are reinforced for vocalizing more than boys are. There have been several attempts to answer this question. In one study, mothers were observed while they nursed their two-day-old babies in the hospital. Mothers of girls talked (and smiled) more to their babies than mothers of boys did (Thoman et al., 1972). Research with older infants and children has yielded similar results. (Several of these investigations were mentioned earlier in the section on "Loquacity.") In the observational study of mothers with their infants during the first month and again at three months (Moss, 1967), throughout the observation period, the mothers of girls "imitated" their infants—that is, immediately repeated the baby's vocalizations—more than the mothers of boys did. Similarly, in the studies of mothers with three-month-olds (Lewis, 1972), six-month-olds (Kagan & Lewis, 1965), and two-and-a-half-year-olds (Halverson & Waldrop, 1970), mothers of girls were found to vocalize more to their children than mothers of boys did.

Other investigations, however, fail to corroborate these findings. Jones and Moss (1971), in their study (also reviewed earlier) of infants at three weeks and three months of age, found no differences in the frequency with which mothers of girls and mothers of boys vocalized to their babies. Similarly, no sex differences appeared in

studies with four-month-olds (Levine, Fishman, & Kagan, 1967), nor with five- to seven-month-olds (Olley, 1973). In the study with four-month-olds, however, although the mothers of boys and mothers of girls did not differ in absolute amount of vocalization to their infants, there were differences in *when* they vocalized. Sometimes, the mother vocalized while she was touching and holding her baby. The authors reason that these vocalizations consequently were less distinctive and therefore less likely to attract the infant's attention specifically to the mother's vocalization. At other times, the mother vocalized but did nothing else to her baby in the periods five seconds before and five seconds after. This kind of vocalization would be more likely, the authors believe, to enhance the infant's use of vocalization as a behavior of special significance in interpersonal situations. And here was where a small sex difference appeared: More girls than boys experienced more distinctive than nondistinctive vocalizations, and this was true whether the mother vocalized a great deal overall or very little.

So in five studies, we find that girls are talked to by their mothers more than boys are. In three other studies, no differences appear, though in one investigation the possibility is raised that mothers vocalize to their daughters in a more distinctive and attention-getting way. On balance, then, there appears to be a genuine, if not wholly consistent, tendency for mothers to stimulate vocal behavior more in their daughters than in their sons.

Fathers and Babies. The mother is not the only adult who spends time with the child, though she generally has the most sustained relationship with the child during the early months and years. (The expression "mother tongue," meaning one's native language, may reflect the view that it is the mother who passes the language on to the infant. In the sixteenth and seventeenth centuries, the expression was "mother's tongue.") About the father's behavior, much less is known, and what we know is hard to interpret. For instance, Rebelsky and Hanks (1971) found that fathers of three- to four-week-old girls talked more to their infants than fathers of boys did. But at three months of age, the differences were reversed, and the boys were talked to more than the girls were.

Birth Order. Some of the discrepancies in existing research findings might be resolved if the birth *order* of the infant is taken into account, though it is not clear why birth order is important. For example, in the study of mothers of two-day-old babies mentioned earlier (Thoman et al., 1972), some of the mothers were multiparous (mothers who had had a child before), others were primiparous (mothers having their first child). It was the primiparous mothers who talked and smiled more to female babies. The multiparous mothers talked no more to females than to males and talked much less overall besides.

So we cannot yet say that either or both parents will inevitably vocalize more to female than to male infants. It depends on the sex of parent, age and sex of child, birth order, and surely other factors too.

ARE GIRLS MORE RESPONSIVE THAN BOYS TO VOCAL STIMULATION?

If girls *are* talked to more than boys, maybe it is not by parental design but simply because girls are more responsive than boys to this kind of treatment. After all, human conversation is a two-way street and is less rewarding for either party when the other person is not responsive. So girls may be more rewarding to talk to, more interested than boys in speech sounds, and more likely to express this greater interest in ways that call out speech from others. A kind of "sphere of influence," therefore, would be established earlier and more intensely in girls than in boys. There is a bit of evidence, still very sketchy, for this possibility. Infants frequently try to imitate sounds made by other people. This does not mean merely making any sound in response, but a particular sound. For this reason, imitation has been called "a refinement of immense importance in advancing speech development" (Valentine, 1930, p. 111). Note this example in a three-and-a-half-month old: "When I said 'da-da' and then 'ba-

ba' very emphatically . . . he looked at me with great interest, and repeated after about five or six seconds, 'da-da'. . . . This speaking seems quite different from his babbling, it is so deliberate, suggestive of effort" (Valentine, 1930, p. 111).

From this example, one can imagine how rewarding the infant's imitation would be for the parent, and how the imitating infant actually could reinforce the parent's vocalizing causing the parent to vocalize still more. Do girls imitate sounds made by others more reliably than boys do? Two early reports, one of infants between a few months and two years of age (Valentine, 1930), another of children through the sixth year (Stern, 1924), conclude that they do—that girls *are* more imitative than boys, especially in reference to language. But subsequently, only a few other studies of imitation in infants have appeared (e.g., Brazelton & Young, 1964; Gardner & Gardner, 1970; Zazzo, 1957; Piaget, 1963, Uzgiris, 1972). Only some included language imitation, and none considered sex differences. As for older children, there have been many recent studies of imitation, and sex differences prove to be negligible, though few if any of these studies, however, have considered linguistic imitation *per se* (Maccoby & Jacklin, 1974).

SEX DIFFERENCES IN RESPONSIVENESS TO COGNITIVE STIMULATION

If girls are more responsive to speech sounds than are boys, the difference may not be in the intrinsic interest in speech sounds *per se*, but in *how* males and females react to any cognitively arousing event, speech sounds being but one instance. This possibility is suggested in two investigations. One is Lewis' (1972) study of three-month-old infants and their mothers, parts of which were discussed earlier. Lewis identified two major categories of mother–infant behaviors: In one, the mother initiates or acts first, for example, by touching or vocalizing, and the infant responds; in the other, the infant initiates, and the mother responds. Though, as noted earlier, girls and boys did not differ in absolute amount of vocalization, there were differences in the pattern of the relationship between the mother's behavior and the infant's. For boys, half their vocalizations were in response to maternal acts, and half were initiators of maternal acts. The scores for girls were 63 percent and 37 percent. The girls thus seem to have been more *vocally* responsive—in proportion to vocalization in general—to their mothers' behaviors than the boys were.

The second study was an evaluation of 12- to 57-week-old infants' reactions to various photographs of human faces. Except at 57 weeks of age, the girls *looked* less at the faces than the boys did, but at all ages *vocalized* to the faces more (Lewis, 1969). Perhaps, then, there are sex differences in neurological organization favoring vocalization in girls as a response-style to *any* cognitively arousing event, whether a voice, face, or touch.

LANGUAGE AND OTHER ABILITIES

So far we have discussed sex differences in various language dispositions and skills, and we have speculated about the origins of these differences. Recently, psychologists have asked whether these differences have implications for a much deeper matter: There are indications that females and males differ not only in language but in certain general aspects of *intellectual* development, with language the key to understanding this difference.

THE ROLE OF LANGUAGE IN GENERAL INTELLECTUAL DEVELOPMENT

Our concern here is with the question of the relation between intellectual development in very early and later life. Most psychology textbooks state that there is only a low relationship between intelligence test scores in infancy and scores even in early childhood. The usual—and generally accurate—explanation is that infant tests primarily assess "sensorimotor" skills such as the ability to pick up a cube, to reach with accuracy, or to build a tower of blocks. Intelligence tests for older children and adults, however, emphasize language ability—and the supposition is that

these two dimensions of intelligence—sensorimotor ability and language—develop in different ways. Infant intelligence tests, however, do include items pertaining to language such as the following measures for the age range from about 5 to 13 months: vocalizes eagerness, vocalizes displeasure, makes vocal interjections, says "da-da" or equivalent, says two words, and uses expressive jargon. When scores on such items are considered independently, the predictive power of the infant test improves—for girls.

Two reports stand as illustrations. In one study, (Cameron, Livson, & Bayley, 1967) females with high intelligence test scores during the period from 6 to 26 years were found to have had high scores as infants on the cluster of language measures; and females with low scores during this period had received low scores in infancy. For males, there was no such relationship: Later intelligence test scores could not be predicted from their infant vocalization scores.

In the second study (Moore 1967), infant language scores (spontaneous babbling at 6 months and use of words at 18 months) were correlated with general intelligence at three, five, and eight years of age. The language scores during infancy predicted later measures of general intelligence in girls only.

These findings suggest that intellectual development in girls takes place, to a greater degree than is true for boys, through *linguistic* channels. In other words, in girls, linguistic skills may play a larger role in general intellectual ability—in their thinking and problem solving. More of their day-to-day experiences may be coded into linguistic forms. We can recognize a certain compatibility here with our earlier proposition that girls are neurologically more disposed than boys to respond vocally to cognitively interesting events. Such a disposition may be the key to understanding the origins of the differences in developmental processes found in the studies just cited.

LANGUAGE AND SPATIAL ABILITY

If language plays the greater role in the intellectual development of females, this may explain still another remarkable difference between the sexes. Although females excel in certain language (left-hemisphere) skills, males have superior spatial (right-hemisphere) skills. This is especially true for "spatial visualization" tests requiring mental rotation or transformation of an object or array so as to recognize it in a new position. The task may be to imagine how a picture of a complex geometric form would look if tilted 90 degrees backwards and 60 degrees to the right. Males also excel on tasks in which the body orientation of the observer is an essential part of the problem, for example, tracing one's way through a complex maze involving many reversals of direction. Sex differences on such spatial tasks appear across a broad spectrum of social classes and cultures, and in adults as well as children (Harris, in press).

Is there a connection between the sex differences in these two kinds of abilities? The girl's lead in language development and the relatively greater role language seems to play in her general intelligence could impede the development of her spatial ability. The implication is that language, or left cerebral hemispheric, modes are *inefficient* for the analysis of spatial, right-hemisphere, problems. Why should this be so? The explanation may lie in a more "process-related" characterization of the cerebral hemispheres than the simple descriptions given earlier.

How the Hemispheres Process Information. The left hemisphere—the "language hemisphere"—is said to work in a logical, analytic, computerlike way, by analyzing stimulus information sequentially or serially, abstracting out the relevant details to which it attaches verbal labels. The right hemisphere, however, is primarily a synthesist—it is more concerned with the overall stimulus configuration, simultaneously analyzes parallel sources of information, and organizes and processes information in terms of wholes.

In light of these characterizations, it has been suggested that the left hemisphere, therefore, is "inadequate for the rapid complex syntheses achieved by the right hemisphere" (Levy–Agresti & Sperry, 1968, p. 1151)—indeed, even that language and perceptual functions are basically in-

compatible. The best-known evidence for this incompatibility has already been alluded to—clinical studies of patients with brain lesions. In some cases the treatment is to surgically remove the affected lobe (lobectomy) or even the entire hemisphere (**hemispherectomy**). This treatment can save the patient's life but not without cost. Thus, removing the left temporal lobe, though having only negligible effects on spatial (nonverbal) tasks such as maze-learning, results in significantly poorer memory for verbal material (Corkin, 1965; Milner, 1965). And after right temporal lobectomy, performance on spatial tasks is impaired though verbal ability is unaffected. The pertinent point for the question at hand is the implication, in the latter case, that the patient's still intact verbal (left-hemisphere) skills are inadequate for spatial (right-hemisphere) problems.

Sex Differences in Hemispheric "Dependency." The important question now is whether the consequence of brain injury for various cognitive abilities depends on the sex of the patient. It appears that it does. For example, Lansdell (1968a) gave intelligence tests to male and female patients who had had either left- or right-temporal lobectomies. Of all the patients, males with operations on the right side scored the lowest on the nonverbal parts of the test. And the more right-hemisphere tissue removed, the lower the men's scores. For women no such relation was found (Lansdell, 1968b). Similarly, the degree of language impairment associated with left-hemisphere lesions was related to visuospatial disability in women but not in men patients (McGlone & Kertesz, 1973).

Such findings suggest that females rely more on left-hemisphere language modes in making visual-perceptual judgments, while males rely more nearly purely on right-hemisphere modes. Consequently, in females visual-perceptual ability depends to a greater extent on the integrity of the left hemisphere; in males there is greater dependence on the integrity of the right hemisphere.

This interpretation is consistent with studies of mental testing in normal individuals. For example, artistic skill is more highly related to competence in verbal reasoning in girls than in boys (Bennett, Seashore, & Wesman, 1959). In other words, a girl who excels in drawing is also likely to have excellent verbal skills. The same drawing (and spatial-representational) skills in a boy are less likely to be accompanied by high-level verbal skills.

It is possible, then, that underlying sex differences in spatial ability in *normal* persons are differences in the very manner in which the detection and processing of spatial information is carried out. If females more usually use left-hemisphere modes, while males use their right hemispheres, then to the extent that spatial problems cannot be solved through language analysis, the female will do less well on spatial tasks.

Of course, we must not overdraw our conclusions from these studies as to the inefficiency of language modes in spatial analysis. There are circumstances when spatial tasks can be solved by "nonspatial" means. The neuropsychologist Moyra Williams (1970) expresses the general point well: "The dysphasic [impaired speech] patient can still communicate, the amnesiac one uses a notebook or some other form of mnemonic to organize his daily life. Even the patient with visuo-perceptual disorders can compensate for his loss by developing new cues to orientate himself by" (p. 124). Williams offers this convincing illustration: " 'One can always use geometry,' said a world-famous mathematician, as he assembled the pieces of a complicated puzzle soon after having lost most of his right cerebral hemisphere as a result of a traffic accident" (p. 124). The mathematician was noting that the rules of geometry are logical rules, expressable in linguistic form. There may be a lesson here for normal individuals.

If there are sex differences in the style of spatial analysis, they probably are set in operation in early childhood. The girl's lead in language development would result in a shorter period of time during which her primary way of encoding information from the environment would be non-linguistic and spatial. So while girls are becoming increasingly skillful in verbal skills and in interacting with other people, boys are still more object-oriented, more focused on things and on spatial-perceptual activities. Perhaps boys never quite catch up with girls, so that having spent absolutely more time in early childhood in the analysis of the spatial features of their environments, boys continue along the "spatial" course, even though they eventually may equal females in verbal reasoning and comprehension, if not in fluency or articulation. Thus even in adulthood, men's conversations continue to reflect their greater "thing" orientation, while women's conversations tend to reflect their greater "social" orientation.

SUMMARY

We have discussed a mass of complex evidence bearing on the question of sex differences in language development. Though one always must bear in mind that today's "fact beyond doubt" has a way of becoming impeachable as new evidence comes in, at least a few general conclusions from existing data seem justified. Girls acquire language earlier than boys according to a variety of measures—acquisition of phonemes, amount of vocalization in infancy, the age of use of the first words, vocabulary size (at least in early childhood), articulation, comprehensibility, and fluency. It is less clear whether girls are also superior in their ability to use language in thinking or reasoning. The girls' early lead in tests of vocabulary size and verbal comprehension is not consistently maintained, and in several cases, where sex differences appear in older children and adults, it is the male who is ahead.

If the facts of at least some of these sex differences are reasonably certain, the explanation is not. Even though the functional specialization of the left hemisphere exists from earliest infancy in both sexes, it is possible that the female's lead in childhood language skills is tied to the greater speed with which her left hemisphere achieves still further specialization. There is little direct evidence: While the anatomical basis for human left-hemisphere specialization may be related to asymmetries in *size* of parts of the frontal and temporal lobes, it is far from certain whether there are further differences within the frontal or temporal speech areas between female and male brains. But the critical difference may be in very fine neuroanatomical structure and organization and not in gross structure.

Are the sex differences a product of social training? Research suggests that parents tend to reinforce girls' vocalizing more than boys', and in a way that may make the caregiver's vocalization more distinctive or attention-getting. Possibly, society, especially perhaps its poorer and less educated members, may be so conscious and accepting of the sexual stereotype about women's "talkativeness" that the fact of sex differences becomes a self-fulfilling prophecy. Neurological and genetic factors and environmental factors thus would work in a complementary way—each strengthening the other from the earliest days of the child's life.

The most critical kind of evidence therefore might be the demonstration of sex differences in the style of infant's response to cognitively interesting or arousing events, and in the nature of these events. If girls are more *vocally* responsive than boys are, not only to the parent's or their *own* vocalizations but to other interesting events as well, then very early a pattern of *linguistic* interactions between the girl infant and other persons is established. Thus, the parents' different treatment of their male and female infants is triggered, or catalyzed, by the infant itself. Initially, differences between boy and girl infants might be very small—but the small initial difference "snowballs," becoming larger as environmental and biological roles become entwined and mutually reinforcing. Eventually language (left-hemisphere skills) may come to play the dominant role in the female's general intelligence, so that in women more often than in men, "intelligence" and "language" become more nearly interchangeable.

Let me emphasize, in closing, that all the foregoing is still just a scenario—an outline of an hypothesized chain of events—but the evidence now at hand at least makes the scenario seem reasonable, if not certain. About human nature there probably can be no certainties.

PART THREE
SOCIAL INFLUENCES ON THE DEVELOPMENT OF SEX-TYPED BEHAVIOR

Contemporary psychologists typically do not maintain that the environment can be arranged to produce any kind of adult from any infant. As discussed in preceding chapters, biological differences between the sexes have varied implications, which may be accentuated or dampened by experiences in a social environment. Few biological differences seem to have *direct* serious implications for behavioral differences. **Socialization** experiences for girls and boys have been too vastly different to allow a conclusion that specific **role** behaviors are direct reflections of innate factors. Generally, females are expected to develop **communal** qualities but not **agentic** ones; males are expected to develop agentic qualities but not communal ones (Chapter 2). Many sex differences are associated with these expectations. Yet, there is **within-sex variation** as well. The chapters of this part are concerned with socialization experiences that contribute both to **within-sex** and to **between-sex variation**.

SOCIALIZATION PRESSURES

Sex differences and role adherence are not all "just natural" but are affected strongly by socialization. Fitzgerald (Chapter 7) discusses research showing sex differences during the first two years, but the differences are not ones that are clearly related to later specific sex-role behaviors. Biological contributors may underlie some differences, but simplistic conclusions about **biopsychological equivalence** are not warranted for adult roles.

Between two and five years of age, children typically show strong concerns about role behaviors. This is hypothesized to be the time when children acquire a concept of themselves as girls or boys and actively try to be what they think a "good girl" or "good boy" is expected to be. They are active participants in their own socialization, just as they were as infants, a process that has been called self-socialization (Maccoby & Jacklin, 1974). Even parents who do not regard sex roles as particularly important may nonetheless interact with girls and boys in different ways. Furthermore, many role pressures are not subject to direct parental control. There are pervasive pressures throughout our society, such as in language, television programs, and school systems, as is documented by Donelson (Chapter 8). The message conveyed is that females are not considered as important or valuable as males; they are often seen as being essentially nonpersons who are expected to assist or admire males.

EXTREMITY

Some evidence indicates that early and distinct sex-typing is of more importance and that agency is more valued in our country than in some others, like England and Scandinavia (Block, 1973). Parent–daughter interactions emphasize relatedness, protection, support; the emphasis is on the girls' developing and maintaining close interpersonal relationships. Girls are encouraged to talk about their troubles and are given physical affection, comfort, reassurance, probably much more than they need for healthy development. Socialization for boys emphasizes achievement and competition, control of feelings and limited expression of affect, and a concern for rule conformity, probably much more than appropriate for healthy development. Authority and control are vital issues between parents and sons.

There is some cross-cultural similarity in pressure on girls toward nurturance, obedience, and responsibility, relative to pressures on boys toward self-reliance and achievement (Chapter 1). However, our American socialization magnifies the differences found in other countries. Furthermore, Americans place greater emphasis on competitive achievement and less on the control of aggression in males than do people in other countries. The **sex-typing** pressures and the strong stereotypes associated with them have disruptive influences that exaggerate differences between the sexes and perpetuate stereotypes that the current differences are "just natural."

ANDROGYNY

A better case can be made for the naturalness of **androgyny** than for extreme sex-typing in defining mature functioning. Donelson (Chapters 8 and 9) discusses a variety of evidence indicating the value of androgyny and the impairment caused by the socialization procedures typical for girls and by the feminine role specifically. It is not regrettable that socialization encourages valuable traits of the feminine role in women and of the masculine role in men. It *is* regrettable that there are fewer valued traits expected of women and that socialization actively inhibits the development and direct expression of the attributes inconsistent with the roles. Males experience greater pressure for role behavior than do females. However, women face more difficulties in many respects than do men. The more conventionally sex-typed a woman is, the less likely she is to see herself as a separate person having an effect upon the world—to feel that she is her own *person*, rather than one defined only through others. An urge toward personal development may be partially responsible for the fact that young

females are not as rigidly sex typed as males.

People of each sex have potentials, needs, and feelings that are considered appropriate only for the other sex; thus they often develop inhibitions about these characteristics. For example, girls are anxious about their aggressive feelings and boys about their dependency needs (Kagan & Moss, 1962). In spite of role pressure, both women and men attempt to express role-inconsistent desires and feelings. Because of role pressures, they often try to do so in indirect ways that are relatively unsatisfying, mask similarities between sexes, perpetuate stereotypes, and possibly impair interpersonal communication. This dilemma is illustrated by selected research areas relevant to agentic and communal development.

ACHIEVEMENT

Our culture tends to value only a narrow kind of achievement that is more consistent with the masculine than the feminine role, as Donelson and Gullahorn discuss (Chapter 11). Because many women strive to meet their own standards of excellence in communal ways, their achievements in interpersonal skills often go unacknowledged. Some women express their needs for more personal, "male," achievement vicariously, through other people, particularly husbands and children who may not necessarily want to achieve another person's goals. As a result of prevalent socialization pressures, many females have low **hopes of success** and high fears about occupationally relevant achievement that interfere with their efforts. An effective personal achievement orientation is facilitated by interactions with parents through which daughters can experience warmth without overprotection or restrictiveness, and encouragement for independence and achievement.

AFFILIATION

Girls and women, compared to boys and men, are thought to be more affiliative and socially oriented in the broad sense of wanting to be with others, cooperating with them, trying to please them and win their affection, being loyal to them, nurturing and being nurtured by them, and so forth. There is both truth and untruth in this stereotype. During younger years, general affiliation is not sex differentiated; children of both sexes are high in "sociability" (see Maccoby & Jacklin, 1974). As Fitzgerald discusses, boy as well as girl infants typically develop an **attachment** relationship with caregivers, an infant form of affiliative behavior. Seeking close contact with and remaining near parents or other caregivers (e.g., teachers) in times of uncertainty does not appear sex-differentiated during childhood. In fact, boys tend to be more gregarious in terms of number of peers with whom they interact and of dependence upon their peers for values and activities. However, dependent responses are punished in males (Kagan & Moss, 1962). Adult men do not approach others for support in times of stress as readily as women. Also, women are more open in giving information about themselves to other people and in expressing their feelings. Both girls and women are more perceptive of the nonverbally expressed feelings of others than are males.

FRIENDSHIP

Psychologists know more about conventional achievement motivation—a "masculine" domain—than they do about the close intimacy of friendship within the affiliative—a "feminine" domain. The greater openness of females and perceptiveness of others' feelings could facilitate sharing in intimate relationships. Indeed, as Strommen points out (Chapter 11), adolescent as well as younger girls are more mature in this respect than are boys. Girls' interpersonal relationships emphasize interpersonal one-to-one intimacy, while boys' relationships are through a gang of boys who provide support against authority. Lack of conformity to peer standards is a cause for rejection of friends for boys more than for girls. Violation of the privacy and sensitivity of the intimacy of their relationships is a prime reason for rejection with girls.

However, assumptions and socialization experiences associated with sex-role typing often inhibit the development of mature friendships gen-

erally, both with members of the same sex and of the other sex. Fears of not being as "masculine" or "feminine" as one "should be" can inhibit honest sharing of feelings, thoughts, perspectives, and the discovery of important similarities and potential shared satisfactions. Interpersonal relationships are often impersonal because they are channeled into narrow and superficially prescribed modes, exemplified by our cultural dating ritual. Also, pervasive definitions of a woman through a relationship with a man often create a competitiveness between women that is a barrier between them.

MOTHERHOOD AND PARENTHOOD

The "mothering instinct" is often the banner under which social responsiveness and inhibited occupational achievement strivings are "justified" as necessary because of biological factors. "It's just natural for a woman to want to get married and have babies." Many women do want to be and take pride in being "just a housewife . . . just staying at home and taking care of the children." However, this is more likely a result of strongly sex-typed socialization than the expression of a "maternal instinct." As Fitzgerald discusses, there is no evidence of a unitary maternal instinct. Nor is one required for species survival. All that is required is that people mate sufficiently to produce offspring and that the young are cared for until maturity.

Furthermore, children seem just as important to men as to women, just as fathers are important for the development of girls as well as boys. Fathers are exuberant with their infants, and women and men college students report strong desires and high anticipated importance of children in their future lives in almost equally high proportions (unpublished data of the editors). In contrast to reports of personal desires, both women and men reported believing that children are more important to women in general than to men in general. People think stereotypes are true even when, as for men in this case, they recognize that they themselves do not fit the stereotype. However, both women and men students tend to believe that men want children to "prove their masculinity" and to carry on their name, and that women want children to fulfill a basic need or purpose in life (Rabin, 1965).

THE INDIVIDUAL'S PARTICIPATION

The obvious effects of socialization do not necessarily imply that biological factors are irrelevant. Rather, as a **psychobiological** perspective emphasizes, there is a complex interaction of biological and experiential factors. Individuals contribute to their own socialization in part through their biological predispositions. A genetically controlled characteristic may be in the form of a greater readiness to learn a particular behavior, or a predisposition to perform given actions. Some sex-typed behaviors may result from a learning process built upon biological foundations. A clear case is aggression. Greater aggression in males seems to involve biological factors, but it is also true that caregivers in this culture do not punish aggression in boys as much as in girls. Similarly, the greater verbal ability in females and spatial ability in males have hypothesized biological foundations that may be reinforced by specific socialization experiences (Chapter 6). Fitzgerald considers sex differences in infants' preparedness to attend to and process information about different kinds of stimuli and thus elicit different kinds of experiences with caregivers.

SELF-SOCIALIZATION

In spite of environmental forces and potential biological predispositions, human beings actively participate in their own socialization by trying to adapt to, or to resist, environmental and biological pressures. Like younger people, adult women, too, participate in their own socialization. They may seek situations that enable desirable experiences or they may remain in unsatisfying situations. They have a choice, despite the difficulties posed by contemporary society for female development.

Stereotypes are unfortunately perpetuated by prevalent views that a healthy "normal" woman is one who functions **reactively** and essentially "gives in" to the demands placed on her, while a healthy "normal" man functions **proactively**. Yet, if we and previous writers are correct in concluding that people are "naturally" androgynous and that the human being is capable of initiating action and effecting change, then the way is open for women (and men) to change life-styles that are not comfortable or satisfying for them. Women can choose to function proactively rather than reactively, as many women already have done. This requires personal courage. However, the support of other people is helpful, and much social change may be necessary for women in general to feel the potential for changing themselves or becoming what they want to be (Chapter 16).

CHAPTER
7
INFANTS AND CAREGIVERS: SEX DIFFERENCES AS DETERMINANTS OF SOCIALIZATION *

SOCIALIZATION

RECIPROCAL SOCIALIZATION

ATTACHMENT

INFANTS' PARTICIPATION

DETACHMENT

A PSYCHOBIOLOGICAL APPROACH

PREPAREDNESS

INFANT PREPAREDNESS

BIOLOGICAL VULNERABILITY

PSYCHOLOGICAL VULNERABILITY

Fear of Strangers

Nonsocial Stimuli

Attention

Learning

PARENT PREPAREDNESS

THE MOTHERING INSTINCT?

SPECIFIC PARENTAL BEHAVIOR

THE ORGANIZATION OF PARENT-CHILD RELATIONS

CRYING

SEX DIFFERENCES

Situational Influences

PARENTS' VOCAL BEHAVIOR

ORAL ACTIVITY

SEX DIFFERENCES

FEEDING MODE

Infant Feeding Behavior

CLINGING

INFANT PREFERENCES

swaddling

PARENTS' BEHAVIOR

Parental Differences

PACIFICATION

* A previous version of this chapter was presented as an invited address at the Congreseo Internacional de Psicologia, Monterrey, Mexico (August 1973), and at the Za Upravni odbor Pedijatrijske Sekcije SLC, Beograd, Yugoslavia (October 1973).

MUTUAL GAZE
SMILING
FOLLOWING
PROXIMITY SEEKING
ACTIVITY

SUMMARY

Girls and boys behave in many similar ways, as do many women and men. However, females and males at all age levels also behave differently. Knowing that there are similarities and differences in the behavior of females and males does not mean that we understand how these behaviors develop, nor does it mean that we know in fact which similarities and differences do exist. Clearly, however, psychology has been more concerned with differences in behavior than with similarities. Some psychologists favor **nativistic** explanations, assuming that sex differences reflect predetermined genetic traits of female and male members of the species. Others favor *environmental* explanations, assuming that all sex differences are acquired via the socialization process (Chapter 1).

In this chapter we will examine sex differences in infant and caregiver behavior while considering the general question: Do infant sex differences influence the early nature of caregiver–infant relations? If extreme nativistic positions are correct, one would expect to find sex differences in infants, but not necessarily in how infants are treated by caregivers, If extreme environmentalist positions are correct, one would expect to find differences in how caregivers interact with infants, but few, if any, sex differences in the infants themselves. We will see that neither pure nativist nor pure environmentalist explanations are warranted. Indeed, since the biological organism always exists in a social-cultural-historical environment, developmental psychologists are fundamentally interested in the *pattern* or process of behavior organization rather than simply biological or environmental explanations of the origins of things.

Working Hypotheses. The long-term consequences of infant sex differences are only beginning to be researched. Nevertheless, many theorists assume a strong continuity from infancy to later periods of human development. Moreover, there is an implicit assumption in developmental psychology that the events of infancy and early childhood influence the events of later periods of development, although they do not fatalistically determine those events.

The existing literature suggests several working hypotheses regarding infant sex differences and sex differences in parent–infant interaction. (1) Psychobiologically, female infants are stronger organisms than are male infants and this difference may influence caregiver reactions to male and female infants' behavior. (2) Female infants receive more sophisticated stimulation from caregivers than do male infants. (3) Differences in sensory–perceptual and learning processes suggest that female infants process auditory information more effectively than they do visual information, while males perform in an opposite manner. (4) There is little current evidence to support the idea that women possess an "instinct" for mothering; however in several respects both men and women seem to be psychobiologically prepared to provide caregiving to the young of the species. (5) There are differences between women and men in the nature of their interactions with infants.

Obviously, there is more support for some of these hypotheses than for others, and there are exceptions to each. Before we consider the evidence from which these working hypotheses were derived, it may be helpful first to briefly review some general aspects of the socialization process. Then we will review the concept of preparedness, and conclude the chapter by considering the organization of parent–infant relations.

SOCIALIZATION

Some definitions of socialization emphasize the acquisition of specific behaviors relevant to social interaction; others emphasize the influences people have on the individual. All definitions of socialization have in common the assumption that the behavior of one organism influences the behavior of another organism and that the influences occur in a social context. Although in a general sense, **socialization** refers to the process whereby one's attitudes, beliefs, values, and behavior are influenced by others, it is primarily parental behavior that is important to the infant.

RECIPROCAL SOCIALIZATION

During the past 15 years there has been unprece-dented, although long overdue, research interest in the early years of human socialization. As a result, many traditional views of the causes of be-havior have been challenged. Historically, psy-chologists have assumed that a child's social be-havior and personality development could be understood readily in terms of a *unidirectional* in-fluence from caregiver to infant. Little attention was paid to the possibility that the infant might play an influential role in determining the quality and/or quantity of caregiving it received. If the task of understanding socialization were merely one of specifying parental behavior, a major por-tion of the task might already have been ac-complished. However, there are *two* active agents, caregiver *and* infant, who *interact* during socialization. Thus, socialization is a reciprocal af-fair; caregiver *and* infant both influence the pro-cess (Bell, 1968).

It does not follow, however, that caregiver and infant necessarily are equal partners in socializa-tion. Obviously the parent provides the infant with an environment, with comfort and security, and with reinforcement that influences the in-fant's behavior. It is the parent who holds precon-ceived notions of what girls and boys "should" be like. And, it is the parent who loves and protects the child, or neglects or abuses the child. The basic claim made within the reciprocal socializa-tion point of view is that the infant does influence caregiver behavior. For example, an infant's shrill and persistent cry may be one stimulus that elicits abusive caregiver behavior; or conversely, an infant's plump and dimpled face may be a key stimulus for eliciting positive caregiver behavior.

ATTACHMENT

Another aspect of socialization of special signifi-cance in infancy is the establishment of an emo-tional-social bond between caregiver(s) and infant. This emotional-social bond is usually called **at-tachment,** a term that refers to a class of behav-iors, ". . . that maintains contact of varying de-grees of closeness between a child and one or more individuals and elicits a reciprocal attentive and nurturant behavior from these individuals"

Figure 7-1.

Time relationships of certain developmental organizational pro-cesses in the dog. Processes are indicated semidiagrammatically in terms of weeks prior to and after birth. (Reproduced from J. P. Scott, J. M. Stewart, & V. J. DeGhett. Critical periods in the organization of systems. *Developmental Psychobiology,* 1974, *7,* 489–513. Copy-right by John Wiley & Sons, Inc., and reproduced by permission.)

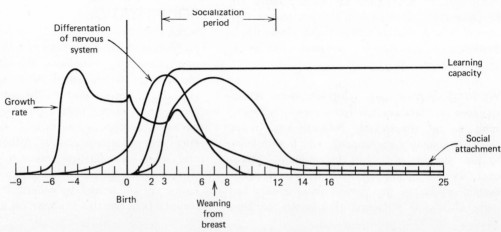

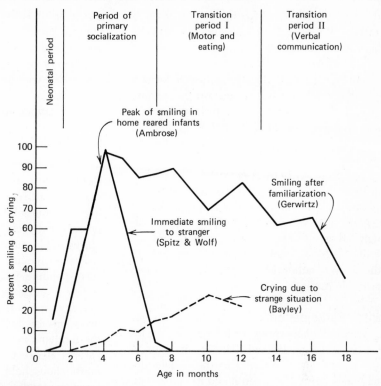

Figure 7-2.
The development of smiling and crying in human infants, in relation to periods of development. The peak of the smiling response to a strange face occurs at about four months and is characteristic of the period of primary socialization, during which the first social attachments are formed. (Reproduced from J. P. Scott. *Early experience and the organization of behavior,* Belmont, Calif.: Brooks/Cole Publishing Company, 1968, p. 95. Copyright by Wadsworth Publishing Company, Inc., and reproduced by permission of the publisher, Brooks/Cole Publishing Company, Monterey, California.)

(Maccoby & Masters, 1970, p. 75).

Attachment occurs in many species, and for each species there appears to be a defined time interval or **critical period** for its formation (Chapter 3). Exactly when the critical period occurs varies from species to species. For example, the critical period for the development of social attachments in dogs is roughly from 3 to 13 postnatal weeks (Figure 7-1), while that for human beings is estimated to range from the 4th to the 12th postnatal months. Within any one species, of course, the timing of critical periods for various aspects of development is different. The greater ability for systematic detailed observation of dogs enables a greater specificity of critical periods than currently is possible for humans. Nevertheless, there are indications that the first 18 months of postnatal life represent a critical period for the development of social attachments in human beings (Figure 7-2).

Attachment has important implications for the continuing social-emotional development of the child, for caregivers, and for the caregiver–child interaction. Whereas in typical environments the primary attachment object is usually the infant's biological mother, attachments are formed with other individuals, including the father. So strong is the father's interest in his newborn infant that his overall reactions have been termed *engrossment* (Greenberg & Morris, 1974). Fathers of newborn infants reported that they enjoyed looking at their newborn, desired to hold their baby, perceived their newborn as perfect and as resembling them, were happy with the newborn's sex, expressed a desire to share the responsibility of caregiving, and were proud to be a father. Although fathers are objects of attachment, infants typically become more strongly attached to mother than to father, at least during the first two years of life (Cohen & Campos, 1974).

Infants' Participation. For attachment as for other facets of infant–caregiver interaction, the infant is an active participant. The infant helps to elicit, maintain, and consolidate the social-emotional bonds formed between it and its caregivers. Specifically, it has been suggested that there are at least six behaviors involving infants and caregivers that are especially influential in the development of attachment (See Bowlby, 1969; Robson, 1968). These behaviors are crying, sucking, clinging, mutual gaze, smiling, and following. All serve to attact caregivers' attention and to initiate an interaction with them. The infant *is* a social organism, one whose behavior influences and is influenced by other human beings.

The most comprehensive and systematic discussion of attachment available is given by John Bowlby (1969). His theory draws heavily from **ethological** and psychoanalytic theory and from the empirical data of **developmental** and **comparative psychology.** According to Bowlby, the basic function of attachment is to assure survival of the species. The maintenance of close proximity (nearness) between caregiver and infant promotes attachment and thereby optimizes species survival. Crying and smiling act as **sign stimuli** that bring caregivers to infants. Conversely, sucking, clinging, and following bring the infant to the

caregiver. It is thought that the attachment relationship provides a foundation upon which subsequent parent–child relationships are built. The question of specific interest in this chapter, however, is whether sex differences play an influential role in the organization of the infant's social relationships and, consequently, in the quality and/or quantity of caregiver–infant interaction.

Detachment. In addition to attachment, normal development requires one to break away from or to *detach* oneself from the attached object(s). The process of *detachment* begins when the infant acquires self-locomotion. As the toddler's locomotor skills become increasingly proficient, there is a corresponding increase in the desire to be self-sufficient and to actively explore the mysteries of the environment. To some extent, the "terrible two's" are terrible because of the conflict between the toddler's insatiable desire to explore and the parents' desire to maintain a semblance of order in the household. Of course, parents may also resist the toddler's efforts toward detachment because of their own desire to maintain the attachment of infancy, or their inability to shift parenting style as the infant–toddler moves toward increasing independence.

A PSYCHOBIOLOGICAL APPROACH

Bowlby's theory is an example of a psychobiological approach to the study of development. The term **psychobiology** encompasses a wide variety of scientific disciplines having as their common objective the intent to understand the mutual development of psychological and biological components of behavior. Viewed from this perspective, behavior cannot be explained by environmental factors alone or by biological factors alone. Rather, all behavior represents the complex interplay of biological and environmental influences (also see Chapter 1).

One assumption of the psychobiological point of view is that much if not all of behavior is adaptive. In other words, much of the individual's behavior will reflect the demands of its changing environment. The specific form behavior takes reflects both the evolutionary history of the species—for example, **species specific behavior** such as language—and the individual's unique interaction with its environment—for example, environmental factors that may constrain the development of language performance. The preparedness continuum (Seligman, 1970) is relevant to this idea of adaptation.

PREPAREDNESS

When the organism is *prepared* to respond, the probability that a response will occur to a given stimulus is high, and learning is rapid and stable—it is easy for the behavior to develop. When the organism is *unprepared,* response probability is low, and learning is slow and unstable—it is difficult for the behavior to develop. Finally, when the organism is *contraprepared,* learning occurs only with difficulty, if at all—the behavior is unlikely to develop even when there are strong pressures for it to do so. Presumably, the organism's preparedness—or lack of it—determines to a considerable extent the degree to which environmental factors influence behavior.

The concepts of preparedness and critical periods can be related. During approximately the fourth to the twelfth month of life the human infant is prepared to develop an attachment relationship to one or more significant caregivers. However, if significant caregivers are not available during the critical period, as for example, occurs in poor institutional care facilities, the attachment relationship cannot develop. Presumably, if social attachments are not formed during the critical period they should become increasingly more difficult to form the further the organism moves away from the terminal point of the critical period. Thus, while once prepared to form attachments, the organism would become increasingly unprepared and perhaps contraprepared to develop social attachments.

Are male and female infants differentially prepared to influence caregiver behavior? Are caregivers prepared to react to female and male infants differently?

INFANT PREPAREDNESS

Infant characteristics relevant to preparedness include its biological sex, its temperament, its total dependence upon caregivers for survival, and the degree to which it is biologically typical or atypical. It appears that females and males do differ in the extent to which they are vulnerable to biological and psychological stress, although the evidence is considerably stronger for biological vulnerability than for psychological vulnerability.

Biological Vulnerability. The number of male conceptions exceeds the number of female conceptions, by approximately 150 to 100 (Rhodes, 1965). However, there is a marked reduction in the ratio during the prenatal months because of more spontaneous abortions of male than of female fetuses (Taylor, 1969). Male newborns exceed female newborns by approximately 105 to 100. Moreover, death rate statistics indicate that males are more likely to die than are females throughout the life span. Even modern techniques of prenatal care are not adequate to reduce the pattern of higher death and disability rates among males (Scheinfeld, 1965). Factors found to be associated with higher death and/or disability rates among males include: susceptibility to infectious disease; cardiovascular, renal and gastrointestinal dysfunction; congenital malformation; chromosomal abnormalities; noninfectious disorders; and blood poisoning during pregnancy (Allen & Dimond, 1954; Braine, Heimer, Wortis & Freedman, 1966). That the greater vulnerability of the male may be universal among the human species is indicated by the fact that incidence of chromosomal abnormality is greater in males than in females across a variety of cultures (Van den Berge, 1970).

Psychological Vulnerability. Does the male's greater biological vulnerability have implications beyond his susceptibility to disease or chromosomal damage? Are males more vulnerable to psychological pressures than females? No clear answer to this question is provided by the current research literature. There are some hints that school-aged boys may be more vulnerable. For example, from three to five times as many school-aged boys have reading or speech problems than girls do. However, it should be clearly noted that the potential for psychological vulnerability exists for girls as well. For example, some investigators have suggested that father absence during the early years of the female's development may have detrimental influences on her later cognitive competence (Landy, Rosenberg, & Sutton-Smith, 1969). Father absence has also been related to social-emotional disturbances in both boys and girls (see Lynn, 1974; Hetherington, 1973).

Fear of Strangers. Some insights into psychological vulnerability during infancy come from studies where infants are exposed to strangers in a laboratory setting. First, it should be noted that *fear of strangers* occurs in less than 50 percent of all infants—it is *not* the universal characteristic of infancy it was once thought to be (Rheingold & Eckerman, 1973).

In general, the literature suggests that fear of strangers occurs earlier and more intensely in females than in males, but occurs more frequently in males than in females (Fitzgerald, McKinney, & Strommen, 1977). This may reflect the females' earlier maturation generally or it may reflect the females' earlier awareness of social objects specifically. One investigator has found that when fear of strangers occurs earlier than usual in boys, it is related to social timidity through preschool and early childhood years, but this is not the case for girls (Bronson, 1971).

Nonsocial Stimuli. Are reactions to unfamiliar people paralleled by reactions to unfamiliar objects and events? In one study boys took longer to "shake off" the effects of an unpleasant auditory stimulus, sounded while the child was playing in a room with mother present (Maccoby & Jacklin, 1971). In another study, females showed a preference for novel stimuli when in a novel environment, whereas males showed a preference for novel stimuli when in a familiar environment (Weizmann, Cohen & Pratt, 1971). Perhaps males require the security of a familiar "home base" (either mother or the physical setting itself) in order

to deal effectively with novel stimuli, including strangers.

Attention. There is reason to think that the differences in reaction to social and nonsocial stimuli are related to differences in other psychological processes such as attention and learning. However, the direction of influence is not clear and there are many gaps in the research. Before one can learn anything about environmental stimulation one must be able to attend selectively to various aspects of the stimulation. Studies of infant and adult *attention* often measure the *orienting* reflex, as indicated for example by heart rate deceleration to the onset of a novel stimulus. The gradual reduction in the strength of the orienting reflex is called *habituation*. Thus, habituation is one measure of the decrease in attention that accompanies repeated exposures to the same stimulus or stimulus situation.

There do seem to be sex differences in infants' preparedness to attend to and process information about different kinds of stimuli. Although there are exceptions to be sure, males tend to be more efficient with visual stimuli than are females, and females tend to be more efficient with auditory stimuli than are males (see Cohen & Gelber, 1975). However, there is more involved, at least when visual stimuli are recurring. It seems that males and females process different kinds of information when given repeated presentations of visual stimuli. Males tend to be more attracted to the specific *physical* features of the visual stimulus itself, such as its color or form. Females tend to be more attracted to the *events* associated with stimulus presentation, such as the consequences of orienting to the stimulus or the reinforcing value of the stimulus. Moreover, females tend to vary the amount of time spent looking at a visual stimulus as a function of the complexity of the immediately prior stimulus, whereas males do not (see Cohen & Gelber, 1975).

Learning. There is some evidence that auditory stimuli are more effective for **operant conditioning** in female infants, while visual stimuli are more effective for male infants (Watson, 1969;

Haugen & McIntire, 1972). That is, if an auditory stimulus occurs, such as an adult saying "cute baby," after an infant response, such as saying "mama," the infant response is likely to occur more frequently in the future. Much of the development of specific responses throughout life can be accounted for by operant reinforcement principles. **Classical conditioning** (essentially the association of two stimuli) is also important for socialization, particularly with respect to emotional behavior. Individual differences among adults have been amply demonstrated for classical conditioning, but infant research is too incomplete to allow any simple statement of sex differences in conditionability (Fitzgerald & Brackbill, 1976).

Basic differences in infant preparedness to respond more efficiently to one type of sensory stimulation than another, and differences in attention and learning generally, very well may influence the nature of the caregiver–infant relationship. Together with the accumulating effects of interaction with caregivers, they may influence much later behavior as well. For example, visual responsiveness and caregiver interaction in visual ways may be related to males' better performance on visual–spatial tasks. Auditory responsiveness and learning and interaction with caregivers in auditory ways may be related to females' better performance on verbal and linguistic tasks (Chapter 6). Note that these suggestions are not ones that indicate validity for sex-role stereotypes, many of which are controverted by evidence from infant research. They do, however, point to differential preparedness of infants in modes of interacting with the environment.

PARENT PREPAREDNESS

If infants are differentially prepared to respond to the world, is the world differentially prepared to respond to infants? Put differently, are parents prepared for parenting? Are they prepared to respond to male and female infants differently? Is there an "instinct" for mothering?

The Mothering Instinct? The usual definition of instinct implies an innate drive or need to be-

have in a rather specific way, common to all or nearly all members of a species. In the context of that definition, there is little empirical evidence to support the notion of an innate drive, need, or "instinct" for mothering. Many people are not good parents, nor does society explicitly see value in good child care. Rheingold (1973) reports that the government classification for child-care attendant and nursery school teacher occupations matches that of restroom and parking lot attendant—all are at the bottom of the occupation rating category. She suggests the development of a new profession, *Scientists of Rearing,* dedicated to the quality of child care and including parents among those who need such specialized training. The government has no rating for parental competence. Nevertheless, programs like the Harvard Preschool Project, though stressing the development of competence in children, promise to provide important information concerning specific behaviors that distinguish competent from less competent mothers (White & Watts, 1973).

Specific Parental Behavior. Whereas there is little evidence to support a general instinct for mothering, some of the specific behaviors involved in caregiving do seem to rely on specific response preparedness, as discussed shortly. However, sensitivity on the part of the caregiver is necessary to adapt caregiving behavior to the particular needs and individual characteristics of the infant. To be sure, caregivers differ in the degree to which they are sensitive to individual differences in infants. Why they differ, however, remains an unanswered question. Part of the answer may lie in the way that parents themselves were reared.

Consideration of the caregiving interaction itself permits an evaluation of parental preparedness for caregiving. Obviously, differences in caregiving can only occur in an interpersonal setting. Moreover, our central question is whether or not infant sex differences can be linked to parental socialization practices. Therefore, the discussion will now turn to caregiver–infant interaction, while continuing to examine infant preparedness and parent preparedness for socialization. We will organize our discussion around the six behaviors that are thought to be especially important for socialization in general and attachment in particular.

THE ORGANIZATION OF PARENT-CHILD RELATIONS

CRYING

The first behavior of obvious social significance is the birth cry, which functions to elicit general and prompt caregiving (Bell & Ainsworth, 1972). Mothers cannot discriminate their newborn's cry from that of others, one piece of evidence against the claim that mothering is a unitary innate characteristic. However, with experience, mothers are able to distinguish their own infant's cry from that of other infants (Michelson et al., 1965), and to distinguish the meanings of different cries. Incidentally, contrary to some popular fears of "spoiling" the baby, during the first three months infants whose cries are not responded to promptly tend to cry *more* in the second half of the first year (Ainsworth, Bell, & Stayton, 1972).

Around three weeks of life a "pain cry" and a "hunger cry" become different and can be distinguished by the mother. The hunger cry begins slowly and gradually assumes a rhythmical quality. The pain cry has a delayed onset, often as much as seven seconds after the pain stimulation has occurred, an initial loud and piercing quality, and is essentially arhythmical (Wolff, 1969). The pain cry continues to elicit prompt caregiving, while caregiver responsiveness to the hunger cry may become less prompt.

Just as the mother comes to distinguish her infant's vocalizations from those of other infants, the infant too comes to respond differently to adults. Initially, nearly any human voice soothes a crying infant. Toward the end of the first month of life a female voice is a more effective pacifier than a male voice; by about six weeks, the mother's voice is almost the only one that can calm the infant (Wolff, 1963). This is probably because the mother's voice has acquired signal value through conditioning by being associated with repeated attempts to pacify the baby.

Sex Differences. There seem to be no sex differences in newborn crying (Fisichelli & Karelitz, 1963). However, sex differences do appear several months later and sex differences in the effect of crying develop too. At three months of age, male infants cry more and sleep less than female infants, whereas there had been no sex differences in the infants at three weeks (Moss, 1967). The three-month-old males received more social attention and physical contact from mother than the girls did. Curiously, however, crying of male infants was negatively related to mother's attention to crying—the more a male infant cried the less mother attended to his cries. The relation had been positive for both females and males at three weeks, and was still positive for females at three months—the more a female infant cried the more mother attended to her cries. This may be because the mothers were relatively unsuccessful in their attempts to calm "fussy" male babies; there is reason to suppose males to be less readily pacified than females, and mothers may also expect that males are supposed to be more "active" in this way than females.

The different effects of crying in female and male infants also is indicated in a **longitudinal study** that looked for relationships between newborn behavior and preschool behavior (Table 7-1; Bell, Weller, & Waldrop, 1971). Male newborns who cried frequently (measured when sucking was interrupted) tended to be shy and to avoid social activities during the preschool years. There were no relationships for females between such crying and later social behavior.

Situational Influences. During infancy and early childhood, the social situations most likely to be related to the crying of either sex are those involving conflict and frustration. A common technique used to study frustration in infants is to place a barrier between the infant and a desirable object. When sex differences occur in barrier–frustration situations, one-year-old females lose

TABLE 7-1.

Behaviors Showing Most Clear Relations Between Newborn and Preschool Periods *

Newborn Period	Preschool Period	
	Males	Females
Applicable to Both Sexes:		
High tactile threshold (low sensitivity)	Vigorous attack on barriers; sustained goal orientation (relations not as strong as for females).	Same as males but stronger relation, also, liveliness, rhythmicity, skill in manipulation, and coordination in gross motor activity.
Low tactile threshold (high sensitivity).	Lethargic and briefly sustained goal behavior.	Same as males; also inactive, clumsy, arhythmic, and uncoordinated.
Rapid respiration (at highest point in sleep)	Inattentive to and inactive in producing auditory stimuli.	Inattentive to music or books (trend in correlations similar to males but nonsignificant).
Slow respiration (at highest point in sleep)	Attentive to and active in producing auditory stimuli.	Attentive to music or books.
Slow respiration (at lowest point in sleep)	Advanced speech, communication, and modeling of adults (relation not as strong as for females).	Advanced speech development, communication, and modeling.
Applicable to Only One Sex:		
Rapid respiration (highest or lowest point in sleep)	Lethargic and passive in free play; unfriendly, uninvolved with peers.	No relation shown for females.
Slow response, few cries after nipple removal	Active and interested in teachers' games and rituals.	No relation shown for females.
Quick response, many cries after nipple removal	Watched others and was inactive in teachers' games and rituals.	No relation shown for females.
High, sustained pronehead reaction	No relation shown for males.	Restlessness; high gross motor activity; negative emotions; easily aroused from sleep.
Many mouth movements during sleep	No relation shown for males.	Advanced speech (statistical basis for relation tenuous).
Large feedings relative to birth weight	No relation shown for males.	Active, assertive, and gregarious in free play (relation based on only nine cases).
Small feedings relative to birth weights	No relation shown for males.	Lethargic, passive in free play; unfriendly, uninvolved with peers.

* *Source.* Adapted from Bell, Weller, & Waldrop, 1971, pp. 115–116. Copyright by the Society for Research in Child Development, Inc., and reproduced by permission.

interest in the object and begin to cry more quickly than do males (Goldberg & Lewis, 1969; Maccoby & Jacklin, 1971).

With this as with many "facts" about sex differences, the meaning of the differences is not clear. Some investigators have suggested that frustration has a greater detrimental influence on persistence of attention in females than males (Kramer & Rosenblum, 1970). However, it is equally plausible that the female infant's crying is an expression of noncompliance rather than a reaction to barrier frustration. Girls tend to reach their peak level of resistance to social pressures around 18 months; boys peak around 30 months (Levy & Tuchin, 1925). Thus, one-year-old male infants may be more compliant than their female peers. Males may persist in their efforts to overcome the barrier not because they especially want the desired object or because of "aggression" toward the barrier. Rather, they may want to comply with what they perceive to be the task demands—to obtain the object—in order to gain the experimenter's approval. This is an interesting possibility since the typical finding for older children is that females are more compliant than males.

In any event, situations that most frequently induce crying shift so that by the preschool years males cry most when manipulating objects, when in conflict with adults, and when in fear-inducing situations. Preschool-aged females cry most when in conflict with other children, especially when their antagonist is a male (Ricketts, 1934).

Parents' Vocal Behavior. There are sex differences in the quantity and quality of parental verbalizations directed to infants. Both mothers and fathers shorten their sentences when speaking to their young children. However, mothers speak more, repeat their own sentences more, and expand their childrens' utterances more than do fathers. Fathers tend to use many single-word declarative sentences and ask lots of questions (Giattino & Hogan, 1975).

There is some evidence for an interesting developmental change in parent verbal behavior during the early months of infancy. Fathers in one study tended to decrease their vocalizations to infants during the first three months of the infants' lives, while mothers gradually increased their vocalizations during these months. Both parents are influenced by the infant's sex. During the first month, parents talk more to an infant of the other sex than of the same sex, but the reverse is true by the third month—mothers talk more to daughters than sons, fathers talk more to sons than to daughters (Chapter 6; Moss, 1967; Rebelsky & Hanks, 1971). Are parents simply disposed to be more attentive to a same-sex infant than to an other-sex infant? Or, are infants differentially prepared to respond to female and male voices, thus reinforcing the same-sex parents's efforts? Although there are no definite answers to these specific questions, evidence about oral activity and physical contact does suggest sex differences in preparedness to respond to varying kinds of other sensory stimulation.

ORAL ACTIVITY

Sex Differences. Female and male infants do not differ in spontaneous sucking rate, whether the sucking is nutritive or nonnutritive. However, in many other aspects of oral activity there are rather clear differences, generally indicating greater oral activity and sensitivity in girl babies than in boy babies. For example, female infants show more rhythmical tongue and mouth movements, are more sensitive to sweetness, show more reflexive smiling; at three months they engage in more hand-to-mouth activity, and from 12 months on, suck their thumbs more than males do. Some of the differences have been interpreted as indicating a more active and earlier appearing search-and-explore activity on the part of females relative to males. This is particularly interesting in light of the widespread conception that males are generally venturesome and more interested in "exploring the world" than are females.

The relationship between oral activity and later development also differ for girl and boy babies. The mouth movements of newborn females are related to advanced onset of speech, while no such relationship holds for males (Table 7-1). In addition, female newborns who consume relatively little (for their birth weight) tend to be low in assertiveness during the preschool years, whereas those who consume more than expected are high in assertiveness. For boys, the only association between early and later behavior is the previously mentioned relationship between crying and frequency of social timidity.

Why do the relationships exist and what significance do they have past the preschool years? Caregivers may be encouraging greater oral activity and attending more to the oral activity of girls than boys. Mothers do use oral pacifiers more with female than male infants (Moss & Robson, 1968), just as girls do suck their thumbs more than do boys. Perhaps mothers want to pacify girls more or are more successful in calming their girls by oral pacification.

Feeding Mode. Without caregivers to provide food, human infants cannot survive. Less obvious but just as important is the fact that the feeding interaction is also a significant occasion for contact between caregiver and infant that can facilitate attachment. Both mother and infant are prepared for the feeding experience. The infant's rooting reflex (a head-turning search response) orients it to the breast or bottle. The sucking reflex predisposes it to suck the found nipple. The mother's lactation (milk producing) reflex and ejection (milk giving) reflex prepare her to provide the nourishment the infant is prepared to seek and take.

The preparedness of both participants for the breast-feeding interaction suggests that there may be psychological benefits to be gained for both mother and infant. Breast-fed infants, compared with bottle-fed infants have lower mortality and morbidity rates, less risk of infection and gastrointestinal disorders, stronger sucking responses, fewer behavior problems such as bed-wetting, poor sleep, nervousness, anxiety, and low activity levels (see Walraven, 1974). Similarly, breast-feeding mothers relative to bottle-feeding mothers, show more rapid contraction of the uterus

after delivery, delay in ovulation after pregnancy, reduction in breast cancer, reduction of menstrual cramping and mood states, and quicker desire to return to active sexual intercourse after delivery (Newton, 1971).

Infant Feeding Behavior. When infants are breast fed, there is an exception to the general rule of greater oral activity by female than male infants. In fact, it has been found in a variety of cultures that male infants receive longer feeding times per feeding session and have delayed weaning compared to females, at least among children who are first-born. The decision to breast or bottle feed does not appear to be related to the sex of infant nor to the mother's expressed preferences for the sex of her child. Thus, the different feeding patterns seem to be more a function of the infant than of the mother.

At least the social implications of feeding differ between female and male infants. This was illustrated by a recent study in our infant research laboratory (Walraven, 1974). Mothers and infants were observed during feeding (breast or bottle) and when an auditory stimulus (a loud buzzer) was presented. The results suggested that mothers are more attentive to male infants than to female infants during the feeding interaction, and are more attentive to breast-feeding males than to bottle-feeding males. Feeding method did not affect mother's attentiveness to female infants. Breast-fed infants of both sexes were more attentive to mother at the time of beginning to suck than were bottle-fed infants, and also seemed more attentive to the auditory stimulus. Breast feeding may be a highly significant contributor to the attachment relationship for mother and son, while visual and auditory contact may be more significant for mother and daughter.

CLINGING

Infant Preferences. Clinging refers to caregiver–infant physical contact, such as holding, handling, cuddling, and snuggling. Infants do not actively cling until about six months of age (Ainsworth, 1967). Clinging as a conscious expression of positive affect, often accompanied by "I love you," is rarely seen before about age two or two and one-half. However, young infants clearly do differ in their preferences for amount of handling and kind of handling (Schaffer & Emerson, 1964). Some infants are *cuddly*, actively seeking close physical contact and responding positively and consistently to caregivers' snuggling, but *do not* protest when put down. *Noncuddly* infants actively resist close physical contact but they also *protest* strongly when caregivers attempt to put them down (Ainsworth, Bell, & Stayton, 1972).

Swaddling. Is it necessary for the contact given to infants to be social contact? An answer is suggested by a recent study of swaddling conducted in our laboratory (Davidson, 1973). Although rather uncommon in our culture, swaddling is used in many parts of the world as a pacification technique. It involves wrapping the infant snuggly from toes to neck in a long, narrow strip of cloth (Figure 7-3). Three-week-old infants with preferences for a low amount of contact with mother protested the motor restraint of swaddling, cried longer, and took more time to fall asleep while swaddled than did infants with preferences for high contact. This is consistent with

Figure 7-3.
A swaddled infant. In pacification research the nipple would not be used. Swaddling is a very effective method of pacification, especially during the first few months of life.

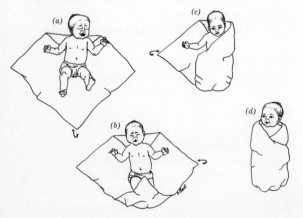

previous suggestions that noncuddlers dislike restriction of movement and close physical contact. However, the effect of swaddling differed depending on the infant's sex. For low contact (noncuddly) females, swaddling was *totally* ineffective as a method of pacification. Both a female stranger and the mother responded to the noncuddly girl infants' preferences by using a more active form of contact than used with cuddly females; the differences did not occur for male infants. However, males were touched more than were females.

Overall, this study and others support suggestions that males receive more *proximal stimulation* (physical contact) during the first six months of life than do females. This may be because males are more irritable or because females are more sensitive to physical contact stimulation than are males. Whatever benefits the infant gains from tactile stimulation, female infants receive more of it in *less time* than do male infants. Both kinds of infant differences may influence the mother's tendency to give male infants more proximal stimulation. In contrast, female infants receive more *distal stimulation* (visual and auditory) throughout the first two years of life. Interestingly after six months, females also receive more proximal stimulation.

Parents' Behavior. Just as infants differ in preferences for handling, mothers also differ in their desire to snuggle and to hold their infants close (Schaffer & Emerson, 1964). *Handlers* are mothers who seek snuggling interactions, while *nonhandlers* tend to avoid close physical contact, preferring instead more active physical interactions with their infants (such as bouncing on the knee, tickling, and tossing into the air). How do cuddling infants react to nonhandling mothers? They seek cuddling from other members of the family, as well as from mother, and through persistent effort generally receive such experience. How does a handling mother typically react to a noncuddling infant? She shifts to noncuddling types of physical interaction. Apparently in many instances, it is not the infant's life-style that changes, but it is the mother who modifies her behavior to meet the needs of her infant.

Not all mothers are sensitive to their infant's desires for physical contact of any sort. Daughters of depressed or otherwise disturbed mothers received little physical contact stimulation from mother during infancy and developed particularly strong emotional ties to their fathers (Murphy, 1973). This may be due to their fathers' having compensated for the attention not given by the mothers. Fathers are attachment objects, even when there are no disturbances in the mother–child relationship, although attachments are typically stronger between infants and mothers than between infants and fathers.

Parental Differences. Mothers and fathers differ in other aspects of the kind of interaction they offer their newborn infant. During the days at the hospital immediately following the infant's birth, mothers smile more at the infant, but father spends more time holding the infant, changing its position, rocking and touching it, and talking to it (Parke, 1974; Parke, O'Leary & West, 1972). If the higher father interaction reflects his engrossment, it is short-lived, limited to first-born infants. Fathers touched later-born infants less than first-born infants, whereas mothers did just the opposite. Thus, some of the father's engrossment with his newborn may be due to the confirmation of his "masculinity," or virility, provided by the birth of "his" first child.

The patterns of interaction were essentially the same for two very different samples, namely, for middle-class families with fathers who attended childbirth classes and were present during the delivery, and for lower-class families with fathers who did not attend classes or delivery.

There are also sex differences among caregivers in where on their own body they hold infants. Whether they are left-handed or right-handed, a majority (55 to 80 percent) of mothers carry their infant so that the infant's head is positioned on the mother's left side, whereas fathers tend to hold infants on their right side (Rheingold & Keene, 1965; Salk, 1973). Both women and men carry inanimate objects, such as grocery bags, on their left side. The left-side position mothers prefer for infants may provide optimal conditions for the infant to "tune-in" to the mother's heartbeat. Salk believes the heartbeat has unique properties as a pacifying stimulus, but there are good reasons to question his contention.

Pacification. Unquestionably, infants are prepared to respond by quieting to holding as well as a variety of other external sensory stimuli. When mother sings to comfort her infant, she applies external stimulation to suppress the infants' internal stimulation underlying crying. Furthermore, up to a point, the stronger the competing external stimulation the more effective is the pacification (Brackbill, 1970). In other words, holding the baby, singing to it, rocking it gently, and keeping it warm provide more effective pacification than any one of these techniques used alone. The preparedness for quieting is adaptive. Unsuccessful pacification attempts by the caregiver together with persistent, continuous crying by the infant can precipitate infant battering and abuse, especially in caregivers who were abused themselves as infants. Successful pacification because of the infant's preparedness to quiet strengthens the caregiver's positive feelings toward the infant and thus promotes the emerging attachment relationship.

MUTUAL GAZE

The mutual gaze of caregiver and infant is their staring at one another, sometimes for time periods (e.g., 30 seconds or more) far in excess of typical adult mutual gaze durations. Although adults and infants are equally able to initiate and terminate mutual gaze, it is the infant who actually controls the visual interaction about 90 percent of the time (Stern, 1974). Indeed, when infants in one study looked at mother or at a stranger, their look was almost always returned but they did not always return a gaze initiated by an adult (Davidson, 1973). Obviously, the infant is an active participant in regulating looking behavior of caregivers.

Although girls spent more time looking at a stranger, they were less likely to return mother's gaze than were boys. This is particularly interesting in light of studies indicating that throughout the first two years of life mothers provide their daughters more auditory and visual stimulation than they provide to their sons (e.g., Lewis, 1972). In other words, mothers talk to and look at their female infants more than they do their male infants even though (or because) female infants are less likely to reciprocate the mother's attempt to establish mutual gaze. In addition, female infants generally are found to be more responsive to social stimulation than are male infants: for example, investigators have reported that female infants begin to talk earlier, smile more, show earlier preferences for looking at faces or facelike visual stimuli, show earlier discrimination of faces, and are more responsive to the cry of another infant (e.g., Chapter 6). Yet, girls are less responsive to mother's gaze than are boys.

SMILING

The baby's first smiles are reflexive and occur more during sleep than when awake, probably reflecting spontaneous neurological discharge in the newborn. There may be sex differences in the way spontaneous neurological discharge is expressed (Korner, 1974). Female newborns show more reflexive smiling, and more overall oral activity (as noted previously), whereas male newborns lift their heads earlier and startle more frequently than do female newborns. The first *social smiles* occur shortly after the baby establishes mutual gaze, for most infants between four and eight weeks of age. There is some indication that older female infants also have more social smiles than their male peers (Moss, 1967); however, no published studies suggest that differences in smiling persist into adulthood.

Perhaps earlier smiling in female infants is merely one example of the more general accelerated maturation of females, and one with important implications for social interaction with adults. Could it be that the girl infants' earlier looking and smiling lead mothers to assume their daughters are very responsive so that they then look at and talk more to their daughters than their sons? Considering the important role that smiling plays in the regulation of social relations with adults, it

is a mystery why its role in the social relations between infants and adults has not been more systematically investigated.

FOLLOWING

Infants do follow their caregivers. However, *following* is a poor term for this behavioral aspect of attachment. Researchers have concentrated on *proximity seeking* (coming to caregiver) and *exploratory activity* (leaving caregiver) rather than on actual following. Proximity seeking is assumed to reflect attachment to caregiver; exploratory activity is often used to measure detachment from caregiver. The research methods used to study these behaviors typically involve placing the child alone in an experimental room or in the presence of familiar and/or strange adults, or else observing the child in a more natural setting such as the school or the home. Using these settings one can study several kinds of relevant behaviors.

Proximity Seeking. Boys are said to be aggressive. Girls are said to be dependent. However, girls are *not* more dependent on mother, as measured by their seeking her or clinging to her. Some studies do not show sex differences among infants (aged nine months to three years) in proximity to mother (Coates, Anderson & Hartup, 1972; Maccoby & Feldman, 1971). When sex differences in proximity to mother are reported, they suggest that when in a *strange* environment, girls take longer to leave mother and begin exploration than do boys (Bronson, 1971; Goldberg & Lewis, 1969). However, sex of parent is important as well. There is some evidence that when in strange situations, children prefer to be near the *same-sexed* parent (Spelke et al., 1973). Overall, however, mothers seem more important than fathers for both boys and girls; when toddlers had a choice between going to mother or to father, they chose mother twice as often as father, but father was clearly preferred over a stranger (Cohen & Campos, 1974).

Activity. Broadly speaking, any behavior is an activity. Thus, all of the literature reviewed thus far could be cited as evidence about infant activity. However, in sex difference research, the term *ac-*

tivity usually refers to gross motor activity, independence, assertiveness, noncompliance, and aggression. *Passivity,* on the other hand, has been equated with submissiveness, compliance, nurturance, affection, and dependence. It has been suggested that males are active and females are passive. On the basis of their review of the sex difference literature, Garai and Scheinfeld (1968) concluded that males have a biologic predisposition to *act* upon the environment whereas females have an inherent tendency to *react* to the environment. This difference was said to account for the male's interest in manipulation of objects and higher need for achievement, and for the female's interest in interpersonal relations and her social-affiliative needs.

Maccoby and Jacklin (1971) have pointed out the logical inconsistencies that arise from such typical and casual uses of the terms activity and passivity. For example, to assert that female infants are passive because they seek help in difficult situations denies the very active nature of the behaviors required in order to obtain help and achieve the goal. Much behavior considered passive in females requires very active behavior!

In other words, there is no evidence that females and males differ in basic activity. There are sex differences in various *specific* activities. Thus, activity may be situation specific in much the same way as sex differences in crying appear to be—males and females do not differ in how much they cry or how active they are, but in when they cry or are very active. For example, in one study 18- to 24-month-old girls spent more time playing with soft toys, dancing, and dressing up like adults, while boys spent more time playing with blocks and manipulating objects (Fagot, 1974). Boys were left alone to play more than were girls, but *both* father and mother were more likely to join in the play of boys than the play of girls. Since fathers tended to rate more children's behavior as appropriate for only one sex than did mother, one might speculate that fathers and mothers were joining the play of their sons for different reasons. For example, father may join his son in play to reinforce what he considers to be sex-appropriate behavior, whereas mother may join her son in play in order to expand what she considers to be rather mechanical and unimaginative play.

SUMMARY

The study of sex differences in infant and caregiver behavior shows promise of clarifying important aspects of early socialization. Although our knowledge of the significance of sex differences as determinants of socialization is not complete, sufficient progress has been made to suggest several working hypotheses or general conclusions worthy of further consideration.

(1). Psychobiologically, female infants are stronger organisms than are male infants. In general, compared to their male peers, female infants are less disease prone, less likely to die, less irritable, less aggressive, more oral, and more advanced in social-emotional and verbal behaviors.

(2). Accordingly, female infants receive more sophisticated stimulation from caregivers than do male infants. Specifically, female infants receive more visual and auditory stimulation earlier than do boys and later in infancy receive more physical contact stimulation as well. It may be that caregivers sense the greater psychobiological vulnerability of the male infant and provide a more comforting and less stressful stimulus environment for him. Although mother may have a "sense" for the psychobiological state of her infant, her sense seems to emerge from actual interactions with her infant rather than from an instinctively based "need to mother."

(3). Since fathers seem to be prepared for parenting as reflected by their engrossment in their newborns and their attachments to their older infants, it seems likely that much of the father's preparedness is suppressed by socialization practices in our culture.

(4). Differences in learning processes suggest that the types of stimulation (visual) male infants are *least* likely to receive from caregivers are those *most* likely to help their attention and learning processes. Female infants do not appear to be as dependent upon specific forms of stimulation. However, investigators have only recently begun to systematically study sex differences in learning so current general conclusions must be viewed with caution.

While many investigators have reported sex differences in infant behavior and in caregiver–infant interaction, there is practically no empirical evidence regarding the significance of these differences for later social behavior or personality development. Nevertheless, one must at least entertain the hypothesis that infant–caregiver interactions provide the foundations upon which later **sex-role** socialization occurs, and the hypothesis that the infant's sex contributes in significant ways to the quality of parenting it receives.

A CASE FOR ANDROGYNY
DEFICIENCIES OF THE FEMININE ROLE
ADJUSTMENT IN GIRLS
COMPETENCE MOTIVATION

TENDENCIES TO ANDROGYNY
FREQUENCY
VALUES OF ANDROGYNY
INDICES OF MATURITY

SUMMARY

People differ greatly in the content and intensity of their sex-typed experiences and in their degree of comfort with the implications of those experiences. However, few people, if any, completely escape **sex-role** pressures. In spite of much current and appropriate questioning of the usefulness of sex roles, most people have lived in environments shaped by them in one way or the other and, thus, have been encouraged to become relatively **sex-typed**. In this culture especially, women are encouraged to be **communal** and men to be **agentic** (review Table 1-1).

By understanding some procedures of sex-typed **socialization**, we may better assess the effects of sex roles in our own and others' lives. In general, the impact of traditional sex-typed socialization tends to be a relatively restrictive and negative one, with members of each sex paying high prices in differing ways. Boys in our culture initially have more pressure for role behavior than do girls, but more freedom than girls within the role toward which they are pressured. Girls are less rigidly sex-typed than boys, but females suffer more for adhering to the sex roles than do males. Some specific means by which the pervasive pressures toward sex-typing occur for both girls and boys are discussed in this chapter. The value of **androgyny** for both females and males, rather than limited sex-typing, is indicated in a variety of ways. The following chapter deals with some facets of conventional socialization that particularly impair the development and functioning of women by discouraging androgynous development.

SEX-TYPED SOCIALIZATION

SEXUAL IDENTITY
Although relevant terminology varies, in this chapter **sexual identity** refers to the extent of a person's definition of self as female or male. Because it refers to one's own physical body, it seems an essential ingredient of one's self-perceptions. To the extent that it is conscious, it is part of the **self-concept** (Chapter 2). Sexual identity also involves attitudes about one's self that occur at deeper or unconscious levels of personality; unconscious and conscious identity are not necessarily consistent. Some people may have a firm sense of themselves as women or men without being considered feminine or masculine by other people. They themselves may feel that they are feminine or masculine simply because they are women or men; or they may consider "feminine" or "masculine" to refer to whatever they are, as persons. They are likely to recognize that their characteristics include both those which others consider feminine and those others consider masculine. Yet, they feel free to be what they are.

However, in a society like ours, where sex roles are so important, people come to think that femaleness or maleness must be defined by selected attributes that are based on sex roles. Thus, **biopsychological equivalence** is assumed, and femaleness and maleness come to have implications they need not have (Chapter 1). To date, many people are likely to have many specific meanings, often very restrictive ones, attached to their concept of being a female or male human being. Sexual identity essentially becomes a matter of sex-role identity. **Sex-role identity** is the extent to which an individual regards the self as feminine or masculine *as defined by sex roles* (Kagan, 1964). Self-perceptions are not necessarily consistent with the judgments of others.

One may have a clear, healthy, sexual identity without necessarily being feminine or masculine in the ways society expects. Even among those whose sexual identity is tightly bound with a sex-*role* identity, there is much room for individual variation. People differ in the importance or centrality of sex-role related evaluations in their self-concepts and in the specific "meanings" of femininity or masculinity. Two persons to whom being feminine is quite important may show very different behaviors, or the same behaviors for different reasons (Figure 8–1). Notice that for another person (Case C), being feminine is just as important and central in the self-concept as for the other persons, yet Case C does not subsume any particular trait or behavior under the label. For that person sexual identity is not a matter of sex-role identity.

Figure 8-1.

Schematic diagrams of different organizations of the content of self-concept, for three people who consider themselves feminine.

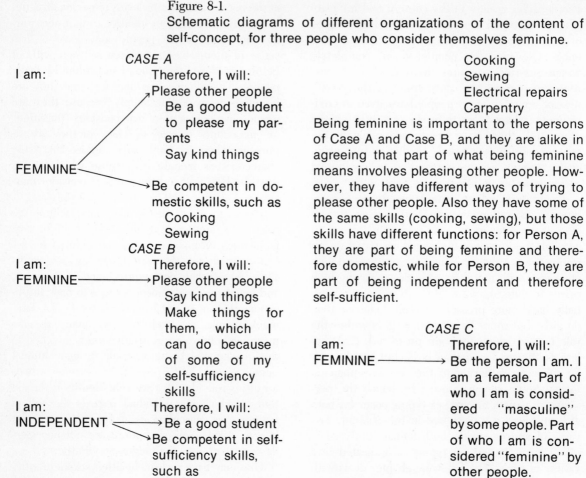

CASE A

I am: Therefore, I will:

Please other people
Be a good student to please my parents
Say kind things

FEMININE

Be competent in domestic skills, such as
Cooking
Sewing

CASE B

I am: Therefore, I will:

FEMININE ⟶ Please other people
Say kind things
Make things for them, which I can do because of some of my self-sufficiency skills

I am: Therefore, I will:

INDEPENDENT ⟶ Be a good student
Be competent in self-sufficiency skills, such as

Cooking
Sewing
Electrical repairs
Carpentry

Being feminine is important to the persons of Case A and Case B, and they are alike in agreeing that part of what being feminine means involves pleasing other people. However, they have different ways of trying to please other people. Also they have some of the same skills (cooking, sewing), but those skills have different functions: for Person A, they are part of being feminine and therefore domestic, while for Person B, they are part of being independent and therefore self-sufficient.

CASE C

I am: Therefore, I will:

FEMININE ⟶ Be the person I am. I am a female. Part of who I am is considered "masculine" by some people. Part of who I am is considered "feminine" by other people.

Adoption and Preference. Sex-role preference is a desire to adopt or display sex-role behavior, or the perception of such behavior as preferable or desireable for one's self (Lynn, 1959; Biller, 1971). Thus, it is a part of the **ideal self.** Display of the role behavior is called **sex-role adoption.** Although one might expect positive associations between role adoption, role preference, and role identity, there is little systematic evidence about their interrelationships, and much room for an individual to have distorted perceptions about their consistency.

Any one person may have some inconsistencies or conflict within and between role identity, preference, and adoption. For example, a person

may want to have characteristics conventionally considered masculine as well as those considered feminine. And, a person may feel, "I am a submissive person," but want to be assertive (Figure 8-2). If the person is male, this aspect of preference is role consistent and identity is not; if the person is female, the preference is role inconsistent while the identity is consistent. Behavior may sometimes be submissive and sometimes assertive, or characteristically one or the other.

The degree of personal discomfort caused by such inconsistencies depends partly on the extent to which the relevant attributes are central in one's own self-view and relevant to significant others. For many people, sex roles are criteria of

Figure 8-2.

Diagrammic representation of high and low consistency among preferences, behavior, and identity.

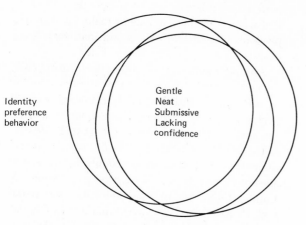

Identity
preference
behavior

Gentle
Neat
Submissive
Lacking
confidence

A. Example of (near) perfect, idealized, consistency between preference, behavior, and identity. For each of the traits, statements of "I am . . . ," "I want to be . . . ," and "I behave . . ." are consistent with each other. All traits listed are considered more in the feminine than the masculine role.

B. Example of lack of perfect consistency between preference, behavior, and identity. For example, for the person depicted, the following are true:

—I am submissive and behave submissively, but I want to be assertive.

—I am gentle and want to be gentle, but my behavior is more likely to be rough than gentle.

—I want to be self-confident, I behave in a self-confident way, but I am not really self-confident.

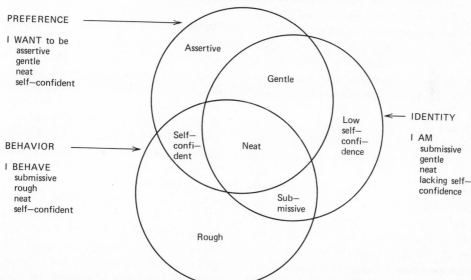

PREFERENCE

I WANT to be
  assertive
  gentle
  neat
  self—confident

BEHAVIOR

I BEHAVE
  submissive
  rough
  neat
  self—confident

Assertive

Gentle

Low
self—
confi—
dence

IDENTITY

I AM
  submissive
  gentle
  neat
  lacking self—
  confidence

Self—
confi—
dent

Neat

Sub—
missive

Rough

evaluation for what Rogers calls conditional regard, so that others are accepted only if they conform to the roles (Chapter 2). Concomitantly, sex roles often form **conditions of worth** for acceptance of self so that people are unwilling to act upon preferences or impulses inconsistent with roles.

The more identity, preference, and adoption are consistent with sex roles, the more an individual is said to be **sex-typed.** Intensity of sex-typing is generally less for girls than for boys. Unfortunately, most research involves indices relevant to only one of these aspects of sex-typing, so that we do not know much about their inter-relationships.

Theoretical Orientation. The range in the extent and specific expression of sex-typing among people is almost paralleled by the range in social scientists' explanations of sex-typing (Chapter 2). The theoretical base implicit in this chapter is a cognitively based social learning theory approach. In this view, people seek information about the world and their relationships in it, including their actual or anticipated relationships with other people. The child learns from other people and is assumed generally to want positive experiences.

The Earliest Years. A major part of the development of sex identity and sex-typed behavior occurs after birth. The first major relevant postnatal event is **sex assignment:** the infant is labeled as a girl or a boy (see Money & Ehrhardt, 1972; Hutt, 1972). For most infants, the assignment is made fairly easily and there is an apparent consistency among the various physical criteria of sex definition (Chapter 4), sex assignment, and the later sex-typed experiences. However, some extreme inconsistencies dramatically illustrate the role of developmental experiences. For example, a male infant whose penis was accidentally ablated during circumcision was reassigned (with appropriate medical treatment) as female. The infant's *identical* twin (and therefore genetically equivalent) brother is developing as a boy and the infant herself as a girl. Similarly, if one genetic female **hermaphrodite** (Chapter 4) is assigned and unambiguously reared as a girl and another one is

assigned and unambiguously reared as a boy, the subsequent medical and social histories differ according to sex of assignment. Hermaphrodites reared ambivalently, so that people do not consistently consider them female or male, have an ambivalent view of themselves and may want a sex change.

Although there are sex differences during early infancy, resulting from parental reactions to the sex assignment and the infants' preparedness, experiences during infancy do not seem to account for major sex-role learning or sexual identity (Chapter 7). Generally, sexual identity is estimated to be established roughly between the ages of 18 months and 3 years (e.g., Hamburg & Lunde, 1966). Sex changes are safest within the first 18 months of life and sexual identity is virtually irreversible after 5 or 6 years. Freud was clearly correct in emphasizing the importance of this age period for sexual identity. But his view, still widely held even by non-Freudians, that femininity in women and masculinity in men are due to identification with (or imitation of) the same-sex parent seems to be in error (Chapter 2). Contemporary evidence about sex typing is fragmentary (e.g., Emmerich, 1973), but some dominant themes are becoming apparent.

THE CHILD'S PARTICIPATION

"Who Am I?". According to cognitive development theorists, after sex assignment, the next major event of sex-typed development occurs when the child is about 2 or 3 years and begins developing a relatively unchangeable cognitive *self-categorization* or *label* of self as girl or as boy (Kohlberg, 1966; Maccoby & Jacklin, 1974). This label may be thought of as the "kernel" of sexual identity. From then on, children become increasingly active participants in their sex-typed socialization, just as they had been active participants with parents during infancy. Children look to other people to try to understand what it means to have the label "girl" or "boy." They look to other people to try to understand who they are and who they "should" be and become. Behavior and self-definitions consistent with the expectations and standards of others are likely to be rewarded by others and increasingly by the *internal* reward of feeling *competent* in being what one is "supposed" to be. There is a continuing reciprocal interaction between the child's emerging view of self and behavior: self-concept guides behavior, and behavior contributes to developing definitions of self. Thus, children internalize expectancies held by others as their own expectancies for themselves, and the relevant behavioral expressions become relatively stable.

If many of the expectancies of others seem to the child to be relevant to the sex lable, then sex-role based dimensions become relatively central in the self-concept and in evaluations of behavior. Sexual identity becomes more and more a sex-*role* identity. Given the presumed importance of the lable, "girl," the child strives for *competence* in being what she thinks she is supposed to be because of that label. Obviously, much within-sex variation is due to differences in exactly what parents and others *teach*, and in what children *learn* about the relevance and implications of the label. However, children typically show role knowledge and behavior quite early.

Role Knowledge. Children do learn the societal importance attached to sex roles and may show sex-typed behavior even before they have a clear label. Indeed, as early as 20 months of age, girls were observed to prefer "girl toys" and boys to prefer "boy toys" (Fein et al., 1975). However, girls were more likely to own boy toys than boys were to own girl toys—even at this age, girls were less sex-typed than boys. By nursery school age, children are quite knowledgeable about sex roles and are themselves fairly strongly stereotyped (Maccoby & Jacklin, 1974). Boys become increasingly more strongly sex-typed than girls, in such matters as avoiding role-inconsistent activities and accepting or preferring role-consistent ones (e.g., Nadelman, 1974).

Parents Teach, Children Learn. Parents differ in the extent to which they are sex-typed, in what they *want* to teach their children, and in what they *do* teach their children. For example,

parents who stressed individualized development rather than strong sex-typing for their children had children who were less rigidly sex-typed than those of other parents; this tendency was more marked for daughters than for sons (Minuchin et al., 1969). However, even parents who think of themselves as nontraditional with respect to sex roles can communicate sex-typed principles to children without necessarily realizing that they are doing so (e.g., Fagot, 1974). Whether conventional or liberal with respect to sex roles, parents are likely to provide many cues that children use in formulating their understanding about themselves and others. Parents, and other adults, *reward* behaviors they consider desirable, *punish* those they consider undesirable, and provide *direct instructions*, such as "Girls don't do that!" and "Good little boys are supposed to. . . ." They are also *models* and *eliciters* of sex-typed behaviors, as discussed shortly.

However, the relationship between parental behavior and children's sex-typing is by no means clear, simple, and direct. Parents are not the only sources of socialization pressures. Nor are children passive organisms, simply shaped by conditioning and instructional principles as often claimed. Studies of preschool children do not report large relationships between the behavior or personality traits of children and those of either parent, though the children are typically strongly sex-typed (Maccoby & Jacklin, 1974). Children's extent of traditional femininity or masculinity specifically is not reliably related to the femininity or masculinity of parents. For example, one 4-year-old girl insisted that females can be nurses but not doctors, although her mother was a physician!

Obviously, the views children develop are not necessarily the same as those of the parents. Parents teach; children learn. Children understand adult concepts at their own level of cognitive development, and their actions vary accordingly. Children simplify a grammatically complex sentence, often retaining most of the meaning, but the structure expresses the child's own level of grammatical competence. Analogously, their understanding of the implications of being a female or male is affected by their stage of cognitive development. Thus, some behaviors of many young children are exaggerations of stereotyped behavior that go far beyond the expectations of even conventional parents. The behaviors may reflect a stronger concern with sex-typing than the parents have intended to teach, particularly when the child has been exposed to people other than the parents. Increasingly the child actively participates in socialization, trying to understand the world and "fit" into it. Consideration of observational learning helps further illustrate this point and suggests some specific sources of variation in the development of role-related behavior and concepts of self.

OBSERVATIONAL LEARNING

Model Characteristics. Theory and research in both naturalistic and experimental situations (with parents, other adults, and peers as models who are observed by subjects) indicate that a model's perceived power or dominance, nurturance and warmth, and similarity to the observer are dominant characteristics eliciting modeling or imitative behavior on the part of the observing subjects (e.g., Mischel, 1970; McCandless, 1970). Each of these three model characteristics increases the likelihood that an observer will perform a response displayed by the model. If parents were themselves clearly exclusively feminine or masculine by traditional criteria, and if same-sex parents were clearly more powerful and warm to the child in addition to being similar in sex, then conventional sex-typing would be rather easily explained. Such is not the case. Complexity is more the rule. In fact, we may be only beginning to scratch the surface of all that influences models' effectiveness (e.g., Waxler & Yarrow, 1975); we are certainly far from understanding all that influences sex-typing.

Observers, children or adults, differ in the extent to which they attribute power, nurturance, or similarity to other people and in their tendencies for imitative behavior (Chapter 9). And, for example, children tend to imitate a warm parent or a dominant parent, regardless of the parent's sex similarity (Hetherington & Frankie, 1967).

Tendencies to imitate a same-sex parent or other model, in preference to one of the other sex, is not particularly apparent in preschool children; nor, as previously noted, are characteristics of preschoolers correlated with those of either parent (Maccoby & Jacklin, 1974). However, slightly older children, such as first and second graders, do recall more about the behavior of a *same-sex* model than one of the other sex; the bias against the model of the other sex is not as strong for girls as for boys (Grusec & Brinker, 1972). Apparently, children learn the societally accorded importance of sex and come to see sex as an important dimension of similarity, though not the only one.

Models' Role Consistency. As they learn the cultural importance of sex, children increasingly respond to the role consistency of the model's behaviors. That is, girls' recall of social and romantic behavior increased when the model was a girl; boys' recall of aggressive behavior increased when the model was a boy (Maccoby & Wilson, 1957). The evaluations made by young children are often rather subtle and somewhat surprising to adults. Five-year-old boy subjects, but not girls, tended to attribute power to an adult male model even though the researchers had gone to some trouble to give the female model clear control over resources, such as toys and cookies (Bandura, Ross, & Ross, 1963). As one boy explained, "He's the man and it's all his because he's a daddy. Mommy never really had things belong to her. . . ." When the controlling woman model later shared with the man, as well as with the child, she became a more "suitable" model, and the boy's imitation of her increased threefold—daddies own, mommies share. Mommies share because they do not really own. Why did the girl subjects not have the same reaction?

Models' Outcomes. Observers often see what outcomes models experience for their behavior. Children are more likely to show spontaneous imitation of models who received rewards rather than punishment, but they can perform a punished response when encouraged to do so (Bandura, 1965). An even more important outcome than the reward or punishment given by others may be how the model *feels* about the outcome. At least with seven-year-old boys the model's pleasure or displeasure with an outcome was more important in influencing the boys' imitation of him than whether the tangible outcome was desirable (a shiny toy locomotive) or undesirable (an old torn book). The boys imitated the pleased model more than the displeased one, regardless of the desirability of the reward (Lerner & Weiss, 1972). If the results are generalizable to girls, and to children of different ages, then it becomes relevant to ask about mother's outcomes and how she feels about them. How does father feel? If mother is unhappy, a girl is less likely to model her behavior than if mother is happy.

Observer's Rewards. Children are likely to experience more rewards for imitating the behavior of a model of the same sex than one of the other sex. The reward not only increases the likelihood of their performing the behavior again, it also increases their recall of subsequent behavior observed in the model (Grusec & Brinker, 1972). However, the tendency for lowered recall of the behavior of a model of the other sex is not as marked in girls as in boys. It has been suggested that even though girls are reinforced for imitating women, men still are very salient as powerful figures (Perry & Perry, 1975). In addition, girls may not be rewarded for same-sex imitation as consistently as boys are and, as noted before, may observe that their same-sex models experience less happiness with outcomes.

Effects of Observation. Observation of adults or peers alone cannot explain strong sex-typing, particularly in the younger years. Modeling is crucial in the child's acquisition of a wide repertoire of potential behaviors, but the complete set of behaviors is not particularly sex-typed to any important degree (Maccoby & Jacklin, 1974). A distinction between *acquisition* and *performance* is necessary. Children acquire many responses, including many consistent with the role of the other sex, but they do not perform all of the responses they have acquired. Observation of other

people contributes information to children's developing sense of the cultural meaning of being a girl or a boy, and to their own predictions of what will happen to them if they themselves perform the behaviors observed in others. They select for performance those responses that they consider appropriate and realistic for them, according to their own developing standards and understanding of themselves and the world. Ongoing interaction *with* parents, in addition to observation *of* parental action, also contributes importantly to the child's perceptions and sex-typed development.

INTERACTION WITH PARENTS

Many parents, including some who do not realize that they are doing so, communicate that they expect role-consistent behavior on the part of the child. They elicit and reward sex-typed behavior in their ongoing interactions with the child. This teaching mechanism may well have greater impact than more explicit parental teaching attempts (Colley, 1959; Biller, 1969). It may also be responsible for the relevance of father for the sex-typing of girls as well as boys. In fact, some developmental psychologists assert that fathers are more important in girls' sex-typing than are mothers. For example, daughters' extremity in traditional sex-typing is not related to their mothers' sex-typed femininity but is related to the degree of their fathers' sex-typed masculinity: daughters of the more masculine men were more sex-typed than those with fathers of lesser masculinity (Hetherington, 1965, 1967; Mussen & Rutherford, 1963). The greater social pressure on a man for role-consistent behavior may make sex-typing more crucial to him than to a woman, even when he is interacting with his children. The traditionally masculine father does not model femininity, but may elicit and reward it in his daughters. Concomitantly, much of the interaction of a traditional mother with a child is general nurturance and maintenance in which sex roles are largely irrelevant. More generally, women are likely to be less concerned than men about sex-typing in their children, just as they were less concerned than boys when they themselves were children. For example, fewer adult women (ages 20 to 25 without children of their own) than comparable men considered behaviors typical of toddlers as sex-typed, particularly for girls (Fagot, 1973). Similarly, women university students who were actually mothers of toddlers rated fewer behaviors as appropriate for only one sex than did fathers; both mothers and fathers placed fewer restrictions on girls' than on boys' behavior (Fagot, 1974). It is also true that fathers were observed to give almost twice as many positive responses to their sons as to their daughters, whereas mothers gave about the same number of positive responses to daughters and sons (Margolin & Patterson, 1975). For whatever the reason, association with their fathers has an effect on daughters' sex-role behavior.

Paternal Deprivation. Some possible effects of absence of the father is illustrated by Mavis Hetherington's (1972, 1973) study of daughters of widowed or divorced mothers who had not remarried. Adolescent girls (aged 13 to 17 years, all first-born, without brothers) who had lost their father felt insecure and apprehensive about male peers and male adults, and the effects were more pronounced if fathers were lost *before* the girls were five years old than later. However, the ways in which they showed their insecurity differed. The daughters of divorced mothers had more negative feelings toward their fathers than did girls of other groups, but they showed a general "approach" to males. They sought out males and were markedly assertive, seductive, or even promiscuous with them. In contrast, daughters of widowed mothers had a general "avoidance" of males and marked inhibition in interaction with them. Both kinds of father-deprived girls, however, were comparable to girls from intact homes in other respects, including traditional feminine interests and role attitudes, security with females, and closeness to their mothers. In trying to understand sex-typing, we may find it important to distinguish between behavior directed toward males and other kinds of behaviors expected of females, a distinction not well developed in research or theory thus far.

Hetherington suggested that the lack of opportunity for constructive interaction with a male contributed to the girls' difficulties in relating to males. Insecurity with males in girls who have *not* been subject to divorce or death of the father may have similar underlying reasons. Fathers in intact marriages may not be at home very much, and simply having a father "around" is no guarantee that he is loving and attentive or that the daughter has a meaningful relationship with him. Other evidence indicates that poor relationships with a physically present father can have other, more subtle effects as well (e.g., Mueller, 1966). Fathers are important to daughters.

However, there are some complexities to keep in mind. Women who do not remarry may have different attitudes about men than do women who do remarry, or than women who elect pregnancy or adoption without marriage. From the child's point of view, to lose a father may not have the same psychological meaning as never having had one, and to have inadequate relationships with an existing father may not have the same meaning as having no relationship because one has never had a father psychologically. Also, sensitive mothers who wish to do so can adequately compensate for the usual effects of paternal absence on sons' development (Biller, 1969). Perhaps they have the capacity to do so for daughters as well.

Employed Mothers. Separation of a child from the mother because of divorce or death has been so infrequent that the effect of this kind of absence has not been well investigated. However, there is a great deal of evidence about "absence" because of maternal employment outside of the home (Hoffman, 1974a; Hoffman & Nye, 1974; Miller, 1975). The exact effects of maternal employment of course vary with factors such as family income and degree of maternal satisfaction, but the results are generally beneficial. The main effects on daughters are a less restricted concept of the behavior acceptable for women, including more approval of maternal employment and a higher evaluation of female competence. For example, young daughters of employed mothers see both women and men as engaging in a wide variety of adult activities, ranging from using a sewing machine to climbing mountains. Adolescent daughters of employed mothers name their mothers as the person they most admire, but they are not dependent upon them (Douvan & Adelson, 1966). These adolescent girls tend to be more self-sufficient, more active in leisure activities, and more involved in general family affairs and household responsibilities than other girls. Both women and men college students with employed mothers saw the positive traits usually reserved for the other sex as appropriate to their own sex as well. Specifically, daughters saw women as competent and effective; sons saw men as warm and expressive (Vogel et al., 1970). This is probably due partially to the modeling of the parents; mothers are behaving in nontraditional ways, and fathers are more likely than other men to be involved in household tasks, including child care. The freeing effect in homes with employed mothers is particularly shown in that daughters have higher than usual educational and career ambitions for themselves (Chapters 11 and 15).

Birth Order. Parents' interaction with any given child varies with the number, sex, and age of other children as well as the parents' own stage of personality development (Warren, 1966; Sampson, 1965; Handle, 1965). In part, because of different kinds of interactions with parents, firstborn children tend to be more anxious, affiliative, adult-oriented, and interested in personal achievement than later borns. These qualities are even more marked in only children. Children are also directly affected by their siblings. Having sibs of either sex can accentuate or minimize sextyping in complex ways not yet clearly known (Sutton-Smith & Rosenberg, 1970). For example, having an older brother reduces the typical difference females show for higher verbal than quantitative scores on aptitude tests.

Some evidence indicates that in two-child families, traditional femininity is more pronounced in the *older* of two sisters than in the younger, although the older child is more concerned with personal achievement, which has been considered masculine (Douvan & Adelson, 1966). How-

ever, girls whose only sib was an older *brother* were the most traditionally feminine of all studied. First-born girls of larger families had the greatest ambivalence about femininity, probably due in part to the many caregiving responsibilities often thrust upon them.

THE SOCIAL CONTEXT

Sex-role socialization is not confined to the home and, in fact, family members' attitudes are influenced by the views prevalent in the larger social system of which the family is a part. Role pressures outside the home are likely to contribute ambiguity and negative evaluations to the perceptions of the attributes expected of females.

Role Valuation. In our society there is a clear strong preference for males and the masculine role. Both children and adults, female and male, tend to express a favorable bias for activities, objects, and traits consistent with the masculine role (Wylie, 1968; McCandless, 1967, 1970; Mussen, 1969). For example, there are more traits considered socially desirable (by both women and men) in the masculine than the feminine role (Rosenkrantz et al., 1968; McKee & Sherriffs, 1957). However, the social desirability ratings of the *valued* characteristics in the feminine role are the same as for those in the masculine role—the problem is that there are just fewer valued traits attributed to women than to men! This may indicate a deficiency of our language and related thought patterns for recognizing and articulating the desirable features of what has been considered "feminine."

Language. Societal devaluation of women is often expressed in mass media, and in fact, in the *content* of the language itself (Chapter 16). The English language has been said to be a masculine one in which women are implied as inferior creatures (e.g., Strainchamps, 1972; Thorne & Henley, 1975). Words associated with males more often have positive connotations, while words associated with females have negative connotations "conveying weakness, inferiority, immaturity, a sense of the trivial" (Thorne & Henley, 1975,

p. 20). A man is shrewd, a woman is a shrew; *shrew* had positive connotations until it came to be applied to women. The generic *he* and *men* to denote the universal and the general, suggest the greater importance of males than of females.

Undervaluation of women compared with men is shown also in the *use* of language in social interaction and in nonverbal language (Thorne & Henley, 1975). First names, rather than titles and last names, are more often used for women than for men of equal status, in situations such as work settings and television talk shows. In mixed conversation, men tend to talk more than women and to interrupt women. A male is more likely to use touch to signal dominance over a woman and to stare at a woman than vice versa. If a woman stares at a man, or touches him, he is likely to intensify his dominance gestures and interpret her gestures as a sexual advance to him, or consider her a lesbian. Touching and staring are related to aggression, dominance, and sexuality in other species as well.

Mass Media. High amounts of television watching are clearly associated with stronger traditional sex-role development, as early as kindergarten years (Frueh & McGhee, 1975; Miller, 1976). This is no surprise in view of typical television content. Portrayal of women in television is unrepresentative at best and often derogatory (Sternglanz & Serbin, 1974). Most women in television shows and commercials are presented in a sexual context, in romantic or family roles. In 10 of the commercial programs most popular with children during the 1971–1972 television season, there were more than twice as many male as female roles, with striking differences in the behavior of the female and male characters. Men were more active, aggressive, and constructive, and were more likely to be rewarded for their actions than the women. Females were more deferent (admiring, complimenting, following directions), and their behavior generally had no particular consequence. What they did made no difference, except that they were punished if they were not sedate. The programs depicted a world in which

it is inappropriate for males to accept another's suggestion or to express admiration for others. It is a world in which it is inappropriate for females to make plans and carry them out, and to receive rewards for that.

Similarly, in prime time network television, the adult male, aged 30 to 54, is the dominant figure in terms of frequency and of competency, prestige, and social acclaim (Miller & Reeves, 1975). To date, adult programs that attempt to break stereotypes still perpetuate them; for example, the woman police officer often is accompanied by and even rescued by her male colleagues. This is unfortunate, as the children who saw special films in an experimental situation of women in nonstereotypic occupations were more likely than other children to see those occupations as appropriate for women (Atkin & Miller, 1975).

Contemporary advertising also bombards people with childish and demeaning images of women (e.g., Komisar, 1972). Commercials depict women as caring little about anything besides shiny kitchen floors and being disappointed mainly about gray washes; they are usually too dumb to cope with everyday chores without instruction, usually by a child or a man, or a supernatural male. Recently, the advertising industry's self-regulatory organization challenged advertisers to put themselves in the place of the people depicted and ask, "How would I like to be depicted this way?" Hopefully, the depictions of women will change.

Schools. The lives of children are clearly affected by their school experiences in pervasive and often profound ways (Minuchin et al., 1969). Schools differ in the content and extent of their teaching of sex-typed behavior, just as parents differ. The effect of schools depends on conditions at home as well, with the greater impact on children when school and home experiences are congruent and mutually supporting. Children, especially girls, who were from liberal homes and attending liberal schools, showed the most individualized development of all studied. When the home and school orientations are not consistent with each other, the home seems the dominant force for sex-role orientation among girls, while schools are the stronger force in other areas, such as intellectual functioning.

Home orientations and school orientations probably have been relatively consistent with each other in the past, fostering sex-typing rather than individualized development. Many activities have been sex-typed, including different activities at recess time and in physical education courses, as well as the segregation of home economics courses for girls and shop courses for boys. Increasingly, people are challenging and correcting this kind of limitation of opportunities offered to children. Similarly, many are challenging sexism in textbooks, but sexism is continually documentable.

The books used in schools, at all levels, including graduate courses in psychology, help instill the view that females are not as important as men (Child, Potter, & Levine, 1946; U'Ren, 1972; National Organization for Women, 1972; APA, 1974). As with television shows, females are not as frequent as males or portrayed as positively as males. Less than 20 percent of story space in children's books is about females. The few girls and women that are portrayed are presented as sociable, kind but timid, inactive, unambitious, uncreative, helpless, and lazy. The legend under a picture of a woman scientist begins, "The project the young woman is working on is not her own idea." Madame Curie is depicted in one text as only a helpmate for her husband. The fact is that her husband had abandoned his own research to aid her in her investigations, for which they received a Nobel Prize. After his death, Madame Curie received another Nobel Prize—the only woman who has twice received the Nobel Prize for scientific achievements. Although most portrayals in mass media of famous women are probably not so erroneous, the treatments of "women in general" are probably just as unfactual and demeaning as for Madame Curie. Many people simply do not realize the extent to which the message conveyed to young children and others is that men are more valuable than women.

PERSONAL IMPACT OF SOCIALIZATION PRESSURES

Children and adults typically have been exposed, in varying degrees, to pervasive pressures for role adherence and to the specific message that women are not as important as men. What is the effect on the individual's self-concept and personal development? Briefly, people have generally accepted roles for themselves and others, but with resistance, and females generally are less rigidly sex-typed than males.

ROLE EFFECTS

Children. Young girls are as knowledgeable about role content as are boys and have as firm a sense of sexual identity at the deeper levels of personality, but there are sex differences in the degree to which girls and boys express their sexual identity in role-consistent behaviors (e.g., Lynn, 1959; Minuchin et al., 1969; Mussen, 1969; Nadelman, 1974). The sexual identity of girls is not as exclusively a sex-*role* identity as for boys. Girls do not show consistent role adoption as early in life as boys do, and boys express a stronger commitment to their sex roles than do girls. For example, most nine-year-old children thought that their own sex had "the most fun and the best life," and that, all in all, it was better to be of their own sex than the other one. However, the allegiance of boys was stronger and more assertive than that of the girls, and the only children who responded with the other sex than their own were girls (Minuchin et al., 1969). Between ages 3 and 10 years, it is unusual to find many boys who prefer the activities or roles ascribed to females. In relative contrast, between ages 3 and 6 years, some girls make predominantly feminine or predominantly masculine choices, while others choose equally among alternatives (e.g., for toys, activities) that are role stereotyped. Between ages 6 and 9 years, the time of "tomboyishness," girls are relatively homogeneous in showing many preferences considered masculine.

Role Resistance? Thus, girls are said to show more role resistance than boys. This is sometimes called a masculine protest, and some people attribute it to penis envy. However, what does the phenomenon called "role resistance" really mean? Curiously, boys are more likely to play with role-inconsistent toys than are girls when an adult authority figure is absent, compared with when the adult is present (Hartup, Moore, & Sager, 1963). And some evidence indicates that two-year-old boys spent more free-play time than girls in other-sex activities (Etaugh, Collins, & Gerson, 1975). Young boys may have a stronger role resistance than realized! Both girls and boys are probably just trying to be themselves and enjoy life. If they are rebelling, as some writers claim for girls, and as connoted by the term "resistance," it is in an attempt to *express* rather than to *deny* their "inner nature."

Several factors seem involved with the reduced resistance of boys. First, boys are typically subjected to clearer and more strongly enforced sex-typing pressures than girls are, even within their first two years of life. This may be associated, as cause or effect, with the greater societal valuation of males relative to females. Girls, then, compared to boys, have more freedom and can be relatively more open in their expression of the role-inconsistent behavior they desire. Second, traits and activities considered masculine are desirable not because they are so labeled, but because they are more suitable and even necessary for personal expressiveness and competence striving in exploring the world and one's place in it, as discussed later. They are also essential in exercising and developing motor skills specifically, such as by running, climbing trees, building tree houses, throwing things—all activities that may help develop spatial abilities as well (Chapter 6). Tomboyishness in middle childhood may be indicative of the difficulty of calming the exuberance of this age especially (Chapter 4). As discussed later, "masculine" activities are necessary for the adult woman as well. Obviously, girls do experience intensified role pressures from puberty on, though still without the consistency of intense role pressures often characterizing male socialization in this culture (Chapter 9).

SELF-CONCEPT

Role Consistency in Self-Descriptions. From the sixth to twelfth grades, both girls' and boys' self descriptions show increasing consistency with sex roles (Carlson, 1965). Girls show an increasing social orientation (e.g., "My friends spend a lot of time at my house") and boys show an increasing personal orientation (e.g., "I'd rather figure things out for myself before asking for help."). Adolescent girls clearly are strongly people-oriented while boys are more concerned about personal achievement and competence (Rosenberg & Simmons, 1975). Similarly, college students describe themselves as closer to their sex role than to the role of the other sex. Self-images of women are largely interpersonal while those of men are largely impersonal and individualistic (Carlson, 1971b). Ideals for others and for self (akin to role preference) also show role influences. For example, women university students in several countries gave higher ratings than did men to communal traits for their ideal self ("The kind of person I would most like to be"), while men wanted more agentic traits than did women (Table 8-1; Block, 1973).

Role Flexibility. However, both women and men have role resistance in wanting for themselves and others some traits considered inconsistent with sex roles. For example, women want to be more vital, active, courageous, dynamic, independent, self-controlled; men want to be gentle, kind, warm, sympathetic (McKee & Sherriffs, 1959). The greater flexibility of women in wanting more role-inconsistent traits for themselves than do men is understandable in view of the greater number of desirable qualities in the masculine role and the relevance of many of these traits for personal effectiveness and expressiveness, as just noted for children as well. But women are also more flexible than men in describing the *other* sex; they want the ideal man to have most of the favorable characteristics of *both* sex roles equally. Men are more limited and inconsistent in what they see in the "ideal" woman.

TABLE 8-1.

Sex Differences in Adjective Ideal Self-Descriptions among Students in Six Countries, "The Kind of Person I Would Most Like to Be" *

Items on Which Females Are Significantly Higher

Orientation	Adjective	U.S.	England	Sweden	Denmark	Finland	Norway
Communion	Loving, affectionate	√	√		√	√	√
	Impulsive	√	√	√		√	√
Communion	Sympathetic	√	√			√	√
Communion	Generous	√		√	√		√
Agency	Vital, active	√		√			√
	Perceptive, aware	√		√			√
Communion	Sensitive	√	√				
	Reserved, shy	√	√				
Communion	Artistic	√				√	
	Curious			√			√
	Uncertain, indecisive		√			√	
	Talkative					√	√
Communion	Helpful		√				
	Sense of humor		√				
	Idealistic				√		
	Cheerful						√
Communion	Considerate						√

Items on Which Males Are Significantly Higher

Orientation	Adjective	U.S.	England	Sweden	Denmark	Finland	Norway
Agency	Practical, shrewd	√	√	√	√	√	√
Agency	Assertive	√	√		√	√	√
Agency	Dominating	√	√	√		√	√
Agency	Competitive	√	√	√			√
Agency	Critical	√	√			√	√
	Self-controlled	√	√			√	√
Agency	Rational, reasonable	√				√	
Agency	Ambitious	√		√			
	Feels guilty				√		√
	Moody		√				
Agency	Self-centered		√				
	Sense of humor				√		
	Responsible					√	
	Fair, just					√	
Agency	Independent						√
Agency	Adventurous						√

The agency-communion classification was judged on the basis of Bakan's descriptions. Items without a classification listed were considered by judges as not clearly fitting either orientation.

√ = The sexes were different, within a given country, at statistically significant levels of .10 or lower.

* Source. Block, J. H., 1973, Tables 3 and 4, pp. 518 and 519. Copyright by the American Psychological Association and reproduced by permission.

Men of varying ages and occupational status depicted the ideal woman as active outside the family, having responsibility, using her talents, being creative and fulfilling herself (Steinmann & Fox, 1966). However, they also believed a woman should put herself in the background and make concessions to her husband's wishes—she should be herself, but not really.

Self-Esteem. Because of role content, women endorse more unfavorable adjectives in describing themselves than do men, and have low esteem on indices relevant to conventional modes of achievement, such as self-confidence about ability (Chapter 11). More generally, women tend to admit more freely than men to attributes considered negative in our society and, for example, are more self-effacing and self-deprecatory than men (Chapter 9). They also accept negative information about themselves, while resisting positive information; the reverse is true of men (Eagly & Whitehead, 1972). The general picture is that women tend to approach the negative about themselves and to avoid the positive, but men do the reverse. Thus, some psychologists conclude that women have little esteem or respect for themselves and are essentially unhealthy. For some women, this is relatively true, as documented in the following chapter.

For many other women, the conclusion is a simplistic over-generalization that does not give them the credit they deserve, especially when they have acted in the face of adversity. People can have an internally sustaining sense of worth and general competence in spite of felt deficiencies and in spite of negative input from others. Many of these people are women. Obviously, maintaining high self-esteem in these circumstances is difficult. Generally, people are likely to have low levels of regard for themselves when a felt deficiency concerns a characteristic central in one's self view or when the characteristic is relevant to important others in the environment who can reward or censure in ways meaningful to the person. Much variation in esteem is likely due to the exact content of one's self-concept and ideals with respect to the attributes rewarded, cen-

sured, or ignored in the environment. Certainly there is variation between stages of life.

Through High School. Between approximately ages 9 and 13 years, girls are likely to have *more favorable* views of themselves than do boys, except for attributes related to conventional achievement. Furthermore, girls' esteem has been shown to increase from the fourth to the eighth grade while that of boys decreased (Soares & Soares, 1969). During these years, girls' performance skills (Chapter 6) and impulse control are likely to be rewarded in the school environment. During the adolescent years, with increased pressure for adherence to conventional sex roles, the content of self-concept of girls and boys has become quite different but the favorability of self-view is now equal (Carlson, 1965).

The dominant areas in which girls and boys have high esteem differ according to roles. That is, girls had more positive views than did boys about themselves with respect to congeniality and sociability (grades 6 through 12); boys were higher than girls in self-views about achievement and leadership, though girls as well as boys had increasingly positive views of themselves in this respect (Monge, 1973). Adolescents who feel successful in the realm they consider appropriate will have support for a favorable self-view. Of course, not all people are comfortable trying to be what others expect. Whereas this is particularly an issue for academically oriented young women (Chapter 11), both girls and boys seem to have some difficulties in this age period in our culture. Both girls and boys had declining esteem levels through adolescence about their general adjustment (e.g., in the extent to which they saw themselves as relaxed, satisfied, stable; Monge, 1973).

College and Beyond. Past high school, no generalization seems clearly justified beyond the limited ones that women as a group do not have higher esteem than men as a group, and conventional environments are not as conducive to women's as to men's personal development. When sex differences are found in self-esteem measures or inferred from related indices, women in college or later years are more likely to score lower than men than vice versa. Similarly, *within* each sex, traditional masculinity is more strongly related to self-esteem than is femininity (Spence, Helmreich, & Stapp, 1975; Wetter, 1975).

Within the typical college environment, the goals and environmental supports are generally consistent with role expectations for men; college success can buttress their esteem on role-related dimensions of the self-concept. However, there is ambiguity and conflict for the woman in college or in professions (Chapter 11; Chapter 15). The publicly stated standards are inconsistent with role expectations and she is not given the consistent encouragement to meet the standards, from either parents, instructors, or professional colleagues. This set of circumstances may contribute to the greater positive changes in concerns about self shown by men than women during college years, although women seem more mature when they enter college (Constantinople, 1969).

However, for some women, academic success is not particularly central in their self-concept so that lack of environmental support or the presence or absence of success does not particularly affect their esteem. Others, for whom academic and future professional potential are important easily can be tempted to *try* to change their self-views to maintain esteem in face of lack of support or of censure. With recent expansion of women's concerns and awareness, more young women seem to be finding support for developing and maintaining their own definitions of themselves, whatever the general environmental pressures.

The same principles about self-esteem seem to apply beyond the college years. Though she may know that she is considered "just a housewife," a woman can have high esteem *if* her environment allows behavioral expression that is relevant to her self-view, and *if* she is rewarded by people important to her in ways she considers meaningful. Unfortunately, difficulties easily occur, especially when conditions of worth prevented a really free choice and when her family takes her for granted and does not give her the rewards she wants and deserves for a job well done. Some detrimental effects of a "housewife" style are dis-

cussed in the next chapter; the beneficial effects of choosing nontraditional life-styles are discussed in several other chapters (Chapters 9, 11, 13, and 15). In general, it seems that environments that encourage and reward androgynous development, whether inside or outside the home, are more conducive to the development of a truly healthy self than those that encourage rather rigid sex-typing and the limitations on personal development associated with it.

A CASE FOR ANDROGYNY

The strongly sex-typed adult, woman or man, is at a disadvantage, but women are at more of a disadvantage than are men. Both females and males potentially can develop and express both agency and communion orientations. Sex roles, however, inhibit the agency of women and the communion of men (Chapter 2). Thus, sex-role based socialization restricts personal development of members of each sex, by encouraging a one-sided development in two-sided human beings. However, the agentic qualities, assigned to the masculine role, are emphasized and valued more in our society than the communal ones, assigned to the feminine role. The androgynous development of both communion and agency in both women and men is desirable. Two broad lines of evidence are consistent with this claim, those showing deficiencies of one-sided development in females and the desirable concomitants of androgyny.

DEFICIENCIES OF THE FEMININE ROLE

Adjustment in Girls. The trend of a variety of evidence about within-sex variation suggests that role adherence is not as advantageous for girls as for boys. For example, through adolescence sex-typing is associated with healthy development in males, but that result does not occur as consistently and often is reversed for girls. Strongly sex-typed behavior may be detrimental to a girl's development, as shown by varying adjustment indices including high anxiety, low self-esteem, low acceptance by peers, and low ratings on other kinds of **sociometric** measures (Gall, 1969; Sears,

1970; Gray, 1957; Johnson, 1963; Webb, 1963; Cosentino & Heilbrun, 1964; Helper, 1955).

Among college students, the healthier women saw themselves as very similar to their mothers *if* their mothers were low in traditional femininity, whereas the least well adjusted were very similar to their mothers if the mothers were high in traditional femininity (Heilbrun & Fromme, 1965). The reverse trend occurred for the men: the healthier sons had greater similarity with their fathers if the fathers were highly masculine than if the fathers were low in traditional masculinity. (However, some evidence indicates high masculinity in men during adulthood is associated with high anxiety, high neuroticism, and low self-acceptance; Harford, Willis & Deabler, 1967; Mussen, 1962.) Also, women who manage best in college have desirable traits from the masculine and feminine roles (Heilbrun, 1968). And, as discussed in the following chapter, it is the women who are most traditionally feminine that are most susceptible to physical and psychological problems.

Competence Motivation. Persons of both sexes have a motivation to be and feel competent in having effects upon the social and inanimate environment (White, 1960). The immediate satisfaction of behavior associated with what is generally called **competence motivation** (or, technically, **effectance motivation**) is a feeling of efficacy; the long-range significance is for the growth of competence and felt *sense of competence.* Curiosity, activity, manipulation of objects, and exploration are clear aspects of competence, though competence motivation can operate in connection with other needs as well. The problem is that the traits most directly related to competence are considered masculine. Although there has been improvement, toys that enable an active interaction with the world have been considered "boys' toys." Creative building blocks and telescopes are advertised for boys, "Because boys were born to build and learn . . . Because boys are curious," according to one advertisement. Thus, it is little wonder that young girls show "role resistance" by liking "masculine" toys and activities!

Attributes relevant to competence and labeled masculine are also necessary for the adult woman in traditional roles. To take care of children, manage a home (which is much like running a small business), and then be an interesting companion for her spouse requires abundant energy, intelligence, activity, rapid and effective decision making, independence, and, as any mother will agree, a few self-survival skills. In short, the successful completion of traditionally feminine tasks requires a sizable share of traditional masculinity. Thus, there is a paradox or conflict in conventional role expectations for women: The "fallacy of femininity" is that a woman cannot do what is expected of her if she is *only* what she is expected to be. She needs to be androgynous to do well even in traditional "feminine" activities.

TENDENCIES TO ANDROGYNY

Frequency. Many people are not strongly sextyped, although group averages show females as scoring generally feminine and males as masculine on trait inventories. The lack of pervasive strong sex-typing is being increasingly shown and investigated, as researchers have developed measuring instruments with separate femininity and masculinity scales and have looked at varying combinations of the two scores. In the past, one score on a single bipolar measure of M–F was assumed useful (Chapter 1). The femininity and masculinity scales of one recent instrument, developed by Sandra Bem (1974, 1975), are equated for the social desirability of the items and also include a separate measure of social desirability with items not related to sex roles (Table 8-2). With this inventory, as others, about as many college students score as *not* strongly sex-typed as do show strong sex-typing in their self-descriptions. Are college students typical of the population at large? Higher education does seem associated with reduced sex-typing (e.g., Gough, 1968). If they are not typical, do they indicate a change that is to come in adults generally?

Values of Androgyny. Androgyny is immensely practical. Androgynous persons can modify their

TABLE 8-2.
Items on Bem's Sex Role Inventory Scale *

Feminine Items	Masculine Items	Neutral Items
Affectionate	Acts as a leader	Adaptable
Cheerful	Aggressive	Conceited
Childlike	Ambitious	Conscientious
Compassionate	Analytical	Conventional
Does not use harsh language	Assertive	Friendly
Eager to soothe hurt feelings	Athletic	Happy
Feminine	Competitive	Helpful
Flatterable	Defends own beliefs	Inefficient
Gentle	Dominant	Jealous
Gullible	Forceful	Likable
Loves children	Has leadership abilities	Moody
Loyal	Independent	Reliable
Sensitive to the needs of others	Individualistic	Secretive
Shy	Makes decisions easily	Sincere
Soft spoken	Masculine	Solemn
Sympathetic	Self-reliant	Tactful
Tender	Self-sufficient	Theatrical
Understanding	Strong personality	Truthful
Warm	Willing to take a stand	Unpredictable
Yielding	Willing to take risks	Unsystematic

* Source. Bem, *Journal of Consulting and Clinical Psychology,* 1974, Table 1, p. 156 in original. Copyright by the American Psychological Association and reproduced by permission.

behavior to be effective in a particular situation, without worrying about whether or not their feelings and behavior are consistent with sex roles or with their own role-related conditions of worth. More important, androgyny is associated with personal satisfaction and a more complete and spontaneous personal expression of basic human potentials than is sex-typing. In this context, it is important to distinguish between two (of many!) definitions of androgyny. By one definition, androgyny means scoring relatively equally on femininity and masculinity scales. By the second, which seems preferable, androgyny is restricted to meaning relatively *high* scores on both femininity and masculinity scales.

Androgynous people, those *high* on both dimensions, are more psychologically healthy according to a variety of indices (Spence, Helmrich, & Stapp, 1975; Berzins, 1975). For example, androgynous college subjects of each sex scored highest of all groups in self-esteem; subjects

equally low in both kinds of characteristics were the lowest of all in self-esteem. The pattern is consistent with a basic claim made repeatedly in this book: The normal human being has potentials societally labeled as feminine as well as those labeled masculine, and personal maturity involves the development and free expression of both kinds of potentials. Some people may be relatively androgynous because they have not been subjected to strong sex-typed pressures. Others may overcome or transcend sex-typing (Hefner, Rebecca, & Oleshansky, 1975).

Maturity Indices. Whether because of practicality or because of growth to fuller personal expressiveness, many people move toward androgyny after conventional sex-typed socialization and the intense role pressure of adolescence. By the criterion of maturity with increasing years, androgyny is "natural." From the middle twenties on, males score increasingly feminine on traditional M–F scales (Chapter 1). Middle-aged people admit to and display traits usually considered appropriate only for the other sex. Women become more self-confident and venturesome; men become more tender and concerned with the feelings of others (Neugarten & Gutmann, 1968).

In younger years even, androgyny is associated with varying indices of maturity. To the extent that lack of extreme sex-typing can imply androgyny, evidence on the problems of very feminine girls is evidence about the value of androgyny. Measures of cognitive development are also relevant. Boys and girls who are strongly sex-typed have been found lower in general intelligence, with greater intellectual development occurring in association with greater than usual masculinity in girls and femininity in boys (Maccoby, 1966). High school and college students at higher levels of cognitive maturity (measured by judgmental maturity, apart from intelligence) used both communal and agentic traits in describing themselves (Haan, Smith, & Block, 1974). They used as many role-consistent traits as did students of lesser maturity, but also more role inconsistent ones. The more mature women used more agentic adjectives (e.g., effective, restless, impulsive, self-centered) and the more mature men used more communal adjectives (e.g., sympathetic, sensitive, responsive, idealistic) than the less mature students.

Evidence about creativity is even more ample. Creative persons, whether prominent in "creative" professions or college students high on creativity tests, have characteristics typically expected of each sex (Donelson, 1973; Dellas & Gaier, 1970). For example, creative women are more open to outer experience and men to inner experience than is typical. The sensitivity and intuition considered feminine are blended with the determination, assertiveness, and confidence considered masculine. Creative women and men are open to their own inner complexity as human beings, just as they are open to the complexity of the world around them. People able to recognize and express both their potentials considered feminine and those considered masculine are more open and self-aware and do not need to defensively deny feelings and desires that are contrary to sex roles. They feel free to be what they are.

SUMMARY

Although androgyny has demonstrated values and some people are more androgynous than sex-typed, conventional socialization of the past has encouraged a sex-typing that inhibits full personal development. In this culture, communion is inhibited in men and agency in women. Pressures toward sex-typing occur at all levels of development and in many different ways, though with less pressure on girls than on boys. After the assignment of an infant as female or male, parents often interact with the child on the basis of sex, rewarding behaviors they consider appropriate and punishing those they consider inappropriate. They are also models of behavior and elicitors of behavior. At least by age five, children are knowledgeable about sex roles and come to imitate models of the same sex relative to the other sex, particularly when the modeled behavior is role consistent. They are also influenced by the outcomes they experience for modeling and by how the models feel about their own outcomes. Fathers play important roles in the development of traditional femininity in their daughters, perhaps because males are generally more concerned about sex-typing than are females, who fairly consistently show less allegiance to their sex role.

Sex-typing is less rigid and consistent in girls than in boys. Girls are not as strongly censured for role-inconsistent behavior as are boys, and many of the attributes considered masculine are relevant for the active and effective involvement with the world that is necessary for full personality development of girls as well as boys. Because of the intensified role pressures during adolescence, girls at that time show more marked sex-typing than in middle childhood, and college women see themselves as more feminine than masculine. However, both women and men want some role-inconsistent traits in themselves and in members of the other sex, with women being more flexible in this regard.

In spite of pervasive cultural undervaluation of the feminine relative to the masculine role and related attributes, females do not necessarily have lower esteem than males. During grade school years, girls have higher esteem than boys; esteem levels are equal during high school and variable afterwards. However, femininity is not strongly associated with healthy adjustment in girls. This may be because the feminine role is less valued in our society and less adaptive for personal expression of competence motivation than is the masculine role. One aspect of the problem that role standards pose for women is the inhibitions on the development of a firm sense of separateness from other people, discussed in the following chapter.

CHAPTER
9

SOCIAL RESPONSIVENESS
AND SENSE OF SEPARATENESS

People experience various degrees of **sex-typed socialization** encouraging one-sided personal development and inhibiting **androgyny,** as discussed in the previous chapter. In this chapter, we shall discuss the broad style of social responsiveness engendered by the typical socialization of girls and strengthened by women's traditional life-style. Women are encouraged toward a **communal** sense of being at-one-with other individuals; men are encouraged toward an **agentic** sense of separateness from others. We will consider the socialization patterns that encourage social responsiveness to the relative neglect of separateness in women. The definition of self through other people that likely results has various deleterious effects for women and for their families, as suggested by mental health data. The complete, androgynous, person is comfortable both with an agentic orientation of self-concern and with a communal orientation of concern with others. It is the separate self that can be most effectively socially responsive and related to other people in meaningful communion.

SOCIALIZATION FOR SOCIAL RESPONSIVENESS

THE IDENTIFICATION PROCESS

A communal sense of relatedness facilitates and is perpetuated by identification with others. **Identification** involves the set of processes through which an individual takes on characteristics or behavior patterns of a model on a long-term basis so that aspects of the model are incorporated into one's own personality (e.g., Ferguson, 1970). Thus, any social process through which one person becomes more like some other person or group of persons in characteristics such as appearance, behavior, attitudes, values, and feelings can promote identification and can be a manifestation of a previously established or ongoing identification. Identification is social responsiveness continuing throughout life. In many ways, infant **attachment** (Chapter 7) is an early developmental form of the more sophisticated attachment of identification that later develops. Identification is also a potential stumbling block to the achieve-

ment of personal identity and sense of self as separate from others if one is defined only by relationships with others, if one is capable only of being attached and never detached.

Learner Characteristics. The chief requirement for identification or social responsiveness generally is that a model be salient to the learning observer; attention is directed to the model. Most theories of identification (and of imitation specifically) consider only characteristics of the model, such as similarity and power (see Chapter 8; Donelson, 1973; McCandless, 1970). However, characteristics of the observer are relevant as well (Akamatsu & Thelen, 1974). For example, a model seen as neutral by one person may be viewed as nurturant or as restrictive by others.

The prime condition for the salience is that the learner feel dependent upon the specific model or upon people generally. Anxiety is a frequent concomitant of dependency. Because of positive feelings about the model (one on whom to depend) and the negative features (anxiety), the learner has contradictory or ambivalent feelings. Thus, ambivalent feelings about the model are often said to be a necessary condition for identification (e.g., Ferguson, 1970). Dependency and anxiety may be temporary and largely situationally induced (a state) or a prolonged and fairly stable characteristic (trait). The stronger the trait, the easier it is for the state to be elicited.

The underlying basic hypothesis of this chapter is that identification and an overly communal style is likely to become relatively habitual for women of traditional socialization. The content of the feminine role is other-oriented. In addition to *what* females are taught in role socialization, certain features of the general socialization process— *how* they are taught—encourage continuing identification and attachments to others.

SOCIALIZATION PROCESS FOR FEMALES

The concept of **defensive identification** (also called identification with the aggressor) tends to be distinctive in the psychology of women. This is paradoxical in view of a prevalent assumption that it is more typical of boys than of girls (Chapter 2). The conditions under which defensive identification seems most likely are ones of *severity* and *inconsistency* of treatment; *restriction on freedom* helps to keep the learner in such a situation. These conditions also are likely to increase anxiety and helplessness and to foster low self-esteem and other developmental problems in children. The restriction on freedom may be an actual physical one or one psychologically inherent in a continuing concern with other people. The contention is *not* that parents of little girls are harsh, cold, and punitive people, while those of little boys are warm, permissive, and nurturant people. However, conventional socialization processes—*how* children are taught whatever they are taught—more often meet the conditions of severity, inconsistency, and freedom restriction for girls than for boys and, thus, increase the relative likelihood of girls' strong identification patterns. This seems true in spite of stronger pressures on boys for behaviors that are specifically sex-role consistent (Chapter 8); children have many more learning experiences than those directly related to role behavior.

The effects of childhood identification experiences is present in adulthood not only in terms of the content of what was learned previously via identification, as frequently noted, but also in terms of adults' identification patterns. There is suggestive evidence that children who have had rather harsh and restrictive experiences identify especially with models who are generally negative and potentially punitive, even after they become adults. Furthermore they identify more intensely than do adults with less severe backgrounds (Balint, 1945; Hartup & Coates, 1967; Sarnoff, 1951; Baxter, Lerner, & Miller, 1965).

Severity *Role Content.* The role content for girls' behavior and parental treatment of the young girl demand more *impulse control* and more obedience to the rules of social *propriety* than for boys. The little girl must become more polite and restrained than her brother. When a boy causes trouble, parents often comment, with a shrug of the shoulders, "Oh well, boys will be boys," and

often chuckle with some relief that "He's a *real* boy!" And of course, boys are pressured in this direction. "Girls will be girls" is not so often heard. Have you ever heard a child referred to as "A *real* girl"? Little girls are expected to be "little ladies." They are expected to become quickly socialized, patient, polite adults in small bodies.

Accordingly, girls are reported to be more obedient, responsible, cooperative, and in general present fewer problems and are better socialized than boys at comparable ages (Sears, Maccoby, & Levin, 1957; Bronfenbrenner, 1961a, 1961b; Becker, 1964; National Center for Health Statistics, 1971). For example, the general picture for girls across four ethnic groups (white, black, Oriental, Chicano, all in the general area of Oakland, California) was one of verbal, quiet control, compared with vigorous, open expression of aggressive thoughts and feeling for boys (Tuddenham, Brooks, & Milkovich, 1974). Boys were more often characterized by their mothers in terms that might be classified as antisocial: they lie more, take things, break things, bully others, show off (but hide their feelings), and ward off affection. Girls are seen as more dependable and mature for their age, and as sharing their thoughts and feelings. Other sex differences occurring in all four ethnic groups are listed in Table 9-1; there were also numerous differences in one or more but not all four ethnic groups.

Severity in Parental Interactions. Although mothers seem to enjoy girls more than boys, some data suggest that mothers also tend to be more demanding and strict with their daughters than with their sons (Sears, Maccoby, & Levin, 1957; Hubert & Britton, 1957). Similarly, women college students were more punitive toward an attractive eight-year-old girl than an attractive boy; unattractive children were not differentially penalized on the basis of sex (Dion, 1974). Also, parents (mainly college students) of children under two years of age gave more praise to girls, but they also criticized girls more than boys; mothers gave both more praise and criticism than did fathers (Fagot, 1974).

Other evidence indicates cross-sex effects, with

TABLE 9-1 *
Items with Consistent Sex Differences in Four Ethnic Groups

Items More Characteristic of Boys than Girls

| | Percent Difference | |
| | "True" for More Boys than Girls | "Not true" for More Girls than Boys |
Item		
Likes to tease others	13.1	16.1
Hates to sit still, restless	11.3	13.5
Hungry all of the time	10.6	10.6
Likes vigorous exercise—athletics	11.8	7.9
Has temper explosions—hits, kicks, or throw things	9.1	11.3
Still wets the bed occasionally	9.0	9.2
Flares up over nothing—gets mad easily	8.6	11.3
Is a "daredevil"; wants to do things that are dangerous	8.5	10.2
Has to be the "winner"; hates to lose in any game	7.3	9.4
Messes up the house a lot	6.5	8.2
Hates to ask for help	6.0	6.6

Items More Characteristic of Girls than Boys

| | Percent Difference | |
| | "True" for More Girls than Boys | "Not true" for More Boys than Girls |
Item		
Fussy about clothes	17.5	16.3
Tries to keep things neat	13.5	13.8
Hates to get dirty	11.3	14.2
Likes quiet activities—reading or watching TV	10.1	10.6
Takes good care of smaller children	13.6	5.0
Doesn't mind losing in a game	8.3	10.3
Acts older than he/she is	10.4	7.0
Feelings get hurt easily	8.4	7.3
Gives in to other children	7.4	4.8
Dislikes being left home when parents go out	6.7	7.2

Note. Listed items show a consistent sex difference in all ethnic groups, a sex difference significant at the 0.01 level for ethnic groups combined, and an absolute difference of at least 5% in six or more of the eight possible subgroup comparisons, that is, four ethnic groups on "true" response and four ethnic groups on "not true" response.
* *Source.* Tuddenham, R. D., Brooks, J., & Milkovich, L., 1974, Table 3, p. 980. Copyright by the American Psychological Association and reproduced by permission.

parents being more permissive and nurturant toward a child of the other sex than of the same sex and, conversely, exerting more power over the child of the same sex (Stevenson, 1965; Rothbart & Maccoby, 1966; Emmerich, 1962). This may be part of a broad tendency for adults generally to have more favorable attitudes to children of the other sex. Although women college student subjects rated a child (on videotape) more favorably than did the men subjects, they were more favorable when the child was presented as a boy than when the same child was said to be a girl; men were more favorable to the "girl" than to the "boy" (Gurwitz & Dodge, 1975). Given that young children are likely to spend more time with adult women than with adult men, girls may end up experiencing less permissiveness, nurturance, favorable views, and more general control than do boys.

The greater socialization severity for girls has been described as due to more love-oriented discipline in treatment of girls than boys (Sears, Maccoby, & Levin, 1957; Bronfenbrenner, 1961a, 1961b). The girl, having been given more blatant affection, experiences a greater threat with the punishment of its apparent temporary withdrawal. The threat increases her eagerness to be obedient to ensure the approval felt to be endangered or lost. And, the more confused she feels by the combination of praise and criticism, the more she may be willing to do to avoid criticism and receive only praise.

Socialization Inconsistencies. Role strain is discomfort with a role. Part of the discomfort likely with the role assigned females is possibly due to severity of role content, as just discussed, as well as the low evaluation of females relative to males and of the traits associated with the feminine role. There are also many kinds of strains caused by various inconsistencies associated with role socialization and expectations for role behavior. For example, *role discontinuity* is prevalent because pressures on the girl to behave consistently with the role are not uniformly applied, and because behaviors called for by role prescriptions may not be compatible with each other,

such as passivity and taking care of others. Girls are allowed more behavior expected of the other sex from infancy through middle childhood than are boys (Chapter 8). During adolescence, pressure for role-consistent behavior increases for both girls and boys. However, for boys, it is continuous with their previous experiences, which have helped to make quite clear what others expect. Role strain on the growing young woman easily continues past high school years, as discussed in the remainder of this and in other chapters (Chapters 11 and 15).

Restriction on Freedom. The final major condition facilitating strong habits of identification in females is restriction on freedom. There is restriction of impulse expression, as already discussed. There is also a relative physical "confinement" and accompanying psychological ties or attachment bonds with other people. The life of the girl and the woman is conventionally expected to be more family centered, with fewer activities outside the home than is true for boys and men. Females are expected to live mainly in an interpersonal environment in which relatedness is fostered; in turn, they have stronger emotional relationships with their families. During adolescence, parents encourage girls to cling more tightly to family apron strings than they do boys; girls take part-time jobs less, go out less, spend fewer nights away from home with friends (Douvan & Gold, 1964). Some parental characteristics and rearing patterns tend to be more closely associated with characteristics in daughters than in sons. For example, conflict between the parents' reactions to their college student children was related to low self-acceptance among the women, as expected, but not among the men (Wyer, 1965).

Within traditional life-styles, women do have restrictions on freedom of movement posed by children and the challenges of running a household. In fact, it is home maintenance, not marriage per se nor maternity that keeps women home. It has been estimated that the average wife and mother spends more than 60 hours a week in household chores, which is about four times as many hours as are spent in interaction with children; her husband receives only about seven hours (9 percent) of her week (Rossi, 1971). Curiously, hours spent in household chores do *not* decrease with an increase in household convenience appliances, perhaps because of an increase in household standards (Szalai, 1973). Thus, by the criterion of hours, the affiliative concerns for which years of socialization have prepared the conventional woman are not directed toward appropriate targets—people—but rather toward dusty tables, grey sheets, and messy rooms—another source of role strain.

SOME EFFECTS OF SOCIALIZATION

Control without Autonomy. Thus, conventional socialization practices for girls compared with boys require greater dampening of behavior, a more restrictive range of intensity and content of behavioral expressions, and a greater control of impulse for the sake of politeness and responsivity to the needs of others. These all restrain the freedom of self-exploration and thwart competence strivings, and development of a sense of independence. Lesser permissiveness, together with the psychological impact of love-oriented discipline and restrictions of freedom of movement help assure that the girl will attempt to meet parental expectations.

The general socialization techniques are effective in controlling children's behavior toward presumably desirable ends, such as obedience, cooperation, and responsibility. They also foster positive aspects of the communion modality of the feminine role. Care of others, understanding, empathy, and love, are all specific facets of the social responsiveness concomitant with strong identification patterns.

However, there are also disadvantages to the general socialization pattern. Love-oriented techniques, such as those applied to girls, tend to increase timidity, sensitivity to rejection, anxiety, and dependency. They involve a strong risk of "oversocialization," which involves an inhibition of the capacity for independence and asser-

tiveness (Bronfenbrenner, 1961a, 1961b). These results are still apparent in adulthood. A study of 30- to 40-year-old women showed that socialization for women, regardless of their level of traditional femininity, is associated with control of impulse and expression and the renunciation of achievement and autonomy. Socialization for women fosters submissive, nurturant aspects of the feminine role without moving them toward desirable qualities considered masculine, such as assertiveness, achievement orientation, and independence (Block, von der Lippe, & Block, 1973). Characteristics that are essential for individuation and self-expression tend to be relinquished in female socialization because these qualities have been defined as masculine.

Certainly sex is not the only factor relevant to the content or process of socialization (e.g., Yarrow, Waxler, & Scott, 1971). Socialization techniques contribute to individual differences *within* the same sex. For example, there are ethnic group variations, and birth order differences. First-born and only children, as groups, differ from later borns in the same ways that girls differ from boys, as groups, in such respects. If other variables besides sex did not contribute importantly to the picture of a child's development, sex differences would be more marked and pervasive than they are. Obviously, sex differences need not be as extreme and pervasive as they have been.

The general outcomes of the socialization practices more typical of girls than boys favor continuing identification. There is a built-in feedback cycle: consequences of identification help to maintain the conditions that promote continuing identification.

Importance of Others. A variety of evidence indicates that other people do seem to be more salient and important as *persons* to females than to males. Infant girls are more interested in people, and less fearful of strangers than are infant boys (Chapter 7). Consideration for others has been found a stronger value for females than for males, both for children (fifth and seventh graders) and adults (parents of the children; Hoffman,

1975). Also, young girls are more cooperative and nurturant than boys, especially with younger children (Hutt, 1972). From age 12 through the high school years, girls cared more than boys about being well liked and worried about what other people thought of them; there were no sex differences among children 8 to 11 years old (Rosenberg & Simmons, 1975). Adolescent girls particularly were also more likely to report inhibiting expression of negative feelings, such as unhappiness or hostility, in the interests of promoting interpersonal harmony. Adult women favor needed welfare more than do men (Steininger & Lesser, 1974), and are more resistant to pressure to harm others (Kilham & Mann, 1974).

Social Cues. Concomitant with the apparently greater importance they attach to others, females seem to be more perceptually sensitive to social cues about other people. There is evidence that women are more sensitive to faces and names, remember them better, and use feedback from the human environment more than men. For example, eye contact is an early and continuing channel of communication; women look more at another person than do men, whether they are speaking, being spoken to, or during mutual conversation (Nevill, 1974; Russo, 1975). Also, some evidence shows that girls and women tend to stand closer together and face each other more directly than do boys and men (Maccoby & Jacklin, 1974). Similarly, women verbally reveal themselves in conversation more than do men. (See discussion of **self-disclosure** in Chapter 10.) Females are also more facially expressive than men and their feelings are more accurately detected from their facial expressions (Buck, Miller, & Caul, 1974), a difference present by ages 4 to 6 (Buck, 1975). Females at all ages from third grade into adulthood appear more accurate in interpreting the emotional meaning of nonverbal social cues, such as facial expressions and body movements (Rosenthal et al., 1974; Zuckerman, 1975). However, men in mental health and art professions are particularly adept in using nonverbal social cues, and we might expect them also to be more socially sensitive and socially responsive

generally than other men—there is always **within-sex** as well as **between-sex variation.**

Conformity? Because of their greater sensitivity to social cues, desire for cooperation, and responsiveness to the desires and feelings of others, women are often said to be dependent, passive, persuasible, and conforming. This reflects a tendency for the unnecessary use of societally negative words when positive ones would do as well or better. It is just as accurate to say that women are better attuned to the social world and have a stronger and more freely open spirit of responsiveness to people other than themselves. Also, the contention that women conform more than men to the views of others in the sense of changing their own attitudes and opinions willy-nilly, is misleading. Actually, through high school at least, boys are more likely than girls to conform to the values and attitudes of their peer groups (Maccoby & Jacklin, 1974). When sex differences in conformity or persuasibility are found among college students, they are likely to be in the direction of greater conformity in women than in men (McGuire, 1969). However, this is partially due to the kinds of research situations in which conformity is typically studied. For example, women conform *less* than men when the issue involved is relevant to the women's own interests and felt competence (Sistrunk & McDavid, 1971). Also, reinforcement for conformity increases conformity. Women with conventional sex-role socialization had had a lifetime of reinforcement for stating agreement with the views of men, as well as for trying to please them.

Seeking Others. The popular assumption that females are more **affiliative** than males is both correct and incorrect (see Oetzl, 1966; Maccoby & Jacklin, 1974). They are more affiliative in the sense of being more sensitive to people and caring about their reactions, but not necessarily in the sense of continually seeking other people out. During childhood, girls and boys are equally sociable. However, women can more easily than men admit to and act upon needs to be with other people. What is more remarkable and regrettable than females' openness of association is males' inhibition. For example, women are likely to approach others when they are fearful. Equally fearful men are inhibited in admitting to their fear and seeking others for comfort (Schachter, 1959; Zucker, Manosevitz, & Lanyon, 1968; Hoyt & Raven, 1973). One example is that first-born men who were alone during the 1971 Los Angeles earthquake reported *less anxiety* than later-born men, *but* they spoke to more people immediately after the quake and offered more help to other people than did the later-born men. In contrast, women admitted anxiety and sought out other people. Apparently, the men were defending against anxiety and felt that they had to "explain" a desire to be with others in ways other than their own fear and affiliative desires.

Punitive Others. Although firm data are lacking, it appears that women are more likely than men to continue attachment to people who are nonrewarding or even punitive. At least, there is evidence that girls are more likely than boys to report that they like the people with whom they interact, even when the other person has not behaved in a rewarding way to them (Maccoby & Jacklin, 1974). Girls (ages 8 through high school) are also more likely than boys to report "acting nice" to people they do not like, and to be more upset, hurt, and disturbed by negative behaviors from others (Rosenberg & Simmons, 1975).

Ethological evidence about other species indicates that attachment to punitive others increases with the punishment (e.g., Kovach & Hess, 1963; Harlow, 1962). It is as if the punishment makes contact and approval more necessary. Thus, the woman typically socialized toward social responsiveness and self-definition through others may increase her efforts to please her family if they do not provide the rewards she desires from them. The family members are continually salient in her psychological environment, just as parents are continually salient in the life of a young child. Thus, some unfortunate women may get caught in a vicious circle: the less reward they get from their family members, to whom they are attached, the harder they try to please and the more the nonreward is experienced as punitive;

and attachment and efforts to please increase. However, unlike the young child, adult women do have more developed capabilities to correct such situations, if they choose. Even when loved ones are not punitive, attachment to family members may be overly intense, for the good of the woman or the others involved, as discussed next.

FULLFILLMENT OR ADJUSTMENT?

Is the strong identification pattern encouraged in women through sex-role content and socialization processes necessarily damaging? Or does it provide a necessary fabric of a woman's personal maturity and fulfillment? The role strains and life-style pressures of traditional women perpetuate the problems of identification and self-definition fostered by the socialization of earlier years and take their toll.

EFFECTS OF LIFE-STYLE CONDITIONS

Self-Alienation. To be maximally adaptive to the desires of others is to be maximally vulnerable to self-alienation. Self-alienation is the noxious feeling that occurs when overt actions are detached from or inconsistent with the concept of self or the ideal self (Gergen, 1971). By probability alone, the more people we respond to and try to please, the greater the likelihood of encountering expectations of others that are inconsistent or irrelevant to our own needs and desires, and the less time we have for self-development and self-expression. The traditional experiences of women encourage self-definition through others and self-alienation.

Societal expectations that women are to define themselves through other people can be seen in the common practice of Miss Me becoming Mrs. Someone-Else, while a man retains his own name after marriage. Although it may seem relatively inconsequential and trivial to many, this practice reflects the deeper problem of pressures toward definition of a woman through other people. It is not without reason that women have recently claimed the rights to use the title Ms. and to use their own names throughout their lives. Our language has helped suggest that women are nonpersons, or persons only through others—Ms. means Myself.

Children can extend the problem. In fact, childfree couples describe their lives in more positive terms than those with young children, and the women have less stress than comparable women with children (Institute for Social Research, 1974; Campbell, 1975). A breast-feeding mother commented, "Sometimes I feel as if the top of me is the baby's and the bottom is my husband's and nothing is left for me at all" (Mary McCaulley, 1970, cited by Bardwick, 1971, p. 146). As children grow, pressures increase for the woman to be only the doer of good deeds for others. She is Susy's mother who can make costumes for the school play, Jimmy's mom who will chauffeur the team to practice, and Tom's wife who can arrange the office picnic. The mother concerned about nurturing her children and husband may not have the time to nurture herself or feel the freedom to request nurturance from them. As long as she is able to be aware of the distinction between her own and their needs, there is still a feeling of an internally located self. However, the danger is that she may try to avoid or reduce self-alienation by an identification with others to the extent that self is defined externally, through others—she becomes nothing but them.

Separation Anxiety and Depression. Self-alienation and definition of self only through other people leaves a person vulnerable. Infants show separation anxiety when separated from their caregivers: initially rage and then apathy and dejection if the separation continues (e.g., Yarrow, 1961). Separation in adulthood has some of the same features. In fact, it was in trying to understand adult mourning that Freud developed the concept of identification: one attempts to compensate for the loss by becoming the other. For adults, the concept of separation and depression involves the actual or fantasized loss of an object upon which the self depended, and includes the attempts and final failures to reestablish or give up the lost or threatened relationships, as evidenced by feelings of helplessness or hopelessness (e.g., Schmale, 1958). Real or threatened loss of a loved one has been cited as a precipitating factor in many forms of psychological and physical disorders.

Separation seems a particularly potent factor in suicide and depression. Many suicidal people feel that their own existence is justified only if the relationship with another person continues, a dependency with lethal potentiality (Farberow & Reynolds, 1971). For others, a feeling of not being in control of one's life is marked (Leonard, 1974). With greater self-definition through others, women are more vulnerable to actual or threatened separation and a feeling of loss of control. Women do report more suicidal thoughts than do men and attempt more suicides. Although women attempt suicide four times more often than men, men complete their attempts three times more often; thus the actual suicide rate of men is about 12 times larger than that of women (Garai, 1970). The attempts of women do not seem appropriately shrugged off as "women just want attention."

Suicide because of interrupted relationships with others may be an extreme physical manifestation of the psychological death of self that occurs when one is defined only through other people. This dependency upon others for self-definition that is encouraged for women is a dependency with a lethal potentiality. Great though the satisfactions of motherhood and marriage may be, children do leave home, and men generally die earlier than women. The "average" woman spends almost a quarter of her adult life without a living husband or children under 18 (Figure 1-2). Thus, socialization toward marriage and motherhood and self-definition through others is insufficient preparation for a meaningful life throughout the life span, even for women who choose the conventional life-style (Chapter 13). Some women pay particularly high prices.

Empty-Nest Syndrome. During middle age, traditional women are especially vulnerable to depression and other symptoms of malaise, and this cannot be attributed solely to hormonal changes with cessation of menstruation. Rather, it is due to the loss of the important role of mother and the feelings of worth it provided (Bart, 1972). The phenomenon is called the **empty-nest syndrome** because of its frequency in women who have defined themselves through their children and then are helpless when the children leave home. Women who have overprotective or overinvolved relationships with their children are more likely to suffer at this time than women who do not, and housewives have a higher rate of depression than women who work outside the home. The depression is *not* more likely in the so-called "masculine-aggressive" women who have not defined themselves exclusively through motherhood. Depressive women score as *more* traditionally feminine than the average woman. Overall, the data suggest that it is the women who "buy" the traditional norms who become depressed when children leave.

Fortunately, not all women "buy" the traditional norms in such extremes, or they manage to outgrow them if they have done so. Parents of older children are generally among the happiest groups of people (Institute for Social Research, 1974; Campbell, 1975). For many couples, the "empty-nest" is a place where they experience more companionship and mutual understanding than they felt as newlyweds. Raising a family seems to be one of those things that is more fun to have done than to be doing! Yet, having children has been seen as the natural fulfillment of a woman's purpose in life (Rabin, 1965), another source of role strain. Marriage itself also provides strains for many women.

MARRIAGE

Recent evidence suggests that marriage and family life are the greatest sources of life satisfactions for adult women and men, 58% of married Americans say that they are "completely satisfied" with their marriages (Institute for Social Research, 1974; Campbell, 1975). Young wives are more satisfied than anyone else. "They are positively euphoric; they are the most likely group to enjoy

doing housework. . . . It appears that marriage is still considered a woman's greatest achievement, and when she marries, the sigh of relief is almost audible" (Campbell, 1975, p. 38).

However, the euphoria fades, and the bulk of the evidence has shown more dissatisfaction with marriage reported by women than by men, while a wife's general life happiness and overall well-being are more dependent upon marital happiness than are her husbands' (Barry, 1970; Ahammer, 1973; Bernard, 1973; Donelson, 1973). Men feel more burdened by responsibilities of marriage (such as financial concerns) than women, but greater and more stressful personality adjustments seem required of the woman by marriage and later parenthood.

Shock of Marriage. Jessie Bernard (1942, 1972, 1973) has proposed a **shock theory of marriage,** a view that conventional marriage introduces genuine emotional health hazards into the life of a woman. Some of the shocks are relatively obvious. The bride experiences conflict between attachment to her parental family and to her husband (Chapter 13). The honeymoon ends; the wife ceases to be catered-to and becomes the caterer. Another kind of shock occurs when women, after years of being taught to expect to lean on a man, find that their husbands are human beings who are not quite so strong, so protective, or so omniscient as culturally romanticized depictions have taught them. Rather, husbands are normal human beings. "For some [women] it becomes a full-time career to keep the self-image of husbands intact" (Bernard, 1973, p. 41).

Several studies indicate that part of the shock to women is caused by the redefinition and active reshaping of personality and styles of interaction to meet the wishes or needs of husbands (Bernard, 1973). Wives conform more to husbands' expectations than husbands do to wives'. Very able young college women lose independence and impulse expression after marriage; they become submissive and conservative. Similarly, women who were quite capable of taking care of themselves before marriage become helpless after 15 or 20 years of marriage—one woman who had managed a travel agency before marriage had to ask friends how to get a passport when widowed at age 55! The psychological costs of the adjustments made by wives are shown in their *increasing* unhappiness and negative and passive outlook on life as the years roll on. Among other things, by middle age, married women are more likely to be alcoholics than single women, although there was no difference between the two groups at earlier ages.

There is also the specific strain on women that the affectional or expressive behaviors women have been taught to be important in meaningful relationships are *not* primary determinants of husbands' marital satisfaction (Wills, Weiss, & Patterson, 1974). Wives' instrumental behavior (such as cooking a good meal or doing household repairs) was found more important to husbands than their affectional behavior (such as asking about his feelings or touching him pleasantly). Thus, the wife who wants to please her husband must readjust the interpersonal style she has been lead to believe would be pleasing.

The Housewife Syndrome. The data do *not* suggest that marriage itself is inherently or permanently "sick." They do indicate that the way in which many people go about being married does not enhance the lives of women. It is being relegated to the role of housewife as it has been defined in our society, rather than marriage itself, that causes problems for women, as shown by comparisons of housewives with employed women (Bernard, 1973). Mothers who work outside the home are less likely than housewives to complain of pains and ailments and not feeling well enough to do all they would like to do. More women working outside the home than expected reported having felt an *impending* nervous breakdown, but more housewives than expected had *actually* had a nervous breakdown. Proportionately fewer employed women and more housewives suffered varying ailments (Table 9-2). Thus, Bernard has suggested that there is a housewife syndrome that might well be viewed as Public Health Problem Number One. Recent evidence shows that particularly housewives who are college graduates are likely to find their lives less rewarding than other housewives, and less rewarding than the lives of college graduate women who were employed (Institute for Social Research, 1974).

TABLE 9-2.

Selected Symptoms of Psychological Distress Among White Housewives and Working Women *

Symptom	Housewives	Working Women
Nervous breakdown	+1.16	−2.02
Felt impending nervous breakdown	−0.12	+0.81
Nervousness	+1.74	−2.29
Inertia	+2.35	−3.15
Insomnia	+1.27	−2.00
Trembling hands	+0.74	−1.25
Nightmares	+0.68	−1.18
Perspiring hands	+1.28	−2.55
Fainting	+0.82	−2.69
Headaches	+0.84	−0.87
Dizziness	+1.41	−1.85
Heart palpitations	+1.38	−1.56

+ indicates higher number of symptoms than expected.

− indicates fewer symptoms than expected.

* *Source.* National Center for Health Statistics, *Selected Symptoms of Psychological Distress* (U.S. Department of Health, Education, and Welfare, 1970), Table 17, pp. 30–31.

Equalitarianism. It must be noted that most marriage research of the past has dealt with marriages of the traditional pattern in which both partners show sex-role stereotypic patterns. It is being increasingly recognized that this is *only one* kind of role patterning in marriage. There is evidence that marital satisfaction is enhanced when husbands and wives perform similar rather than stereotypically divergent roles (Ahammer, 1973). The typical man *can* be less demanding of service and conformity from his wife, and the typical wife *can* be more assertive in countering the demands. Societal expectations of the nature of marriage *can* be restructured to be less stereotypic and more realistic than the current idealistic picture of ". . . and they lived happily ever after." Generally men do seem to live happily; that women do so is subject to debate.

What is Fulfillment? Certainly, the happy, healthy, fulfilled housewife does exist. Many housewives report themselves as being very happy and satisfied with life. However, it is not clear that even these have found personal fulfillment or psychological maturity. They report happiness, but they also report more specific problems, such as worries and other symptoms. Perhaps they are happy and fulfilled in spite of their specific problems. After all, they have been taught to value the nurturant role of mother and homemaker and to be satisfied with rewards and obligations different from those thought applicable only to men.

However, an alternative interpretation has serious enough implications to deserve attention: Women, and perhaps men as well, are confusing "adjustment" with happiness. Adjustment and health are not necessarily the same thing, nor is happiness the same as fulfillment or psychological health and maturity. That is, some women have married, as they were expected to, and are trying to adjust to marriage and please their husbands. So it follows to them as a "logical" conclusion that they must be happy—they interpret their conformity to societal expectations as a signal or assurance of happiness and health (Bernard, 1972, 1973).

Conformity does not necessarily lead to psychological growth. True, the healthy person must sometimes come to terms with the inevitable and simply "adjust" to a reality that cannot be changed. Many women may feel that even if it is not what they were led to believe, their life as housewife is better than alternatives for which they have not been prepared; they really feel no choice. There are an increasing number of alternatives to the conventional life-style of the past, and increasing support from women and men in seeking them. **Proactive** functioning, rather than **reactive** functioning, is possible (Chapter 2). Women can be, as many are, origins of their behavior rather than pawns. However, therapists often judge their success with a woman client in terms of the degree to which she functions reactively, which is consistent with the feminine role: she accepts her life-style as a "must" and "stops complaining about it." Clinicians often have a double standard of health and of "sickness."

What is Sick? More women than men are hospitalized for psychiatric treatment or receive outpatient treatment from public hospitals (Chesler, 1971; Broverman et al., 1970). Female patients are more self-deprecatory, depressed, perplexed, and prone to sucidal thoughts and attempts than are male patients (Zigler & Phillips, 1960). Healthy women *not* receiving treatment do report more distress, worry, fear of breakdown, and need of help than do healthy men. Are women then really "sicker" than men? One problem of interpreting mental health data is that typical socialization makes it more likely that females will recognize and admit their problems. Women more freely admit emotionality and emotional problems than do men, and are aware of traits and experiences considered negative, irrational, or unhealthy in our society (Silverman, 1970). Also, they are censured less for the overt expression of emotionality. A man's tightly clenched fist in his pants pocket is not the sign to others of his feelings as are a woman's freer, more open verbal and facial expressions. The man is taught to portray self-confidence, even to the point of cockiness, rather than to admit the self-doubt that women can. Thus, a woman's problems are more likely to be noticed by herself and others than are a man's. Are unrecognized problems less of a problem?

Double Standard. Another problem of interpreting mental health data is simply that women are expected to have characteristics that in a male are considered abnormal. Curiously, women are expected to resemble a "normal child" or a disturbed adult, and at the same time to be an effective companion for a mature normal man and an effective mother for children. For example, the depiction given by both female and male mental health experts, of the normal mature adult, sex unspecified, match well with that given for the normal, mature man (Broverman et al., 1970). However, healthy women were considered different from the healthy adult and the healthy man by being submissive, emotional, easily influenced, sensitive to being hurt, excitable, dependent, concerned about appearance, not very adventurous, noncompetitive, and unaggressive. Why are these traits considered healthy in women but not in men?

Women are expected to function reactively and accept the "givens" of an unhealthy life-style. Attributes of the male role and of healthy males encourage a proactive change of undesirable environments. The researchers made a plea for a definition of mental health that emphasizes self-actualization and competence in dealing with the environment, which they recognized is in conflict with becoming "adjusted" to the social environment associated with restrictive stereotypes, for both women and men. Although many therapists are men or women who do not understand the situation of women and feel the "healthy" woman must make herself happy with her current life, times are changing. Therapists, both women and men, are questioning conventional views of psychological health generally and becoming more sensitive and inventive in therapeutic work with women (e.g., Franks & Burtle, 1974).

THE FAMILY PRICE
The woman's family also pays for her socialization and resulting inclination to define herself through other people. She may seek an outlet for her self-expression and agentic qualities through domination in the home (see discussion of Jung, Chapter 2), including pressures on children and husband to provide her with vicarious achievement satisfactions (Chapter 11). A woman who is as homebound as the "average" woman may become an omnipresent mother who inadvertently but subtly and pervasively interfers with her children's struggle for autonomy, for privacy, and the right to worry things through for themselves (Rossi, 1964). "It is, after all, feminine women, the ones who play the traditional roles, not the career woman, who are likely to dominate their husbands and children" (Bart, 1972, p. 185). The domination may be a very subtle matter of manipulation and guilt induction. Nonetheless it is domination and restricts the freedom of daughters, sons, and husbands. If she is not immediately successful in getting them to do as she wishes and to keep them close to her, she may intensify her efforts to be "a good wife and mother." By being more patient or working harder than is reasonably expected, she places a moral debt on family members that their normal adequacy does not satisfy (Turner, 1968). Children and husbands become susceptible to their own self-alienation as they try to please someone who tries so hard to please them.

THE PARADOX OF SEPARATENESS AND RESPONSIVENESS
Identification is social responsiveness. It is being attentive to others, caring with them, and learning from them and with them. Social responsiveness is necessary for a social life of benefit to all and for the full personal development of all. "The common basis of loving and of understanding is identification, and without it, both would be impossible" (Balint, 1945, p. 321). Identification makes possible communication and empathy, tenderness, concern and caring, as implicit in everyday expressions such as, "I can really identify with you."

However, the problem is that the responsiveness to others may well not be effective. To give effectively to others requires being separate from them and having the firm sense of self and self-knowledge that the separateness from them allows and demands. Bonds between people without a sense of separateness and completeness in themselves are likely to be ones of distortions and projections. So frequently does the "shadowy love" of union without separation occur that it has been cited as the typical love of the "Adjusted American" with "Normal Neuroses" (Putney & Putney, 1964/1966).

The union of creative love, in contrast to neurotic love, demands the separateness, individuality, and self-affirmation of each party, and in turn develops the potential of each. Union exists only between distinct entities. The complete person is the one who experiences complete love.

"Love is the union with somebody, or something outside oneself, under the conditions of retaining the separateness and integrity of one's own self" (Fromm, 1956, p. 37). By such a union, one may truly become more individualized as a separate self.

The request, then, is that both women and men be encouraged to develop both a sense of separateness and of social responsiveness. Until they do, neither can well understand other people nor be complete in their giving and receiving. When they do, both may be more completely what they are, apart from and with other people. This requires overcoming sex-typing in favor of the openness of androgyny and will further foster full androgynous development.

SUMMARY

Everyone loses because of sex-typed socialization, with women losing more because of the lower valuation placed on the feminine than the masculine role and the necessity of traits considered masculine for self-development, personal expressiveness and competence striving, as discussed in the previous chapter. In addition, the method of socializing little girls and the content of the feminine role encourage patterns of overrelatedness and overidentification and discourage the development of a firm sense of self as separate. Although this seems to contribute to women's social responsiveness, shown for example in social sensitivity and attitudes of cooperation and caring for other people, it also promotes a sense of a self-out-there rather than self-in-me.

Specifically, the typical methods of dealing with girls are more severe, inconsistent, and restrictive than those of dealing with little boys. This socialization style inhibits spontaneity and independent assertiveness and fosters continual attention to other people, even if they are nonrewarding. The typical life-style of traditional homemakers further encourages self-alienation and definition of self through others, often resulting in anxiety and depression with separation or lack of acceptance from the self-defining others. The shock of marriage and the housewife syndrome are fairly clear examples of the damaging effects of conventional sex-role socialization and particularly of the expectations held for girls and women. It is women of traditional femininity and lifestyles who show more specific symptoms such as worries, and fears. Yet these women often report themselves happy, perhaps because some of them are equating happiness with meeting expectations. Even some mental health experts have applied a double standard of health, expecting "healthy" women to adjust reactively to their sex roles and conventional expectations, but expecting men to be energetically proactive in changing unsatisfactory ways of life.

A woman and her family can reap the satisfaction of her social responsiveness. However, they all can also pay high prices for her diffuse self and the attempts to function as a reactive, other-defined person that undermine and inhibit interpersonal satisfactions. It is more likely to be an androgynous person functioning with both relatedness and separateness than one who is strongly sex-typed who can give and receive effectively in meaningful relationships.

CHAPTER
10
FRIENDSHIP

WHAT IS FRIENDSHIP?
FRIENDSHIP AS LOVE
FRIENDSHIP AS ADMIRATION
FRIENDSHIP AND OTHER FORMS OF LOVE
CONTRIBUTIONS OF LOVE RELATIONSHIPS

FRIENDSHIP IN EARLY YEARS
RELATIONSHIPS IN CHILDHOOD
SEX-TYPING IN PEER GROUPS

ADOLESCENT FRIENDSHIP
CHANGES DURING ADOLESCENCE
Limits on Family Guidance
Turning to Friends
SEX DIFFERENCES IN SAME-SEX FRIENDSHIPS
Young Girls
Older Girls
Teenage Boys
REASONS FOR DIFFERENCES
FRIENDSHIP, LOVE, AND DATING
The Dating Ritual
Courtship and Romantic Love

ADULT FRIENDSHIP
IMPACT OF SIMILARITIES
INFLUENCE OF PERSONALITY ATTRIBUTES
DOGMATISM
SELF-DISCLOSURE
Nondisclosure

FRIENDSHIP CHOICES
BETWEEN-SEX FRIENDSHIPS
FRIENDSHIPS WITHIN MARRIAGE

WOMEN AS FRIENDS
RELATIONSHIPS BETWEEN WOMEN
THE "QUEEN BEE"
CURRENT DEVELOPMENTS

FRIENDSHIP AND PERSONAL GROWTH IN ADULTHOOD
NEED REDUCTION
ENRICHMENT

SUMMARY

It may be true of friendship as it is of jazz: If you need a definition for it, you'll never understand it. We could leave the issue of definitions at that and go directly to the topics of how friendship develops, its importance during adolescence, its manifestations in adulthood and the ways in which it may be important in women's lives, except for one major problem. People often mean different things when they speak of friendship, though their meanings may overlap; and they apply the term to a variety of different relationships. A central thesis of this chapter is that friendship is a relationship of dynamic importance in personal growth and development, but it is often undervalued. However, this is not equally true for all relationships people call friendship. Therefore, we must clarify at the outset what we mean by friendship in this chapter.

WHAT IS FRIENDSHIP?

FRIENDSHIP AS LOVE

The working definition of friendship in this chapter is that friendship is a form of love. It is an intimate, personal, caring relationship with attributes such as reciprocal tenderness and warmth of feeling; reciprocal desire to keep the friendship; honesty and sincerity; trust; intimacy and openness of self; loyalty; and durability of the relationship over time. Friendships having these attributes are relatively rare. Most of us do not experience many of them over a lifetime.

This definition may seem self-evident to many readers, but people do use the term in other ways. Most often, they say "friend" when they mean more casual, less intimate relationships that may be based upon some shared external interest or concern, rather than upon mutual regard of two persons. Some of these less intimate relationships are listed in Table 10-1. Friendship as love can, and does, often develop out of these less intimate relationships, each of which is of value in its own right. However, they should not be confused with friendship as love.

FRIENDSHIP AS ADMIRATION

Another source of confusion is that there is a second tradition of defining friendship (dating back at least to Cicero, the Roman orator and statesman) in which the emphasis is placed on respect and admiration for the friend rather than upon mutual choice and intimacy. A friend is seen as the realization or embodiment of some set of values. One feels admiration rather than affection; feelings may not be reciprocal as they are in friendship as love; and the continuation of the friendship depends upon whether the friend continues to live up to the set of values. That both friendship as love and friendship as admiration are alive and well among people today was demonstrated when college students were asked what they would do if a friend violated generally accepted standards of behavior (Nesbitt, 1959). Some said that they would be consistently loyal to the friend, some would consistently uphold the standard of behavior, and some would be influenced by both types of considerations.

Of course friends may feel both love and admiration for one another, and both types of feelings may contribute to personal growth in different

TABLE 10-1.
Different Relationships Often Called Friendship

Relationship	Definition
Casual Acquaintance	Someone one "knows to speak to"
Companions	Persons with whom social activities are shared
Colleagues	Persons who work together and share professional concerns
Comrades	Persons who share commitment to some common cause

ways. But it is the reciprocity, trust, and personal intimacy of friendship as love that will concern us in later discussion.

FRIENDSHIP AND OTHER FORMS OF LOVE

Of the many ways in which friendship as love may differ from other love relationships, three seem especially relevant. These are, first, the importance of sexuality and sexual attraction, regardless of whether it is directly expressed in an overt, physical relationship; second, the degree of mutual choice about the relationship; and third, the importance of psychological intimacy or personal closeness. A high degree of personal closeness and mutual choice are essential for friendship as love, but sexuality is secondary or absent. In marked contrast is a love relationship in which sexual attraction is primary but one-sided, and there is minimum psychological intimacy. Intense feelings for another person are not always reciprocated, as many people know from painful experience.

Although there are many combinations between these two extremes, there has been a tradition of dichotomizing sexual love and friendship. Many have questioned whether the personal closeness of friendship could be combined with sexual love. Men especially were likely to feel that they could not, on the grounds that women were not capable of the qualities important for close friendship (see Montaigne, 1580, 1588/1960, and the counterargument of Alger, 1879). The dichotomy has been breaking down. Increasing numbers of people believe that sexuality and psychological intimacy are combined in the ideal love relationship, the one most worth seeking and working for. Contemporary young people particularly are likely to emphasize the necessity of a close personal relationship as part of their sexual love (e.g., Conger, 1973).

Contributions of Love Relationships. All relationships can make valuable contributions to our lives. Through sexual relationships we may explore, express, and come to know our sexual and emotional selves in ways not possible in other relationships—a process of major importance since we are sexual and emotional beings. Yet, friendship as love, with sexuality secondary, has other strengths and flexibilities. For one thing, friendship is likely to be shared, whereas sexual relationships typically exclude others. As C. S. Lewis said, "In each of my friends there is something that only some other friend can fully bring out . . . [within limits] we possess each friend not less but more as the number of those with whom we share him increases" (1960, p. 95). We speak of "our mutual friend," but few people are comfortable with the idea of "our mutual lover."

Perhaps more important, friendship as love encourages the development of objective assessment and tolerant understanding of another person, including those with whom we form sexual love relationships. Because we care about our friends and want to maintain the friendship, we are likely to work to understand them and to accept even those attributes we might consider unacceptable in other people. Such understanding can develop in sexual relationships, especially when psychological intimacy is also important. However, the nature of sexuality sets limits. Sexual feelings can be strong and intense. They can easily interfere with the capacity to see the loved one clearly, resulting in an inability to see faults and in an attribution of positive traits that do not exist ("love is blind").

Similarly, lovers' sexual feelings may not encourage the honesty and sincerity that is the bond for friendship as love. Although honesty is important for sexual relationships, it is not essential to them in the way that it is to friendship as love. Indeed, honesty and sincerity are demanded, as the main bond, of friendship. "Eros [sexually based love] will have naked bodies; friendship, naked personalities" (Lewis, 1960, p. 103). Much of the potential of friendship is that of developing awareness and sensitivity to oneself and to others, as friends reveal themselves to one another and thus learn more about each other and themselves. (See Lepp, 1966, for an extensive discussion of related ideas.)

FRIENDSHIP IN EARLY YEARS

For friendship as love to develop, people must have a fairly high level of interpersonal and intellectual maturity. They must be able to recognize and value other persons as separate from themselves, having their own needs and values; they must have sensitivity to others and ability to communicate effectively. These are quite sophisticated requirements that children develop only gradually.

RELATIONSHIPS IN CHILDHOOD

Although empathy and sensitivity to others begin to develop during preschool years, young children have difficulty distinguishing their own needs, feelings, or thoughts from those of others. Their own immediately experienced reality dominates their social perceptions. Consequently, they are more like companions than friends. Their relationships are relatively unstable, based more upon shared interests and activities than upon the attributes of the friend as a person, and dependent on external factors such as where they live.

Once children enter elementary school, their social awareness and responsiveness to others develop rapidly. Peer groups and peer norms become more and more important, and conformity to peer opinions increases steadily, reflecting the increased awareness of the expectations of others and concern over being accepted (Berenda, 1950; Iscoe, Williams, & Harvey, 1963, 1964). Friendship choices become more stable, probably reflecting a general stabilization of preferences and interests over this period (McKinney, 1968). The reasons given about why someone is their friend shift from the predominantly impersonal attributes of earlier years (e.g., has a nice home, has nice clothes, has lots of toys) to more personal attributes (e.g., friendly, cheerful, clean; Dymond, Hughes, and Raabe, 1952).

Changes in social awareness and responsiveness to others take place as children grow more experienced in dealing with the conflicts that inevitably arise between their own interests and wishes and those of others. In dealing with peer interactions, children improve their communication skills as they adapt what they say to another person's information or point of view. They also improve in role-taking skills, which require recognizing how another person might think, feel, or act, and reflecting that awareness in one's own behavior (Flavell et al., 1968). In short, children become more responsive to other children as persons.

Sex-typing in Peer Groups. Athough the general changes occur for both girls and boys, there are differences in peer group experiences that both refect previous **sex-typed** experiences and provide a basis for further sex differences. Sex-typing is evident in preschool children (Chapter 8) and **sex-role** consistent behavior is one major determinant of peer acceptance (e.g., Hartup, 1970). Thus, as the importance of peer acceptance and conformity to peer norms increase, girls and boys are increasingly encouraged to display sex-role behavior. Although girls and boys learn sensitivity to others through peer interactions, girls' experience is primarily with other girls and boys' experience is with other boys. The "sex cleavage" or separation between girls' and boys' groups begins in preschool years, intensifies once children enter school, and persists until well into adolescence. Similarly, during preadolescence as in adolescence, girls are likely to group together in twos and threes, whereas boys are more likely to group together in larger groups, or gangs.

ADOLESCENT FRIENDSHIPS

At the same time that adolescents must cope with rapid and far-reaching changes in themselves, limits are developing on the ways in which their families can provide understanding and assistance in coping with these changes. They turn to friends to fill this void. Friendships are as much a matter of necessity as of choice during this period.

Changes During Adolescence. Physical changes are most obvious. The body, which up to adolescence was taken largely for granted, now changes with a rapidity and a visibility that require a major shift in body image. Maturing sexuality brings with it new urges and emotions to be dealt with and understood. With these changes, adolescents begin to elicit new expectations from others and to develop new expectations for themselves. They must begin to act more like adults. The transitions that adolescents go through are not easy in this culture.

Less obvious than physical changes but equally important are intellectual changes that result in new ways of conceptualizing themselves (e.g., Elkind, 1970). Adolescents become capable of a self-awareness and self-criticism that is foreign to younger children, who take their own attributes pretty much for granted. This new self-awareness is probably the source of much of the self-preoccupation seen in adolescents. It is also the source of a new awareness of the possibility of changing one's attributes. Given the new self-criticism, the uncertainty of their in-between, neither-child-nor-adult status, and armed with their new openness to change, the possibilities of personal growth through friendship may be greater during adolescence than at any other time of life.

Limits on Family Guidance. Continued love and emotional support from parents are crucial for adolescents. At the same time there are ways in which parents may be part of the problem confronting adolescents. During adolescence young people in this culture typically redefine relationships within their families and move toward a greater independence of them. For this, they need support from outside the family. Also, habitual patterns of family interaction that have been practiced for years are difficult to overcome for either parents or children.

The new emotional intensity of adolescence also creates problems. There is little room within the family for working out erotic and aggressive feelings, so adolescents may seek more neutral ground on which to explore them. Adults are likely to have forgotten or repressed the reality of the conflicts and uncertainties of their own adolescence. They may be unwilling or unable to deal with the conflicts and uncertainties their children are experiencing.

Finally, parents can be of little help to adolescents in learning to get along in the rapidly changing peer subculture. Only from other adolescents can one learn about acceptable ways of dressing, speaking, and acting within that peer group.

Turning to Friends. With a friend facing similar conflicts, there can be shared recognition of reality. The friend can provide a "safe haven" for exploring one's own thoughts and feelings. The **"imaginary audience"**—the tendency of adolescents to feel that they are the focus of everyone's attention—is overcome. Through the honest interchanges of friendship, adolescents discover that the social blunder or physical blemish that seems so conspicuous actually is trivial to the friend, and also that the friend has her own concerns (Elkind, 1970). Honesty and sincerity in friendship are critical for this process of self-discovery and increased understanding of others. To adults, adolescent friends often seem overly critical of one another. But, ". . . their job is not to be nice to each other, but to be real to each other" (Friedenberg, 1959, p. 51).

Sex Differences in Same-Sex Friendships.
Pressures toward friendship are much the same for both girls and boys. Nonetheless, there are subtle but important sex differences in friendship patterns, as one might expect given previous **socialization** experiences. The following summary is based chiefly on an extensive study of adolescents from a variety of different social backgrounds, types of schools, and communities (Douvan & Adelson, 1966).

Young Girls. Friendships of the youngest girls interviewed (11–13 years) focus largely on shared activities, as in childhood. The qualities sought in a friend are mostly those that facilitate cooperative activity (does favors, easy to get along with) rather than personal qualities. Issues such as dating or sexuality are not often discussed with friends yet, though the girls do express interest and concern about beginning to date.

By 14 to 16 years of age, friendships have become more personal and emotionally interdependent. When asked what qualities a friend should have, sensitivity to the needs of others is one main theme in the girls' answers. A second theme is security: Friends should be loyal and trustworthy, a source of emotional support in times of crisis, should not gossip behind your back. The strong concern with security evidently stems from developing sexuality. Sexual feelings are new and unfamiliar. Girls this age are still unsure of themselves in their relationships with boys, although most have begun to date. Instead of exploring sexuality directly with a member of the other sex, the emotional energy of sexual feelings is diverted into same-sex friendships through which the girls explore feelings, relationships and morality. Under this heavy emotional load, friendships are intense and prone to disruption because of jealousy. Girls of this age want to be popular with boys, but more for high status among girlfriends than because of interest in boys as persons.

Older Girls. By 17 to 18 years of age, the intensity of same-sex friendships has declined markedly. Older girls have begun to establish their identity; they have more understanding and control of their impulses; they are more comfortable with boys as people. For the first time, these young women begin to mention interpersonal sensitivity and mutual trust as important in *het-ero*sexual relationships, as they did previously only for same-sex relationships. As the capacity for closeness and intimacy with another person begins to generalize from like-sex friendships to heterosexual relationships, friendships become more neutral, playful, open. There is less concern with security and loyalty, although girls still want a friend with whom they can share important confidences. At the same time, there appears to be a greater ability to tolerate differences, and an increased interest in the individuality of the friend.

Teenage Boys. Boys do have intimate friendships similar to those of girls (e.g., Friedenberg, 1959), but generally they are less concerned with interpersonal intimacy than are girls. Only 14- to 16-year-old boys were included in the major study we have been considering; these boys were more like the younger girls (ages 11–13) in the ideas they had about the meaning of friendship and in the relatively impersonal qualities they considered desirable in a friend.

There are also sex differences in the structuring of groups of friends. For boys, the gang is the focal point of friendships. Girls' groups are loose coalitions of intimate twosomes and threesomes, seldom reflecting the "gang spirit" typical in groups of boys. Consistent with the greater importance of the gang, boys more frequently than girls cite failure to conform to peer group standards as a reason for unpopularity or rejection. The gang is the boys' basis of support against authority. Far more often than girls, boys mentioned that a friend should stand by when you are in trouble, and should not "rat" or go over to the side of adult authority. The emphasis is upon mutual support in case of conflict with adults, rather than upon the emotional support in personal crises stressed by girls.

Reasons for Differences. Boys generally develop more slowly than girls, and this difference in developmental rate may be one reason for boys' relative lack of sophistication concerning friendship compared to girls'. However, other factors that relate to physical differences and to differences in cultural learning may be more important.

Anatomical differences influence the ways in which boys and girls learn to recognize their own sexuality (Chapter 12). Adolescent boys have little doubt when they experience sexual feelings. They must learn to regulate their sexual impulses, and sessions with friends may help with this, but boys are unlikely to confuse sexually related feelings with other feelings. In relative contrast, the physical signs of girls' sexual feelings are less obvious, though they are clearly recognizable once girls know what these are. Also, there are stricter prohibitions on sexuality for girls than boys, and sex education provides girls with no information about the indicators of female sexuality. Under these circumstances, more girls than boys may confuse sexual feelings with other emotions. As a result, girls' sexual feelings may be more easily channeled into friendships, where they begin to be clarified.

In addition, a dominant relevant aspect of cultural learning is the strong fear of homosexuality among men in this country. For this and other reasons, boys and men experience pressures toward inhibiting intimacy (Douvan & Adelson, 1966; McCandless, 1970). There is more social pressure upon boys to keep sexual feelings separate from other emotions as well as to avoid intimacy in relationships with other boys, lest sexuality influence the relationship.

Sex-role socialization also affects adolescent friendship patterns in more general ways. *Identity* and *sexuality* are central themes in adolescent development of both sexes. However, for girls *interpersonal relations* are the third interrelated theme, whereas for boys the third interrelated theme is *autonomy*, which includes assertiveness and achievement. Consistent with this interpretation, interpersonal maturity was clearly related to other attributes of personal development, such as self-confidence for girls but not for boys (Douvan & Adelson, 1966). Girls are socialized toward the interpersonal—the communal—throughout their lives. Empathy, intimacy, sensitivity to others, need for love, and need to nurture become part of the fabric of girls' personality in ways they do not for boys. Boys are socialized toward independence—an agentic orientation—and against emotional expression and emotional interrelationship throughout their lives. To become independent, boys must assert themselves against authorities. Thus, the differing emphases in girls' and in boys' friendships reflect the different needs and different habits of interaction that have been developing over previous years of sex-role socialization.

Friendship, Love, and Dating. Theorists writing on friendship (Lepp, 1966) and on personality development (Sullivan, 1953) stress the importance of friendship in preadolescence and adolescence as apprenticeships necessary for developing the capability for love in adulthood. At the same time that they are beginning to date (about 14 for girls, 15 for boys) most adolescents have entered puberty or are sexually mature. Dating presents a potentially stressful and demanding conflict. Adolescents have had little experience with their own sexuality and they are unsure of themselves in interactions with the other sex. Yet, they are expected to cope with a situation involving a member of the other sex, in which there are strong prohibitions against overt sexual behavior, and in which they are given a great deal of freedom.

The Dating Ritual. The potential stress of the situation is reduced because in early adolescence especially dating is highly ritualized and structured. Although the specific forms of the dating ritual differ over time and locale, a ritual that clearly prescribes roles for the "good date" always exists (e.g., Smith, 1962). The dating **persona** (see discussion of Jung, Chapter 2) is fun to be with, easy to talk to, has a good sense of humor but is not silly, and is neither moody nor too serious. These kinds of attributes encourage pleasant, congenial companionship, but not interpersonal intimacy. The safety provided by the ritual has a price. If the dating persona becomes too firmly attached, it may later inhibit the development of the intimacy important to a successful marriage or a good friendship. Thus, the structure of dating in early adolescence may *prevent* rather than foster interpersonal intimacy.

A second factor, homoeroticism, may also limit the potential for developing intimacy through dating. **Homoeroticism** is engaging in heterosexual activities as a means of acquiring or maintaining status with same-sex peers, rather than out of interest or concern for persons of the other sex. It is evident among 14 to 16-year-old girls. However, it appears to be more prevalent and more long-lasting among boys, for whom it may persist throughout adolescence and perhaps into adulthood. The strong socialization toward achievement and against the interpersonal, the widespread cultural view that sexual behavior is an achievement for men, and the male's need for acceptance within the gang are all likely to accentuate male homoeroticism. There are some suspicions too that recent emphasis on sexual "liberty" has fostered homoeroticism in college populations of both sexes; sexual relations have become a standard to meet, even if one does not particularly want them (Chapter 12).

Courtship and Romantic Love. Courting (seeking a spouse) usually becomes a realistic function of dating only later in adolescence, after young people have become sufficiently comfortable with themselves and with members of the other sex to move beyond the dating ritual toward more personal, intimate relationships. There are still hazards (Chapter 13). With their relative inexperience, adolescents may be more prone than adults to idealize the loved one, failing to recognize faults as well as strengths. The higher divorce rate for young marriages may relect the difficulties of mate selection on the basis of the intense romantic love of adolescence. The intensely committed passion of romantic love is also shown in rebuff of parental counsel against what the parents consider an ill-chosen partner or premature marriage decision. The parental criticism intensifies the adolescent's devotion to the chosen partner and the need to demonstrate responsible independence. The effect is to increase the young couples' feelings of being bound together against outsiders who "just do not understand." Thus, "Don't interfere" is in many ways well-taken advice for parents. Romantic lovers must discover each other's faults on their own. When this happens, the outcome may be the breakdown of the relationship. It may also be a transition to a more objective and close psychological intimacy.

ADULT FRIENDSHIP

Relatively little is known about the dynamics and patterns of friendship from adolescence on. For that matter, research on interpersonal relationships in the earlier years is scanty compared to the amount of information about other aspects of human behavior, such as aggression, achievement, and intelligence. In part, friendships may receive little attention because they are not visible and institutionalized in our culture, in the way that love relationships between women and men are institutionalized in marriage, for example. There may also be discomfort with intimacy. Observers from other countries have often commented that people in this country, compared with people in their homelands, are remarkably easy to "get to know" superficially, but difficult to get to know well. This could be partly a matter of culturally different styles of friendship. Still, if there is discomfort with intimacy, it may inhibit interest or willingness to study friendship.

There are numerous studies of peripherally related topics, such as interpersonal attraction. In these studies, a person is usually asked to respond to an unfamiliar person on the basis of a brief interaction or of a brief description (often false) of the unfamiliar person. This approach is valuable for understanding factors that contribute to first impressions. However, these factors are not the same as those that contribute to a longer relationship, even when the relationship is only a few weeks or months old (e.g., Newcomb, 1961; Rosenfeld & Jackson, 1965; Halverson and Shore, 1969). Such studies, then, are not of much help in understanding the more enduring relationship of friendship. Thus, although there is some relevant research, much of our discussion must be speculative because information is not available.

IMPACT OF SIMILARITIES

Why does friendship develop between some pairs of persons but not others? Whether friends are similar to one another—"birds of a feather flock together"—or whether they complement each other—"opposites attract"—is a question that has been studied. There are definite similarities between adult friends, including spouses, and perceived similarities are positively associated with attraction (e.g., Byrne, 1974). Furthermore, the longer two people have been friends, the greater their perceived similarity; in fact, *perceived* similarity may be greater than *actual* similarity (e.g., Newcomb, 1961; Lott & Lott, 1965). However, the *content* of prominent similarities varies with the duration of the friendship. There are relatively obvious similarities in personality attributes and social background in newly formed relationships (Rosenfeld & Jackson, 1965; Newcomb, 1961). In older relationships, similarities in attitudes and values are more apparent (Richardson, 1940; Newcomb, 1961; Lott & Lott, 1965; Fiebert & Fiebert, 1969). Friends probably have complementary attributes too, but the evidence is unclear.

Similarities between friends may not be large, nor do they by themselves explain friendship. We know many people who seem similar to ourselves; only a few of them become close friends. General similarities seem to serve as screening devices, specifying groups from which friends are chosen. Which specific persons will become friends may be determined by the discovery of more specific similarities. Friendship arises when ". . . two or more of the companions discover that they have in common some insight or interest or even tastes which the others do not share, and which, till that moment, each believed to be his own unique treasure (or burden). . . ." (Lewis, 1960, pp. 96–97). The "shared uniqueness" may provide the impetus for friendship to develop.

INFLUENCE OF PERSONALITY ATTRIBUTES

Several personality attributes that have been studied appear to influence friendship patterns. As one might expect, traits reflecting *openness* to others are relevant to friendship. Here we will consider two forms of openness: openness in the sense of accepting that another person differs from oneself, and openness in the sense of willingness to reveal oneself.

Dogmatism. **Dogmatism** is close-mindedness, an opinionated insistence on the correctness of one's own opinions without sensitivity to others' views. Dogmatic persons lack the openness of accepting another person's differences from themselves. Dogmatic people are less well-liked than nondogmatic people, though this effect may appear only over time. Among college freshman women living in dormitories, dogmatism made little difference during the first five weeks of the term. However, by the 10th week, the dogmatic students were less well-liked than others, and desire for contact with them had declined (Rosenfeld & Nauman, 1969). Very likely, lack of openness to the views of others discourages people from approaching or attempting to develop friendships with intolerant people, while openness can mitigate the effects of dissimilarity. A laboratory study demonstrated that a dissimilar dogmatic stranger was disliked, whereas a dissimilar open-minded stranger received neutral or mildly positive reactions (Hodges & Byrne, 1972).

Self-Disclosure. Conversely, openness in the sense of willingness to reveal oneself facilitates

being liked by others. It may also foster discovery of what we are calling unique similarities. "**Self-disclosure** is the act of making yourself manifest, showing yourself so others can perceive you" (Jourard, 1971, p. 19). More specifically, it is the explicit communication to someone of some personal information that the person would be unlikely to learn from other sources, and that the disclosing individual would not give to everyone who asked. Self-disclosure in appropriate situations is positively related to liking (Certner, 1973). However, the positive effects of self-disclosure, like the negative effects of dogmatism, require time to develop. For example, Peace Corps trainees (sex unspecified) who were high in self-disclosure were better liked than others by the sixth week of training, although they had not been during the first week of training (Halverson & Shore, 1969).

There are exceptions, but women generally report themselves as higher on general tendencies to self-disclose (e.g., Jourard, 1971; Littlefield, 1974; Cozby, 1973). Also, women volunteer more intimate information about themselves, and answer and ask more intimate questions than do men (e.g., Sermat & Smyth, 1973; Janofsky, 1971). Both men and women show a *reciprocity* effect (also called a dyadic effect): once someone self-discloses, the other person is likely to do so as well, and the intimacy level of the second disclosure is likely to match that of the initial disclosure. Despite the reciprocity effect, college men still tend to disclose less than women. For example, there is more total disclosure between pairs of women than between pairs of men (Brooks, 1974). Furthermore, men view other men who disclose more than they themselves do as acting atypically; they perceive the high disclosers as *dis*similar to themselves and like them less (Sermat & Smyth, 1973).

Nondisclosure. Self-disclosure is not always appropriate, of course, and whether it facilitates liking or perceived similarity depends upon its perceived appropriateness. Whether or not self-disclosure is considered appropriate depends on how well the two persons know one another, how long they have known one another, their relative ages, the topic of the disclosure, and the physical setting in which it takes place. Perhaps because of the complexity of estimating when disclosure is appropriate, nondisclosure is considered more appropriate in most situations (Chaikin & Derlega, 1974).

Something more fundamental than complexity of decision making may be responsible for the widely perceived appropriateness of nondisclosure. "Self-disclosure . . . requires courage . . . the courage to be known, to be perceived by others as one knows himself to be" (Jourard, 1971, pp. 6–7). It is threatening to disclose oneself. Disclosing when one does not know what the other's reaction will be carries a risk of being misunderstood, rejected, or exploited—a potentially terrifying experience. Low self-esteem, or self-esteem depending upon support from others, can increase the fear. So, too, can the defensive climate created by dogmatic attitudes, evaluative behavior (cf. conditional regard, Chapter 2), or expression of superiority by the other person (Sermat & Smyth, 1973; Yalom, 1970). As willingness to disclose oneself decreases, for whatever the reason, so also does the likelihood of discovering unique similarities that may foster friendship.

Lepp (1966) suggests that when friendships occur between persons who hold very different beliefs, the persons involved ". . . have attained a relatively superior degree of psychic maturity and are for this reason better able to understand those who do not share their faith and convictions" (p. 24). Neither low dogmatism nor self-disclosure are themselves definitive indices of psychological maturity. However, both are consistent with general conceptions of maturity and both seem likely to widen the range of persons with whom one might become friends, as one is better able to tolerate differences from others and to open oneself to them.

FRIENDSHIP CHOICES

What differences are there in the people chosen by women and by men for self-disclosure? Within the family, both women and men disclose more to their mothers than to their fathers, though men do not disclose as much to their parents as women do (Jourard, 1971; Littlefield, 1974). With peers, friends of the same sex are clearly preferred over those of the other sex, both by high school and college students. Thus, genuine friendships with members of the other sex may be limited by reluctance to disclose, at least into the college years. But from the college years through the fifties, disclosure to a friend of the other sex or to one's spouse increases, while disclosure to same-sex friends declines (Jourard, 1971). Apparently, the personal intimacy of friendship is increasingly incorporated into heterosexual love relationships.

Between-Sex Friendships. Friendships can and do exist between women and men, within and outside of marriage. However, there are obstacles to realizing the potential of friendships between women and men. Simple contact is one. Most people seem to have contact with more members of their own sex than of the other sex. Even when contact is made, self-disclosure is less likely to take place between women and men.

Another obstacle is that friendships are most likely to be initiated between persons who see one another as equals. Social roles depict women as less important than men, and either women or men may accept this view although there are also people who consider women superior. Either way, the perceived inequality may prevent friendships from developing.

In view of the screening function of general similarity and the difficulty many people have in dealing with differences, actual or assumed differences in attitudes, interests, or personal styles can also be obstacles to the development of friendships between women and men. Although there are some differences between groups of women and men, there are many similarities between the sex groups and certainly between *individual* women and men. Any individual woman and individual man may share many interests, activities, or enthusiasms. Problems arise when *perceived* differences, which may or may not actually exist, prevent the discovery of the distinctive similarities out of which mature friendships may grow. These obstacles *can* be overcome. Initiation of friendship between a woman and a man may be made more difficult because of them, but many women and men do form close friendships.

Friendships Within Marriage. Married couples sometimes form fourway friendships with another couple. These friendships are very demanding, because there must be mutual liking and respect among all four participants. However, when such friendships work they are very satisfying (Brenton, 1974). Wives and husbands may also form independent friendships outside the marriage. Some people seem to believe that the happier the marriage, the less need there should be for independent friends. But adults have needs for many kinds of relationships (Weiss, 1969; also see Chapter 14). Wives and husbands frequently cannot meet all of one another's interpersonal needs. Independent friendships may be very important even to happily married people. In addition, the capacities for friendship, love, and intimacy are closely related. Those persons capable of forming happy marriages may also be those most likely to form meaningful independent friendships as well.

WOMEN AS FRIENDS
Given the socialization of women toward interpersonal concerns and their greater self-disclosure, one might think that women would be considered better friends than men. Historically, this has not been true. There have been occasional male writers who have argued that women are capable of friendship (e.g., Alger, 1879) but the typical view has been that they are not. The deprecatory view of women's capacity for friendship has not disappeared. There are more jokes and cartoons about ladies' clubs, bridge games, and the kaffeeklatch, than there are about fraternal organizations, the Friday night poker game, and "beer with the boys," though it is hard to see why men's versions of such activities should be any more important or meaningful than the women's. The devaluation of women's relationships with one another also may apply to more intimate, personal relationships.

Unfortunately, many women themselves appear to accept devaluation of their friendships with other women. Many young women unhesitatingly break commitments to a woman friend to accept any invitation from a man—an ordering of priorities that many men expect as their due, but that leaves some men (and women) dubious about the value of friendship to these women. Possibly the devaluation of friendships between women reflects a more basic devaluation of women as persons.

Relationships Between Women. Devaluing women may very well be one reason why college women often prefer men and deprecate women as friends. For some women, preferring to be with men may be less a matter of friendship than of desire to seek a spouse, or to seek status. Popularity can provide status among one's same-sex friends in college as well as in high school (homoeroticism). But other women may seek association with men because they themselves deprecate other women, or because they do not trust other women. Women themselves may share popular stereotypes, seeing other women as gossipy, or assuming all women are in competition for the attention of men. Some college women report that they prefer men friends simply because they find men more interesting than other women, who are interested only in men—itself a demeaning stereotype despite its kernel of truth.

The "Queen Bee." A different kind of competition sometimes occurs when women who have "made it"—who have achieved good jobs and social success—show no sympathy at all with younger women working toward similar goals, or with current women's movements (Staines, Tavris, & Jayaratne, 1974). These women typically worked hard to get where they are and resent efforts to ease the way for others. Even though their status places them in a position to advance the cause of women, they ironically choose not to do so. Thus their attitudes generally inhibit meaningful friendships with other achievement-oriented women.

These women are popularly called **"Queen Bees,"** by analogy to the special status of the queen in bee colonies. Unfortunately, this analogy is false. In bee society, the queen's special status serves functions crucial to survival of the hive: the continuing production of worker bees. The queen is selected and raised by workers; when her performance declines, they kill her and replace her with a new queen. The complete interdependence of queen and workers in maintaining the hive presents a picture totally at variance with the refusal of human "Queen Bees" to act interdependently with other women.

Current Developments. One concomitant of the Women's Liberation Movement is that increasing numbers of women are challenging the traditional devaluation of women in general and of women as friends in particular. Movement activities contribute to friendships among women in several ways. They provide an occasion for contact with other women, single and married, that might not occur otherwise. Consciousness-raising groups (CR, or "rap" groups) are especially helpful (Gornick, 1971). With the mutual self-disclosure they encourage, important similarities in experiences, problems, and satisfactions can be discovered: "We share the same uniqueness." There is mutual personal support, and a gang spirit similar to the one adolescent boys develop that serves much the same function of self-protective defense against a power external to the group. Sometimes these processes break down, unfortunately, and women who are "trashed" or ostracized by other women to whom they have opened themselves may find the experience exceptionally painful (Joreen, 1976). More typically, many women find valuable support in new-found friendships with other women.

The availability of mutual support may be especially important in the rapidly changing times we are experiencing. Adults as well as adolescents like to have friends in times of change. A friend who understands may be especially valuable when one is in the process of challenging old structures and habits of thinking, and in understanding and choosing new alternatives. Many men provide some of the support that women want, but many women need the help and the

deeper sense of shared similarity in attaining a shared vision that they are likely to get only from other women. More and more they are getting it. Men's groups are also increasing. Hopefully one outcome will be more and better friendships between women and women, men and men, and women and men.

FRIENDSHIP AND PERSONAL GROWTH IN ADULTHOOD

While many people previously assumed that personal growth is completed by adulthood, it is becoming increasingly clear that this is not so. People continue to grow and develop, and friends can continually play an important part in growth. It is true that much about an individual stabilizes with adulthood, and some personal attributes may have a great deal of stability over many years (e.g., Woodruff & Birren, 1972). However, personal characteristics can alter dramatically if environmental circumstances change (e.g., Useem & Useem, 1963) or when new problems and challenges are encountered. Certainly, ours is a time of change.

Need Reduction. Friends may be helpful in meeting stresses of adult life, just as they are for adolescents. Shared stress and need reduction can be powerful forces in initiating friendship (Fiebert & Fiebert, 1969). The need for friends may differ from one adult to another. Need will also be greater at some period of any person's life than at others. Beginning a new job, coping with problems such as social rejection or bereavement, or periods of intense intrapersonal conflict require changes in patterns of feeling, thinking, and living. These times of stress are also times of potential personal change, and friends may be invaluable in meeting the challenge of growth. So obvious is the value of friendship for need reduction that it is tempting to evaluate its importance primarily in these terms. However, to do so would be to have an incomplete view of human beings and their interpersonal relationships. Friendship is perhaps more important for what it can *add* to a person's life, for expanding and growing, rather than for helping with personal deficits.

Enrichment. With adulthood, there is less uniform pressure toward friendship than there was in adolescence. At the same time adults have developed more adequate strengths for coping with life. According to personality theorists such as Maslow and Rogers, mature people do not *need* friendships. However, they will usually *choose* to develop friendships as a spontaneous expression of their interest and involvement in the world around them. To the degree that adult friendships are based on mature choice rather than need, they may grow in importance for the enrichment of life through discovery and pursuit of new interests and ideas as well as through increased understanding and acceptance of self and others, beyond what is required for simple existence. Friendships may contribute to the *enhancement* of life as well as to its maintenance.

SUMMARY

Friendship is defined here as a form of love, an intimate, personal, caring relationship. The capacities necessary for friendship develop during childhood. In adolescence, friendships play a crucial part in helping young people to cope with change, to clarify their own identity, and to develop understanding of others. Although this is generally true for both girls and boys, there are some differences: girls' friendships tend to focus on two or three close relationships while boys' first loyalties tend to be to their gangs. Interpersonal exploration through friendships may be more prevalent among girls than boys. Adolescent girls are likely to show more mature understanding of friendships than adolescent boys. The capacity for intimacy develops first in same-sex friendships and then, in later adolescence, generalizes to other love relationships. Consequently, love relationships in adulthood are facilitated by successful adolescent friendships.

Friendships are most likely to develop with persons with whom one shares particular similarities, so that there is a sense of "shared uniqueness" between the friends. The formation of friendships is facilitated by personality attributes that promote openness to others, either openness to differences from oneself (low dogmatism) or willingness to reveal oneself (high self-disclosure).

Some people believe women are incapable of friendship, and some women themselves accept this view. Yet women do form close friendships with one another, maybe increasingly so with the strengthening of bonds encouraged by the women's movement. Close friendships also develop between women and men, although some obstacles make between-sex friendships less likely than within-sex friendships. Throughout adulthood, friendships continue to provide both support in times of stress and, perhaps more important, enrichment and expansion of self for both women and men.

CHAPTER
11
INDIVIDUAL AND
INTERPERSONAL ACHIEVEMENT

COMPONENTS OF ACHIEVEMENT MOTIVATION
HOPE OF SUCCESS
SOCIAL CONCERNS
EXPECTANCIES AND ASPIRATIONS

FEAR OF FAILURE
SEX DIFFERENCES
IMPLICATIONS

FEAR OF SUCCESS
FAILURE CAN MEAN SUCCESS
INCIDENCE AND MEANING
OTHERS' REACTIONS TO A WOMAN'S SUCCESS
MEN'S SUPPORT

PERSONAL RESPONSIBILITY
SELF VIEWS
IMPLICATIONS OF ATTRIBUTIONS
OTHERS' PERCEPTIONS OF RESPONSIBILITY

DEVELOPMENT OF ACHIEVEMENT ORIENTATION
PARENTAL BEHAVIOR
MATERNAL WARMTH VS. HOSTILITY
Measurement Problems
PERMISSIVENESS-RESTRICTIVENESS
ENCOURAGEMENT OF INDEPENDENCE AND ACHIEVEMENT
MODELING

THE IMPACT OF SEX ROLES
COMPETITION AMONG ACHIEVEMENT GOALS
AMBIGUITIES ABOUT ACHIEVEMENT REALMS
BRAINS VS. POPULARITY
FOCUSING ON INTERPERSONAL ACHIEVEMENT
The Marriage Connection
OTHERS' MIXED MESSAGES

ACHIEVING WOMEN
ACHIEVING WITHIN THE TRADITIONAL FEMININE ROLE
VICARIOUS ACHIEVEMENT
Implications

ACHIEVING WITHIN CAREERS
CAREER RELEVANT ATTRIBUTES
ABILITY
INTERESTS, VALUES, AND NEEDS
COMMUNAL INTERESTS

PERSONAL AND SOCIAL ADJUSTMENT

SUMMARY

Achievement is conventionally defined by psychologists as competition with a standard of excellence, or the desire to accomplish something difficult, to master objects, people or ideas, and to do so as rapidly and as independently as possible (e.g., Murray, 1938). Doing well is a goal. Obviously, there are many kinds of activities in which one may strive for independent mastery and many ways of demonstrating personal competence and **effectance** in dealing with the world (see, White, 1960). However, most people in our society—including psychologists—have a relatively narrow view of achievement, centering on academic and occupational success as well as personal victory over others in competition for the "top rung." By this narrow definition, women do not achieve as much as men. Instead, women typically are encouraged to express their personal competence and achievement concerns in interpersonal behaviors that are not culturally defined as achievements in our society.

COMPONENTS OF ACHIEVEMENT MOTIVATION

Women are markedly underrepresented in various lists of "achievers," such as lists of people of eminence, genius, and American Men of Science (recently changed to include women in the title). Even in fields considered traditionally appropriate for women, the leaders often are men rather than women. Typical **socialization,** based on **sex roles,** interposes a series of red lights for women, and green lights for men on their routes to conventional achievement goals. Not all women want the delay of the red lights, nor do all men want to be pressured to take advantage of the green light opportunities. The specific traits included in role stereotypes reflect the societal pressures on men to achieve (e.g., competitive, dominating, assertive, independent) and on women not to attempt independent achievement (e.g., dependent, passive, compliant). We can better appreciate some of the ways in which women's achievement striving is unnecessarily inhibited by considering some basic components of achievement orientation as well as some relevant developmental antecedents. The typical "high

achiever" has high hope of success, assumes personal responsibility for success, and also displays low fear of failure and low fear of success. Women often show the reverse pattern.

HOPE OF SUCCESS

A major requirement for effective performance is that a **hope of success** be aroused: The person perceives the situation as one providing an opportunity for a success that is personally meaningful. People differ in their ability to see the opportunity for success as well as in what kind of success is most meaningful to them (e.g., Veroff, 1965). In a discussion situation, for example, a typical "high achiever" is likely to see the opportunity to demonstrate competence and intelligence (or to brag about previous achievements!). A person with different achievement goals might see the same situation as providing an opportunity to use social skills, to discover what another person is really like, or to offer comfort. Both individuals are concerned about success, but they have different personal definitions of what is meaningful success. Within the conventional perspective of achievement, however, only the first person is likely to be considered an achiever.

Social Concerns. Women's achievement needs have often been said to be "channeled into" or "in the service of" their **affiliation needs**—that is, their needs to be close to accepting others and to please them. This contention has been based in part on the early work with the McClelland procedure of assessing and studying achievement motivation (McClelland et al., 1953; Atkinson, 1958). Achievement motivation is defined according to the amount of achievement imagery (themes related to achievement) occurring in stories told by subjects about pictures like those from the **Thematic Apperception Test** (TAT). Typically, men's achievement motive, or hope of success, is aroused when they are told that a task done immediately before the TAT measurement is relevant to leadership, intelligence, and occupational success. Women's scores do not consistently increase in such a situation.

Furthermore, the achievement concerns that

do occur in stories told by women usually are for *males* in the pictures rather than for females. Thus, women's achievement motivation has been said to be projected onto men. However, women's achievement scores *are* increased by instructions that call attention to interpersonal success (popularity) rather than to occupational leadership, whereas men subjects are not influenced by information about social acceptance.

From such findings, one need not conclude, as many have, that women achieve only to win social approval or that they are not *really* achievement oriented. One can equally well conclude that women prefer to achieve in ways they consider personally relevant, such as affiliation, and that other expressions of their achievement needs have been inhibited. The importance of relevance to **self-concept** is shown by the fact that women who define conventional achievement behavior as an acceptable part of a woman's role do in fact show the expected increase in achievement scores to "standard" (i.e., male) instructions, engage in achievement behaviors, and see their own achievement as important (Donelson, 1973). Furthermore, these women attribute achievement concerns to the females in the TAT pictures.

Expectancies and Aspirations. To expect to succeed facilitates performance. Across various age groups and many measures of conventional achievement, females have lower expectancies of success than do males (Stein & Bailey, 1973; Wylie, 1968). This is true even when the actual performance or task ability of females and males is equal, or even when the females are superior by objective standards (such as being more intelligent and having better grades but expecting lower academic performance). Obviously, females can and do achieve at higher levels than they expect to, but their expectancies interfere and pose internal pressures that contribute to unrealistic self-deprecation and lack of confidence.

Girls and women also tend to have problems with aspirations. **Level of aspiration** (LOA or LA) is the level of accomplishment that people attempt or want to attain (rather than what they *expect* to accomplish). In general, men, and espe-

cially men high in need for achievement, have realistic LOAs. For example, they select tasks of moderate difficulty so that success is possible; this reflects their own skills rather than the ease of the task. Furthermore, they shift their LOAs realistically on the basis of feedback about their performance. In contrast, women generally and low achieving men are more likely to choose either very high or very low LOAs and to make unpredictable, inappropriate shifts when given feedback, such as *lowering* LOA after a *success*. Such patterns in expectancy and LOA are likely to be associated with fear about both success and failure.

FEAR OF FAILURE

A person may be high on hope of success, but also high, or higher, on **fear of failure.** Such a person may want to succeed but has severe fears about consequences (e.g., shame, embarrassment) of possible failure. Fear of failure is most likely to occur when it is clear that performance will be evaluated, when failure is a distinct possibility, and when the failure may be viewed as a result of lack of abilities. It is shown in anxiety about performance and a tendency to withdraw from achievement situations. If the withdrawal desire is acted upon, the act of withdrawing is reinforced by anxiety reduction; thus, one is likely to continue to withdraw. The withdrawal may be physical; one simply does not get into situations in which achievement is relevant. Or, it may be psychological, for example, by coming to perceive fewer situations as relevant to achievement.

When a person with a high fear of failure must confront an achievement situation, psychological avoidance may be shown by extreme LOAs and risk taking. On the one hand, if LOA is low enough, or if the task is an easy one, then success is virtually assured. On the other hand, failure to meet a very high standard or to master a very difficult task is "nothing to be ashamed of." In fact, there may be some social approval for aiming high and trying the impossible. In brief, people whose hope of success is higher than their fear of failure have moderate, realistic LOAs and choose tasks of moderate, realistic difficulty. The reverse is true for people whose fear of failure exceeds their hope of success.

Sex Differences. Females tend to be more anxious about failure than are males, and their anxiety increases during elementary school years more than that of males (Stein & Bailey, 1973). Thus, their expression of hope of success will tend to differ because of the differing levels of competing fear of failure. Some evidence suggests that simply stating an expectancy about performance heightens girls' anxiety about evaluation and results in a drop of later expectancies (Dweck & Gilliard, 1975). However, girls can deal as effectively as boys with perceived failure under many conditions. Under other conditions, anxiety about evaluation may be debilitating, particularly when lower levels of anxiety are required for optimum task performance.

Many young girls and women obviously do achieve in spite of their anxiety about failure. However, generally, the fear has more easily observable effects on the behavior of females than of males. Sex differences appear early and are relatively persistent (e.g., Kagan & Moss, 1962). Withdrawal from potential failure situations was stable for girls over ages 6 to 14 years, but not for boys; similarly, the relations of withdrawal in adulthood with indices from childhood were generally high for women but negligible for men.

The stability of fear of failure for females relative to males is likely to reflect the fact that withdrawal brings social censure for males and comes to be unacceptable in their own views of themselves. The boy who avoids is noticed. Socialization pressures push him to deny the anxiety or to control it sufficiently to face the feared challenge, possibly mastering it and gaining rewards that moderate the anxiety. In contrast, the girl who avoids is more likely to be neglected. Her achievement strivings often are not taken seriously anyway; so her avoidance of achievement situations is more easily accepted as "the way girls are," or "the way girls are supposed to be." As with other aspects of sex-role socialization (Chapter 8), boys experience greater pressure for

role adherence, but the girls' temporary luxury of freedom from pressure may cause later problems for her, and for her family.

Implications. Fear of failure can obviously influence vocational decisions, choices of college and of curriculum, and other career related decisions. Without realizing they are doing so, many college women aim "beneath their abilities" because they fear failure. Among women who fear failure, those who suffer low risks are likely to be eliminated during college and early occupational involvement, leaving a preponderance of high risk takers (e.g., Bernstein, 1974). There is anecdotal evidence that seriously committed undergraduate students, as well as graduate and professional women, tend to have higher LOAs and be more perfectionistic than comparable men (e.g., choose a particularly difficult term paper topic or research project). This takes the burden of responsibility for failure off of them, since lack of success may be attributed to the task difficulty rather than to lack of ability or conscientiousness. However, when they succeed, as they often do, they do so at the cost of an increased psychological burden relative to easier success on tasks of more moderate and realistic difficulty levels.

Fear of failure also has clear implications for women who are not involved in academic or career situations. It can interfere with effectiveness in performing the traditional role of manager of the household, caregiver of children, and partner of a spouse. The fear may be shown in apprehensions about *any* position of responsibility, low confidence in decisions about the family members and family purchases, and anxiety in social situations in which negative judgments are possible (Kagan & Moss, 1962).

FEAR OF SUCCESS

Failure Can Mean Success. **Fear of success** is the expectancy of negative consequences as a result of success in achievement situations, particularly competitive ones. The fear may sound bizarre. However, any task performance occurs in a broad social context, or within a person who has more than one concern in life. A task success, or failure, has implications for other facets of a person's life. Of immediate relevance is the fact that success on a conventional achievement task does not always bring social success, especially for women. Thus, fear of success is closely associated with fear of failure: To succeed in one way, on an achievement task, is felt to mean failure in another task, causing censure from other people or from one's self. The response to task success is often a result of role-related expectations. Some people are expected to fail and their acceptance is contingent upon failure; they inhibit their performance so that they *do* fail (Klinger & McNelley, 1969). Individuals for whom success is not expected may come to fear success; they may also hope for failure (the rewards of failure outweigh the rewards of task success). The hopes and fears may be conscious. With repeated experience, however, people may automatically decrease effort or undermine their own effort toward success without awareness of their actions.

Incidence and Meaning. Negative concerns about the success of a woman are expressed by some women in the stories they tell to **verbal leads** (rather than pictorial stimuli as in previously mentioned research). One frequently used lead is, "After first term finals Anne finds herself at the top of her med school class." There is continuing debate about the incidence of such fear and its meaning (e.g., Levine & Crumrine, 1975; Bernstein, 1974). Some investigators report a high frequency (65 percent or higher) among college women and among young girls (e.g., Horner, 1972; Hoffman, 1974b; Monahan, Kuhn, & Shaver, 1974). Others report a fairly low incidence and note that women give more positive than negative themes in such stories (Spence, 1974).

There is reasonable consensus, however, that when the fear does occur in women, it is because of fear of social rejection. (When it occurs in men, for men's success in the verbal leads, it is usually a matter of questioning the value of success, for example, "What does it mean?") Some psychologists interpret the negative reaction to women's success as a result of women's feelings that success is "unfeminine," and therefore to be avoided. This may be true for some women. However, it is clear that sex-role expectations are social *realities*. Women do experience pressures against achievement, even by the same loved ones (or professional colleagues) who may also be encouraging achievement. They also face instrumental problems of integrating achievement and affiliative concerns, as discussed later. Thus, many of the negative concerns expressed in stories about a woman's success deal with such practical matters (see Spence, 1974). The woman must weigh the benefits of success against the costs, part of which involve the reactions of others.

Others' Reactions to a Woman's Success. Females' fear of social censure for success is quite realistic. Often even the "success" is denied. As discussed in Chapter 15, identical credentials or professional products are evaluated lower when a woman's name, rather than a man's, is attached to them. Furthermore, a female with an acknowledged success often is deprecated. Male subjects (10-year-olds and college students) have been shown to react negatively to female success, just as some women fear (Monahan, Kuhn, & Shaver, 1974; Spence, 1974). The young boys showed clear hostility about a woman's success (in a verbal lead), often with rather bizarre sexual themes: The woman who did well in medical school was depicted as later becoming a prostitute! College men were especially negative about the success of a single female: She succeeded out of loneliness and was often visited by a physical catastrophe that ended her career or her life.

Men's Support. On the brighter side, not all men react with censure to women's success, and many actually encourage and reward it. Men college students did not react as favorably as women to a verbal lead of a woman succeeding, but they were less demeaning and more accepting of her success than images of chauvinists would suggest (Spence, 1974). Additionally, in many of the men's stories, the negative aspect was threat to self-image or self-doubts created in her husband or boyfriend, rather than adverse statements about the achieving woman herself.

Support by a boyfriend or husband does decrease fear of success (Horner, 1972). Whether the man encourages the woman's personal achievement striving or not, attachment to a man (being engaged or married) lowers fear of success in women (both black and white; Puryear & Mednick, 1974). Similarly, older married women returning to college had significantly less fear of success imagery than did the younger unmarried women of typical college ages; women who had children had less fear imagery than those without children (Tomlinson-Keasey, 1974). The conditions under which these two groups showed fear also differed. The older women were most fearful when either a male or a female cue figure was in a role-inconsistent situation. In contrast, female success in either a role-consistent or role-inconsistent area elicited fears from the younger women. Thus, the younger women are apparently rejecting roles as a basis for making decisions, but still have concerns about success. Some women see achievement as conflicting with affiliation; some comfort of success in affiliation with men enables a freeing of their achievement concerns.

PERSONAL RESPONSIBILITY

Assuming personal responsibility for success is another ingredient of successful achievement orientation. When people do not accept personal responsibility for their success, their experience of gratification is minimized, and the success does not influence future behavior in advantageous ways, for example, in increased self-confidence, realistic shifts in LOA and expectancy, or seeking more success. Recent research on sex differences in attributions, or "explanations," for the reasons for success or failure holds much promise for illuminating some of the specific ways in which achievement is facilitated or impaired. Again, generally the pattern for females interferes with effective achievement strivings.

Self-Views. Girls and women tend to approach the negative and avoid the positive, while the reverse is true for boys and men (Chapter 8). Gen-

erally, females seem more ready to assume responsibility for their failures relative to their successes than are males (Stein & Bailey, 1973; Nicholls, 1975; Dweck & Reppucci, 1973). Throughout the school years, girls assume more responsibility for failure than do boys; the gap increases in adolescence, congruent with the findings that girls become more anxious and concerned about failure as they progress through school. For example, girls think it is their fault (e.g., not studying enough) when they do not do well on a test, while boys "explain away" their deficient performance (e.g., the test was too hard or unfair). Essentially, girls' attributions for failure are self-derogatory while those of boys are defensive and self-protective. For example, fourth grade girls, but not boys, attributed perceived failure on preliminary trials of a laboratory task to their poor ability more than they attributed successes to their ability (Nicholls, 1975). In contrast, boys more than girls attributed failure to bad luck, and luck was more relevant to them after failure than after success.

Similar results have been reported with college students, though there is also evidence that women feel personal responsibility for neither failure nor success (Feather, 1969; Deaux & Emswiller, 1974). Often college women "excuse" hard earned honor grades by claiming, "I really lucked out on that one." Concomitantly, women prefer chance tasks while men prefer skill tasks, as shown by observations of the kinds of games they select at country fairs as well as in laboratory situations (Deaux, White, & Farris, 1975).

Implications of Attributions. The pattern of self-derogatory attributions for females and self-protective ones for males is likely related to some of the sex differences in specific ways of dealing with achievement situations and reflects the content of social pressures. For example, the differences in explanations of success and failure may contribute to the previously mentioned differences in expectancies of success after preliminary failure (Nicholls, 1975). If males can see their failure as due to bad luck (even on a task defined as one of skill!) and assume that luck can change, it will be easier for them to have higher expectancies for later trials and to persist. Conversely, girls' self-denegration of their abilities in response to early failure would be a basis for lower expectancies for performance and withdrawal from a skill-achievement situation when possible. Yet, when females (college women) are winning at a skill game, they are inclined to quit while ahead, perhaps "before luck runs out." Fear of failure seems responsible, in conjunction with attributing success to luck and failure to poor ability.

In view of the extensive pressures on the typical boy and man for recognized achievement, their self-protective attitude is facilitative. In view of social expectations about girls and women, their reactions in achievement situations are not surprising.

Others' Perceptions of Responsibility. Although a woman's views of responsibility may not be realistic by criteria of "objective facts," they do match well with the "social facts" of how other people react. Women and men subjects attribute the success of a man's doing well on a masculine task to his skill; a woman with the same performance on the same task is considered "just lucky" (Deaux and Emswiller, 1974). The reverse is *not* true for a feminine task: Males are generally seen as more skillful than females, regardless of what they are doing and in spite of equal attainment. Different perceptions of male and female performances appear to be well established in both girls and boys by the fifth grade; subjects in the fifth, eighth, and eleventh grades and in college did not differ in their attributions (Etaugh & Brown, 1975).

Furthermore, apparently a woman must use a "masculine" way to accomplish what she does if she is to be given credit for her achievement. That is, performing a "masculine" task in a logically assertive way was seen as indicative of a better performance and more deserving of reward than accomplishing the *same* consequence in a sensitive, intuitive way societally seen as a "feminine" mode of performance (Taynor & Deaux, 1975).

The low perception of a woman's level of accomplishments and the denial of the contribution of her skill and intelligence is reflected in perceptions of occupations. Ratings of prestige and desirability of selected occupations (architect, college professor, lawyer, physician, scientist) decreased when subjects were told that more women will be entering the occupation than previously (Touhey, 1974). On the positive side, the emphasis of the past few years on redefinitions of what is possible and appropriate for women may be having an effect in increasing women's positive feelings about success, which suggests an attribution of their success to themselves, rather than "just luck" (Feather, 1975).

DEVELOPMENT OF ACHIEVEMENT ORIENTATION

So far, we have seen that women are less likely than men to exhibit high hope of success, personal responsibility for success, or low fear of failure and success. Some light is cast on why this is so by evidence about socialization, much of which is related to sex-role expectations.

PARENTAL BEHAVIOR

Even young infants exhibit an **effectance motive** (White, 1960) within which achievement orientation develops. Parents can facilitate their child's achievement striving and sense of competence and self-confidence by providing guidance, appropriately timing opportunities for the child to practice new skills, and by demonstrating their approval for success. For both girls and boys, achievement orientation is enhanced by **authoritative** parental behavior. The authoritative pattern involves sensitivity to the individual child's maturity and abilities, clear communication of expectations, and use of reason with some punishment but not with restrictive or coercive behavior toward the child (e.g., Baumrind, 1971). A parent with this style realistically encourages the child to perform at increasingly higher levels and effectively reinforces successful efforts. More specific parental behaviors that affect the development of achievement orientation include warmth, permissiveness, independence and achievement training, and modeling.

Maternal Warmth vs. Hostility. Since the child development literature focuses mainly on the traditional socializing agent—the mother—most studies of "parental" warmth actually concern the mother's behavior. Much of the evidence indicates that a *moderate* level of warmth or nurturance fosters achievement behavior in girls. Perhaps it is readily understandable that cold, rejecting, and punitive parents generally will have dependent, low achieving children who have many other problems as well (Chapter 9). It may not be so obvious that parents can overdo their nurturing: too much affection and protection diminishes children's achievement effectiveness.

Mothers with high levels of babying, protectiveness, and warmth generally have daughters who later tend to be passive and conforming and to withdraw from achievement tasks (Kagan & Moss, 1962; Crandall & Battle, 1970). Less affectionate and nurturant mothers, on the other hand, tend to have high achieving girls. The results for boys seem to indicate the opposite pattern. The sons of highly protective mothers later became higher achievers than the sons of less nurturant mothers. Since researchers label this nurturant aspect of maternal behavior "warmth vs. hostility," these findings often have been interpreted to mean that different dynamics are involved in girls' and boys' achievements, and that high achieving girls had "hostile" mothers whereas high achieving boys had "warm" ones (Bardwick, 1971). One might thus conclude that a mother should reject her daughter to help her become a high achiever! Such a conclusion, in addition to violating humanistic ideals, masks the subtleties involved.

Measurement Problems. First, the full range of the "warmth–hostility" dimension probably was not represented in the research. Parents willing to cooperate in such a **longitudinal study** are not likely to be people with extreme hostility and rejection toward their children. Therefore, mothers who scored as hostile were probably at a level better considered moderate in terms of the amount of warmth exhibited toward their children; they seemed "hostile" because truly rejecting mothers were not in the study. Other studies of **authoritarian** parents, who often use coercive punishment, indicate that hostile parental behavior actually is associated with very low autonomy and low achievement-oriented behavior in the children (Baumrind, 1971).

There is also a possibility that the same behavior on the part of a mother may be coded differently by psychologists, according to whether it is expressed toward a boy or a girl (Hoffman, 1972). At the time much of the early data on child-rearing practices were collected, researchers were less aware than currently of possible biases from their own stereotypes. Given the popular but incorrect belief that a girl is more fragile than a boy, an interaction that appears to be "high hostile" with a girl might be considered "moderate" or even "low hostile" with a presumably more lusty young boy. Conversely, given cultural expectations about the appropriateness of protection for girls, what seems "low protective" of a girl may seem average or even high for a boy. Keeping in mind these concerns, we conclude that mothers with a moderate level of behavioral warmth and protectiveness are more likely to foster achievement in their daughters than are overly nurturant or overly rejecting mothers. Perhaps a somewhat higher level of warmth enhances achievement in boys, because it counteracts the severity of general social pressures for high performance (Stein & Bailey, 1973).

Permissiveness–Restrictiveness. The dimension of parental permissiveness or restrictiveness involves the number of rules imposed about aggression, sexual expression, damage of property, and so forth. Children of highly restrictive parents often are overly obedient and conforming, or are defiantly rebellious. They generally do not develop independence, responsibility, or leadership qualities, and they tend to have low achievement aspirations (Bronfenbrenner, 1961a; Douvan & Adelson, 1966). On the other hand, children of more permissive parents tend to be more achievement oriented, particularly when the permissiveness is associated with demands for mature behavior.

Encouragement of Independence and Achievement.

Realistically timed independence pressures facilitate achievement behaviors. However, when independence training involves unreasonable expectations or parental rejection for failures, the children are likely to become fearful and reluctant to participate in achievement situations. In fact, fear of failure occurs when parents encourage achievement, but do not reward success while punishing failure (Teevan & McGhee, 1972). Mothers of highly achieving girls and boys attempt to accelerate the children's development by expecting realistically higher levels of achievement and explicitly reinforcing achievement efforts, often with affection (Kagan & Moss, 1962; Crandall & Battle, 1970). Fathers of highly achieving sons apparently behave similarly in providing general encouragement but expecting the boy to perform on his own at a reasonably high level (Rosen & D'Andrade, 1959; Hermans, ter Laak, & Maes, 1972). The father's role in his daughter's development is less clear, although there is some indication that his encouraging and rewarding achievement helps a girl integrate achievement in her self-concept, particularly if the mother is a rather traditional woman (Stein & Bailey, 1973).

Modeling.

Throughout their development children are bombarded with models of achieving *men*. The scarcity of models of women whom society defines as achievers conveys a message about the appropriateness or likelihood of conventionally defined achievement for girls. Generally, girls who identify with mothers conforming to the traditional feminine role show low achievement aspirations (Douvan & Adelson, 1966). However, if the mother is a dissatisfied housewife, she may be a negative model who provides a powerful incentive to the daughter to avoid such a life for herself (Lipman–Blumen, 1972). The daughter who observes frequent unhappy housecleanings may have as much impetus to seek a career as the one who observes a happy mother who works outside the home.

Career commitment among girls frequently is related to having a mother who works outside of the home (Astin, Suniewick, & Dweck, 1971). Among career-oriented university women, for example, four-fifths reported that their mothers had worked outside the home, compared with one-half of the noncareer women (Almquist & Angrist, 1970). Among women doctorates, the most productive in all fields tended to be daughters of working mothers (Astin, 1969).

Why should the mother's working or not matter? As a group, mothers who seek outside employment may initially be more independent and assertive than their homebound counterparts, or they may develop these qualities through the work experience. Whatever the working mothers' motives or qualities, she does demonstrate in a tangible way to her daughter that women can take independent action and exhibit competencies outside of the home while still being "true" enough to the maternal role to have a home and child. In addition, the sheer absence of the mother during work hours may provide opportunities for the daughter to develop her own independence and assume personal responsibility for her own activities and perhaps those of siblings as well.

THE IMPACT OF SEX ROLES

Parental behavior that overemphasizes traditional **sex-typing** can inhibit children's achievement behavior. This is pronounced for girls but also true for boys. Because of sex-role expectations, parents often consider female infants as more fragile and more in need of protection than males, despite the girls' greater maturity and sturdiness (Hoffman, 1972). Although such parents may not actually discourage their daughter's early independence and achievement strivings, they generally do not encourage or apply effective pressure for the behavior as much as for a son.

As a result of culturally sanctioned overprotection and too much nurturance, many girls do not experience achievement opportunities until success is virtually assured. For example, mothers tend to set later ages for granting girls autonomy on such tasks as using scissors without adult supervision and playing away from home for long periods (Collard, 1964). Parents also report allowing boys to cross busy streets by themselves earlier, although boys generally are not motorically more advanced than girls—in fact, their greater motoric impulsivity might actually make this more dangerous. Such delayed achievement opportunities tend to reduce the girls' pride in the accomplishment and the likelihood of their developing realistic achievement goals and finding such striving satisfying. With inadequate opportunity to practice achievement behaviors in challenging situations, girls also will not learn to cope with the stress involved in mastery striving. Thus, they are more likely to avoid conventional achievement situations.

Though they sanction different treatment for boys, cultural expectations can also damage a boy's achievement orientation. Fearing that nurturance will make their son a sissy, some parents provide too little warmth and encouragement, thus depressing their boy's achievement behavior. In addition, when parents expect accomplishments before their "little man" is sufficiently mature, he often fails and thus does not develop positive feelings about achievement endeavors. If they also punish his failure and do not reward his successes, he is likely to develop fear of failure (Teevan & McGhee, 1972).

COMPETITION AMONG ACHIEVEMENT GOALS

Though they may be influenced to varying degrees by sex-typed expectations, achievement-oriented parents tend to encourage and reward both their daughters and their sons for mastering bodily coordination, learning basic skills, and performing well in school. But even in early socialization there are different emphases in the content of achievement expectations for girls and boys. Girls are expected to develop social skills—to be able to assess others' feelings and respond to them in helpful and supportive ways. Interpersonal sensitivity is not emphasized for boys, who are encouraged to focus more exclusively on developing specific personal skills relevant to later occupational achievement.

The socialization pressures produce the intended effects. Females do tend to develop greater affiliation and interpersonal skills than do males (Chapter 9). But the negative cultural bias about communal attunement relative to individualistic agentic concerns appears in some theories of achievement motivation. As noted earlier, some psychologists claim that female achievement behavior results from a need for social approval rather than from "intrinsic," or internal, achievement motivation. In this view, females achieve in order to gain others' approval and love, whereas males achieve in order to satisfy their own standards of excellence.

If this were true, then females would exhibit low achievement effort in situations where they received no social rewards, and they would show high effort when they received praise. But there are no consistent sex differences reported in the large research literature on the effects of social reinforcement (Stein & Bailey, 1973). Others' approval and self-approval from meeting internalized standards are involved in the achievement behavior of both females and males. What has not been acknowledged in the past is that interpersonal relations are often major areas of achievement for females. Women develop internal standards of excellence about social relations and strive to attain these.

AMBIGUITIES ABOUT ACHIEVEMENT REALMS

The message that women should develop social skills comes through loud and clear. It is less clear whether they should develop these skills *in addition to* or *instead of* other competencies that apparently have more direct occupational relevance. At least until early adolescence, it appears that girls are expected to develop social skills *in addition to* other school-related skills. School achievement alone is considered inappropriate for girls. In one study of fifth- and sixth-grade children, for example, teachers rewarded bright girls who exhibited socially oriented achievement behavior, whereas they tended to reject the bright girls who focused only on school work (Sears, 1963). Among high school students, the girls who hoped to combine career and marriage were more popular with their peers than were the career-oriented girls who were not interested in marriage (Turner, 1964).

Brains vs. Popularity. At about the time of adolescence, however, messages about girls' achievement goals seem to get more mixed and confusing. Fear of success becomes more likely, as does withdrawal from achievement situations because of fear of failure. Girls are experiencing increasing pressure to be nonassertive, dependent, and noncompetitive—qualities that are in conflict with achievement efforts in intellectual and occupational contexts. Of course, these qualities also interfere with effectiveness in interpersonal relations, although the conflict is not so immediately obvious as in the occupational sphere (Chapter 9).

Focusing on Interpersonal Achievement. In an attempt to cope with the pressures and conflict and to be rewarded by others—especially boys—some achievement-oriented girls focus on social skills *instead of* other school accomplishments. For example, one study reported sex differences among high school underachievers (students whose grade performance was below the level expected of them on the basis of aptitude). The girls had shown normal levels of achievement until junior high school, when their grades began to drop; the boys, however, had been chronically poor in school from third grade on (Shaw & Mc-Cuen, 1960). Thus, underachieving girls and boys appear to have different problems, and the girls' problems seem related to sex-role conformity and to their perception that "brainy" girls are less popular with boys (Matthews & Tiedeman, 1964).

The Marriage Connection. The increased emphasis on achievement in social skills to the relative neglect of occupationally relevant ones is consistent with the belief of many adolescent girls that marriage is to be their major, if not only, life commitment. At least in surveys prior to the

1970s, girls do not report realistic career plans (Douvan & Adelson, 1966; Turner, 1964). This is probably due in part to their assumption that they must remain flexible enough to fit the plans of their usually unknown future spouse. Because of the desired flexibility in self-definition, adolescent girls' identity remains diffuse and ungelled while that of boys solidifies with the help of their need to make specific career plans. It is also true that girls are simply not taught to think seriously or realistically about any career other than marriage. Whatever response they give to "And what do you want to be when you grow up?" that is other than "A mommy" is likely to bring adult chuckles rather than encouragement and guidance. With career education more prevalent now in school curricula, hopefully fewer college women will be unprepared to make decisions between major lifestyle alternatives.

Others' Mixed Messages. Even young women who begin college with career objectives find it difficult to cope with mixed messages from parents and others. One girl who was in the top 1 percent of her university class commented: "First my parents encourage me to get grades and then they worry I'm not meeting any boys or having any fun. When I do go out and have fun, they worry about my grades. I feel pulled two ways" (Ross, 1963, pp. 23–24). As their daughters progress through college, many parents apply greater pressure toward marriage goals. Professors, too, deliver ambiguous messages. Sometimes they encourage women's intellectual performance, but they may be reluctant to facilitate women's actual professional involvement (Chapter 15). Women graduate students report put-downs such as the following from male faculty (Harris, 1970):

You're so cute. I can't see you as a professor of anything. A pretty girl like you will certainly get married; why don't you stop with an M.A.?
Why don't you find a rich husband and give all this up?

The impact of such discouragement may be far-reaching, particularly if the women's career goals are not supported by the men important to them. Consistent with concepts about fear of success, the career commitment of many women wanes during college years, whereas their desire for the conventional marriage life-style increases (Cross, 1968). In addition, according to a recent study, adult women involved in the homemaker role exclusively and those in traditional feminine occupations reported that the "significant men in their lives" tended to hold the conventional view that gender roles should be distinctly different. However, women in nontraditional occupations reported that their partners shared their **androgynous** view of gender roles and supported their life-style (Hawley, 1971).

ACHIEVING WOMEN

As a result of differences in their competencies and life experiences, women develop a variety of techniques for engaging in achievement activities and integrating their achievement striving with their roles as women. Some women emphasize achievement in various aspects of the traditional feminine role and accompanying life-style. Others pursue academic and occupational goals instead of, or in addition to, the goals traditionally expected of them.

ACHIEVING WITHIN THE TRADITIONAL FEMININE ROLE

For some women, focusing their achievement strivings within the traditional domestic role is a genuine preference and a source of continuing challenge and satisfaction. They value themselves and what they do even though they may describe themselves as "just a housewife." But given society's narrow, agentic view of achievement and lack of recognition of the competencies involved in the housewife role, these women need a strong sense of personal worth as well as the continued respect of their families to counteract the social devaluation.

Other women who adopt the traditional role may also appreciate its challenges and satisfactions but still feel frustrated because their other potentialities are underdeveloped. Many of these women take advantage of opportunities to develop and apply their skills outside the home by seeking employment, taking courses, or engaging in political or volunteer community work. Some dissatisfied housewives, however, do not pursue or find satisfaction in such activities. They remain homecentered mainly from a fear of failure or a fear of success, such as a belief that competing with males is inappropriate or that success may cause rejection by others. Their sense of personal "unfinished business" may have serious consequences for themselves and their families (Chapter 13).

Vicarious Achievement. A woman whose growth is frustrated in the domestic role may engage in **vicarious achievement** behavior: Feeling she cannot directly express her own achievement needs, she may try to gain satisfaction through the accomplishments of her husband and children. Traditionally in American culture this has been considered an appropriate way for a woman to gain recognition—women often attribute achievement concerns to males, not females, in TAT pictures. In this social system, a woman's social status is anchored to her husband's occupation—for example, "the doctor's wife." The woman often encourages this state of affairs by delaying development of her own self-definition and identity until *after* she selects a husband.

Paradoxically, her husband's job might call for less diversified executive skills than she herself uses in monitoring the household, in planning family expenditures, time budgeting her many tasks, supervising the children's activities, and coordinating a complicated car pool to get the children to music lessons, scout meetings, and so on. By performing all of these family support tasks, she makes a crucial contribution in freeing her husband's time and facilitating his occupational productivity. Often, however, her contribution is not fully appreciated and she does not receive credit for her many jobs well done. What *she* achieves is *not* considered an achievement. Her reward is to bask in the reflected glory of her husband's accomplishments. What *he* achieves is an achievement. Thus, it is not surprising that in studying "Some Aspects of Women's Ambition," a sociologist measured women's eminence ambitions by inquiring about their standards for their future husbands' success (Turner, 1964). Even highly educated women seem to accept the societal standard (e.g., Lipman-Blumen, 1972). Most alumnae studied in a national survey of college graduates indicated that the kind of success they most desired for themselves involved being the "wife whose husband becomes very prominent" and being the "mother of several highly accomplished children" (Rossi, 1965).

Implications. The capacity to feel deep pride and pleasure in the accomplishments of loved ones and to share their satisfaction represents a communal togetherness that seems worth encouraging for all persons, male and female. But the capacity for love and respect of others presupposes a love and respect for oneself. If gratification in the achievement of others is a *substitute* for gratification with one's own achievement, then there is likely to be damage to self as well as to the people on to whom the achievement is projected. Vicarious achievement striving easily involves pressure on others to achieve at high and perhaps unattainable levels the success one really desires for oneself. Many husbands and children thus become unwitting victims of achievement pressures that are not their own, and they experience the internal turbulence from striving to reach the goals of another person. The person who relies on vicarious achievement experiences a loss of personal pride and an inhibition of the sense of mastery that comes from personal action. This damaging vicarious achievement pattern is not so much a consequence of the personal "neuroticism" of some women, as it is a predictable result of social devaluation of women and of the competencies involved in the traditional feminine role.

ACHIEVING WITHIN CAREERS

Although some women express achievement strivings only within the traditional homecentered role, others pursue academic and occupational goals (Chapter 15). They act on both agentic and communal values. Obviously, things are stacked against women in the areas of societally recog-

nized, agentic, achievement. Yet women do achieve in these ways, and in numbers surprising in view of the internal and external pressures they experience. Women do write books, make scientific discoveries, own businesses, perform surgery, get elected to Congress, become ambassadors and college presidents. Only recently has research focused on such women, and the picture is incomplete. But available evidence does not support negative stereotypes and folklore. Rather, the data indicate such women have strong ability, committed interests, and sound psychological health.

CAREER RELEVANT ATTRIBUTES

Ability. Women who want careers and those who have them are clearly of high intellectual ability. Girls with career goals tend to score higher on aptitude and achievement measures than those without such plans, and the differences appear fairly early in their academic history (Tyler, 1964). College women have better high school records than do college men; women professionals tend to have been top achievers in their classes and often score higher than male colleagues on measures of intelligence (Bernard, 1964). The relevance of ability to career orientation was shown even more dramatically with a sample already highly selected on intelligence, namely National Merit Scholarship winners (Watley, 1969). Those who planned an immediate career, with or without marriage also, scored significantly higher on both verbal and mathematical aptitude than those planning on marriage only or marriage with a deferred career.

Interests, Values, and Needs. To develop and maintain a serious career interest, young women must not only have ability, but also a pattern of interests and agentic traits that encourages and enables them to use their abilities in a career. Interest tests in conjunction with aptitude are predictive of high school women's career plans; for males, interest measures alone can be adequate predictors (Astin, 1968). Career-oriented young women score higher than homemaking-oriented ones on need for achievement specifically, and on related attributes such as responsibility, self-control, well-being, dominance, and intellectual efficiency (Hoyt & Kennedy, 1958; Tyler, 1964). Similarly, first-year college women who were planning doctoral training, relative to those for whom finding a husband was more important than vocational preparation, were more concerned with obtaining recognition, having responsibility for other's work, becoming an authority, and helping others in difficulty (Rand, 1968—a national survey of over 6000). In fact, these women were higher than comparable men on intellectual self-confidence, research ability, achievement drive, independence, and perseverance.

Communal Interests. Career-oriented woman often have *both* communal and agentic orientations in career concerns and self-definitions (Chapter 15). In a national survey of over 30,000 college graduates, over two-thirds of white women, compared to about half the men, regarded opportunity to work with others important in choosing a job or career (Davis, 1964). Less than half the black women did so, a possible reaction against stereotypes of domestic service that may be changing with an increase of mutual support among blacks. Furthermore, like future homemakers, career-oriented young women consider it important or essential to make sacrifices for the happiness of others (Rand, 1968). Perhaps some women basically feel that they are unimportant compared to other people; others may feel equally important but from their sense of personal acceptance and confidence are more willing and able to give to others, even in a sacrificial way. All in all, many career-oriented women seem to be relatively androgynous, combining agentic and communal traits and values.

PERSONAL AND SOCIAL ADJUSTMENT

Can the women who deviate from traditional role expectations be happy and psychologically sound? Few differences between career and homemaker-oriented women are found in traits presumed relevant to psychological maturity and health. When they do occur, they suggest a greater psychological health of the career-oriented rather than in exclusively home-oriented women. For example, career- and homemaker-oriented high school women did not differ on social presence, sociability, self-acceptance, flexibility, or femininity (Tyler, 1964). College women interested in realizing their own potential or women planning to enter career fields previously dominated by men do not differ from those of a more traditional orientation in general happiness, nor in romantic and friendship relations with men (Gump, 1972; Tangri, 1972). In fact, the more liberally oriented women tend to be more autonomous, individualistic, and motivated by internal standards—all characteristics attributed to mature healthy adults in our society (Chapter 9). Undoubtedly, some women who pursue careers are as unhappy and maladjusted as some men who pursue careers, and as some women who do not. But available evidence suggests they are not a majority among career-oriented women.

In contrast, there is evidence that an exclusive homemaker orientation may take its toll, especially among able women (Chapters 9, 13, 15, and 16). For example, middle-aged women who had performed with distinction during college and were currently pursuing traditional homemaking roles had low self-esteem and saw themselves as neither attractive to men nor competent (Birnbaum, 1975). Married professional women had high self-esteem, felt personally competent and attractive, and felt productive and worthwhile in their work.

SUMMARY

Our society's limited view of achievement inhibits personal development of both women and men.

Women are expected to express competence in marital and maternal roles within the home; men in occupations outside the home. However, women's home-oriented achievement strivings typically are not considered achievement; furthermore, women seldom receive direct recognition from others for the competencies they use in these roles. Typical socialization patterns discourage conventional achievement striving in women so that they tend to have low hope of success and low expectancies of success. Fear of failure is also more detrimental for girls than boys. Girls are more anxious about failure and more able to withdraw from achievement situations or to choose unrealistically low or high tasks and goals. Girls also learn, particularly as adolescents, that traditional achievements can bring negative consequences, such as social censure and reduced popularity—reactions that foster fear of success. In addition, when women succeed, the success often is attributed to luck rather than to personal ability. Young girls are not encouraged to develop realistic expectancies and career plans for themselves. Rather they are encouraged to define

themselves only through their husbands and to seek vicarious achievement through husbands and children.

This socialization pattern can be changed. Parents can encourage achievement in their daughters by moderate rather than excessive warmth and permissiveness, by realistic independence training, and by modeling. Women who do accept conventional achievement for themselves achieve as well as men. Indeed, career-oriented women are likely to be more intelligent than comparable men and to value personal achievement and accept personal responsibility for achievement strivings. At the same time, they are concerned for others and may be more happy than exclusively home-oriented women. Many achieving women thus seem androgynous and display a good deal of personal stability and self-direction in "bucking the system." Perhaps future societal views will encourage women and men to express their achievement concerns through both agentic and communal contributions.

PART FOUR

ADULT INVOLVEMENTS AND THE QUEST FOR ANDROGYNY

Earlier chapters considered the varying degrees of overlap between females and males, even in physical sex characteristics. Yet, as noted repeatedly, **sex-role** expectations often overlook actual and potential similarities by categorizing women and men as opposite sexes with divergent destinies. (Thus we have deliberately used the term *other sex* in this book, rather than *opposite sex*.) The chapters in this section further examine the impact of sex-role expectations on various facets of the involvements of adult women, including sexual relationships, social relationships within married and single life-styles, and occupational pursuits. Attention is given to possibilities about coming changes that could facilitate **androgynous** development within each sex.

IDENTITY AND SEXUALITY
Cultural expectations about sex differences are embedded in theories of sexuality and in the scripts through which people express their sexuality. In developing their sex identities as well as their sense of themselves as sexual persons, children integrate their bodily experiences with information from others. As Gullahorn notes (Chapter 12), caregivers' labeling practices and cultural modesty taboos often foster girls' incomplete and negative concepts regarding their genitals and reproductive functions. The emphasis on concealing evidence of menstruation and on deodorizing "offensive" natural odors further reinforces females' self-images as sex objects who are only conditionally acceptable to others. Undoing such hang-

ups by helping women develop accurate and positive images of their bodies and themselves has become a major goal of recently organized women's self-help clinics.

The difficulty some women experience trying to see themselves as agents with choices about their sexuality partly reflects their uncrystallized identity formation. With adult encouragement and pressure, adolescent boys plan and begin enacting their adult identity primarily in terms of occupational goals. This is a mixed blessing, since there are dysfunctional consequences of the tendency for men's identity to be fused with occupational status. Even their roles as husbands and fathers, for example, are evaluated in terms of their agentic success as breadwinners (Chapters 15 and 16). Adolescent girls, however, are urged to preserve their flexibility lest premature identity formation interfere with their ability to adapt to their future husband's needs and to complement *his* identity.

AND SHE LIVED HAPPILY EVER AFTER?
Ferguson (Chapter 13) describes the recurrent problems, even in a traditional marriage, that ensue from deferred identity development. Sometimes the decisions early in a marriage that postpone identity issues for women snowball during subsequent stages of the family life cycle. Unresolved issues do not disappear. For example, a young wife might curtail her own education to take a dead-end job that supports her husband's

advanced training. Then, he may become disillusioned with her lack of growth compared to his own and seek divorce. If not, she can easily become immersed in childcare and everyday family obligations and may never really take time to find out who she is. Women who develop only a relational identity often become the depressed casualties of middle age (Chapter 9). In fact, the "housewives' syndrome," involving depression and feelings of futility, is the most frequent complaint treated in mental health centers. Children, too, often are thwarted in developing autonomy by current family patterns involving too much maternal nurturance.

LIFE-STYLE CHOICES

There is much current discussion of the viability of traditional marriage and the **nuclear family.** Increasingly, people are seeking nontraditional living arrangements. The percentage of single women in the 20 to 24 age group has risen markedly since 1960. Whether the long-term effect of this change will be a later marriage age or a growing commitment to lifelong singleness remains to be seen. In exploring some costs and benefits of a single life-style, Donelson (Chapter 14) demonstrates that the possible range of experiences and need satisfaction (or deprivation) does not necessarily differ for a single and a married woman. She also notes that contemporary patterns of social relations pose unnecessary problems for single people.

Many motives underlie current life-style experimentation. Some people "sleep around," "make the scene" at swinging singles bars, engage in group sex, or experiment with bisexual chic in order to avoid personal involvement. For some men this pattern not only reflects the traditional macho renunciation of tenderness and relatedness, but also expresses their distrust and hostility toward women who have become competitors on traditional male turf. Recent studies report overt hostility by college men toward achieving women (Lockheed, 1975 and Chapter 11). Some women avoid personal involvement to emulate the male "success" style or to protect themselves from the "compassion trap" they perceive many women to

be caught in. These "cool" men and women seem to value the ability to confront potentially meaningful emotional experiences with the depersonalized, mechanical nonchalance of a Kurt Vonnegut (1969) character, shrugging, "So it goes."

Instead of moving away emotionally from people, some other life-style experimenters are seeking more authentic relationships than those based on the scripted sex roles embedded in many conventional arrangements. Many couples now formulate their own marriage vows, and some write contracts specifying mutual obligations. For two or more adults sharing a communal household, Margaret Mead and Shulamith Firestone, among others, have proposed instituting renewable contracts. The purpose of contracts is to stimulate clear communication about expectations for the relationship and to formalize mutual commitments: The contracts necessitate review and reappraisal of the extent to which the relationship promotes the development of the partners. Whatever its structure and contractual basis, hopefully the psychological unit that is the family of the future will be more successful than the contemporary American family in developing the potential of *all* of its members. This will require objective consideration of the current impact of sex roles on peoples' lives.

THE FUTURE OF SEX ROLES

Adult life-style experimentation has profound implications for sex roles. We are witnessing a variety of reactions, including defenses of the status quo, trends toward unisex, and quests for androgyny. What will women and men be like? Will they be alike? The answers will depend on individual and group decisions. In Chapter 16 Gullahorn speculates about outcomes of different policies.

There is evidence that strong **sex-typing** is associated with poor psychological and social functioning in both sexes (see Part 3 and Chapter 16). Our socialization often produces females and males who are psychologically half-persons—and the two halves do not make a viable whole in marriage or in other relationships. But the masculine **agentic** trait pattern is more valued than the feminine **communal** pattern in this society. Furthermore, prestigious occupations are structured to accommodate agentic males (Chapter 15). Thus some young women believe they will be treated as persons in their own right only if they win in competitive academic and occupational pursuits. Such assimilation to the agentic male model could eliminate much of our current sex-typing. However, it also would ignore many of the desirable communal traits now associated with the feminine role. This kind of unisex really is the ultimate in sexism: It would develop only *one* kind of half-person, with both sexes becoming like strongly sex-typed contemporary males.

The quest for androgyny attempts to encourage fully functioning "whole" people who incorporate the positive agentic and communal qualities that now tend to be separated by sex. If androgyny were the prevalent pattern, women and men would be similar in both having at least some minimum level of both agentic and communal characteristics. Beyond this core similarity individuals very likely would exhibit a range of trait differences, with considerable overlap between the sexes. The goals of androgyny are not likely to be achieved, however, with our current patterning of family and occupational role relationships. Modifications in our social system are necessary to facilitate androgynous adult life-styles and androgynous socialization of children

SOCIETAL CHANGE

The women's movement has been both praised and blamed for actual and suggested changes in family structure and increased female participation in the workforce. Actually, demographic changes in women's roles preceded the feminist upsurge of the 1960s. During 1950—in the era of the so-called feminine mystique, glorifying women's homemaker role—one-fourth of all the women in intact marriages who had school-age children were employed (Van Dusen & Sheldon, 1976). In a sense, then, the women's movement was necessary to formulate new directions for women's changing roles and to address the discrimination women were facing (Chapter 15).

Today, a majority of working women are married; over two-thirds have children.

However, working outside the home is not synonymous with "liberation." Employed mothers frequently carry double burdens when their husbands do not share home and family tasks (Chapters 15 and 16). Sometimes the lack of male assistance reflects the structuring and time demands of many managerial and professional jobs that husbands have. Often it takes two people to make one successful career—one person devotes more than full-time to the career; the other acts as a life-support system, maintaining the career person.

So long as occupations continue in their present structure, increased communal experience for men and increased agentic opportunities for women are unlikely. In view of the dysfunctional consequences of strong sex-typing and current social structural impediments to androgyny, we maintain that social modifications are necessary. Human beings develop in social contexts that can facilitate or impede their growth.

Presently there are few models of modern societies whose occupational structures and social policies clearly foster healthy androgyny. Gullahorn uses some facets of Sweden's experience to explore the possible modifications in work schedules and child-care services that could provide more choices toward androgyny for both sexes (Chapter 16). Avowedly, this exploration is not simply social-psychological. It has political implications. But the discussion is not political in the sense of subscribing to a particular ideology—be it capitalism, socialism, or something else. Nevertheless, some readers have suggested that such "polemics" are inappropriate in a psychology book. Some facets to this objection are instructive.

First, we question whether other ostensibly "neutral" scientific theories impinging on the psychology of women really are not polemic. Perhaps they seem noncontroversial because they reflect cultural biases and perpetuate the status quo. It is noteworthy that so much psychological literature has endorsed strongly sex-typed behavior as "sex-*appropriate*," in the light of evidence indicating

dysfunctional consequences, especially of traditional femininity. Yet, ironically, professionals active in the psychology of women are accused of
polemics as they examine previously unquestioned assertions and attempt to substitute facts
for implicit assumptions.

Is it nonpolemic for mental health experts to
characterize the mentally healthy woman in "unhealthy terms" that are vastly different from those
used to characterize a mentally healthy "adult"
whose sex was not specified (Chapter 9)? And
some psychoanalysts' response to Masters' and
Johnson's data regarding female sexuality are particularly revealing (Chapter 12). Clearly some
aspects of psychoanalytic theory that are widely
held as documenting women's passivity and inherent deficiencies are not simply an impartial
systematization of empirical facts.

Many changes in conventional habits of thinking and theorizing are necessary. Furthermore, to
overcome the dysfunctions of extreme sex-typing
and realize the benefits of androgyny, concomitant structural changes are needed. Some general
policy recommendations to promote androgynous
life-styles are included in Chapter 16. Final decisions about the merits of these proposals and
their implementation call for considerations
beyond the scope of this book. For example, if
more day-care facilities are developed, how are
they to be supported? The issue of who pays is
not a trivial one, especially for childless taxpayers.
But at the same time we should raise the question
of who *already* pays for the $12,000 or so of ser-
vices now "contributed" yearly by housewives.

The quest for androgyny will not be easy, but
it seems necessary for the personal and social fulfillment of people of both sexes. We are now confronting the twilight of our myth of unlimited natural resources and unbounded economic growth.
We may also be confronting the twilight of our
myth that the strong sex-typing of our culture is
"just natural," necessary, or beneficial. To cope
with environmental, financial, social, and personal changes and to promote effective, meaningful, and compassionate lives, we need people who
are competent, flexible, caring, and sensitive to
both their independence and their interdependence. We must be open to the facts about our
current situation and to the possibility for change
if we are to grow, separately and together.

CHAPTER
12
SEX ROLES
AND SEXUALITY

Few aspects of human life approach sexuality in the depth and complexity of its individual and social significance. Although sexual behavior is an exercise of biological capacities, it is not simply an automatic enactment of an "instinctual" drive (Chapter 3). We create our sexuality as we learn what females and males are supposed to be in our social worlds. Cultural learning and unique life experiences interact with our "biological selves" so that sexuality becomes an expression of non-sexual as well as distinctly sexual desires, fears, and joys. Sexuality may be enriched because of its relevance to our total lives or it may be constricted and impoverished. Many contemporary Americans, for example, regard sex as another achievement arena where success or failure—however they are defined—have crucial implications for their sense of personal worth. In this chapter, we shall examine some facets of women's sexuality and the implications it has and could have in their lives. As with many other kinds of behavior, there are many mistaken assumptions about "the way women are."

ANATOMY AND DESTINY

A NECESSARY LINKAGE?

In asserting that "anatomy is destiny," Freud linked anatomical sex differences to differences in adult sexual behaviors and social roles. Beyond obvious biological functions like child bearing, are the associations inevitable? As demonstrated repeatedly in this book, appeals to "It's just natural" are not valid justifications for current **sex-role** standards or the prevalent undervaluation of women. With respect to sexuality specifically, research has not confirmed Freudian assumptions that females envy penises and desire maternity to compensate for their presumed genital deficiency (Chapter 2). Yet, "anatomy is destiny" has become entrenched either blatantly or subtly in the thinking of contemporary laypersons and professionals alike. Despite contrary evidence, and Freud's own example of stating his views to be tentative and incomplete, his theory has become dogma to many—particularly the view that, because of anatomy, women are essentially passive

and men active. One contemporary psychoanalyst even claims that the mandate for women's sexual passivity is in the act of conception itself: ". . . the spermatozoon swims actively, whilst the ovum passively awaits its penetration . . . anatomy and physiology form the inescapable substratum upon which the emotional difference between the sexes stands firm" (Storr, 1968, p. 62). Needless to say, the conservative dogmatic members of the psychoanalytic community are not "receptive" to evidence, presented later, refuting the Freudian-based claim that "mature" women experience a "passive, vaginal orgasm" rather than an "active, clitoral orgasm."

Further disconfirmation of a belief that sexuality and other sex-role behaviors inevitably follow from anatomic sex characteristics comes from data regarding **transexuals,** whose anatomy conflicts with their identity and desired sexual behavior. We shall also see that cultures disagree on what sexual behaviors are "natural" for women and men. Thus there is a strong case against the view that anatomy *must be* destiny. Yet for many people within many cultures, anatomy *is* destiny because they adhere to specific cultural interpretations of femaleness and maleness.

To Reproduce or to Enjoy? In many cultures women have been almost exclusively defined as reproducers and instruments for male sexual pleasure. Meanwhile, there is ambivalence and distrust of the mysterious power of women's reproductive organs and marked attempts to maintain their purity of function and to curb their powers. Nineteenth-century critics claimed that higher education would deflect blood to women's brains from their generative organs, causing them to lose touch with their sacred primitive destinies. In Victorian society, "good" women were supposed to serve as the indifferent, passive instruments of their husbands' satisfaction in order to beget children. Thus, women's destinies often have been limited to the roles of wife, mother, or nun (a woman who marries her god)—or else to roles as prostitute or witch (a woman who allegedly sleeps with the devil). These roles reflect the recurring theme of purity versus pollution in

Western civilization's views of women's sexuality.

In Victorian days, presumably only "bad" women, who were unfit for marriage and motherhood, enjoyed sex. The polarity of purity versus pollution is apparent still in pervasive **double standards** about sexual conduct and a lingering "virgin–prostitute" syndrome. Contemporary English reflects the preoccupation with women's reproductive functions and their potential impurity: there are over 200 English terms connoting female prostitution and only about a tenth as many describing male sexual promiscuity (Stanley, 1973).

Recently, segments of Western society have acknowledged that women have a right to sexual pleasure and that women's destinies need not be limited by their reproductive biological capacities. Many agree that women are entitled to as much sex as men—and to even more orgasms, if they wish to act on their unique capability. Some radical feminists, however, argue that sex is oppressive to women and urge that they abstain from heterosexual encounters. With such contrasting visions of female sexuality, many women feel their intimate feelings are being tossed about on an ideological playground. Thus achieving a comfortable definition of themselves as sexual persons requires considerable self-awareness, sensitivity, honesty, compassion, and courage.

RESPONSES TO SEXUAL ANATOMY

The Double Standard of Shamefulness. Our cultural double standard in evaluating sex organs as well as sexual practices communicates a feeling of shame about female genitals. This standard is reflected in derogatory labels for adult female genitals and in the lack of labels or vague regional references for little girls' genitals. Frequently parents in this culture instruct their daughters to wash "down there" or to wash "your bottom," referring to the genital organs, rectum, and buttocks. In contrast, they clearly acknowledge the existence and importance of their sons' genitals. While a little boy's penis may not be identified correctly by its anatomic label, parents and sons

often share an approving nickname, such as "widdler," which reinforces a boy's pride of ownership. Displaying this pride is approved. Males often sit with their legs spread apart, making obvious the bulge in their trousers.

Other experiences reinforce the double standard, making it more difficult for girls than for boys to incorporate positive concepts about their genitals into their physical images of themselves. Some adult women are unaware of the actual appearance of their genitals. Their learned feelings of shame or even disgust have prevented their using a mirror to explore their relatively hidden clitorises, inner labia, and vaginas.

Feelings of aversion about female genitals are further reinforced by advertisements for scented douche mixtures or vaginal deodorant sprays that are promoted not for any purported health benefits to women (in fact they often cause vaginal irritation) but in order to protect others from "offensive" natural feminine odors. No comparable sprays are marketed for men's use, even though men potentially could be more "offensive" to the other sex because women typically have a more sensitive sense of smell than men (Chapter 4).

Concealment Rituals. For many females, therefore, their "unseeable," unlabeled, or negatively labeled genitals become a thing of mystery and shame. Rituals of concealment encourage and perpetuate this reaction. "Unmentionables" is a term for female, not male, underwear. Girls are admonished to keep their legs together when wearing a skirt, lest someone glimpse their panties. This shameful event is documented in some children's chants, such as "Jane, Jane (or any girl's name), fine and fair; I can see your underwear. . . ." And lifting a dress to expose the forbidden, hidden area becomes a challenge for many little boys. This childish scenario depicts pervasive elements of traditional sex-role interaction in our culture, with the daringly active male "scoring" mainly for praise from his peer group, and the fearfully passive female remaining helplessly humiliated.

Females' secondary sex characteristics are to be concealed also—even before they develop. Bra tops are included in bikini outfits for infant and toddler girls, and it is considered inappropriate for preadolescent girls to appear with their chests uncovered. However, there is a double message. Once they do develop, breasts are highly valued for their "sex appeal." They are not supposed to be concealed entirely; instead they should be tantalizingly outlined under clothing as a sort of promissory note to be enjoyed by men. This attention, however, does not really enhance the body images of many women: few "measure up" to the standards depicted by *Playboy* centerfolds and displayed in topless bars. Among those who come to regard themselves as inadequately endowed, some wear padded bras, and some even undergo plastic surgery or silicone injections to appear "acceptable." In our culture, growing up female can easily mean developing an incomplete body image or one that focuses on the "necessity" of making sexual elements acceptable to others.

Most other human groups do not share our culture's enormous concern about women's breasts, nor do they regard female genitals as shameful. According to a survey of 190 societies throughout the world, most cultures do, however, impose some restrictions about female genital exposure (Ford & Beach, 1951). Where people wear any clothing whatsoever, adult women are expected to conceal their genitals, whereas men and children of either sex are not necessarily expected to do so. Apparently no peoples reverse the clothing taboo by insisting that men but not women cover their genitals. In the few societies where both sexes usually are nude, rules of etiquette prevent looking at an adult female's genitals, but not a male's.

Signaling and Scripts. Cultural norms restricting female genital exposure seem to function to control sexual encounters. In many species, genital exposure ("presenting") is an important preconsummatory display in a copulatory sequence (Chapter 3). Women in a number of societies also deliberately display their genitals to men to initiate sexual intercourse. In some cultures the structuring of power relations between the sexes enables a man to have intercourse with a woman

even though she unintentionally exposed her genitals, such as during sleep; therefore, women keep their legs close together and their skirts down if they do not desire intercourse. Our cultural modesty taboos also function to regulate sexual encounters. However, because of negative evaluations of sex, the control procedures have focused on female sex organs as shameful rather than alluring.

Why are female but not male genitals emphasized? Recent research that we shall discuss next indicates that both sexes are aroused by nude portrayals of the other sex. Why then do women in nude societies not continually "turn on" to the men? Sexual displays alone do not explain sexual behavior.

Cultures incorporate the basic elements of sexual display into more or less elaborate scripts (Gagnon & Simon, 1973). As illustrated, in some cultures female genital exposure under almost any circumstances can lead to intercourse; in others the woman's display must be a deliberate, intentional act for intercourse to ensue. In still other settings, partially clad *Playboy* Bunnies or completely nude striptease dancers intentionally expose themselves but are not considered available for sexual contact with their viewers. Therefore, even though individuals may be aroused by certain displays, they will not act on that arousal if other cues in the complex total stimulus situation are not part of their learned script for sexual behavior. Before considering other aspects of sexual scripts, let us examine data about responsiveness to sexual stimulation.

RESEARCH ON SEXUAL RESPONSIVENESS

Because of Western civilization's long tradition of viewing sex as a somewhat shameful and potentially sinful activity, there has been a paucity of accurate information about sex and a multitude of erroneous myths, particularly about female sexual functioning (or nonfunctioning). Even though research on sexuality has increased considerably in recent decades, the legacy of the past is still with us. Because of shame, shyness, desires for privacy, or other reasons, many people are reluctant to disclose information about their sexual behavior. And some researchers have made erroneous assumptions about female sexuality rather than investigate it.

REACTIONS TO EROTIC STIMULI

Women and Men as Sex Objects. Female displays in advertisements of nonsexual products ranging from soft drinks to computer hardware are familiar stimuli in our social landscape. Researchers also have emphasized women as stimulators of men with little concern about women's reactions to either male or female stimuli. For example, Ford and Beach (1951) catalog the diverse female physical characteristics considered beautiful in different societies, but they present no information regarding women's preferences about men's features. In this culture, some psychologists use female silhouettes with varying-sized anatomical features to demonstrate that some men are distinctly more responsive to breast size, some to buttocks, and some to women's legs (Wiggins & Wiggins, 1969). Women, too, have somatic preferences, but these have yet to be researched systematically. Women's reports of "boy watching" indicate comparable distinctions among those who attend to shoulders, to apparent penis size as indicated by the bulge in the trousers, or to buttocks.

Pure Eroticism vs. Romance. Until recently, females have been neglected also in investigations involving "hard-core" pornography, in which there is an absence of feelings of affection and relatedness. Beliefs that women, at least the "good" ones, *should* not be aroused by such erotic stimuli contribute to the assumption that women *are* not so aroused. Often it is claimed that women need romance to turn them on, but men do not—and the male way is "real" sex. In some surveys fewer women than men reported feeling aroused by purely erotic pictures and stories (Kinsey et al., 1953). However, many women may have been unwilling to admit to the excitability that has been considered "abnormal" for "good" women. Thus the relief many have experienced

in recognizing their own fantasies in the heroine's fantasies may help account for the popularity of Erica Jong's *Fear of Flying* (1973).

Both women and men can be aroused by erotic or by romantic stimuli. Contemporary research shows similarities in sexual arousal. In one investigation, both female and male university students reported similar levels of arousal to each of two stories—one about a couple's mutual affection and their vividly described sexual relationship; the other about a couple who were bound together only by the sexual encounter (Schmidt, Sigusch, & Shafer, 1973). Similarly, married women and men did not differ in their overall total reported arousal to erotic pictures and stories or to many of the specific heterosexual erotic themes of the stimuli (Byrne & Lamberth, 1971). However, the themes that were most arousing to the women involved a male in undershorts, a nude male, a male masturbating, or homosexual fellatio (oral stimulation of a penis). These stimuli are unlikely in the typical erotic story or movie. Until recently, stimuli with explicit sexual content have been aimed almost exclusively at heterosexual males. Thus, it has been easy to underestimate women's responsiveness to "hard core porn," which is really male porn.

Physiological Response to Erotic Cues. Are self-reports about sexual arousal accurate ones? Female volunteer subjects might have exaggerated their reactions to demonstrate how "liberal" they were, and males might have done so to "prove their masculinity." Only recently have unobtrusive recording devices become easily available to measure sexual physiological responses (such as **vasocongestion**). A small tamponlike device inserted just inside the vaginal entrance measures changes in females' blood volume; a band around the base of the penis measures the blood volume changes associated with male erection. Self-ratings of arousal and physiological measures gave similar results, for both sexes, to a variety of tape-recorded stimuli: purely erotic explicit descriptions of sexual encounters, combinations of affectionate expressions and physical relationships, purely romantic scenes of tender expressions without explicit sex, and neutral conversations without romantic or erotic elements (Heiman, 1975). The great majority of subjects of both sexes were aroused, according to physiological and subjective measures, by erotic and erotic-romantic stimuli but not by the purely romantic or neutral stimuli. Clearly, the assumption that women must have romance for sexual arousal is not valid.

Although sex research is becoming more meaningful and effective in dispelling some prevalent misconceptions, there are problems still. We do not know that the subjects who volunteer for sex research are representative of people at large. Neither has the full range of hard core pornography been examined, including the sexually violent portrayals and glorifications of rape that apparently appeal to some men but evoke terror rather than lust in women (Brownmiller, 1975). An additional limitation to date is that we do not have sufficient information about the images, thoughts, and fantasies that get embedded in sexual scripts and influence whether or not arousal will be maintained and heightened so that the full sexual response cycle is experienced.

HUMAN SEXUAL RESPONSE

Until the latter part of this century, the sexual response system was the only system of the body that had not been investigated with the technology available for careful laboratory research. In the 1950s, William Masters and Virginia Johnson observed and recorded the physiology of sexual response in almost 700 women and men. Many of their detailed findings are as interesting to the layperson as details about the physiology of digestion—the information may not necessarily enhance one's pleasure in the activity. But since sex has been a taboo topic for so long, intellectual discussions help many people to use terms like clitoris, penis, and orgasm. Such a small step in clear labeling is an important one.

One major contribution of the Masters and Johnson research has been to demonstrate the fallacies in theories about sex *differences* in sexual response. Aside from obvious anatomic variants, women and men are *similar* in their physiological responses to sexual stimulation (Table 12–1).

There is, however, one major exception: following orgasm, women are capable of repeated orgasmic experience, and many women report that their second or third orgasm is even more intense than their first. Men, however, experience a refractory period of varying duration following orgasm, during which they cannot be restimulated to erection.

Phases in the Sexual Cycle. The *excitement phase* of the sexual cycle is initiated by whatever is sexually stimulating for a particular individual, including the kind of stimuli mentioned previously. If stimulation is strong enough, the excitement mounts rapidly and the genital organs swell because of vasocongestion. Vasocongestion in the vagina causes some of the fluid in the tissues to pass through the membranous walls, lubricating the canal. Women who are clothed during arousal often experience damp underwear as a result of the lubrication.

If effective sexual stimulation is continued, individuals experience the increased sexual tension of the *plateau phase*. Some people can escalate their arousal and even go on to orgasm through their fantasies alone. More typically, however, people use some type of genital friction to supplement their erotic thoughts. For women the clitoris has a particularly important role. During the plateau phase the clitoris retracts under its hood and becomes relatively inaccessible. However, clitoral stimulation still occurs when friction in the vagina or on other parts of the genitals causes a traction on the clitoral hood that stimulates the clitoris.

Other physiological changes during the plateau phase include increases in heart and respiration rates, in blood pressure, and in muscle tension (myotonia), along with both voluntary and involuntary muscle contractions. Some people exhibit a "sex flush"—a rash that begins just under the rib cage and spreads rapidly over the chest. In females a more pronounced color change, the "sex skin reaction," occurs late in the plateau phase: the labia minora of women who have never given birth change from pink to bright red;

TABLE 12-1.
Bodily Reactions During the Human Sexual Response Cycle *

Female	Male
I. Excitement Phase	
Vaginal lubrication	Erection of penis
Lengthening and distention of vagina	Partial elevation of testes
Nipple erection	Nipple erection
II. Plateau Phase	
Elevated blood pressure	Elevated blood pressure
Fast heart rate (tachycardia—100–175 beats per minute)	Fast heart rate (tachycardia—100–175 beats per minute)
Rapid breathing (hyperventilation)	Rapid breathing (hyperventilation)
"Sex flush" (75 percent incidence)	"Sex flush" (25 percent incidence)
Vivid color change in labia minora	Sometimes deepened color reaction in head of penis (glans)
Glandular emission of lubricating mucous into vagina	Glandular emission of lubricating mucous from penis
Retraction of clitoris	Increased circumference in ridge at the penile glans
Decrease in size of vaginal opening	Full elevation of testes
Elevation of uterus	
III. Orgasmic Phase	
Increased blood pressure elevation	Increased blood pressure elevation
Rapid breathing (hyperventilation)	Rapid breathing (hyperventilation)
Tachycardia—110 to 180 beats per minute	Tachycardia—110 to 180 beats per minute
Rhythmic vaginal contractions, beginning at 0.8-second intervals	Rhythmic penile contractions, beginning at 0.8-second intervals
IV. Resolution Phase	
Loss of vasocongestive size increase in vagina, labia majora, and labia minora	Loss of vasocongestive size increase in penis, scrotum, testes
Return to normal breathing, heart rate, and blood pressure	Return to normal breathing, heart rate, and blood pressure
Rapid disappearance of "sex flush"	Rapid disappearance of "sex flush"
Perspiring reaction (about 33 percent incidence)	Perspiring reaction (about 33 percent incidence)
No refractory period—capable of repeated orgasm if stimulated	Refractory reaction—temporary loss of stimulative susceptibility

* Source. Data compiled from Masters & Johnson (1966).

and in women who have had children, from red to a deep purplish color. Some men have a comparable deepened color reaction in the head of the penis. Once a woman develops the sex skin reaction she is almost certain to go on to orgasm. People who are aroused to the plateau level but do not go on to orgasm experience a sometimes uncomfortable gradual reduction of vasocongestion and muscle tension.

As the *orgasmic phase* proceeds, a person's breathing increases to at least three times the normal rate, heart rate is more than double, and blood pressure increases by a third. Most of the body muscles tense, and the orgasmic response begins with rhythmic contractions. Physiologically, orgasm is a release of the muscular spasm and reduction of the blood vessel engorgement built up by stimulation. Subjectively, orgasm is an experience of peak, all-encompassing pleasure.

Following orgasm there is a *resolution phase* during which the body gradually returns to its pre-excitement state. Before completing the resolution stage, some women prefer continued stimulation to additional orgasms. As noted before, men experience a refractory period during which they cannot have an erection.

Physiological reactions in this four-phase cycle are the same whether sex stimulation is from heterosexual intercourse, homosexual stimulation, autosexual activity, or from erotic fantasies alone. The intensity and duration of the responses vary, however, and in the laboratory situation women's orgasmic responses were less intense from heterosexual intercourse than from masturbation or from their partner's manipulating their genitals under their direction. Perhaps the women's lower physiological response to intercourse is due to poor communication about the stimulation that most enhances their sexual pleasure. Poor coital technique probably also accounts for the frequent report that the female takes longer than the male to reach orgasm in intercourse. This has been erroneously generalized into a conclusion that females are inherently slower in response than males. If this were so, then females also would take longer to reach orgasm from masturbation, but research evidence indicates that females and males take the same average length of time—between two and four minutes.

VARIETIES OF SEXUAL ACTIVITIES

Although the physiological components of the sexual response cycle are virtually the same for all people, there are tremendous variations in preferred practices and in the evaluations of the psychological significance, desirability, morality, and consequences of various types of sexual behavior.

AUTOSEXUAL ACTIVITIES

Because of learned reluctance to explore their genitals, young girls in this culture take longer

than boys to use their genital excitability. Only about one-fifth of American females report masturbating prior to adolescence; the incidence increases during adolescence so that two-fifths have masturbated by age 20; and over three-fifths have done so by age 40 (Kinsey et al., 1953; Sorenson, 1973; Stern, 1975). Higher proportions of American males report masturbating, especially during adolescence. Kinsey notes, however, that among preschool children who masturbate, more small girls than boys reach orgasm. Probably the girls' earlier development of muscular coordination facilitates the rhythmic manual movements leading to orgasm. Some women discover the pleasures of self-stimulation only after they have experienced sexual intercourse; and masturbation rates generally are higher among women who have had intercourse than among those who have not.

For many older women in our society, autosexuality becomes their main sexual activity. These women find relatively few male partners because of differential longevity, the incidence of impotence among older men, and societal discrimination against older women who are judged "old" (and sexually unattractive) 10 or 15 years sooner than men. Men are at a greater *biological* disadvantage in aging; women are at a greater *social* disadvantage because they are defined as erotic objects, whose luster quickly fades. Although the mass media glamorize and legitimate the liaison between an older man and younger woman, the opposite type of relationship is considered "unnatural."

Attitudes Toward Autosexuality. For many people the satisfactions of self-stimulation are undermined or prohibited by feelings of guilt, anxiety, or fear of harmful effects. Despite modern evidence that masturbation relieves sexual tensions and has no adverse physiological consequences, prevalent assumptions link the practice with nervousness and even "insanity." A long history of medical support for persecuting the masturbator, persisting well into this century, has contributed to the stigma (Spitz, 1952). Medical treatments have included blistering thighs, cauterizing the genitals and spine, and circumcising (removing part of the foreskin of a penis or of the clitoral hood). One surgeon who believed masturbation caused convulsive diseases even introduced clitoridectomy (surgical removal of the entire clitoris). He did not propose the analogous technique for treating masturbating boys. Psychoanalytic theory of childhood sexuality did much to modify medical views about masturbation and to rescue many children from the "cures." However, psychoanalytic thinking has also supported the view that masturbation is an infantile response to be given up, rather than one of many means of enjoying one's sexuality.

Cross-Cultural Attitudes. Adults in many other societies also regard masturbation as inferior to intercourse, and only the South Pacific Lesu tribe seems to lack prohibitions against adult autosexuality. Nevertheless, it occurs despite social censure. Usually women stimulate their genitals with their hands and fingers, but some use other instruments, such as a reindeer leg muscle (Siberian Chukchee women), a wooden root (the African Azande), or a banana (South Pacific Tikopia women). American women have the advantage of modern technology, and many use electric vibrators or handheld shower massagers.

While autosexuality generally is considered inappropriate for adults in most societies, less than one-tenth of those surveyed by Ford and Beach have restrictions about children's masturbation. Some parents fondle infants' genitals (South Pacific Alorese) and sexually stimulate young children (North American Hopi and South American Siriono). In such permissive societies, children masturbate freely and openly in public, stimulate each other's genitals manually and orally, and imitate adult copulation, which they often are permitted to observe.

HETEROSEXUAL ACTIVITIES

Part of our societal censure of childhood sexuality and autosexuality for children or adults reflects an assumption that adult heterosexual intercourse is the only "normal" sexual expression and that other kinds of activities will inhibit the likelihood of "success" (or enjoyment?) of this specific adult activity. Actually freedom and enjoyment of sexual expressiveness in one way tends to be associated with freedom and enjoyment in another. Women who have masturbated generally enjoy intercourse more readily than those who have not. In the cultures just described, early sexual exercise is considered beneficial and necessary for healthy maturation and for later begetting of offspring. As the children mature, their sex play consists predominantly of heterosexual intercourse, with occasional homosexual encounters also approved in some cultures.

The Girl's Responsibility. A minority of societies, including our own, are highly restrictive about sexual matters. Adults try to prevent children's gaining sexual knowledge and punish sex play; prohibitions against sexual activities continue until after the girl's menarche or the boy's puberty ceremonies, or until betrothal or marriage. When pregnancy results from the "forbidden" premarital relationships that do occur, the double standard typical of our culture often is evident: Generally the girl is blamed. Within our society adolescent intercourse has been considered "immoral" in a girl, but "masculine" in a boy; promiscuity by girls but not by boys is considered delinquent behavior; female prostitutes, but not their customers, are targets of legal persecution; and adultery is more condemned for a woman than for a man.

Why are females censured for the violations of general restrictive standards that are "winked at," praised, or at least tolerated in males? Do we assume that women but not men are capable of resisting the temptations of the arousal they feel when encountering a sexual display? Do we assume that women are less arousable than men, so that "giving in" denotes more weakness to be more censured? Does the woman have the destiny of more responsibility because of the greater mystery and reproductive power of her anatomical genitals? Or does our sexual script decree that a woman can be only virgin or prostitute, pure or polluted, while men have more freedom of choice about where they will be on an evaluative continuum?

Types of Activities. Despite the official morality, people in our society do indulge in many forms of sex activity, and females are far more active than the social code prescribes. We have already noted the frequency of masturbation. According to studies conducted mainly with unmarried college students, heterosexual premarital sexual experience tends to follow the sequence listed in Table 12-2. That is, experience 1—kissing—is likely to occur first, then experience 2, then 3, and so on, on a continuum from "necking" (above the shoulders), to "petting" (above the waist), to "heavy petting" (below the waist), to intercourse. The activities before intercourse (foreplay), often occur alone and sometimes lead to orgasm themselves. Of the students reporting each experience in a recent survey of over 800 college women, about 4 percent had experienced orgasm from kissing alone; 11 percent from breast stimulation; over half from a man's manually or orally stimulating their genitals; and over three-quarters from coitus (Stern, 1975).

Foreplay. As decreed by traditional etiquette, most of the foreplay activities listed in Table 12-2 are initiated by the male; yet females are blamed for "illicit" activity. Our social norms set up sexuality as a conflict situation. Very few other societies consider it appropriate for a female to initiate sexual advances; but some, like the Pacific Maori, regard women as "naturally" more amorous than men. In a few societies either a woman or a man may solicit intercourse by initiating foreplay.

While most foreplay activities are engaged in by different subgroups in our society as well as in other cultures, the relative frequency varies, and the sequence is by no means universal. Prolonged foreplay, with various forms of oral stimulation, is particularly popular among college-educated Americans. Grooming activities also are sometimes included in the preliminaries. For example, South American Siriono couples extract and eat lice and wood ticks from each other's bodies. Similarly, many American couples undress and

TABLE 12-2.
Types of Heterosexual Experiences Reported by College Age Women and Men *

Type of Behavior	Percentages of Women	Percentages of Men
1. Kissing	100	100
2. Male feeling female's covered breasts	85–98	92
3. Male prone on female, no penetration	77	77
4. Male manually stimulating female's nude breasts	75–86	80
5. Male orally stimulating female's breasts	74	73
6. Male manually stimulating female's genitals	71–91	71
7. Female manipulating male's penis	60	72
8. Male orally stimulating female's genitals (cunnilingus)	48–53	43–69
9. Coitus, male on top of female	40–52	53–58
10. Female orally stimulating male's penis (fellatio)	40	52
11. Coitus, female on top of and facing male	30	42
12. Coitus, vagina entered from rear	22	29
13. Coitus, partners lying side-by-side and face-to-face	19	36

* Percentage ranges based on studies by Hunt (1974), Kinsey, *et al.* (1953), Packard (1968), Sorenson (1973), Stern (1975), and Zuckerman (1973).

bathe one another as part of their precopulatory activities.

Virginity. Some unmarried females in our society restrict their heterosexual activities to foreplay in order to preserve their virginity. Sometimes they define virginity specifically and narrowly as lack of penetration of the vagina by a penis. By this definition, the following activities do not violate virginity: the soixante-neuf or 69 (simultaneous oral stimulation of each other's genitals), interfemoral intercourse (penis between the women's thighs), or anal intercourse (insertion of penis into the rectum). Paradoxically, many married people consider some of these "substitute" methods much more advanced or even immoral than simple intercourse, but many unmarried couples view these as "moral" substitutes.

Variations in Intercourse. There is tremendous variation across cultures, within cultures, and within individuals from time to time in preferred positions, frequency, and duration of intercourse. However, the most frequent position in most societies is for the woman to lie on her back with the man on top of her, with the reverse position being next in relative popularity. Many women find that being on top of the man is highly satisfying because they are better able to control the amount and timing of clitoral stimulation and depth of penile penetration. Many couples enjoy experimenting with a diversity of positions.

Frequency is highly variable. In some societies couples regularly have intercourse twice a day. In our society weekend "orgies" are common among college couples separated during the week. Many couples have periods of abstinence and vary the frequency of intercourse.

In some societies men are trained to delay ejaculation so that women regularly experience multiple orgasms. "Premature ejaculation" is considered a problem in this culture, partly because some couples end intercourse when the man "comes." Thus some women do not experience orgasm in intercourse because of lack of sufficient stimulation to get beyond the plateau phase. Labeling these women "frigid" is not only inaccurate

but also exacerbates the problem by encouraging the women to conclude that they are "incapable" of orgasmic response. The seemingly more neutral term "nonorgasmic" is little better: "preorgasmic" is a more desirable and accurate term. Modern sex therapists demonstrate that treating sexual "inadequacy" as learning and communication problems of a couple is more efficient in promoting satisfying sexual relations than is treating only one part of the twosome.

Transexuals. An unusual form of heterosexual activity occurs in the case of transexuals. Technically, transexuals are in a homosexual relationship when they are having sexual relations with a person of their own sex. However, generally both parties consider the liaison heterosexual, because they accept the transexual partner's self-definition. Obtaining sex organs consistent with their sexual identity generally is important to transexuals, often with the explicit intention that their sexual relationships be unquestionably heterosexual. So far there have been more genetic male than female transexuals requesting sex changes, and surgeons have been relatively successful in creating sexually responsive vaginal canals for males. However, because genetic females do not have the erectile tissue required for a typical male penis, surgeons have so far been unable to construct for them a penis capable of erection; even urinary capacities tend to be inadequate.

The press of the desire to have an anatomy that matches identity is so strong that female transexuals nonetheless endure the physical hardships involved with constructing a penis (including disfigurement of the abdomen and removal of a portion of the colon to obtain tissue to make the penis). Even though heterosexual intercourse may require cradling the penis into a synthetic penis and holding it to stimulate the clitorine tissue at the root of the new penis, former transexuals and their partners report satisfaction with their sexual relationships (Money, 1973). The "transformed" women can be satisfactory husbands and fathers by adoption.

Would the original anatomy that is discrepant

with the identity be so disturbing if our society did not insist on strong differentiation between the sexes in traits and choice of partners (Chapter 16)? Jan Morris, formerly British journalist James Morris, raises these issues in her poignant autobiography:

Would my conflict have been so bitter if I had been born now, when the gender line is so much less rigid? If society had allowed me to live in the gender I preferred, would I have bothered to change sex? Is mine only a transient phenomenon, between the dogmatism of the last century, when men were men and women were ladies, and the eclecticism of the next, when citizens will be free to live in the gender role they prefer? (1974, p. 172).

Although homosexuals typically are comfortable with the anatomy that is consistent with their sexual identity, they too experience needless problems because of societal role expectations.

HOMOSEXUAL ACTIVITIES

Biologically, only reproduction requires heterosexual activity. However, many people in our culture typically assume that romance, marriage, and sexual enjoyment also require heterosexual relationships. They do not understand people who are sexually attracted to members of their own sex. A sexual component is normal in relationships between any individuals, particularly strong relationships. Because the sexual script decrees otherwise, many people are unable to detect and clearly label their sexual feelings for someone of their sex. For these "forbidden" feelings, as well as for the heterosexual ones that are subjected to fewer societal constraints, the individual always has a choice about communicating them or acting upon them. Many considerations influence whether an individual wants to or does follow through on either heterosexual or homosexual attraction. It probably would be too complicated a world if people directly expressed *all* of their sexual attractions. However, it would be an uncomfortably impersonal world—as some claim it now is—if people failed to at least recognize their feelings and their possibilities.

Incidence. Homosexuality and heterosexuality are points on a continuum rather than being sharply differentiated, and homosexuals and heterosexuals have much in common. For example, Kinsey used a 7-point scale ranging from exclusively homosexual to exclusively heterosexual behavior, with 4 as a **bisexual** midpoint. Many people find this conceptualization a more meaningful and accurate depiction of reality than the restrictive dichotomy of *either* hetero- or homosexual. According to Kinsey's data and criteria, about 4 percent of white American adults are exclusively homosexual throughout their adult lives; 13 percent of females and 37 percent of males report some overt homosexual experience leading to orgasm between adolescence and old age; more report fantasies and strong attractions to one of their sex, and the incidence for females increases with age and education. Given our restrictive sexual codes, the figures are conservative estimates of the extent to which people have and act upon homosexual feelings. Many homosexuals remain "in the closet," passing as "straight" (heterosexual). Many people who choose to behave exclusively heterosexually have dreams or fantasies of sexual encounters with others of their own sex. Conversely, some overt homosexuals also enjoy fantasies about heterosexual activities. Some people are bisexual in behavior as well as in fantasy. In behavior and in fantasy, many homosexual activities are the same as heterosexual activities, such as embracing, kissing, caressing. Contrary to pornographic descriptions by male authors, lesbians generally do not use a dildo (penis substitute). They prefer manual or oral stimulation of the genitals, along with foreplay.

Homosexual Relationships. In a large number of cultures, male homosexuality is accepted as a normal variation from the normative heterosexuality. As is the case with many other topics, there is comparatively little information about the corresponding phenomena in females—a fact that lends itself to many interpretations. In the societies where homosexuals of either sex are socially accepted, the life circumstances of homosexual couples are in many ways comparable to those of heterosexual pairs, though conventional role pressures are apparent. Among the American Mohave Indians, for example, one lesbian acts as "husband," assuming a male name as well as the dress and occupational role of a man in that society (Devereux, 1937). The other woman behaves like a typical Mohave wife. Should the wife be pregnant at the time of the homosexual marriage, the lesbian husband is socially recognized as the father of the child. Thus, the Mohave apply labels—husband, wife, mother, father—to people in societally important roles without restricting the sex of the role incumbent. A male Mohave homosexual who is enacting the wife role feigns menstruation by cutting his thighs monthly. He also fakes pregnancy by stuffing rags under his skirt and imitates labor, claiming to have buried his stillborn baby whose death is mourned by husband and "wife." Thus while they deviate from the norm, Mohave homosexuals still conform to some sex-based expectations for their chosen sex role.

Although things are changing, some older lesbian couples in this culture have had butch–femme relationships in which one woman, the butch, dresses and behaves rather masculinely while the other, the femme, dresses and behaves in a stereotyped feminine manner. Younger lesbians involved in the women's movement generally reject the intrusion of traditional role patterning into their relationships and emphasize egalitarian sharing for the full **androgynous** development of each member of the couple. They must do so against a background of previous socialization and current societal attitudes which assume that adult sexual relationships must be heterosexual.

Gayness in a Straight Society. Some women who are relatively exclusively lesbian in behavior made a choice for lesbianism during their maturity, perhaps after sexual experience with men. Others recognized their attraction to women and considered themselves homosexual during adolescence. In view of cultural stigmatization of homosexuality on top of the many other problems of adolescents in our culture, some of these young

women felt they were "sick" and were exposed to a stressful and unsuccessful psychotherapy in which "cures" for their "abnormality" were attempted. It is only as recently as 1973 that the American Psychiatric Association removed homosexuality from its list of mental disorders so that a homosexual with no generalized impairment in social effectiveness is no longer considered "disordered." Some homosexuals, like some heterosexuals, are emotionally disturbed, but the disturbance may not primarily involve their sexuality. Often homosexuals are anxious and unhappy because of parents', relatives', and friends' reactions to their sexual orientation. Several studies support the contention that homosexuals are not any more unhealthy psychologically than heterosexuals, and some writers claim superiority for gays in some respects (Freedman, 1975; Thompson, McCandless, & Strickland, 1971). Some therapists and many more participants in homophile organizations are helping homosexuals learn to enjoy their gayness in our straight society. However, there still are therapists who disagree with the 1973 decision. Some will not treat a homosexual who does not wish to change orientation. Others are not so open about their beliefs and attempt "cure" without an explicit communication of that to the client.

"Coming out" (publicly revealing homosexual orientation) is still a difficult decision because it can bring psychological or physical harassment. Job discrimination is still a problem and blackmail a danger to the public gay in spite of advances by Gay Liberation groups in seeking legal protection. Because lesbian women usually do not have husbands to provide financial support, losing their jobs could be economically disastrous. Lesbian mothers fear their children will be taken away. Many overt lesbians frequently are harassed by sexual propositions from men who "magnanimously" offer to set them "straight." Thus, homosexuals need not only legal protection, but understanding from an educated public who will acknowledge their right to conduct their private sexual lives and their public social lives with whatever consenting adult partners they choose.

MEANINGS OF SEXUALITY

Both informal and formal theories about sex differences in sexual behavior are embedded in theories about differences in personalities and assumed social destinies. Theories of sexuality seldom stand apart from other dimensions of complex human behavior, nor should they. Sexuality is related to many or all other aspects of personality in its social context. However, the topic of sexuality too often is twisted to the mold of preconceptions about how the sexes are *assumed* to differ. Sexual theories, like sexual behavior, often serve nonsexual purposes. This is illustrated by reactions to sex research and by the "achievement" or "rebellion" themes that are prevalent in contemporary sexual scripts.

REACTIONS TO MASTERS' AND JOHNSON'S RESEARCH

Challenges to the Dual Orgasm Theory. Freud claimed that infantile female masturbation involves clitoral stimulation and therefore a "clitoral" orgasmic experience. He argued that to achieve psychosexual maturity, females must relinquish the active, "masculine" sexual pleasure of clitoral orgasm to experience "vaginal orgasm." The vaginal orgasms he considered maturely feminine presumably depended on the thrusting penetration of conventional heterosexual intercourse. Thus, the assumed passivity of the vagina dictated the passive receptivity Freud believed to be an essential aspect of a mature woman's personality.

Freud admitted that the clitoris continued functioning in adult life in a manner he did not fully understand, and he recognized the incompleteness of his view of female sexuality. Many contemporary psychoanalysts have not emulated Freud's scientifically appropriate caution and instead have proclaimed this aspect of psychoanalytic theory as a dogma. They virtually ignored Masters' and Johnson's findings that female orgasm involves clitoral stimulation and is experienced in both the clitoris and vagina. Female sexual "inadequacy" is shown by the research to be attributable not to "vaginal frigidity" and "clitoral fixation," but to the cessation of the

response cycle at the plateau stage. When psychiatrist Mary Jane Sherfey challenged the dual orgasm theory on the basis of sex research findings, the initial response was derogation of her "heresy" (see Sherfey, 1973 for an elaborated account; Heiman, 1968). Eventually, however, the Masters and Johnson research has lead to careful questioning of traditional assumptions, resulting in improved treatment of sexual problems.

Interpretations by Radical Feminists. Some radical feminists have been as adamant as some psychoanalysts in politicizing the clitoral–vaginal issue for their own purposes. While these women accurately emphasize the necessity of clitoral stimulation for orgasm, they inaccurately deny any role for the vagina. Apparently in their selective interpretation of the Masters and Johnson research, they incorrectly assume that a thrusting penis is necessary for vaginal response—and they reject any dependency on a "male oppressor." For some of these women, therefore, autosexuality or homosexuality is not simply a means of gaining sexual satisfaction. Rather, such activity is used to assert independence from males in a sexual script that has more to do with achievement than with sexuality.

What's in an Orgasm? Views about what an orgasm is and what it means are as subject to personal and cultural bias as are views about its induction. Because of cultural views of sex as pollution and motherhood as purity, there is a strong cultural force to desexualize women who are mothers. Sherfey (1973) reports that during pregnancy the entire pelvic area increases in vascularity (blood vessels), which increases sexual tension and the intensity of orgasm. Pregnant women and those who have given birth (if their pelvic organs are not damaged obstetrically) often are more physiologically primed for sexual response than are other women. And in the very act of giving birth women who are not anesthetized or drugged often experience intensely erotic sensations. Nursing, which stimulates the uterus, also can be sexually arousing to the point of orgasm (Newton, 1973). Yet the potential erotic

bonuses of pregnancy and lactation are not included in our pronatalist (favoring childbearing)
folklore, because of assumptions about the impurity of orgasm.

People have sex for many reasons other than
physical pleasure, and the meanings of orgasm
are likely to vary with these. Sexual activity can
be a peak fulfillment of love; it can also be a way
of *proving* something or of *being* something. For
some women sex is symbolic of dependency; for
others it represents liberation from conventional
morality. Indeed, some young men use the taunt,
"Aren't you liberated?" in attempting to persuade
a woman to have intercourse. Pressures to conform to new norms often make it as difficult for a
person to choose virginity or celibacy as previous
restrictions inhibited a choice of direct sexual expressiveness. Although we live in a time of increased sexual liberation, sexuality is still a slave
to many other human motives. The achievement
motive is particularly salient in our society.

ACHIEVEMENT IN SEXUAL SCRIPTS

Males in this culture experience fairly consistent
and continuous pressures to prove themselves as
successful achievers in the occupational realm and
in many other life pursuits, including sexuality.
As an achievement arena in which he must perform and succeed, the sexual arena can be particularly threatening in evoking a man's fear of
failure because sexual achievement is considered
an integral part of his worth as a person. Impotence suggests failure *as a man.* A woman can
fake an orgasm and conceive without one. A man
cannot fake an erection. Although he can lie
about his sexual and other competencies to other
males, he must *perform* with females.

Even though women probably did not make
up the definition of male sexual achievement,
they bear the brunt for men's anxiety about potential or actual failure. The anxiety some men
experience seems to underlie their hostile
derogations of women as *tramps, sluts, whores,
tails,* or *pieces of ass.* Denying a woman's personhood by defining her in derogatory terms of
her sexual functions and apparatus eases the pressure on a man to perform—a woman is not a per-

son anyway. Knowing the rules of the sexual
achievement game, some women retaliate by
taunting men about inadequate performances or
impotence, thus eliciting additional titles such as
castrating bitches and *ball-busters.*

"Scoring" Sexually. Socialized to be achievement machines and to view "real" men as high
sexual scorers, some men exploit women sexually
to confirm their manhood to themselves, to their
imaginary audience (Chapter 10), and to their
nonimaginary audience of other men who will be
regaled with stories of their actual and fantasized
sexual exploits. Definitions of what constitutes the
achievement of "scoring" with a woman vary
across time and cultural groups. The traditional
"macho" Don Juan score is a simple tally of the
number of women a man has "seduced" (or
raped). However, especially among college-
educated men, sexual success and prowess now
are defined more often in terms of the woman's
response. The criterion is how turned-on the
woman got and how many orgasms she had.
While this criterion of success is an improvement
over the usual one, since it acknowledges the
woman as a sexual human being, the acknowledgment often is only superficial. Frequently, the
woman is still an object, as in the macho script:
her orgasms are "given" her by the skilled lover.
In the new script, she must not only receive the
male; she too must "perform" to validate *his* performance.

This success criterion may be part of the reason why pornography for heterosexual men often
includes elaborate descriptions of women's sexual
feelings. It also may explain why males in a previously noted study were most aroused by erotic
descriptions of the woman's (not the man's) sexual
feelings (Heiman, 1975).

Faking the Score. The women in the above study
also were more aroused by descriptions of the
woman's, not the man's, sexual responses. Perhaps they simply experienced a vicarious pleasure. But achievement overtones in sexual scripts
probably are involved as well. A male's sexual
response generally is viewed as a "natural" result

of his presumably greater biological "sex drive." His response is not considered an achievement for the woman. It is not even an achievement for him since he "should" be able to do it. In the cultural sexual script, the woman's achievement comes from attracting the man into a permanent relationship and pleasing him. To do this, she must confirm his virility and may therefore become overly concerned about her orgasmic response because of its significance to him. Unfortunately the anxiety in both partners may produce the feared failure. Certainly, it is hardly conducive to future pleasurable relations for a woman to confront a humiliated lover's angry, "What, you didn't come this time, *again?*"

To protect their lovers from a "defeat" and themselves from rejection, some women fake sexual pleasure and orgasm. Because deception undermines their achievement, some men attempt to expose fraudulent feedback on their performance. In his manual of sexual gymnastics, Dr. David Reuben (1969) suggests that after a possible orgasm, men look for sexual flush and nipple erection as "accurate indicators" of female orgasm. Actually, these reactions occur *early* in the response cycle and end abruptly with orgasm (Table 12-1).

SEXUAL INSTRUMENTALISM

Sexual scripts encourage both sexes to use sexuality as an instrument for obtaining nonsexual goals and expressing nonsexual needs. Some scripts and some nonsexual goals—such as needs for affiliation, union, and love—can be mutually enriching and can enhance the sexual experience. Other scripts can be dishonest and destructive. Even among the young, liberal, and well-educated respondents to a recent *Psychology Today* survey (Tavris, 1973), over half of the men admitted to using deception to have sex (Table 12-3). More than one-fourth of the women reported using sex to bind a person into a relationship, and two-thirds of them had on some occasion pretended to have an orgasm. These responses lend some support to Kate Millett's (1970) view that some women seek to control more socially powerful males by manipulatively using sex to attract and

hold men. Although men, too, are objects in the sexual game, the impact of deception in leading a person to feel like a "used" sexual object is far greater on women than on men.

Sexual Objects and Sexual Agents. Whether or not they deliberately use their bodies to attract a man, it is hard for women to avoid adopting the cultural view that they are *objects* of erotic desires rather than self-directed *agents* who can act on their sexual attraction to others. Fantasies as well as behavior reflect the cultural conditioning.

In one study over half of the middle-class married women who had fantasies during intercourse reported thinking of being overpowered by a dominant man (Hariton, 1973). The fantasies did not involve violence or abuse: They were not "rape fantasies" (although that label often is misused in such a context). Contrary to myths of female "masochism" that are used to justify rapists' sexual violence, women do not crave humiliation and violation of their bodily integrity (Brownmiller, 1975). The reported fantasies generally were of a stereotyped dominant–passive heterosexual encounter, frequently following a sexual display (such as a striptease dance) by the women. Curiously, the women's fantasized displays indicate their sexual power; however, the power is used to elicit an episode in which the women are receptors or objects of the men's dominant sexual agency.

Responsibility for Contraception. Many women do not use contraceptive techniques. For some women, this is because they lack the encouragement to view themselves as agents with choice and responsibility about their own sexuality. As "objects" they expect to be suddenly "swept off their feet" by dynamic male sexual agents (who might or might not use some type of contraception). If the encounter is romantically "spontaneous," it is somehow more "genuine" and pure than if it was a sufficiently planned possibility to warrant preparation. Avoiding the responsibility for contraception helps maintain a view of self as pure, not polluted, and as an object, not an agent. Survey data from sexually active un-

TABLE 12-3.
Sexual Instrumentalism *

	Women (Total = 544)	Men (Total = 763)
Have you ever told anyone that you cared more for him or her than you really did in order to have sex?		
Frequently	7%	25%
Rarely	9	27
Never	84	48
(Women only) Have you ever felt compelled to act less knowledgeable than you are in order to please or impress a man?		
Frequently	11	—
Occasionally or rarely	53	—
Never	36	—
(Women only) I have often felt that men were more interested in my body than in me as a whole person.		
Strongly true	15	—
Moderately or slightly true	46	—
False	39	—
Have you ever used sexual intercourse to bind a person into a relationship?		
Frequently or occasionally	12	5
Rarely	16	13
Never	72	82
Have you ever pretended to have an orgasm?		
Almost every time I have intercourse; frequently; frequently with some partners, not with others	16	0
Occasionally or rarely	51	31
Never	33	69
Have you ever felt used in sexual intercourse?		
Almost every time I have intercourse; frequently; frequently with some partners, not with others	17	5
Occasionally or rarely	62	48
Never	21	47

* Data from Tavris, 1973.

married women indicate that 16 to 21 percent never use contraceptives, and 28 percent claim their partners use withdrawal, which is a relatively unsafe method since semen might already have been deposited in the vagina (Stern, 1975; Zelnick & Kantner, 1972). While these women are not accepting responsibility for intercourse,

they will be held responsible by others should pregnancy ensue.

In some ways the contraception issue can be a "no-win" situation for women. Whatever they do, they take risks—of pregnancy, abortion, childbearing, or contraceptive effects. If they do not take responsibility for contraception and get pregnant, they are blamed for the pregnancy. If they do use contraceptives, they may unwittingly be subjects in contraceptive "experiments" where the main "testing method" is the passage of time. For both the birth control pill and the intra-uterine device (IUD), possible long-term dangers are unknown, although some short-term side effects already have been identified (Table 12-4). There is concern about the incidence of blood-clotting disorders, especially among older women taking "the pill" (Seaman, 1975). Pelvic inflammatory disease and, more rarely, uterine perforation do occur with the IUD (Katz, 1975). The diaphragm is highly recommended for its overall safety in preventing conception (when used properly) and in not harming a woman's body (Weideger, 1975). For permanent protection from pregnancy ("sterilization"), various surgical interventions for either females or males are available. None of the contraceptive methods mentioned thus far offer protection against venereal disease: Condoms are recommended for that purpose (Seaman, 1972).

Sexual Rebellion. Women who take responsibility as sexual agents choose active decision making about their sexual activities and celibacy. An apparently small number who are resisting sexual objecthood act out a rebellious emulation of the exploitative male sexual success pattern. These women, called *ball freaks* on college campuses, are Donna Juanitas who score with lots of males and proudly outdo their partners in the number of orgasms they "achieve." Not only do these women also boast about their sexual exploits, they sometimes have to "prove" their liberation by having sex while their roommates are present. There is a market for earphones among dormitory residents that is not related to stereo usage.

The Zipless Fuck. When former "victims" assume the behavior patterns of former "aggressors," we simply have a change of characters in the sexual power script—not a liberation from oppression in human relationships. Of course, some women who experiment with promiscuous or with non-private sexual relations are not after power.

Rather, they are trying to "keep it cool" and avoid emotional involvements. Avoidance of emotionality and of the restrictions of sexual scripts may both heighten the attraction of Erica Jong's (1973) "zipless fuck": A sexual encounter with literally no strings attached, neither physical ones like zippers and girdles, nor emotional ones, such as feelings of anxiety, guilt—or even of love. The fun and games of a zipless fuck can be a playful diversion, but not a satisfying long-term substitute for the deeper involvement of real sexual sharing:

. . . the absence of love in our lives is what makes them seem raw and unfinished . . . There is something comforting, then, about being in the regular presence of one person who can adapt to varying dosages of your capacities and incapacities and for whom you can do the same. The thought of loving someone whom you can see for four or five hours every day and spend the night with, sharing the daily accumulation of simple, silent warmth, both sexual and nonsexual, is one of the more inspiring aspects of life, whenever it can be achieved (Bengis, 1972, pp. 208, 252–253).

SEXUALITY AND SEX ROLES

For sexuality to be meaningfully expressed in emotionally open and personally equal relationships, there must be liberation from the scripted interactions based on sex roles. Role-based constraints on feeling and acting are so strongly ingrained for many people that liberation from them will not be easy for either sex. Possibly, however, the change will be more difficult for men because it requires shifting from patterns of dominance and emotional stoicism to egalitarianism and personal self-disclosure (Chapter 10). Just as women have been disadvantaged in developing **agentic** orientations by the lack of achieving female role models, men are perhaps even more deprived of male models who demonstrate honesty and mutuality in their relations with women. Those men who have such sensitivity to women often hide their feelings from other men because of the expected facade of male machismo. Many male professors serving as "father

TABLE 12-4.
Pros and Cons of Contraceptive Measures

Advantages	Disadvantages

Diaphragm with Spermidical Cream or Jelly
You must know how to use the diaphragm and use it consistently with a spermicide.

Advantages	Disadvantages
1. Diaphragm (with effective spermicide and *consistent* use) is 98 percent effective as a contraceptive.	1. Pregnancy rate of 2 to 12 percent, depending upon which study you read and type of population surveyed.
2. No side effects. Does not add chemicals (like the Pill) or irritants (like the IUD) to the body's system.	2. Currently requires fitting by a physician. (This could be done by a trained assistant.)
3. Insertion is before intercourse (can be up to four hours ahead) and need only be used at the time of intercourse. This need not interfere with spontaneity.	3. Often physicians do not make sure that users know how to check the proper placement of diaphragm.
4. Cost of the diaphragm is only about $6 and may last up to two years. Spermicidal cream or jelly (such as Delfen, Ortho, Ramses) costs only around 10¢ to 15¢ per application.	4. Fitting needs to be rechecked periodically.
	5. Some women object to inserting or carrying it around. This is at variance with some common assumptions about female sexuality.

Condom
You must know how to use it. Space should be left at the end of the condom for sperm collection. Hold it onto penis while withdrawing so there is no leakage.

Advantages	Disadvantages
1. It is the only method of male contraception that is currently available and effective.	1. Occasionally the condom breaks or leaks. (This is a rare occurrence.)
2. Especially when used with a spermicidal cream or jelly, it is around 98 percent effective as a contraceptive.	2. There is a slight loss of sensation for the male.
3. It is the only contraceptive that provides some protection from venereal disease.	3. Intercourse must be planned for and the condom brought along.
4. It does not add chemicals or irritants to the body's system.	4. Possible embarrassment on purchasing at the drugstore. (Really a needless worry since the pharmacist usually is glad to sell anything.)
5. Can be bought at any drugstore without prescription.	5. Some couples feel foreplay is interrupted when it is put on.
6. Application can be incorporated into foreplay; thus it does not necessarily interfere with spontaneity.	
7. Good for infrequent or "unexpected" intercourse.	

Advantages	Disadvantages

Birth Control Pill

1. Almost 100% effective in preventing pregnancy when taken consistently.
2. One of the contraceptives whose use is independent of sexual intercourse. Thus no interference with foreplay.
3. Often eliminates menstrual cramps (dismenorrhea), lightens menstrual flow, and regulates menstrual periods.
4. Sometimes helps with acne.

1. Long-term effects of artificial hormones on body system still unknown.
2. Must be prescribed by a physician, who should perform a pelvic examination and get a thorough medical history as well as give instructions about possible effects. Serious complications or fatalities are associated with a history of blood-clotting disease, psychiatric problems such as severe depression, cancer (and even family history of breast or uterine cancer), heart disease, endocrine disease (such as diabetes or thyroid disease), liver disease, sickle cell anemia, kidney disease, asthma, epilepsy, and migraine headaches.
3. Incidence of blood-clotting disorders (such as thromboembolism, pulmonary embolism, and stroke) higher among pill users—especially women over 40. Suspicion of higher diabetes rates and gall bladder disorders among pill users. Extent of risk of cancer from synthetic hormones will not be known for some time.
4. Frequent "nuisance" side effects include spotting between menstrual periods, nausea (similar to "morning sickness" of early pregnancy), and fluid retention, causing tender breasts, bloated feeling, and weight gain. Vaginitis (inflammation of vagina) and vaginal yeast infections may be more frequent (but are treatable).
5. Pill cannot be started the minute a woman decides to have intercourse. Not fully effective until after the first month's usage.

TABLE 12-4. *(Continued)*

Advantages	Disadvantages
Birth Control Pill (Continued)	
	6. Ovulation and menstruation may be delayed after stopping pill usage. This may cause problems in trying to plan timing of pregnancy.
The Intrauterine Device (IUD) 1. About 97 percent effective in preventing pregnancy among women *over 30 who have previously given birth.* 2. One of the contraceptives whose use is independent of sexual intercourse. Thus no interference with foreplay. 3. After initial cost of insertion, no additional expenses except for an annual checkup. 4. Method is reversible and does not impair fertility. 5. The IUD does not interfere with sensations and is not felt at the time of intercourse.	1. Long term effects still unknown, particularly regarding the newer copper IUDs. 2. Less effective than diaphragm or pill among women under 30 who have not given birth. High expulsion rate for these women. 3. Must be inserted by a physician who should perform a complete internal gynecological examination and give instructions about possible effects. Should not be used if woman has a pelvic inflammatory infection, if her uterus is markedly retroverted (tipped backwards), if she has excessive bleeding or cramps during her normal periods, if she has uterine or cervical cancer or heart disease, if she is pregnant, or if she has given birth or had an abortion within the past six weeks. The insertion is painful, especially in women who have not given birth. 4. Side effects frequently involve menstrual-like cramps, heavy menstrual flow, and bleeding or spotting between periods. 5. Pelvic inflammatory disease (infection of uterus and fallopian tubes) has a higher incidence among IUD users. This is serious and without treatment can be fatal. 6. In about 1 case out of 2500 the IUD perforates the uterus,

Advantages	Disadvantages

piercing the uterine wall and sometimes going into the abdominal cavity. This is life-threatening and requires surgery.

7. If the IUD fails as a contraceptive, the resulting pregnancy may be ectopic—occurring outside the uterus in the fallopian tubes or on an ovary and thus requiring major surgery. Even pregnancies within the uterus are likely to be aborted when an IUD is in place and may necessitate surgery.

Vaginal Spermicides (Foam, Creams, Jellies)

Advantages	Disadvantages
1. Effective *if combined* with other methods like the diaphragm or the condom.	1. When used alone, foams are more effective than creams or jellies; but all have high failure rates.
2. The chemicals do not interfere with sensation nor with body's system.	2. A few women experience minor allergic reactions to the chemicals.
3. Available at any drugstore without prescription; therefore does not require pelvic examination.	3. Use must be anticipated and prepared for because an application is required before each act of intercourse. Thus, some couples feel it interferes with foreplay.
4. Need only be used when intercourse is to occur.	4. Some women object to inserting the applicator or carrying it around.
	5. Can be runny and messy.
	6. Can interfere with oral–genital sex.

Rhythm

You must know how to estimate the fertile period and keep accurate records, preferably with basal temperature data.

Advantages	Disadvantages
1. Has approval by religions that prohibit other types of birth control.	1. "Off-beat babies." *Highly unreliable* as a contraceptive.
2. No expense.	2. Requires long periods of abstinence from conventional intercourse.
3. No side effects or internal system changes.	3. Requires regular menstrual periods and careful calculations.

TABLE 12-4. (Continued)

Advantages	Disadvantages
Sterilization	
1. One hundred percent effective for contraception.	1. Permanent. Rarely reversible, though this possibility is being researched.
2. No fear of pregnancy.	2. Surgical risk (usually very low).
3. Possibly cheaper than other measures in the long run, depending on when it occurs.	3. Female sterilization requires short hospitalization.
	4. Some males anxious about loss of potency or "virility," though potency not affected by vasectomy.
	5. Initial expense is high.

figures" perpetuate the hunter–pursued model of heterosexual encounters by boasting of their (usually fantasized) adventures with coeds they consider "fair game" who will "do anything for a good grade."

Although many men accept equal opportunity for women in some spheres, the dominance script frequently is still their model for sexual relations. They admit having trouble being sexually attracted to a woman they consider their intellectual equal. When she is not particularly troubled by their trouble, they may proposition her anyway in hope of becoming "on-top" of her symbolically as well as literally.

If sexual expression can come to be motivated by authentic concerns for the persons involved, then enacting or escaping from exploitative and manipulative sexual scripts will not be the prime reasons for sexual activity. Thus freed, sex could be enjoyed in a variety of contexts. Sometimes sex might be simply a playful diversion; at other times it might express the affection of a developing friendship; and sometimes it might fulfill desires for psychological and physical merger and affirmation within a love relationship. Prescriptions that "good" sex must be limited to certain practices in certain relationships to express only certain feelings perpetuate dishonest scripts and dishonest people.

SUMMARY

Through their sexual practices people express a vast range of sexual and nonsexual motives, as well as cultural values regarding sex-role behavior. Both informal and formal theories of women's and men's sexuality often are embedded in assumptions about their separate social roles. In disconfirming the psychoanalytic dual orgasm theory, the Masters' and Johnson research also challenged views regarding females' inherent passivity and prescribed social destiny. For some radical feminists, however, these findings became a bulwark for their separatist ideology.

Because of Western civilization's long history of viewing sexual behavior as shameful and potentially sinful—especially for women—expectations about women's sexual and sex-role behavior have focused on a purity–pollution dimension. "Good" Victorian women were not supposed to enjoy the sexual duties that enabled them to reproduce, and only recently have many people acknowledged women's right to sexual pleasure. There still is, however, a strong cultural force to desexualize and keep motherhood pure by "overlooking" the erotic bonuses of pregnancy, childbirth, and lactation. Concerns about women's purity also appear in our double standard for evaluating not only sexual practices but also genital organs, as expressed in a variety of concealment rituals for females.

Modern sex research has dispelled many myths claiming that women and men differ markedly in responsiveness to various erotic stimuli, but the research has yet to explore the full range of "hard core porn," including sexually violent materials. With respect to the physiological sexual response itself, research has demonstrated that women and men differ essentially only in the fact that women, but not men, are capable of repeated orgasmic experience within a short time interval.

Various surveys indicate that despite social restrictions, people engage in a variety of autosexual, heterosexual, and homosexual practices. Sometimes these activities are enactments or escapes from exploitative or manipulative sexual scripts that are based on sex-role expectations. Liberating women from their scripted casting as sex objects and men from their casting as sex agents will require that both women and men become more androgynous. Only then can sexuality be freed of destructive scripts and based instead on authentic concerns for the persons involved in an encounter that may be a simple playful diversion, an expression of affectionate friendship, or an affirmation of love.

CHAPTER
13
THE WOMAN
IN THE FAMILY

COURTSHIP AND EARLY MARRIAGE
COURTSHIP DURATION AND INTIMACY
PARTNERS' EXPECTATIONS AND ASSUMPTIONS
OLD AND NEW FAMILY LOYALTIES
IMPACT OF COURTSHIP MYTHS

THE CENTRAL ISSUE: INDIVIDUALITY PLUS INTIMACY
EDUCATION AND CAREER OPPORTUNITIES
MATURE INDIVIDUALITY

CHILDBEARING AND EARLY PARENTING
TIMING OF CHILDREN
SHARING LOVE AND RESPONSIBILITIES
RESISTANCE TO SHARING

ORIENTATION TO MOTHERHOOD
PRACTICAL AND EMOTIONAL SUPPORT

CHILD REARING
EARLY PARENTHOOD
CHILD-REARING ATTITUDES

SHARING RESPONSIBILITY WITH THE SCHOOL
THE MOTHER AS AUTHORITY
REACTIONS TO THE CHILD'S PEERS

DECISIONS ABOUT INCREASED FREE TIME
EXTERNAL INFLUENCES

MIDDLE AGE AND CHILDREN'S ADOLESCENCE
FATHER-CHILD RELATIONS
MOTHER-DAUGHTER RELATIONS
RELATIONSHIPS WITH OLDER ADOLESCENTS
FAMILY CONFLICT
SEPARATION EXPERIENCES

RESPONSES TO VALUE DIFFERENCES

OLD AGE
RETIREMENT

SUMMARY

Earlier chapters have considered the influence of many social institutions, including the **family of origin,** on the individual woman's development. Now we shall discuss how the adult woman is affected by her **family of procreation.** A number of authors, most notably Erik Erikson (1963), have described individual development in terms of a series of stages, roughly related to successive periods of chronological age. To each stage Erikson assigns a crucial set of emotional and interpersonal issues that must be resolved if individual development is to proceed satisfactorily. Such a development framework can also be applied to stages in the life of a family group (Worby, 1971; Duvall, 1958). The five stages relevant to this

chapter and some of the issues typical of each stage, at least for the middle-class American family, are listed in Table 13-1. Readers can easily add others from their own experience.

Through her involvement in each phase of family life, the woman is successively confronted with new roles, responsibilities, opportunities, choices, and emotional experiences. Her specific resolutions for the typical issues of each developmental stage are influenced by her previous experiences and by other family members. In turn, her decisions markedly influence the problems and solutions of later stages. Partial or unsatisfactory resolutions get carried forward as "unfinished business" to later periods, when resolution may

TABLE 13-1.
The Family Life Cycle

Stage	Issues
1. Courtship and early marriage	Intimacy–Isolation
	Freedom–Commitment
	Individuality–Merger
	Cooperation–Subordination
	Family loyalties–old and new
2. Child-bearing and early parenting	Nurturance: Giving–Receiving
	Symbiosis–healthy and pathological
	Possession–Sharing
	From the dyad to the triad
	Shifting generations–loyalties realigned
3. Child-rearing (Socialization)	Patterns of parenting
	Family and society (or, the parent goes to school)
	Styles of mastery: Achievement, competence, conformity, and creativity
	Separateness–Integration
	Separation: Phase 1
4. Middle age (and children's adolescence)	Menopause and puberty
	Accomplishment and disillusion
	Values of Authority: The conflict of generations
	Separation: Phase 2
	Intimacy and individuality renegotiated
5. Old age	Retirement: Fulfillment and loss
	Loneliness versus continuity of generations
	Dignity–Despair

entail greater psychic cost. If a woman has satisfactorily resolved earlier crises she can meet the challenges of later stages with greater self-confidence and more available options.

Much of the following discussion assumes relatively traditional marriage patterns. At the time of writing (early in the 1970s) most research on family life and much of the author's experience as a clinical and developmental psychologist involve people with traditional patterns. We shall note, however, possibilities of alternate career options, marriage styles, and arrangements for child care. Increasing women are postponing or deciding against marriage, deferring childbearing, and planning smaller families (Van Dusen & Sheldon, 1976). There now are more dual-career families in which both spouses work. Probably the family of the future will be less traditional and more open than the one described here.

COURTSHIP AND EARLY MARRIAGE

Marriages arranged by parents or tribal elders are relatively rare in our culture, where the selection of marital partners is generally a matter for individual choice. Although romantic love is idealized as a basis for marriage, there are important implications to consider about this basis of selection. The early phases of "falling in love" may provide an unlikely atmosphere for open and honest exploration of mutual compatibilities and differences. The couple who are strongly sexually attracted to each other and are forming a compelling attachment will tend to idealize each other into unrealistic perfection and to minimize the differences that may later cause them problems. Over time, as the strength of passionate feelings begins to subside, some of the discoveries of unsuspected personal idiosyncrasies ("Why does she always have to use up *all* the hot water when she takes a shower?"; "Why does he *never* clean up the kitchen after making a sandwich?") as well as deeper differences in expectations about husband's and wife's roles may come as a considerable shock. The first real test of the affection on which a marriage is based is surviving this inevitable process of partial disillusionment.

COURTSHIP DURATION AND INTIMACY

One important variable in the courtship process, which may be significant later, is simply the amount of time the couple have known each other before making a commitment to marriage or to some other more or less permanent living arrangement. Currently more unmarried couples are living together. Some of these relationships become "trial marriages" and eventually legal marital relationships. Whether having lived together is an ideal preparation for marriage is debatable. The sense of commitment ensuing from a religious or legal marriage can significantly alter perceptions of the relationship.

Some short courtships are terminated by a set of circumstances that force a hasty or coercive decision to marry—for instance, the imminent departure of one of the couple into a new job, or the discovery that the woman is pregnant. Especially among high school couples, pregnancy may be a planned device for securing parental consent that might otherwise be withheld. A decision for marriage made in a coercive situation often leads to stored up resentments that later erupt into open conflict.

PARTNERS' EXPECTATIONS AND ASSUMPTIONS

Whether before or after marriage, there is a crucially important process of mutual acquaintance and adjustment that must occur if the marital relationship is to "gell." Partners typically must explore and work out expectations about the division of roles in the family. Traditional assumptions that the husband must be the provider and the wife the homemaker currently are being challenged. The couple needs to be clear with each other about their own expectancies. Differences in the partners' two families of origin may be reflected in specific assumptions about rights and responsibilities (e.g., who carves the roast at family gatherings, who manages the budget and pays the bills, and who is responsible for household repairs). Though some of these issues seem trivial, they tend to be invested with the sanctions of custom and tradition—"the way we do things"—and may be unexpectedly hard to compromise.

Other differences involve more subtle assumptions about the marital relationship. Inevitably, the woman compares her prospective or new husband to her own father and the kind of relationship exemplified by her parents' marriage. This does not necessarily imply an "unresolved **Electra complex**" as many psychoanalysts would assume. Quite simply, over the past 20 years or so she has observed and been emotionally involved in her parents' marriage. The kinds of comparisons the young woman makes between father and husband will depend on her experiences as a daughter. Even if she consciously chooses a man very different from her father, she may still have expectations, of which she is not fully aware, that her relationship with her husband will be similar to that of her parents. A daughter who resented a domineering father, for instance, may choose a gentle, somewhat passive husband; and then, as the years wear on, become progressively more impatient with his lack of assertiveness and initiative. Meanwhile, by similar processes, the husband may come to perceive his wife as increasingly like his dominating mother, and become even more passively resistant in return. The potentialities for escalating mutual frustration and resentment are obvious.

Old and New Family Loyalties. In an emotional sense, the separation from one's family of origin is never complete, and from that family one carries images and fantasies that color all future relationships. While some ethnic groups in this culture preserve traditions of extended family life, with several generations living together, young couples generally establish a household that is *physically* separate from parents. This physical separation minimizes in-laws' interference, but it may cause a young wife to feel emotionally isolated. She might resolve this problem by simply transferring her earlier dependence to her husband. He may then be confronted with emotional demands that initially may gratify his sense of "masculinity," but may grow to be burdensome in later years. Thus the husband may

come to resent his wife's passive clinging and lack of personal independence. At the same time, the wife may become increasingly haunted by the sense of having submerged her own individuality to her husband's and let herself be dominated by him.

Impact of Courtship Myths. A related problem arises from our cultural courtship myths. Traditionally it is assumed that the man takes the initiative, both in dating and arriving at the decision to marry, whereas the woman has only the power to assent or refuse. Actually, the woman is expected to exert a great deal of control in *covert* ways, by being sexually seductive and guileful. Thus, roles prescribe a lot of game-playing that may leave the woman feeling somewhat deceitful and the man with a sense of having been entrapped into marriage, with his ostensible initiative something of a sham. When couples continue to enact stereotyped roles, the man may find himself wishing that he did not always have to be the initiator of sexual relations, and other actions and decisions. Yet he will feel inhibited from saying so, for fear of being "unmasculine." The wife, on the other hand, may find the passive role increasingly irksome, but will be fearful of being "unfeminine" if she makes sexual demands more directly or takes the initiative in other areas. Where partners engage in open communication they usually can renegotiate roles to allow for a more balanced and flexible assumption of initiative and assertiveness. A noticeable change in this direction seems apparent among college youth, where young women feel freer to initiate social and sexual contacts, and young men feel freer to accept.

THE CENTRAL ISSUE: INDIVIDUALITY PLUS INTIMACY

The central developmental problem for most women (and men, too) in this initial phase of forming a new family is how to preserve and enhance a sense of their own individuality and self-esteem, while at the same time making the compromises and sacrifices necessary for building an enduring intimate relationship. This process is more complicated, and more likely to leave unresolved conflicts, for the many women who have not been developing a sense of individual identity (Chapter 9). In our society a wife traditionally acquires status and a sense of personal worth *vicariously* through her husband (Chapter 11).

Education and Career Opportunities. The tradition of derived status and identity generally implies that a wife's vocational and educational goals are secondary to those of her husband. Thus many couples who marry before completing their education manage their economic problems by having the wife drop out of school to work at a relatively unskilled job to support the household, while the husband completes college or professional training. If children then come along as soon as the husband is earning enough to support a family, the wife may not for many years have the opportunity to complete her education. For some young women, the decision not to pursue their own goals may be a real sacrifice of personal ambitions and satisfactions. For others, the decision may be a relatively easy one because it avoids the necessity of forming an independent identity.

In either case, the woman may feel she missed some important opportunities and have a sense of unfinished business in her personal development that contains the seeds of some of the crises of middle life. Furthermore, if one member of the couple—typically the man—becomes much more highly educated and socially mobile than the other, a widening communication gap is likely. Paradoxically, the sacrifices the young wife makes of her own vocational goals or intellectual interests for the sake of the relationship may serve eventually to alienate her husband from her because they no longer have much in common except the responsibilities of home and children.

One significant impact of the Women's Liberation Movement is a clear departure from traditional assumptions that the husband's education or career must come first. Many young couples now consider the wife's educational and vocational goals as significant as the husband's. These couples plan applications for graduate school, job hunting, timing of children, and other aspects of

their lives accordingly. Although this more egalitarian planning may necessitate more complicated decisions, harder work, and less immediate gratification for both partners early in the marriage, it seems well worthwhile if it leads to a sense of more satisfying mutuality in later married life. Also, many young women and men find considerable relief in being liberated from one-sided assumptions about the responsibilities of married life.

Mature Individuality. In the development of a truly intimate relationship, there is always a certain degree of shared identity and emergence of a sense of "we-ness." The values, needs, and purposes of the partner assume an importance equal to one's own. This sense of shared identity is necessary for a new family, in a true sense, to emerge from the formal partnership of the couple. Such sharing is also a large part of what we mean by love. Our culture, however, places an extremely high premium on individuality. Often, therefore, people confuse self-centered independence and exclusive control (which seems necessary for identity formation in adolescence) with a truly adult identity and personal worth. In truth, a sense of personal identity and intrinsic worth includes and is enhanced by deep attachments to others. "I-ness" allows for a true sense of "we-ness," and "we-ness" can enhance "I-ness." Thus "intimacy *versus* individuality" is a pseudo-conflict in mature individuals.

On the other hand, distortions of intimacy occur when partners are not sufficiently differentiated as persons to maintain a sense of separateness and of self-worth somewhat independent of ongoing interactions with other family members (Boszormenyi-Nagy & Framo, 1965). True intimacy is possible only when partners engage in genuine "dialogue," respecting personal differences and freely communicating feelings and ideas. In this kind of relationship, both partners can develop toward greater maturity, and neither is enhanced at the expense of the other. For this kind of productive intimacy to occur each partner must have a fairly well-developed individual identity before marriage. Otherwise, identity formation will be stalled or bypassed in the apparent interests of the marital relationship. If both partners begin marriage with a clear sense of separate identity, then their further development as individuals can be enhanced by a truly intimate, sharing, and mutually supportive relationship.

CHILDBEARING AND EARLY PARENTING

Becoming a mother is a major transition in a woman's life (Rossi, 1968). In fact, parenthood involves much greater changes than marriage itself, and is more likely than marriage to be considered a sign of achieving adult status for both the woman and her husband (Hill & Aldous, 1969). The stress of parenthood is reflected in the reported decline in couples' happiness and satisfaction during early child-rearing years, followed by an increase as children get older (Chapter 9).

TIMING OF CHILDREN

If children come before the wife has established an occupational role and before the couple can afford paid help, the young woman may become totally absorbed in the tasks of housework and child care. Of course, women are subject to strong social pressures, even from some psychologists, to be full-time mothers (Bowlby, 1969). In many cases women adopt the full-time role as a retreat from the problems of developing a vocational identity, in the same way that deferring one's educational goals may be.

While early parenthood can have advantages, the potential problems are more obvious. In later marriage greater financial stability may make parenthood more of a pleasure than a burden. But more important, a delayed pregnancy enables the young couple to have more time to establish their own identities and become more comfortable in their relationship with each other. Couples in which the wife becomes pregnant during the first year of marriage tend to use more coercive and less rational modes of resolving their conflicts than those who defer pregnancy (Raush et al., 1974). Couples who have their first child later have more time in which to increase their skill in making compromises and understanding one another.

SHARING LOVE AND RESPONSIBILITIES

A woman's transition into motherhood is influenced by her ability to share, her feelings about motherhood, and the support she receives. With child-care help from her husband, the new mother generally does not feel trapped by many new burdens, and the father develops closer relations with his children. Fathers of newborns normally show immediate, strong affective responses to the infants (Greenberg & Morris, 1974). Traditional role expectations, however, deprive men and their children of continuing meaningful intimacy.

Resistance to Sharing. A woman may resist sharing children with their father if *she* needs his parenting for herself. Many women are attracted in part to their husbands' fatherly qualities. A husband's capacity for fathering is evident in his desires for parenthood, his solicitude toward his wife, his willingness to take on responsibilities, and his overall reliability. As previously discussed, when a wife has incompletely resolved her dependence on her parents, she may transfer her feelings about them to her husband. Or a woman may hope to find in her husband the paternal affection she felt she never received from her own father. In this case her psychological equation of husband and father may be so close that she has difficulty sharing him with her own children and to some degree she competes with them for paternal care. The reverse situation is perhaps even more prevalent, where the husband values his wife particularly for her maternal, nurturant qualities, and then has the problem of sharing her mothering with the baby.

If the partners have learned to *share* important relationships with others and to experience sharing as enriching, then having children will be rewarding and will deepen their bond. But if the parents' earlier experiences, for example, in competition with siblings for parental love and attention, led mainly to a sense of loss and deprivation, then these feelings will be rearoused with the advent of their own children. The resulting emotional stress, and possible **regression** in one or both marital partners may seriously strain their relationship with each other and with their children.

ORIENTATION TO MOTHERHOOD

Ideally a couple will be prepared for parental roles before the family expands. Preparation for motherhood begins, not in the nine months of pregnancy, but in the woman's own infancy. Her relationship with her own mother and the kind of "mother image" she has internalized will significantly influence her attitudes toward motherhood. If the relationship has been a difficult one, the woman may find disturbing early memories and fantasies reactivated during pregnancy (Anthony & Benedek, 1970; Caplan, 1957). Normally, however, the little girl who has a reasonably positive relationship with her own mother begins maternal role practice early and plays out the nurturant role with dolls and younger children. She then encounters the "real thing" with a sense of competence and pleasurable anticipation.

PRACTICAL AND EMOTIONAL SUPPORT

A third factor influencing a woman's transition into motherhood is the extent of support and help she receives, especially in the early stages of mothering. Aside from her husband's involvement, this help may come primarily from her own mother and other members of the extended family such as aunts and sisters, or from close friends. Help and support are crucial in avoiding the sense of isolation or depression that many new mothers experience. The new mother who has adequate support develops a strong emotional bond to her infant, and some of the beneficial psychological **symbiosis** of pregnancy will persist into the child's early years.

As the baby becomes more responsive and satisfying and less demanding of total care, the young mother still needs practical help and social support to avoid feeling isolated and entrapped in a baby-centered world. Various alternatives are becoming acceptable. Fathers are sharing increasingly in the responsibilities of child care. Many working couples can also afford a housekeeper, who, if all goes well, becomes almost a third parent. More day-care centers are becoming available. Nontraditional family patterns, such as group marriage, also offer alternatives for child care.

CHILD REARING

The child-rearing stage of family life is really a series of subphases, since the joys and problems of parenthood constantly change with the development of the child and with the addition of new children to the family.

EARLY PARENTHOOD

The developmental issues and the responsibilities of this early period will be the same whether the mother spends 168 hours a week with her child or not. The mother must come to terms with the meaning to *her* of her infant's total dependence. She needs to gain confidence and satisfaction in her ability to nurture and protect a new infant, as well as to continue to give care and affection to her husband and the rest of the family. Caring for a new baby can be intensely gratifying in itself and may bring many secondary rewards in the extra attention and tenderness lavished on the new mother. However, women whose babies are more temperamentally "difficult" (Thomas et al., 1963) may experience mainly burdens and interference with their personal freedom.

For parents the development of the child brings with it a continuously emerging mixture of feelings and experiences—some regret at the passing of one phase with its pleasures and gratifications, balanced by enjoyment of the challenge of the new stage and fascination with the unfolding of the child's capacities and individuality. As the baby becomes a toddler and more assertively explores the environment and practices a new-found bodily mastery, the parents must support the child's needs for autonomy and growing sense of self-confidence. They also must begin to socialize the child toward patterns of behavior acceptable in the family group and ultimately in the wider society.

Child-Rearing Attitudes. Parents show different degrees of warmth, or acceptance of their children, and of restrictiveness, or need to maintain control over the children's behavior (Chapter 11; Schaefer, 1959). A mother's acceptance of her child is related to her self-esteem and relationship to her husband (Winder & Rau, 1962). Her restrictiveness regarding certain behaviors reflects her degree of comfort with her own impulses and her relative acceptance of traditional sex-role stereotypes. For example, parents have tended to be more permissive of aggression in boys and of dependence in girls (Sears, Rau, & Alpert, 1965). Shifts toward viewing ANDROGYNY as more desirable for both men and women will probably reduce some of the sharp sex-typed socialization currently typical in this culture. Changes are slow, however. Indeed, a recent study of college student parents of toddlers (Fagot, 1974), indicates that parents react differentially to children of different sexes even though they *believe* they would not do so.

Inevitably the mother's feelings and attitudes will reflect her own socialization experiences, although her behavior may be a conscious or unconscious reaction against the treatment she received as a child. Many mothers look to popular authorities only to find that they disagree over time in child-rearing prescriptions. Still the emphasis on the importance of parental influences for the child's development has tended to increase parents' sense of the responsibility of their role, without necessarily making it any easier for them to carry out.

SHARING RESPONSIBILITY WITH THE SCHOOL

A further transition period in the life of the family begins when the oldest child enters school and ends when the youngest does so. Part of the responsibility for socialization is handed over to another major institution of society, whose goals and values may or may not correspond to those of the family. For families with different cultural traditions, the school may be an alien territory, whose values and demands bear little relationship to their own goals or life-style. The middle-class family, on the other hand, typically shares the school's orientation that academic education is important for life success and satisfaction.

Parents not only share responsibility with the school, but their effectiveness as parents comes under scrutiny and will inevitably be judged by the child's ability to conform to school requirements and achieve successfully. Many parents continue to see the child mainly as an extension of themselves, so that the child's achievement, or lack of it, is important mainly for their *own* rather than the *child's* needs. This is especially likely if the mother has "unfinished business" about her own educational or vocational aspirations. If, for instance, she stopped her own formal education to help support her student husband, then her school-aged children may well be burdened with her frustration. This is the situation in many families where the children become "underachievers" or develop other school-related problems. It is a poignant example of how failure to resolve adequately the issues of an earlier period in the life of the family may interfere with role relationships at a later stage.

For other women, the critical issues when their first child starts school mainly involve regrets over the loss of what may have been continual contact with the child. Such nostalgia, though, can be balanced by the increased freedom a mother now has to pursue her own activities as well as her enjoyment of the child's excitement in exploring a new world.

THE MOTHER AS AUTHORITY

The child's entry into school has implications also for a woman's view of herself as a person of authority. The child encounters less intimate relations with authorities than those thus far experienced. For example, the teacher's attention must be shared with perhaps 25 other children, and classroom rules must be followed. The ease with which the child negotiates relations with early extra-familial authority figures generally reflects the nature of family experiences. Children tend to be more trusting and cooperative, but not overconforming, in relations with other authority figures if their mothers have been **authoritative** rather than **authoritarian** (Chapter 11). This means the mothers have set firm and fair limits for the child while also maintaining open communication and recognizing the reality of the child's own feelings. For many women socializing their children is their first experience in the role of an authority.

Reactions to the Child's Peers. During the succeeding years of elementary school, the peer group gains increasing influence in children's lives. If a mother's own peer relations have been problematic, she may attribute greater significance to the slights and conflicts her children experience and become over-involved in their peer relations. Thus she may try to assert her authority in unhelpful ways. Her current social relationships are important as well. The mother who is secure in her own social world will be supportive rather than obtrusive as her children find their way in theirs.

DECISIONS ABOUT INCREASED FREE TIME

The developing independence of children facilitates the life-style of a woman who has combined a career with motherhood. But the mother who has been involved in "total parenthood" may find herself again at a choice point when her youngest child begins school. This may be an even more acute transition than when her first child entered school. Many late-born children may be conceived at this point in the life of a mother who decides to continue focusing on child-centered activities. Other mothers engage in an expanded social life or community involvements, seek employment, or return to school. Reentries into the community as a person somewhat separate from husband and children will have profound implications for the woman's identity formation. For many women, this stage in their lives involves a reopening of the individual identity issues of late

adolescence, which may have been foreclosed by an early commitment to marriage and parenthood. This reopening can easily evoke feelings of anxiety and depression. For other women, the transition proceeds more smoothly with a sense of renewed freedom and pleasurable excitement in new possibilities to be explored.

External Influences. The nature of this transition in the woman's life depends a great deal on community resources for adequate help in child care and housekeeping, and for employment and educational opportunities suited to the needs and schedules of women with family responsibilities. Here again the Women's Liberation Movement has been a constructive force in urging necessary social changes. If the values and institutional arrangements of the community do not support combined roles for women, or if the woman's own socialization does not facilitate growth in this direction, she may continue to be involved primarily or even exclusively in the family. In more traditional groups this may be an effective pattern for the rest of the woman's life. She may prolong the period of motherhood with additional pregnancies until it almost merges into grandmotherhood. For other individuals, however, the prolonged immersion in being a mother and housewife may be less functional. It may represent the postponement of a developmental crisis to the next period in the family's life cycle, when it may surface with a more disruptive impact than it would have earlier both for the woman herself and for the other family members.

Resistance to the woman's more individualized development sometimes comes from the shared but unexpressed fear that her involvement in a career will lead to the dissolution of the marriage. This fear occurs primarily when there has been conflict and polarization regarding issues of intimacy and individuality so that enhancement of one individual's identity is experienced as being at the expense of others in the family. As we have seen, the greater differentiation and enrichment of individual identity *contributes* to the capacity for true intimacy and does not detract from it. Thus a marital relationship can be enhanced by the wife's widening horizon of interests and experiences that she can share with her husband.

MIDDLE AGE AND CHILDREN'S ADOLESCENCE

Parents in our society are typically entering their forties as their children become teenagers. The conjunction of middle age in one generation with adolescence in the next can introduce new stresses and strains in family life. This period actually is neither brief nor sharply delimited in time; rather it stretches over at least 10 years, whether it is defined primarily in terms of the development of the offspring or the parents. Although defining adolescence is difficult (Ferguson, 1970), for our current purposes we may consider it as beginning with puberty. The end point is less clear since adolescents may not become economically and emotionally self-sustaining adults until some time in their twenties, possibly even later if they undertake advanced professional training. Many adults think of their fortieth or fiftieth birthday as the "great divide" between maturity and middle age; however, many women do not experience the *physiological* changes of menopause until some time in their fifties, and many men continue to think of themselves as "middle-aged" until retirement around age 65. Psychologically, the onset of middle age is less a matter of biological aging than of that point in life when people consider themselves "not so young" as they used to be. At this time some individuals experience a "crunch" in comparing youthful hopes with the reality of actual attainments.

FATHER–CHILD RELATIONS

The fact that children tend to reach puberty as parents enter their forties means that there are emergent concerns about sexuality for both generations in the family. Although these concerns are very different in nature, they interact in ways that profoundly affect family relationships. Father–son feelings at this time about waning and waxing virility often are expressed in contests of athletic skills, arguments about the use of the family car, and so forth. In contrast, father–daughter relations tend to have a greater balance of affection and mutual satisfaction. It is important to daughters that fathers appreciate their emerging adult identity, even though they occasionally resent the critical paternal eye cast on boyfriends. At this stage, too, the father's acceptance of the girl's achievement strivings may be very important in helping her to integrate such goals into her identity. Many high-achieving girls have experienced particularly close relations with their fathers.

MOTHER–DAUGHTER RELATIONS

Mother–daughter relations typically are smoother than those of fathers and sons (e.g., Bronson, 1966), and most adolescent girls do not overtly challenge parental authority as much as boys generally do. However, teenage daughters nevertheless get into conflicts with their mothers, particularly in areas related to the girls' sexual maturity and dating. The mother may, in a more or less benign way, be attempting to relive the romantic fantasies of her own adolescence. At the same time, parental warnings about the dangers of sexual promiscuity and premarital pregnancy may reflect, in part, a heightening of the mother's anxiety about her own sexuality. According to professionals who work with pregnant teenagers, a young girl's sexual "acting out" frequently is an expression of her mother's fantasies as much as of any needs or desires of her own.

The potentiality for conflict, which may propel the daughter into unfortunate sexual encounters or instill inhibiting anxieties, is greater when the mother is struggling with unresolved feelings about her own sexuality. The mass media depict the enormous concern in our culture with retaining a youthful appearance in order to be attractive as a sex object. In responding to this glorification of youthfulness, a woman may experience middle age as a time of waning fertility and sexual attractiveness. The intensity of her reaction and the potential for conflict with her daughter will depend on two interrelated sets of factors: The extent to which the woman's sense of identity and personal worth is integrally associated with her role as a mother and her ability to produce children; and the current state of her marital relationship and her relations with men in general.

Women who feel insecure in their marital relations and lack other sources of self-esteem and personal satisfaction are likely to experience emotional stress and physical symptoms during menopause. The previously discussed issues of "intimacy–individuality revisited" gain even sharper relevance here. In contrast, if the mother feels comfortable with her self, and feels loved and appreciated in intimate relations, particularly with men, and if she also has a variety of sources of personal security and fulfillment, then she can supportively accept and appreciate her daughter's maturity and initial ventures into heterosexual relations.

RELATIONSHIPS WITH OLDER ADOLESCENTS

If problems of intimacy have not been worked out between the parents, and have even become more severe during the busy years of raising and providing for a family, the offspring's later adolescence period can present another developmental crisis. The issues here are likely to come into focus as the family anticipates the oldest child's departure to school, to work, or into marriage. While writers on adolescence typically focus on the crisis of separation and **individuation** from the child's point of view, they tend to neglect the implications of this period for the parents' development. A major exception occurs in the literature on family process and schizophrenia, a severe form of mental illness (Boszormenyi-Nagy & Framo, 1966). The "schizophrenogenic" family is seen as an extremely disturbed system that strongly resists the individuation of the child defined as "sick" so that the parents will not have to confront their own serious difficulties.

Family Conflict. A series of referrals to the university psychological clinic some five years ago demonstrated to us that similar dynamics may exist in the families of late adolescents exhibiting much less severe problems. In each of these cases a seventeen- or eighteen-year-old child, usually the oldest in the family, was engaging in delin-

quent activities or otherwise getting into serious academic or social difficulties. The parents were expending a great deal of energy and concern attempting to control and cope with the deviant behavior, and usually they were at odds with each other about how to handle the situation. During group therapy with these parents we found that the parents' controversy over the children's problems was an indirect way of expressing aggression toward each other. Because communication between the parents was being channeled largely around the children, the presence of the problem child in the family was functioning to hold the marriage together. The prospect of the child's growing individual autonomy and separation from the family was a source of intense, if unacknowledged, anxiety to the parents, because it implied that they would be confronted with the emptiness of their relationship and the shakiness of their own self-esteem.

In therapy, the couples explored ways of being more honest and direct with each other about anger and other negative feelings and how to assume greater individual responsibility for self-esteem and personal satisfaction. It became evident that all the wives had important "unfinished business" in the area of individual identity formation that had been shelved at the period of early marriage and childbearing and never satisfactorily worked out. Some concrete expressions of working out this unfinished business were individual decisions to go back to school and complete a college degree, to drop an unsatisfying job in order to pursue more satisfying personal interests and eventually other career alternatives, and even the move of one whole family to a new community where the husband secured a more suitable job and the wife had greater opportunities as a professional artist. In each case, the child's behavior improved dramatically as the parents began to focus on the underlying problems in their own relationship. Usually within the next year the child began the process of separation from the family in an age-appropriate manner.

Some couples find that once their children are gone they indeed no longer have much in common. Thus, the incidence of divorce after about

20 years of marriage, while not as high as in the early years, is still substantial. This period is a relatively easy transition for couples who have continuously readjusted to the children's growing independence and developed other shared interests.

Separation Experiences. There are large differences among family systems in the extent to which older adolescents actually separate physically and emotionally from the family. Among Italian-Americans in Boston (Boutourline-Young & Ferguson, in press), there were many instances of extended families of three generations in which young married couples and their children lived in the same neighborhood or in the same household as their parents. In these situations the mother of maturing children can rather easily expand her existing set of roles to include that of grandmother. Readers can find an interesting and appealing account of a grandmother's central family role, her preservation of her psychological integrity and vivid personal identity, and her profound influence on a famous granddaughter in Margaret Mead's autobiography, *Blackberry Winter* (1972). A sharply contrasting picture is presented in Pauline Bart's (1972) study of middle-aged Jewish mothers who had been hospitalized with severe depressive reactions. Because women in this cultural group often are so heavily invested in the maternal role that they have become a stock subject of social satire, Bart hypothesized that they are particularly vulnerable to the **empty nest** phenomenon. She did indeed find that most of her sample had experienced separation from their children and loss of self-validation through the maternal role. Her material provides poignant illustrations of the catastrophic quality of middle age for women so overwhelmingly invested in motherhood (see also Chapter 9).

RESPONSES TO VALUE DIFFERENCES

Much has been written about the "generation gap" between adolescents and their parents, ranging from dress styles and tastes in music to more fundamental values as sexual **mores** and beliefs about human nature. Surveys of adolescent beliefs and values (e.g., Douvan & Adelson, 1966) disconfirm popular beliefs that there are wide differences in values between parents and the adolescent peer group. Nevertheless, parents of adolescents are likely to be confronted with many challenges to their life-styles and perhaps their more basic values. Parents respond in many ways, ranging from rigidly authoritarian attempts to preserve control of the child's behavior and avoid changes in the family's life-style, to sometimes ludicrous attempts to join the youth culture and deny any real differences between themselves and the teenagers.

In the first kind of response, we often see a revival of the struggles over authority and impulse control that characterized socialization battles with toddlers during early parenting. Only now the stakes are higher, and in the battles of this stage the parent is much less likely to win. Rather, attempts to maintain repressive control are likely to lead to an escalation of rebellion into various forms of delinquency. Parents in the 1960s who attempted to assert more traditional patterns of control over their adolescent children were likely to discover serious drug users or flight from home into youth culture "undergrounds." In the 1970s, such a break with the family is more likely to result in residence in some type of youth commune.

Not all parents of adolescents experience such painful confrontations, but to some extent all of them are pressed to reexamine their own values and patterns of life and, thus, to revisit some of the identity solutions of their own adolescence. Some parents find, to their own surprise, that reexamining their basic assumptions is refreshing and liberating, and they may thus grow up with their children, gaining a new self-definition. In the past few years many young women have discovered that their mothers were at first cautiously, but eventually enthusiastically sharing their participation in the women's movement.

OLD AGE

Aging presents many practical and social problems such as illness, reduced financial resources, and the need to move from a life-long home that has become too large and hard to care for. However, a central psychological problem is likely to be loneliness (Lynd, 1961; Fromm-Reichmann, 1959). Statistics on the prevalence of widows in our society speak for themselves. Particularly for the woman whose marriage has been the primary attachment of her adult years and whose children are no longer immediately available, the bereavement of widowhood may be sharp indeed.

Specific reactions to the loss of husband in later life depend on the dynamics of the marital relationship, earlier reactions to loss, and also on current environmental supports (Parkes, 1972). After the period of acute mourning, vulnerability to loneliness varies with the woman's inner resources, including her interests, hobbies, skills, and sources of entertainment, as well as on her surviving social network. Every community has its "LOL" (little old lady) groups, and women who have had wide and varied friendships will continue to enjoy them and perhaps count on them even more in old age. Observations of "senior citizens" make it clear that the capacity to form new attachments, including romantic ones, is not lost in old age.

The nature of the social network within the family may be even more important. It is a great source of comfort for old people to be surrounded by respectful and solicitous children and grandchildren. Currently, however, many "senior citizens" in our society are segregated in retirement communities or nursing homes. There is now a voluminous literature on the social problems of aging indicating that this segregation not only alienates the aged but also further splinters the **nuclear family.** Without a sense of the continuity of generations within the family, children grow up with little understanding of aging or of death. This contributes to their tendency, as adults, to cling to the semblance of youth and to avoid recognizing the inevitability of their own death. There is much to be said for radical social changes that would modify this pattern, although they may be difficult to achieve in modern urbanized society.

RETIREMENT

While many married women spend their last years as widows, some experience a more or less prolonged period of old age with their husbands. This situation may present its own problems. When the husband has been the principal or only wage-earner, his retirement marks the beginning of what the couple consider old age; and many older men actually age rapidly after retirement.

For both men and women who have been employed, retirement frequently involves a loss of social contacts and a reduced sense of competence and usefulness; thus it is a developmental crisis, and it may be a mortal trauma. Loss of self-esteem and depression are common reactions to retirement, and the intellectual deterioration and personality disorganization afflicting many "senile" persons probably should not be attributed solely to brain cell degeneration. Many couples compound the retirement crisis by moving to a new community without realizing that the "dream home" removes them from their familiar social network and may bring other unanticipated practical problems.

Women not only live longer than men and have superior physical health in old age, but they also show less intellectual deterioration (Young, 1971; Blum, Fosshage & Jarvik, 1972). This may create shifts in the husband–wife relation. Even women who had shared decision-making responsibilities with their husbands may need to take over many functions their husbands no longer can perform. For women who have been dependent on others all their lives, the need to make many new decisions may be a very difficult transition. Some women may have experienced a similar crisis earlier when they had to assume more responsibility as their aging parents became increasingly helpless.

For some older women, the need to assume more initiative and responsibility gives them a new lease on life and they remain enthusiastic and vigorous into extreme old age.

Even in the face of physical deterioration and imminent death, old age can be a time of personal fulfillment and dignity (or in Erikson's term, ego integrity) rather than a time of loneliness and despair. This positive culmination depends very heavily on the degree to which the older person is still a valued and contributing member of a family system and thereby experiences the sense of the continuity of generations. Many women who have not had children gain this same kind of gratification from continuing mutually enriching relations with students or other members of a younger generation. In old age, as well as earlier, experiences are a continuation, a recapitulation, and sometimes a significant reworking of previous solutions to the issues of personal identity, of competence and self-worth, of intimacy and sharing, of love and hate, which are the essence of being human.

SUMMARY

The family of origin is our first social group and for most of us remains the core of our social world throughout our lives. For women who choose to marry and have children, the network of intimate relationships includes her family of procreation, which continually changes during successive phases of the family life cycle. At each phase of this cycle, from courtship, through parenthood, to old age, a couple confronts a major challenge in developing a relationship that fosters and enhances each family member's individual development while also promoting intimate sharing among all. We have focused on the ways in which a woman can meet this continuing challenge as well as with the new experiences, new problems, and new opportunities for personal growth that occur at each stage of the cycle. If a woman makes a partial or unsatisfactory resolution of the emotional and interpersonal issues at one stage, the problems are likely to be carried forward as unfinished business in later periods. More satisfactory solutions may be found later, but often with greater psychic cost.

Developing a fulfilling and sharing relationship is particularly important during the courtship and early phases of marriage. Extending this sharing and coming to terms with issues regarding authoritative behavior and shared socialization responsibility become salient during the parenting stages. The simultaneous occurrence of middle age for parents and adolescence for offspring introduces a number of issues related to waning and developing sexuality, in addition to posing specific problems involving value differences. With old age come possible shifts in responsibilities, and a need to experience acknowledgment of one's contribution to the continuity of generations. To the extent that the individual woman finds creative solutions to these developmental problems and challenges, she becomes more fully a person and contributes to a richer family life.

The American family has many critics and many who question its viability as a social institution. The traditional roles of women in the family have often presented barriers to personal happiness and the realization of human potential. Whether this will continue in the future, or whether newly emerging patterns of family roles and relationships will support the healthier individual development of all family members, is largely up to the next generation of women as they go about making the important choices in their own lives.

CHAPTER 14
BECOMING A SINGLE WOMAN

Many people are increasingly questioning the suitability of conventional role expectations and life-styles for themselves. However, the expectations that people must be married if they are to be considered mature and fulfilled individuals is questioned much less frequently and more fearfully than others. A life as a single woman does not yet seem clearly accepted as a personally relevant and viable alternative to marriage. For many people, love, happiness, maturity, and purposefulness in life seem dependent on marriage. Thus, many young women tend to view the possibility of being a single woman much the same way that most people regard the possibility of their own premature accidental death—it can happen to other people, but it just can't happen to me! Some of the fears about singleness are relatively realistic and some are not, just as people have both realistic and unrealistic beliefs about marriage.

In this chapter we shall examine some implications of being single. On the one hand, our aim is to dispel some prevalent misunderstandings and raise consciousness about the unnecessary disadvantages and discriminations directed toward single people. On the other hand, the purpose is to enable readers to make more informed choices about marriage and singleness in their own lives, with a better understanding of potentialities for personality development and life satisfaction within either life-style.

WHO IS A SINGLE WOMAN?

Why are some women single women? What do they want in life? Do they have meaningful lives? There are as many answers to such questions as there are single women. Given increasing social change, the considerations relevant for the mature women of tomorrow may be different from those for women of today. However, some of the basic variables to consider are likely to remain much the same.

SCOPE OF THE ISSUE

There are Many. It is highly likely that every woman will at some time in her adult life be sin-

gle in the sense of not being married to a (living) man. First, divorce frequency is increasing. In 1970, 10 percent of all women who had been married were divorced or separated, a jump from 7 percent in 1960 (Rossi, 1971). The increased incidence of divorced people *may* mean a tendency for them to remarry less frequently than they did in the past. Second, differential longevity makes singleness because of death of a spouse likely for a woman currently married; most married women can count on several years of being a widow. For example, there are more than 100,000 widows aged 25 to 34 years old; there are almost 2.5 million widows aged 45 to 64 years old (1970 Census Data). Some women have never married, and it is these with whom we shall be most concerned here.

And There are Few. Approximately 3 to 7 percent of the United States population are single women. (See Figure 14-1 for absolute numbers of working single women of varying ages.) This is not a high percentage. However, the percentages of recent years are low relative to *past* years and are likely to be low compared to the projected trends for *future* years (Rossi, 1971; Giele, 1971; Bernard, 1973; U.S. Census Bureau, 1976; Van Dusen & Sheldon, 1976). The proportion of American people who marry increased over the first half of the century. Then, at the end of the 1960s, the marriage rate began to falter and was leveling off, if not beginning to decline, by the early 1970s. There were proportionately more single women and men in 1970 than in 1960, and a continuing increase of singles in 1975 relative to 1970.

The increased incidence of singleness is particularly strong among people under 34 years of age: the number of persons between 25 and 34 years of age who have not married has increased by about 50 percent since 1970, from 2.9 to 4.2 million persons. Concomitantly, the proportion of young single persons, particularly women, who are living away from their parents' homes and who are establishing their own households has increased: in 1975, 28.5 percent of young adults aged 25 to 34 years old were living alone, com-

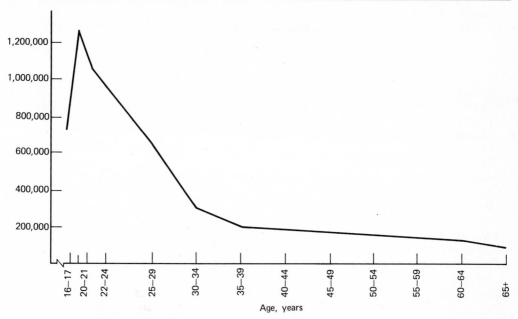

Figure 14-1.
Number of employed single women, by age.

pared to 21.2 percent in 1970.

The data may represent only a delay of first marriage or a trend toward lifelong singleness. Some sociologists are clearly predicting, with appropriate caution, that the marriage rate will indeed go down. As will become apparent in following pages, many of the unnecessary problems for single women are associated with the relatively low numbers of them. Part of the hope for the future of single women lies in an increase in their numbers.

TO STAY OR TO BECOME—A DEFINITIONAL COMMENT

The definition of "single" seems at first glance quite simple, aside from a few problems of distinguishing the never-married from the once-married (widows, divorcees). Is not a single woman simply one who is not married? No, not by psychologically meaningful criteria. Being a single woman cannot be defined negatively, as the absence of marriage. It must be defined positively, as the presence of singleness. Three cri-

teria of being a single woman have been suggested (Adams, 1971): (1) The capacity and opportunity to be economically self-supporting, which provides social independence from which many other features of singleness derive; (2) social and psychological autonomy; emotional independence from relationships requiring commitment or subjugation of her own personal claims; and (3) a clearly thought through intent to remain single by preference (a criterion that will be modified slightly in this chapter). These criteria are not likely to be met before about age 30. Notice the sharp drops in single employed women between ages 25 and 35 in Figure 14-1, indicating high marriage rates during these years. Women who are not married past this time are likely to be professional women (Table 14-1). Thus there is a **bimodal** distribution of working single women, with one age group being young and uneducated and one group being older and better educated. Many of the younger group, working in clerical positions, are likely to marry, whereas many of the more educated group are more likely to meet the positive criteria of singleness.

TABLE 14-1.
Occupations of Employed Single and Married Women *

	Total	Single	Married	Widowed	Divorced
Total employed women 16 years and older	30,534,658	6,810,944	19,101,511	2,543,567	2,078,636
Professional, technical	4,674,716	1,142,470	2,960,326	294,892	277,028
Such as:					
Accountants, computer specialists, engineers, lawyers, librarians, mathematicians, physicians, dentists, nurses, religious workers, social workers, teachers, writers, artists, entertainers.					
Managers and administrators	1,083,601	162,076	688,068	135,393	98,064
Such as in:					
Purchasing, sales, restaurants, schools					
Sales workers	2,249,259	501,269	1,412,459	216,866	118,665
Clerical workers	10,515,431	2,766,757	6,409,431	618,648	720,595
Such as:					
Bank tellers, bookkeepers, file clerks, counter clerks, keypunch operators, receptionists, secretaries, telephone operators.					
Craftsmen	547,761	88,807	346,215	68,196	44,543
Operatives	4,430,853	635,090	3,110,932	376,363	308,468
Such as:					
Assemblers, dressmakers, packers.					
Transport equipment operators	138,979	16,973	101,383	12,656	7,967
Such as:					
Bus drivers					
Laborers (except farm)	307,688	72,099	188,476	28,426	18,687
Farm laborers, foremen	181,044	40,506	122,945	12,808	4,785
Service workers	5,061,340	1,118,241	3,060,730	497,506	384,863
Such as:					
Maids, cooks, waitresses, nursing aids, hairdressers, housekeepers					
Private household workers	1,186,369	252,635	591,392	252,731	89,611

* *Source.* United States Census Bureau, 1970.

In this spirit, we suggest that the relevant topic is not women who *stay* single (actually unmarried women), but women who *become* single. Single women do not necessarily have a negative view of marriage; rather, they have a positive view of being single. In many ways, the purpose of the chapter is to explain why such criteria are set for becoming single and the intertwined advantages of singleness that encourage a woman to choose to become a single woman.

CHOOSING

Promarriage and Antisingleness Pressures. The pressures toward marriage and away from singleness are so pervasive and intense in contemporary society that many people have not in fact freely chosen the marriage they have or intend. There has been an idolatry of marriage as the only way to find peace and fulfillment: "And they live happily ever after. . . ." The external pressures from other people are often strongly internalized, so that many young women and men feel an unexamined compulsion to get married. They assume that marriage is desirable for themselves without considering that assumption, or they have difficulty admitting even to themselves that they have some reservations about marriage.

Supporting the assumption of the necessity of marriage are strong assumptions about the disadvantages of not being married—although most single women are not particularly antimarriage, most other people are antisingleness. A prominent cultural definition of happiness for a woman is "escape from being 'an old maid' " (Bernard, 1973, p. 55). The fact that the marriage rates in teenage years are negatively related to the income of the young women also suggests that young women often marry because they feel it is the only thing they can do. Thus, marriage has often been sought not because of its positive features but because of the presumed negative features of singleness. Among students recently taking a psychology of women course, for example, many women felt that marriage is the only way for them to be happy, and that singleness means only a loneliness and despair they think they can

avoid by marriage. Some of their comments reflecting this, and relevant in later discussion as well, are given in Table 14-2.

Women's Marriage Expectations. Most young women expect to marry, and most older single women initially were little different in assuming marriage for themselves, although they may now vocally reject marriage (e.g., Fallaci, 1974). The percentage of women during high school and early college years who state an intention not to marry is fairly consistently reported to be around 5 to 6 percent, both in this country and in Great Britain (e.g., Douvan & Adelson, 1966; Fogarty, Rapoport & Rapoport, 1971). Similarly, among highly gifted women who had been winners of National Merit Scholarships between 1956 and 1960 (interviewed in 1965), 6 percent stated that they were planning on a career and no marriage; another 6 percent were uncertain; almost half planned marriage and an immediate career (Watley, 1969). More recent evidence gathered by the editors in 1973 and 1975 does not indicate any marked increase in the number of young women planning not to marry.

Education increases the frequency of intention not to marry (to around 20 percent in women graduate students), or postpones the desired time for marriage (Davis, 1964; Ginzberg et al., 1966). However, the percentage of educated women who expect to be single is lower than the percentage who actually are. Why do so many of those who expect to marry not do so? The stereotyped answer, "They didn't have a chance," seems applicable to few, if any.

Competing Concerns. For most single women, the lack of marriage is not a result of an early clear, explicit decision, but of drifting into singleness through many small choices that are not necessarily made with thoughtful awareness (McGinnis, 1974). For some women, avoidance of marriage is based on such factors as fear of rejection, anxiety regarding the intimacy or the commitment expected in marriage, or rebelling against expectations. A larger number of single women, however, have no particular need to

TABLE 14-2.
Views of Young Women about Marriage *

Responses to the items, "Estimate the extent of your confidence that you want to be married at some time in your life, relative to being single (on a 0% to 100% scale)" and "What do you most value or like about marriage for yourself?"

100%. Because we all need someone that is going to stand by you. Marriage fulfills this need of dependence and the ability to love and have someone rely upon you. *Value:* The idea of depending, loving, and helping someone who equally depends, loves, and needs you. Age 19, no major declared yet.

100%. I need someone special, who cares about me and loves me and I need to love and care about somebody. I like the satisfaction and joy that a serious relationship gives. I find a mutual sharing and caring for each other is very reassuring. *Value:* The companionship. Age 20, junior, Nursing Major.

100%. I have learned so much through relationships with women as well as men. But since a male/female marriage is my only societal option open, and since I feel that sex is a beautiful male/female activity, I wish to share the majority of my life with a man. *Value:* LOVE AND COMPANIONSHIP! I want to be able to do my thing and at the same time let him do his. I feel that this continual growth process of becoming rather than being with him will fascinate me for the rest of my life (and his)! Age 20, Sophomore, Psychology Major.

98%. Having someone around permanently who understands me and loves me . . . the security of somebody who will care about me. To be alone in the world seems very scary to me. I didn't put quite 100% because if I never meet the person who would fit ideally with me, I'd rather be alone than fool myself or push it. *Value:* The security of being loved and cared about. Age 18, Liberal Arts Major.

avoid marriage. Rather, placing primary value on some involvement such as a career, they simply do not get around to marriage. Lack of marriage is a by-product of their choices, not a major part of their definitions of the ideal life. They very well may visualize married life as desirable, though not markedly more desirable than what they already enjoy.

Even among older single women with years of happy experience as a single woman, most have not definitely ruled out marriage as a possibility for themselves. They occasionally may say, "I won't get married," but few mean this as an absolute irreversible, "Never!" They are not rejecting men or avoiding marriage; rather they are affirm-

ing and enjoying their current life. Such single women do not say, "I *will be* single," but rather "I *am* single." And they say so with pride, self-confidence, and satisfaction with life.

"*Moment of Truth.*" At some point single women are likely to experience a "moment of truth" during which they confront the reality that they are single and possibly will remain so. This realization may provoke a personal crisis of varying duration in which a woman may feel utterly alone in confronting stark reality. Many women experience this "moment" shortly after achieving a major goal, such as completing professional training and settling into a job, or getting a promotion that

90%. The companionship and sharing with someone who means very much to you, Age 19, Freshman.

85%. I do want to get married. The reason for 85% is because there are some reservations in my mind about what marriage will be like. *Value:* A person to share my life with. Someone I love enough to spend the rest of my life with. Age 18, Social Work Major.

75%. I seem to be heading in that direction right now. I haven't had any very positive experiences or feelings as far as being single goes. If I had, I might change my mind. *Value:* The togetherness, and, unfortunately, I think security would be a big part of it for me. Age 20, junior, Urban Development Major.

50%. If I could get married, share a relationship which encourages my and my spouse's growth, and retain my individual freedom I would be pretty sure of getting married (80%). Right now, I'm not sure a husband like that will come along. Age 19, Premedical Major.

10%. The more I meet different types of men and ask myself, do I want to actually live with them for the rest of my life, the more I'm inclined to say 99% of the time, no. I'm not going to say that I don't need a man, but the more education I receive, the more capable I am of providing for myself. As long as I have a few men in my life at certain intervals of time, I'm satisfied. That's another thing, men are nothing but a bunch of hassles with their childish games, their inconsideration, their ego, and the fact that they have to have their way because they've gotten their way all their lives. *Value:* Having someone on my level of intelligence and therefore able to understand and accept me as I am. Having a child. The experience of for the first time considering someone else's feelings and working together to achieve something meaningful and everlasting. Age 18, First-year student, Business Major.

* *Source.* Students in a psychology of women class at Michigan State University, Spring, 1975, were asked to answer a variety of questions about marriage and singleness. These are responses to two items of all students who returned the forms.

offers clear career potential; with typical career patterns, this is likely around age 30, but occurs also in older women. The critical nature of this time of life is indicated by higher than usual suicide rates among young single professional women compared to married professional women (Mausner & Steppacher, 1973). However, most single women do not choose death, physically or psychologically, as the mean for resolving quandaries about themselves at this time of life.

The outcome of the "moment" for most women involves deciding to change the current life-style or views about it. Some women may decide to actively seek marriage. Others may experience a change from being a woman of drift to one of decision: "Oops, I'm single . . . but it's not so bad. In fact, it's O.K.—I like it!" The feeling is not, "I will be single," but "I *am* single." A similar confrontation with reality can occur with married women as well, when they realize, "I *really* am married!" Such a confrontation seems valuable in demanding an awareness and definition of who one is and wants to be. Reactions during the moment of truth may mark the transition from being an unmarried woman to being a single woman, or to being a married woman. Who will make which choice cannot be firmly predicted, but certain factors are likely to influence the decision.

SELF-DEFINITIONS

Socialization Antecedents. The probability that a woman will become a single woman seems to be increased by (1) any factor that decreases the centrality of **sex-role identity** as a central dimension in her concept of self or that decreases the relevance of marriage in her sex role or her **sexual identity** and, closely related to this, (2) any factor that increases the ease with which she can or expects to have self-acceptance, self-respect, and meaning in life without marriage. Because of a complex set of factors, women come to differ a great deal in how central sex-role evaluations are to them and in the traits and behaviors they believe are appropriate and comfortable expressions of their own identity (Chapter 8).

Even for women to whom traditional femininity is important, traits they consider feminine may be expressed through life-styles other than marriages. Not all young girls experience sharp sex-role training from their parents. Also, for some, observations of unhappy married women or happy single women may ease the other pressures they experience toward a focusing of **self-concept** around marriage. A young girl may observe her mother's laments about a maiden aunt but also observe that the aunt owns her own business and takes long vacations to exotic places. What is important to her mother may not be what is most important to her. The growing child and the growing woman evaluate their experiences in light of their own evolving conceptions and values in ways not completely understood. That education is highly relevant to becoming a single woman is fairly clear.

Socialization for Education. Education and its correlates are chief factors encouraging a young woman to question whether marriage is necessary for her. She may find other dimensions in self-view of equal or greater importance than marriage. Other avenues of personal expression are open. Parents often start the ball rolling by expecting college or other career-relevant education for their daughters. They do so for many reasons. Some simply value education for itself. Some

want their daughter to "make a good catch," to escape the small town, or to gain financial security, perhaps within marriage, "just in case . . ."

Whatever their motivations, parents strongly concerned about education or career preparation for their daughter may not clearly and *explicitly* communicate that they expect her to marry as well. It can be quite a shock to them when they realize that their educated daughter does *not* share their implicit belief that marriage is "just natural" for her. As a consequence of her training, a woman can experience many opportunities that might not be available in a traditional marriage.

The educated woman can support herself in a job that she has chosen because of its interest to her and her competencies in it. She can find support for self-esteem and satisfactions of **competence motivation.** Her career may provide many satisfying side benefits, such as travel, meeting interesting people, making important decisions with an immediate social impact, evolving a realistic image of herself as an inventive scientist, effective administrator, thoughtful scholar, creative poet, beneficient humanitarian—or simply, an interesting and attractive person. Her career may also provide many opportunities for developing warm interpersonal relationships. As a consequence of her many experiences she may become more selective about the men who attract her for temporary or more permanent relationships (Chapter 15). Marriage thus becomes more a choice and less a requirement for her happiness, self-esteem, life enjoyment, and sense of purpose. This is sometimes difficult for parents and other loved ones to realize.

Parents' Concerns. Lack of marriage is often fairly traumatic for her parents in ways the single woman may have trouble understanding. Expecting their daughter to find "a nice young man," parents often feel guilty that "Somehow we failed; what did we do wrong?" or feel angry at their child for disappointing them. A strong core of their feelings is simply concern—they want a happy and a meaningful life for their children and do not understand how the single life can be that.

Thus, as a young woman becomes increasingly a single woman rather than an unmarried woman, she has an ongoing challenge of educating her parents and other loved ones about the advantages of singleness for her. My observations suggest that parental responses to their unmarried *child* typically progress from subtle or blatant pressure for marriage, through resigned sympathy and concern, to respect for this single *woman* who is "doing her own thing" and well so. The extent to which their feelings of respect become dominant over those of sympathy is a matter of the degree to which the woman herself is able and willing to experience more advantages than disadvantages in both her life alone and in her life with other people.

A LIFE ALONE

For many women, all or a sizable portion of their lives may be spent living alone, with concomitant advantages and disadvantages. Some women come to live alone because of divorce or widowhood, which may accentuate or reduce some of the specific advantages or disadvantages experienced by women who have never been married. Over the decade from 1960 to 1970, there was a sharp upturn of about 50% in the number of women living alone, to about 7.6 million women (see Rossi, 1971). Although part of the increase is due to population aging, the sharpest increase was among women between 20 and 24 years, a 109% increase. The increase may be due to factors such as rise in age at first marriage, a reduced tendency to prompt second marriage after divorce, or a rise in women in higher education. In addition, women differ in what specific features of living alone are most relevant to them and in the ways they experience the consequences of a life alone. Aloneness is not the same as loneliness.

ADVANTAGES

The advantages of being single and living alone are vastly overlooked and misunderstood by most married people and many younger people who have grown up in a culture dominated by marriage. A life alone can provide exceptional freedom and opportunities for developing a sense of personal competence and individuality.

Freedom. One who lives alone is less encumbered by the necessity of having to plan around other people and to make decisions to solve the interpersonal conflicts that normally occur. Indeed, even women who say that they are "100% sure" that they want marriage see personal freedom as a clear asset of being single. The freedom contributes to day-to-day peace of mind that can be enjoyable, refreshing, and often necessary. One does not have to contend with the petty aggravations of conflict about which TV show to watch, what kind of coffee to use, what color to paint the living room, and so forth. The woman alone is also free to pursue her own hobbies and interests without worry about disturbing someone else's plans. Similarly, the moments of solitude that everyone needs are easily guaranteed to the person living alone. When one is too tired or distracted to perform the usual social courtesies, they need not be attempted. It is rather pleasant to come home, prop your feet up in your favorite chair without having to listen to someone's problems of the day or to decide who gets what section of the evening paper first, or when to start dinner. There is, of course, also freedom in planning vacations, expenditures, where to live, and what friends to invite over. One need not worry about fitting the needs or preferences of other people.

Probably the largest drawing card of interest to many women is freedom in career choices and decisions. The single career woman can work nights and weekends without feeling guilty for depriving her husband, children, or other housemates. She can consider taking a promotion that requires moving to another town or being away from home more without worrying about uprooting the family. In this sense, she has more career freedom than the typical married person.

Individuality. A single life-style also provides potential for growth toward the mature individuality that comes from knowing you can use your freedom well and be self-sufficient and can enjoy aloneness. There is a greater demand and opportunity for developing self-sufficiency and a firm sense of separateness (Chapter 9). By choice or by necessity, the single woman may develop many practical fix-it skills typically assumed present or appropriate only in the husband in traditional marriages. A healthy woman can fix the lamp plug, build a bookcase, or saw a broken branch from a tree. She can have pride that she is "keeping things going." High school shop courses and readily available how-to-do-it books can help develop competencies relevant to some practical implications of living alone.

Developing and recognizing self-sufficiency have profound effects on self-development and self-definition. The woman alone must have or develop a thorough knowledge of herself, an acceptance of herself, and a commitment to herself as a worthwhile person. She must be capable of psychological survival as a separate, independent person. What one does with personal aloneness is an issue most married people do not face until the actual or anticipated death of a spouse. Nonmarriage thus can be a vehicle for developing personal autonomy: "I see that there is some work on the self that can only be done alone, independent of relationships. That work is the affirmation of one's self. *You are the only one who will never leave you,* someone once told me. Curiously, it is a thought that reassures me" (Kwitney, 1975, p. 71).

A woman who values the peace of mind possible without restrictions on her freedom posed by responsibility to other people may seem extremely selfish, stubborn, and snobbish. Before considering why this is not necessarily so, let us consider the other side of the coin, the disadvantages of living alone.

PROBLEMS

Minority Status. The most obvious and influential disadvantage of singleness is that it is neither expected nor is it frequent, compared to marriage. Our social system has not allowed the single person a role position of clear definition and value. The problem can become self-perpetuating

if not interrupted: The low incidence of singleness inhibits recognition of its values, perpetuating negative stereotypes; the stereotypes inhibit getting to know the single people who do exist so that stereotypes are not broken and the implicit equation of marriage, personal desirability, and happiness continue. Thus, many of the problems currently experienced by single people could be reduced or eliminated if there were more single people or if they were responded to as the persons they are instead of on the basis of negative preconceptions, which often operate without awareness.

Others' Role Confusion. The single woman often makes other people uncomfortable; she seems incongruous to other people, who expect a woman to be married. If she also seems happy, she is even more incongruent. People are simply confused by her while they think they know about "the typical American woman," who is Mrs. Someone-Else, with two or three children. Often they lose touch with their usual reasonableness and social sensitivities when they first meet a single woman; they offer unnecessary sympathy, ("It must be hard, dear"), inappropriate consolation ("There's still time"), or attempt a meaningless flattery, ("Why aren't you married, you're so pretty!"). Such comments can undermine a woman's self-esteem and pride, if she lets them, and lead to unpleasant interchanges; they can also be an occasion for informing people of the facts and sharing one's own personness. Widows and divorcees tend to fare better on such matters than women who have always been single. However, the longer a divorcee stays that, the more susceptible she becomes to comparable problems.

When Two's Company. The social patterns of most married adults, and unmarried adults as well, perpetuate problems. Our society tends to pay extensive lip service to values of individuality and self-sufficiency. Yet social functions typically are set up for couples rather than for individuals, even when pairing is not necessitated by the activity involved, such as eating at a dinner party, spending an evening of pleasant conversation, or watching vacation movies. Well-meaning hostesses often close their invitation to a single woman with a "permission" that is really a request, "And you can bring someone." If the single woman brings a male friend, both she and he easily become uncomfortable targets of speculation and misinformed gossip; bringing a woman friend causes even more problems. Although Noah had good reason for selecting creatures two-by-two for his ark, one can question the applicability of his example for most contemporary guest lists.

Given the problems involved, the single woman and her married acquaintances are likely not to develop friendships—a regrettable restriction potentially affecting the personal growth of all concerned (Chapter 10). For women in professions where much professional business is conducted informally at social gatherings, there may be interference with her career progress also (Chapter 15).

Companionship. Because of the likely exclusion from married social circles and because of her own desire for friendship with others who understand and value her single life-style, the single woman wants to know other single people. In view of their small number, this is difficult in some communities. Thus, the single woman needs to be able to do things by herself. Again, societal conditions do not facilitate this. At present, a woman cannot go alone to a cocktail lounge or movie with much safety. There is often a problem of finding someone who can share interests and hobbies; one friend may share a golfing interest, but have no interest in gardening or visiting museums. Probably much the same problem exists in many marriages, as one spouse "goes along" with an activity of interest to the other, but without zest or enthusiasm. The single woman may have to celebrate important occasions or holidays alone. Such celebrations are not necessarily better or worse than shared occasions. They are simply different, and potentially very rewarding and valuable. Alone does not mean lonely.

Because of the greater incidence of singleness in the 20- to 30-year-old age bracket, younger people have fewer problems of finding single companions than older singles. Hopefully, increased incidence of singleness will improve the situation for more mature singles. For singles of any age, it is difficult to find the other singles that do exist. Large city apartments for "singles only" and clubs for singles (or divorcees or widows) may bring new opportunities. Sometimes, however, they are often only a collection of people who have nothing in common other than being not-married.

Professional and social activities associated with the women's movement are facilitating contact among single women and between single and married women. Contacts made in such contexts of free and open acceptance foster increased mutual understanding and respect among single and married women (Chapter 10). One may hope that both women and men may come to benefit from such interchanges.

Aloneness. Some problems for the single person will continue, no matter how many single people there are. The unavoidable disadvantage of a life alone is also the basis of the advantages: there is just one of you. The advantages may be better enjoyed if the disadvantages are also recognized and affirmed. Some of the disadvantages revolve around the simple fact that the single person has only two hands. The working woman who lives alone must do for herself things the married woman's husband does for her *and* things that a wife does for a married man. Given the unrecognized and pervasive ways in which a homemaker wife keeps the mechanics of life running smoothly in a household, the single woman is likely to find the absence of a wife a greater inconvenience than the absence of a husband! In any case, she has two sets of energy-consuming jobs to do at home, while working full time. Some single women can afford help for household chores; others cannot. And, their salary is likely to be less than that of a man in a comparable job, while their expenses are *not* half the amount for two people living together.

Living alone also has implications for self-maintenance. There are none of the occasional prods or reminders often needed to get an appointment with the dentist, and no help for day-to-day monitoring of bad habits—smoking a little more and eating a little less, working a little more and sleeping a little less. Reminders from others can be nagging criticisms; they also can be useful. What was once a matter of occasionally bringing work home for the evening can become a compulsive drive that erodes weekends and all evenings. In times of illness, there is no ready caregiver, and the possibility of a protracted illness or permanent disability is a concern. If the single woman loses her job, there is no one else's check to meet the necessities. She may now be self-sufficient financially, physically, and psychologically, but the future is unknown. Some issues of life must be confronted whether one is single or married, but the practical implications can be more severe for single than married people.

IMPACT ON MENTAL HEALTH

Given the potential benefits and costs of a life alone, how psychologically healthy are single women as a group? Generally, data do not support stereotypes about the misery of single women, and there are sex differences in the ef-

fects of marital status. Marriage tends to be associated with marked benefits for men and impoverishments for women; singleness is associated with impairment for men and benefits for women. Depending on the populations surveyed and the criteria used, sometimes single women may score highest on mental health indices or married men may score highest; single women are better off than married men in terms of some psychological distress symptoms (Table 14-3). Married women generally are third in the rankings, and single men invariably are at the bottom of almost any psychological or sociological criteria relevant to life success. Single men certainly are not carefree, happy, or swinging bachelors.

Life-Style Comparisons. Married women are more likely than single women to report that they are very happy with life. However, as discussed previously (Chapter 9), the high incidence of reports of specific worries and fears suggest that married women, housewives particularly, have problems not reflected in their reports of happiness. That is, on specific indices, rather than global reports, the housewife has more problems

TABLE 14-3.
Selected Symptoms of Psychological Distress Among White Single and Married Women and Men *

	Single Women	Married Women	Single Men	Married Men
Nervous breakdown	− .86	+ .57	+1.00	− .76
Felt impending nervous breakdown	−4.48	− .18	− .07	− .51
Nervousness	−3.04	+1.05	−1.05	+ .31
Inertia	−6.34	+1.00	+ .29	− .76
Insomnia	−1.68	+ .60	+1.92	−1.17
Trembling hands	− .76	− .54	− .52	− .23
Nightmares	−2.35	0.00	+1.28	− .75
Perspiring hands	−1.18	+ .38	−1.18	+ .55
Fainting	+ .09	+ .26	+ .81	− .11
Headaches	−1.63	+ .97	−1.96	+ .80
Dizziness	−2.97	− .10	− .79	+ .24
Heart palpitations	−3.43	+ .46	−3.87	+ .02

+ indicates higher number of symptoms than expected.
− indicates fewer symptoms than expected.
* *Source.* U.S. Department of Health, Education and Welfare, 1970.

than the wife who is employed outside the home (Table 9-2). Similarly, married women are more bothered than single women by feelings of depression, feelings that they are about to go to pieces, strong irrational fears, passivity and so on (Table 14-3). The favorable depiction of single women relative to married women may well reflect the **housewife syndrome** characteristic of many wives who are not employed outside the home (Chapter 9). It probably also is affected by the associated factors of the higher education levels, and perhaps higher intelligence levels, of single women.

The life-styles of single women and employed married women apparently foster their capacities for developing a healthy sense of separateness and other agentic characteristics that often are neglected in more traditional married women. Single women, like employed married women, are also likely to seek a balance to their agentic traits through communal concerns in a life with other people.

A LIFE TOGETHER

Aloneness does not necessarily imply loneliness. The dichotomy of marriage *versus* singleness is misleading for a psychological understanding of human beings. Requirements for well-being, growth, and meaningfulness are the same, whether a person is married or single. A person needs both an independent identity and meaningful interpersonal relationships. Both "the day alone" and "the day together" have critical functions in personal growth (Bonhoeffer, 1949/1954). The woman who is single and lives alone is no different from others in this respect. Obviously, her life alone demands a sense of separateness and provides opportunities for "the day alone." Does it also allow for social responsiveness and "the day together"?

SOCIABILITY NEEDS

Actually, little is known about specific needs for social relationships in adulthood (Chapter 10). Some relatively basic motives (such as needs for achievement, affiliation, and nurturance) involve other people in their expression and satisfaction.

There also may be needs that are specifically sociability needs, such as those described in Table 14-4. Marriage and parenthood are conventionally assumed to be the prime, often sole, vehicle for such needs. However, even happy, successful marriages are not necessarily efficient or appropriate for meeting all sociability needs. Happily married women may feel unhappy and socially isolated after a move to a new community (Chapter 13; Weiss, 1969). Conversely, the needs can be met without conventional marriage.

The woman who elects singleness *may* have generally lower sociability needs, but she is not likely to be without them. She encounters some difficulties in meeting her needs, but the difficulties are not inherent in singleness; rather they are manifestations of social patterns just discussed, and can often be overcome with some effort. Many kinds of people can and do make meaningful contributions to the life of a single woman and she to theirs. Colleagues can help with shared concerns, reassurances, and some assistance and guidance. Close friends clearly can meet many needs, and another single woman, particularly one in a related career, can be particularly important. Many needs may be met by family, and perhaps some are likely to be met only by family (for example, prolonged assistance needs in times of illness or financial crisis). Perhaps because of this, some career women choose jobs geographically close to their **family of origin.** *Any* meaningful relationship allows opportunity to express needs to give to and care for others. However, the relevance of children requires separate comment.

THE SINGLE MOTHER

For some women, absence of children is a marked advantage of being single, and fear of children a deterrent to marriage. However, many other women who might otherwise consider becoming a single woman are not comfortable with the idea of not having children; successful single women are more likely to lament the lack of children than the lack of a husband. Why concerns about parenthood are so strong is not clear. An "instinct" to bear and raise children is clearly not

TABLE 14-4.
Sociability Needs of Adults *

Intimacy. Need for emotional integration in which people can express feelings without self-consciousness. In an intimate relation there is trust, effective understanding, and easy accessibility. A successful marriage is a frequent source of intimacy satisfactions, but there is no necessary relation between marriage and intimacy, and there is no necessary relationship between physical and psychological intimacy.

Social integration. Need for sharing concerns with people who are in similar situations or are striving for similar objectives. "We're in the same boat." "We want the same things." Experience, information, and ideas are shared in the relationship.

Nurturance needs. Need to be needed, to take care of, and minister to another. Taking responsibility for the care of a child is an obvious example. Married people often nurture each other.

Reassurance of worth. A need to have evidence of competence in some role of central concern. If a professional role is important, colleagues can provide reassurance. Husbands and other friends may provide assurance of competence to a woman for whom being a competent housewife and mother is of central concern.

Assistance. Needs for time, energy, and money of other people. Most likely to be met by close relatives.

Social-emotional guidance. Needs that can be met, for example, by ministers or priests or mental health experts, or, more generally, by experts in an area of concern.

* *Source.* Adapted from Weiss, R. S. The fund of sociability. *Transaction,* 1969, *6,* 36–43.

a defensible concept (Chapter 7). Yet, young women and men do consider their anticipated children an important part of their potential life satisfaction, and both women and men want more children than they expect to have (Donelson & Gullahorn, unpublished data).

The single woman who wants children has several alternatives. Single women and men are increasingly adopting children and providing homes for children who otherwise would be institutionalized. In Scandinavian countries, there has been a recent trend for women who want to be single and mothers to elect intentional pregnancy without marriage. The women often select the father on the basis of genetic considerations to maximize the chances of having a child with desired attributes such as high intelligence and good health. They have little trouble finding willing sperm donors of diverse characteristics. Ample child-care facilities enable career freedom during the day.

Artificial insemination by a man not her husband is available to married women in this as in other countries. Why should single women not take advantage of this technological opportunity? Is the absence of love for the sperm donor at conception more a problem for a single than a married woman? Is the presence of love for the potential child less real in a single than a married woman? Whether or not single women in this country will more frequently choose to bear children is hard to predict. Increasing child-care facilities make it increasingly practical. Class discussions, however, indicate that adoption still is the only procedure most college women say they would consider were they to be single.

Is Fatherlessness Fair? For the case of adoption, another question is equally relevant: Is it more fair for a child to have *no* parent than to have *one?* More broadly, the physical capacity to conceive and bear children is no guarantee of adequate parenting ability (Chapter 7). The single mother can be a more satisfactory parent than many women and men who are married. Some detrimental effects of paternal absence specifically may be due more to the conjunction of having-and-then-losing a father than to the sheer fact of paternal absence. To know that "mother adopted (or bore) me when she wasn't married because she wanted me" may have very different effects on a child's development from those of knowing that "my mommy and daddy don't live together anymore." Children often feel rejection or guilt at the divorce or the death of parents. Data simply are not yet available about the effects of good parenting by a single parent.

In the meantime, many single women enjoy casual interactions with others' children, without the demands and strains of parenthood. Other women find that their needs to contribute to the continuity, maintenance, and enhancement of life can be satisfied in a professional and personal life that does not directly involve children. With or without children, the single woman can have many marriages relevant to her interpersonal expressions and growth.

THE MARRIAGES OF THE SINGLE PERSON

Responsible Commitment. The single person can be married, and often is, in the psychological sense of marriage. Marriage requires responsibility, care, sacrifice, and the faith of creative love (Bonner, 1965). The creative love that characterizes true marriage may occur in any meaningful interpersonal relationship. In the process of expressing themselves and meeting their own socia-

bility needs, single people form many small marriages, and often some rather large ones. The paradox is that for every step taken to fulfill social needs, a piece of singleness is forfeited and a piece of marriage obtained. The friend who meets your own intimacy needs is also one with intimacy needs to be met. The friend you call for assistance is also one who will call you for assistance, perhaps at inconvenient times. Developing and maintaining any good relationship requires concern and responsibility comparable to that required for a successful marriage. The other person, or cause, with which one has an authentic relationship may well be described as a "marriage partner." What kinds of partners are possible for the single woman?

A Cause. Some single people, as some married people, find that their integrating core of life and their dominant marriage "partner" is a cause rather than a person. The cause may be politics, religion, the women's movement, or the cause of the "truth" that presumably is served in a scientific, administrative, artistic, or humanistic career, for example. The cause may be so viable, vibrant, and alive that a commitment to it is a relationship with a living organism. Other people also devoted to the cause contribute to its meaningfulness and may therefore become marriage partners on their own. Career commitment is often cited as a reason for singleness. For other people, religion is their marriage, not necessarily expressed in public means such as entering a convent or taking clerical vows of celibacy. Such people are not rejecting conventional marriage; they just have chosen the one marriage that is most important to them (Should you be single?, 1975; McGinnis, 1974; Sister Edna Mary, 1968).

Living-in Love. For most people today, the surest way of expressing and satisfying social needs involves living with other people on a day-to-day basis—a living-in love. Marriage, as conventionally conceived, is one style of life that can, when successful, provide this. Other styles are possible.

The Household Surrogate. Communal living is one variety of marriage and of living-in love that deserves serious consideration. Shulamith Firestone (1971) has proposed a household surrogate as a plan of communal living that, unlike other plans, provides for the concept of "home" as a stable place to be counted on for continuing security. The household she proposes as a replacement for conventional marriage might be legalized, with 10 or so adults of varying ages obtaining a license, much the same as a couple applies for a marriage license today. However, the license would apply only for a limited time, such as 7 to 10 years to provide some stability; it could be renewed if desired. Both adults and children could transfer out of the household, but within restrictions necessary to assure a continuing stable unit for the period of the license. Both adults and children could profit from the variety of interpersonal relationships and avoidance of exclusive dependency on one or two people that is possible in such an arrangement. Whether this or other plans of communal living will be widely instrumented is not known. Meanwhile, many single people opt for a "room-mate" to provide both marriage and living-in love.

Men as Partners. Calling a roommate or housemate a marriage partner might seem far-fetched. However, if the relationship is one of responsible care, marriage partner is the appropriate term in a psychological sense. Perhaps "life partner," or simply "partner" might be better terms both for the single person and the married person. Some single women choose to live with men for brief or prolonged times, sometimes with an acknowledged prospect of a prolonged commitment or with a clear intention to end the relationship at an appropriate time (e.g., Fallaci, 1974).

Other women who would value an egalitarian partner relationship with a man find that there are few prospects desirable to them because of the pervasiveness of sex-typed male socialization. It will take time and effort, especially by men, for truly egalitarian partner relationships to evolve. But many couples, both within temporary living-in love relationships and in legal marriage roles,

are genuinely striving toward this goal of open, honest, and sharing equality.

Women as Partners. From the viewpoint of social needs, two women may be as happy together as any other combination of two people. From the viewpoint of the psychological essence of marriage, they may be as genuinely married as a woman and a man, and their commitment need be no less permanent. Living together can have many practical advantages. Together they may be able to afford the house or the farm that neither could alone. Together they may share chores around the house that are "too much busy work" for either alone to enjoy. Each can count on the other and be counted on by the other. The actual or planned permanence of the interpersonal commitment and joint living arrangements between women is not necessarily different from the intended or actual permanence of formal and informal marriages between men and women. Some women find women easier to live with than men.

SEXUALITY

Choice. People generally seem extremely curious about a single woman's sexuality but are afraid to ask explicit questions. Meanwhile their subtle investigatory attempts are amusingly blatant to the woman herself. The incorrect assumptions they make out of ignorance are similarly blatant but not always amusing. The typical single woman is neither neurotically repressing her sexuality nor is she the promiscuous libertine fantasized by some people. She is neither pitifully frustrated nor does she carelessly "sleep around." Facts indicate that, like other people, the single woman makes choices about her sexual expressiveness. She can choose not to engage in overt sexual activities or to do so.

Potentially she has more freedom of choice than a married woman about her sexuality. While some couples are experimenting with "open marriages," the married woman typically experiences pressures that limit her choices. The single woman can choose among autosexuality, heterosexuality, or homosexuality. Autosexuality is the largest source of total sexual outlet for single people (and also a large source for married people); heterosexuality is a very close second; homosexuality is a substantial third. All alternatives are chosen by some women; some women choose all (Kinsey et al., 1953; McCary, 1970; Boucher, 1975). Each choice may be made with or without a psychological marriage commitment.

Celibacy. Some single women choose celibacy (abstaining from sexual activities with another person) for short or long times. Historically, celibacy and singleness were assumed one and the same, an assumption that probably was never particularly accurate. Today, many single women do not consider complete sexual abstinence mandatory for them, as implicit in the facts referred to above. They make choices about what forms their sexual activities will take, just as they made choices about singleness and marriage. Although some single women have always been celibate, others with previous meaningful sexual experience decide on temporary or permanent celibacy, as do some married people, too. As with the issue of singleness or conventional marriage, they are not rejecting a negative state (marriage or sexual activities), but are affirming a positive state (singleness, celibacy). However, because the term *celibacy* is still highly loaded with negative connotations, many people hesitate to use it to describe themselves, even when it is in fact applicable.

Reasons for periods of celibacy among single or married people vary, but peacefulness is often paramount (Bernard, 1973), as noted by a contemporary poet, Ellen O'Donnell: "It does seem that celibacy would be worthwhile in order to preserve the quietness . . . needed for graceful loving." In the past, religious celibacy was the only socially acceptable life-style for a person desiring the peacefulness (or devotion to a cause) that can be associated with celibacy or with singleness. Perhaps some people still implicitly assume that the stigma of celibacy, or of singleness, is relieved only when it occurs in association with religion.

Periods of freely chosen celibacy can enable not only the peacefulness of abstinence, but also more meaningful sexual expression. Even a single person who lives alone may become embroiled in sufficient "marriages" or other kinds of relationships with distinctively sexual overtones that a "time away from it all" is necessary. While a single woman may have more *access* to freedom, she may also find, as do married women, that in the process of expressing her social responsiveness, she needs to *protect* her freedom. This kind of value—or necessity—of celibacy was well recognized by a woman reporting that a period of celibacy enabled her to be free in later sexual relationships because during celibacy she had become freed of the demands of sexuality: ". . . the longer I was celibate, the more centered I felt. My celibacy was for me a body-and-psyche meditation, a retreat inward. It made me peaceful, it made me stronger, it expanded my sense of myself as myself, without husband or lover or partner" (Kwitney, 1975, p. 71).

For the single woman, as for other people, meaningful living and growing involve a continual working toward the combination of psychological marriage and psychological singleness, of separateness and of togetherness. There is no one life-style that guarantees success in this venture. Neither does the life-style of a single woman prohibit it. Some women may need singleness for growth; for no woman need singleness be a barrier in growth.

SUMMARY

Single women do *not* match the negative stereotypes carelessly held about them. Although currently the percentage of single women is low, many women who marry will become widows or divorcees, and there are signs of a trend for an increase in the number of unmarried people. With an increase in the number of singles, many problems of the single woman will diminish: the choice of singleness can become recognized as a viable and attractive alternative to marriage, married people can become more knowledgeable about single women and less confused by them, and the single woman can find other single people with whom to share. Even now, singleness is a choice, and the preferred choice of many women, who are not necessarily rejecting marriage so much as they are affirming singleness.

Mature single women who are in fact single women rather than only unmarried women are likely to be over 30, highly educated, financially independent, and emotionally independent and healthy. They can enjoy the benefits of freedom and a sense of independent individuality. They must also deal with often demeaning treatment by other people who do not understand them or their lives, and they must learn to enjoy their aloneness. Single women can and do, however, have many marriages in the psychological sense of sharing and commitment. Some have a dominant marriage to a cause, as well as to friends. Some women elect to live with another woman, a trend that will probably increase. Sexually, single women are neither promiscuous nor particularly frustrated; they are likely to use their sexuality responsibly and may freely select celibacy as their preferred choice. Single women can and do often have their social needs met by other people and enjoy the warmth and sharing of interpersonal relationships. The tally sheet provided by mental health data indicates that single women are clearly healthier than single men and generally healthier than married women, particularly housewives. Singleness is a desirable and beneficial state for many women. It is not "just second best" to marriage. For many, it is "first best."

CHAPTER
15
THE WOMAN PROFESSIONAL

Many of the facts cited in this chapter are discouraging. A variety of myths support the **sex-typing** of occupations and other discriminatory practices that have hampered many working women in pursuing their goals. While the myths die hard, and the social practices they support are slow to change, progress is occurring. In Chapter 16 we shall suggest some social structural changes to facilitate **androgynous** life-styles for both women and men. Here we discuss the current situation of employed women. The focus on professionals is not intended to be elitist but rather to highlight careers planned by increasing numbers of college student readers. Moreover, many of the problems that women professionals face and the solutions they adopt are relevant to all working women. Hopefully, in a few years some of the present discussion will have mainly historical relevance.

WOMEN IN THE LABOR FORCE

About 36 million American women—more than half of those between 18 and 64—are in the labor force. Although the average woman and the average man worker have the same amount of education (slightly more than 12 years of schooling), 1970 census data reveal that four out of five salaried women are on the bottom rungs of the job and pay ladders—as domestic, service, clerical, and sales workers. The concentration of women in their categories denotes an underutilization of talent. For example, at the beginning of the 1970s, almost half of the employed women with one to three years of college were clerical workers, and 9 percent were service workers. Among comparably educated men, only 12 percent were in clerical fields and 5 percent were in service occupations (Bernard, 1971). Even in 1974, women college graduates who worked full time averaged only 60 percent of the income earned by men graduates. Thus, in many instances a college-educated woman earns less than a man who has not gone past elementary school.

SEX AND OCCUPATION

Most cultures assume that only certain occupations are appropriate for women. However, cul-

tures vary in what they consider appropriate work, just as they vary in other aspects of **sex roles** (Chapter 1). The premise that women should be protected against heavy labor is by no means universal; 80 percent of farm laborers are women in Japan and Romania (Cook, 1975). Especially in Eastern European countries where women have done agricultural work, they are employed also as road builders, street cleaners, construction workers, and parks and grounds maintenance workers. Work allocation by sex also varies over time. Although the first secretaries and bank tellers were men, now most are women. Men used to teach in American schools; then women took over; and now men are returning, especially as elementary school principals and high school teachers.

Sex Segregation. In the United States job segregation is so extensive that half of all women workers are in occupations that are over 70 percent female, and most men are in occupations that are over 70 percent male (Deckard, 1975). The current sex segregation of adults in educational levels and occupations is indicated in Tables 15-1 and 15-2. Notice the declining percentages of women at several key points of academic advancement. Only one woman in a hundred with a bachelor's degree attains the doctorate, as compared with about one in every ten or eleven of the male bachelor's degree recipients (Folger, Astin, & Bayer, 1969).

Women's Work. Similarly, women are drastically underrepresented in high prestige (and high paying) scientific and professional fields. Even within these fields, there is sex-typing. Women constitute 40 percent of the professional work force; however, they tend to be concentrated in fields calling for nurturing and servicing qualities, such as nursing, teaching young children, and social work (Table 15-2). Although the percentage of women receiving doctorates in 1970 increased by 2.5 percent over 1960, less than 3 percent of women doctorates were in engineering, business administration, agriculture and forestry, physics and astronomy, and earth sciences (Astin, 1973).

Many more women are in less prestigious jobs

TABLE 15-1.
Percent of All Persons at Selected Levels Who are Women *

Levels of Educational Attainment		1970
High school graduates		50.4
Bachelor's degrees		43.1
Master's and doctor's degrees (combined)		36.5
Faculty members		24.0
Doctor's degrees		13.4
Full professors		8.6
Major Occupational Groupings	1960	1970
Domestic service	96.5	96.9
Other service workers	61.9	60.0
Clerical and kindred workers	67.9	73.6
Sales workers	36.2	38.6
Factory operatives	28.7	31.5
Laborers, except farm	5.1	8.4
Farm workers	9.6	9.5
Managers and administrators (except farm)	14.8	16.6
Professional and technical workers	38.4	39.9

* *Source.* Data from The Carnegie Commission on Higher Education, 1973, and from U.S. Bureau of the Census, 1960 and 1970 *Census of Population.*

that incorporate aspects of women's traditional household and social roles, such as domestic service, food service, laundry work, and hairdressing. In offices, secretaries often are expected to give their male bosses the subservient, watchful, and admiring attention traditionally expected of wives.

Sex-typing in occupations is often "explained" as due to different skills and interests. Such average differences are not the whole story, however. There is also discrimination against women. Many jobs that are considered "women's work" call for finger dexterity: typing, fine parts assembly, or work in textile trades. However, women are underrepresented in the higher prestige occupations that also require manipulative skill: watchmaking, dentistry, or surgery.

Although the absolute numbers are too small to effect much change in the census data, some loosening of sex-typing is occurring in occupations. There are increasing numbers of male nurses, secretaries, teachers, and telephone operators as well as increasing numbers of female professional athletes, bus drivers, law enforcement

officers, and telephone repairers. Yet, given the characteristics of sex-typed professions that are summarized in Table 15-3, it is unlikely that substantial changes can occur without some major social changes permitting more androgynous lifestyles (Chapter 16).

The Wage Gap. To a large extent the wage gap in men's versus women's salaries ($11,835 median income for men in 1974 vs. $6,772 for women) stems from the sex segregation of occupations, with women employed predominantly in the lower paying job categories. But even when women are in the same job categories as men, they earn considerably less: Women sales workers average only 40 percent of the amount men earn; women service workers earn 59 percent of the pay men get; and women in clerical jobs as well as those in professional and technical jobs earn only 65 percent of the amounts paid to their male colleagues (U.S. Dept. of Labor, 1971).

Do these figures represent unequal pay for equal work? Some evidence that this is so comes from a systematic nationwide study of employed

TABLE 15-2.
Percent of All Persons in Selected Professional-Technical Occupations Who are Women *

Predominately Female Professions	1960	1970
Nurses	97.5	97.3
Dietitians	92.7	92.0
Teachers, elementary	85.8	83.7
Librarians	85.4	82.0
Dancers	86.0	81.3
Health technicians	68.2	69.7
Therapists	63.4	63.5
Social workers	62.8	62.8

Mixed Male and Female Professions	1960	1970
Religious workers (other than clergy)	63.3	55.7
Farm and home management advisers	47.2	49.7
Teachers, secondary	49.3	49.3
Recreation workers	51.2	42.0
Editors and reporters	36.6	40.6
Musicians and composers	38.6	34.8
Personnel and labor relations workers	33.1	30.9

Predominately Male Professions	1960	1970
Authors	25.5	29.1
Teachers, college and university	23.9	28.6
Accountants	16.5	26.2
Radio operators	16.7	25.9
Designers	19.3	24.2
Social scientists	25.4	23.2
Life and physical scientists	9.2	13.7
Engineering and science technicians	11.1	12.9
Pharmacists	7.5	12.0
Physicians, medical and osteopathic	6.9	9.3
Draftsmen (sic)	5.6	8.0
Lawyers and judges	3.5	4.9
Architects	2.1	3.6
Clergy	2.3	2.9
Engineers	.8	1.6

* *Source.* The Carnegie Commission on Higher Education, 1973.

workers in a variety of occupations (Levitin, Quinn, & Staines, 1973). The relative importance of various achievement factors such as education, time on the job, and occupational prestige in determining income was established for half of the men in the sample. With this base, predictions were made for the income of the other half of the men as well as for the women in the study. The average difference between predicted and actual income for the men was $27. For the women it was $3458! Thus the average woman in that study would have to earn 71 percent more than her current salary to equal the income of a man with her achievement scores. These data contradict the two myths that women are "legitimately" paid less because they achieve less than men, and that

TABLE 15-3.
Characteristics of Sex-Typed Professions *

Women's Professions (e.g., Nursing, Teaching, Librarianship)	Men's Professions (e.g., Law, Engineering, Medicine)
1. Require large numbers of skilled, but cheap workers.	1. Require limited numbers of highly skilled, expensive workers.
2. Do not require extensive schooling or great investments of time, energy, and devotion.	2. Require extensive schooling and great investments of time, energy, and devotion.
3. Most of the training is acquired before employment and thus requires virtually no investment by the employer.	3. Employers often provide or contribute to additional professional training.
4. Do not require continuity in employment or a long-term commitment.	4. Generally require continuity in employment and long-term commitment.
5. Do not generally expect overtime work (paid by employer or contributed by employee for personal development).	5. Often expect a lifetime of overtime work. Frequently this presupposes the unpaid maintenance services of the employee's wife.
6. Worker's mobility or immobility (often accepted as contingent on her husband's job expectations) not important: These jobs exist all over the country.	6. Mobility may be required for advancement. Thus employee's family expected not to have commitments that interfere with mobility.
7. Rarely place women in supervisory positions over men.	7. Frequently place men in supervisory positions over women.

* *Source.* Based on discussion by Oppenheimer, 1975.

women who perform equally do receive equal compensation.

Combatting salary discrimination continues to be a priority of the National Organization for Women. Some evidence of progress comes from 1973 data (National Research Council, 1974), indicating that women doctoral scientists and engineers averaged 83 percent of the amounts paid to male colleagues—a considerable gain over the 65 percent previously noted, though still a long way from equality.

CHARACTERISTICS OF
WOMEN PROFESSIONALS

Similarities of Women and Men Within Disciplines. Women professionals and their male colleagues share abilities, interests, and training experiences. For example, both women and men engineering students have interests and abilities in science, mathematics, mechanical things, and outdoor sports. Women and men law students have high interests and competencies in verbal activity, writing, and debating (Mitchell, 1957). Women and men in the social sciences, both beginning graduate students and seasoned professionals, tend to be highly liberal politically and unconventional socially. Those in humanities typically are next on these dimensions; natural scientists tend to be the least liberal and the most conventional of these groups (Davis, 1964).

Thus, it is not surprising that women's recent activism in the professions typically started among sociologists, political scientists, and psychologists in the late 1960s, then spread to women in literature and other humanities, and finally rippled to those in mathematics and the natural sciences (Rossi, 1973). There are also discipline-related variations in communication styles. For example, among American professors who received Fulbright awards for teaching or research abroad, the women and men social scientists usually engaged in the most frequent and extensive contacts with colleagues and other people overseas. Faculty members in the humanities were next; and those in natural science typically were the lowest (Gullahorn & Gullahorn, 1962).

Communal Emphasis in Personal Ambition.

Because women generally are socialized to develop **communal** qualities, they not only tend to select professions rewarding these qualities, but they also often emphasize them even in more traditionally **agentically** oriented occupations. According to a recent study of 50 women state legislators who had proven records of effectiveness in government (Kirkpatrick, 1975), the women resembled their male colleagues in their willingness to fight for their convictions. Both the women and men tended to come from families who were active in community and political organizations. Unlike the men, however, the women were late starters: Three quarters of them first ran for office after they were 40, presumably after their major "family responsibilities" had been completed. Ninety percent of the men had their first political campaign earlier in life. The women tended to immerse themselves in their jobs and to see power as an instrument of public purpose rather than as a tool for personal ambition. Generlly they did not consider their activities as legislators as advancing law careers, building business contacts, or even as stepping stones to higher political office. Thus, despite within-sex differences in political ideology, the women tended to concentrate on citizen needs—a communal focus in their personal ambition that is probably consistent with their past socialization.

Work Involvement vs. Competitiveness.

Women professionals tend to be assertive, but they do not often manifest the same type of competitiveness as more agentic males. In one study of almost 450 zoologists, women and men were equally productive in terms of research and publications; however, they gave different explanations for their productivity (Bernard, 1964). Three-fourths of the women scientists claimed "fascination with a problem" as a prime motivation for their research and writing; less than half of the men did so. Instead, almost two-fifths of the men cited competitive "publish or perish" pressures spurring their productivity; only one-fourth of the women mentioned this concern.

The differing reasons given for productivity may reflect conventional stereotyping that it is "appropriate" for men to say they are competitive and for women to say they are noncompetitive. However, people often come to believe and act on what they say, especially when they receive relatively consistent rewards for saying it. Since a man's identity is so wrapped up in his occupational role, he is under extreme pressure to prove himself to his colleagues ("show us you're one of the boys"), to his family ("we expect you to surpass your father"; and "I know you're better than my friends' husbands"), and to himself ("I've got to prove I can make it"). Women professionals are not likely to experience the same degree of pressure to prove themselves in competition with others, and thus may feel freer to pursue intrinsic interests.

Other Personality Traits.

Although many women professionals do not emphasize the competitive aspects of their work roles, as a group they have demonstrated their ability to cope with tremendous competitive pressures. As already noted (Table 15-1), there is a greater selectivity operating for women than for men in higher education. Thus only the intellectually "fittest" of the women tend to survive, as demonstrated by the fact that women graduate students and professionals rather consistently score higher on intelligence tests than do their male peers (Bernard, 1964; Astin, 1969).

Women professionals also seem to have personality characteristics that are helpful in deviating from traditional sex-role expectations. For example, compared with women in the general population, women authors, artists, and psychologists are more aggressive, adventuresome, imaginative, unconventional, and self-sufficient, as well as more intelligent (Bachtold & Werner, 1970, 1971, 1973).

Some of the personality characteristics on which women professionals differ from the general population of women are also shared with male colleagues. However, there are some interesting sex differences within fields. In one study of almost 400 authors and artists, the women generally scored more aloof, emotional, and less self-confident than the men on a self-report personality inventory. Among almost 500 psychologists who answered the same inventory, the women tended to be more aloof, more radical, and *higher* in superego strength than their male colleagues, as well as more intelligent.

An interesting generational difference appeared among the women psychologists. The younger women, whose formative professional training occurred after World War II, were comparatively more insecure and impulsive than the men, and even than women in general. The older women psychologists, who were near retirement, were similar to male colleagues on these measures. Are the older women from a different population than the younger ones? After all, these pioneers invaded a male-dominated profession, which might have led to a preselection of very self-assured and highly self-controlled women. The spirit of these gate crashers is illustrated by Vassar's psychologist Margaret Washburn, who was "intrepid enough to invade the sacred precinct of the men's smoker at psychological meetings. Marching uninvited into its midst, she sat down and lighted a cigar. None questioned her privilege to enjoy a smoker thereafter" (MacCracken, 1950, p. 74).

Will the younger women become more like their older colleagues as they gain further professional experience? Their low confidence could inhibit their professional activities and lead to further aloofness in an attempt to separate themselves psychologically from the social discrimination we shall discuss shortly. Thus these women could get caught in a vicious circle. But the situation for women professionals is changing. Young women now have the benefits of support provided by women's professional groups and movement activities generally. Others' support and group action toward social structural change may well bolster their confidence and opportunities.

STATUS INCONSISTENCY

The relative insecurity and aloofness of some young women professionals may stem from and be exaggerated by others' difficulties in responding to them apppropriately in terms of their competency. Such confusion results from inconsistencies in criteria of social status.

CRITERIA OF STATUS

If social status were based solely on a person's relation to the means of production, then a women professional would have a higher social status than a male laborer. This is not the case in mature industrial societies because there is a series of hierarchies of ascribed and achieved status rather than a single criterion.

Ascribed status indicators consist of fixed personal attributes such as sex, race, and age, which generally are beyond the control of the individual. Although times are changing, blacks, women, and the elderly experience discrimination based on expectations that they possess less valued personal qualities than do people in other ascribed status categories (i.e., whites, men, and the young).

Achieved status criteria include education, income, and job classification—attributes that are not fixed at birth and that an individual can control to some extent. As with ascribed statuses, people generally agree in evaluating the relative worth of different levels of these indicators. There is much consensus, for example, regarding the relative prestige of different occupations.

Inconsistency of Criteria. Persons who are high in ascribed and achieved status characteristics know where they stand, and others know how they are expected to behave toward them. For instance, there is no confusion about the status of an Episcopalian white man from a Mayflower family who is president of a large corporation and who wields political influence in his community. But when a person is high on some status criteria and low on others, then uncertainties and difficulties arise. A black male physician is inconsistent in status because of the racist devaluation of his ascribed characteristic of skin color.

Similarly, the achieved status of a woman professional's position is higher than the ascribed status of women. Since others are confused by the inconsistency, they often simply avoid or reject the status of the inconsistent individual. Another reaction involves failing to recognize or "explaining away" the achievement in order to maintain consistency and justify treating the woman professional as "only a woman." A variety of myths express this **conditional regard** (Chapter 2) and help in rationalizing inequitable treatment of status inconsistent women professionals.

MYTHS REGARDING WOMEN'S COMPETENCE

If It's By a Woman, It Can't Be So Good. The popularity of the "dumb blond" stems not only from her sex appeal, but also from her assumed portrayal of women's "innate" incompetence. The stereotype of women's incompetence is reflected in studies of job recruitment discrimination, where screening committees in various organizations are sent identical resumés of applicants' credentials, with female and male names randomly assigned. The general finding is that the *same* credentials are evaluated less favorably when they are attributed to a woman than to a man. Thus women applicants often are offered lower ranking and lower salaried jobs than are men with the same credentials. Even psychology department chairpersons exhibit this discriminatory pattern (Fidell, 1970). Apparently many personal decision makers are influenced by sex-role stereotypes that they either do not recognize or do not question. Students, too, have manifested similar stereotypes. College women and men rated professional articles less favorably on their value, persuasiveness, and profundity when the alleged

author was *Joan* T. McKay as opposed to *John* T. McKay (Goldberg, 1968; Bem & Bem, 1970).

Modifications of the Incompetence Myths. At times myths seem to be discouragingly self-perpetuating. Even when they are confronted with evidence of women's competent performance, some people regard the achievement a matter of luck; whereas they attribute men's success to the men's ability (Chapter 11). Truly exceptional performance or endorsement by an authoritative source, however, can lead to acknowledgment of a woman's competence (Taynor & Deaux, 1973). For example, although students generally rated identical artistic works with female names less favorably than those with 'male names, this difference was eliminated when the paintings were presented as contest winners (Pheterson, Kiesler, & Goldberg, 1971).

Perhaps the women's movement challenges to sexist myths and the increased visibility of competent women professionals are having some impact. In a recent repetition of the Joan vs. John study of authors, women students showed less undervaluation than previously of works attributed to women. Daughters of employed mothers, unlike those of nonemployed mothers, showed no undervaluation (Baruch, 1972). In another study both women and men judged successful women in male-dominated occupations as being happy with their success (Feather, 1975).

The positive effect of actual experience with women professionals is demonstrated in a recent survey involving almost 1300 state university students (Ferber & Huber, 1975). Overall, the students favored their same-sex professors. However, favorable experience with women professors significantly decreased the men's preference for men professors, suggesting that competent faculty women may expect support from both women and men students.

MYTHS REGARDING WOMEN'S WORK COMMITMENT

A Pretty Girl Can't Be Serious. Even when a woman is deemed qualified for a position, questions often are raised about her work commitment, especially if she is young and attractive. Is she only husband-hunting in graduate school? Won't she just stay home once she has children? These expectations appear to be confirmed by the higher drop-out rates of women compared to men doctoral and medical students (Lopate, 1968; Mooney, 1968). Such data provide apparent support for male faculty members' reluctance to select even exceptionally qualified women graduate students as protégés. Thus women often are denied the special training advantages and later job opportunities that come from sponsorship by experts in their fields. Nonreinforcement from their professors, therefore, may be the main *cause* rather than an effect of the women's drop-out rate. Women who do complete the doctorate exhibit a high degree of career commitment, with 91 percent employed. Furthermore, those who interrupt their careers do so for only a short time (Astin, 1969).

She Only Works for Money. Myths regarding the sincerity and economic necessity of women's work commitment have very real consequences for how female ambition is treated. One "justification" for assigning women to lower paying positions is the belief that women work only for "pin money" whereas men are "breadwinners." Actually, a recent nationwide survey indicates that fully 40 percent of working women are economically independent of men, and a third of these women are the sole wage earners in their households (Crowley, Levitin, & Quinn, 1973). Are women, then, working only because they have to? This belief makes as little sense for women as it does for men. Although people may *need* the income from work, they may also *want* to work for other reasons. Most working women and men state that they would continue to work even if they had enough money available to live comfortably the rest of their lives (Crowley et al., 1973).

She Only Works for Sociability. Suspicions regarding women's work commitment stem also from myths that women are more concerned than men with making friends and socializing on their

job and less concerned than men in gaining self-actualization through their work. In fact, survey data indicate that women and men equally value the opportunity to make friends at work, and both attach more importance to having a *competent* supervisor relative to a *nice* supervisor who is concerned about their welfare (Crowley et al., 1973). Furthermore, women are just as concerned as men about the meaningfulness of their work and the opportunity it provides to develop their special abilities.

There seem to be sex differences in ambition: 64 percent of the men versus only 48 percent of the women indicate they want to be promoted. However, women's stated desire for promotion is based on their *expectation* of promotion. Two-thirds of women never expect to be promoted. To avoid frustration, many scale down their stated ambitions. Those who believe they have a realistic chance of being promoted want promotions just as much as men do. Of course, in some instances women's perceptions of being in dead-end jobs may be distortions because of their low expectations (Chapter 11), which also may lead them to select or accept dead ends.

In general, then, myths about how women differ from men in work competence and commitment are not supported by facts. Most people do not know the facts to begin with; furthermore, they are not easily convinced by evidence that their beliefs are not valid. Still, some modifications give hope that times are changing. Until further changes occur, however, the work world remains largely a man's world where women have problems because of status inconsistency.

THE "MASCULINITY" OF THE WORK WORLD

A gentleman's world is not gentle. As an industrial psychologist notes, the managerial model involves agentic masculine traits, not communal feminine ones:

The model of the successful manager in our culture is a masculine one. The good manager is aggressive, competitive, firm, and just. He is not feminine, he is not soft and yielding or dependent or intuitive in the womanly sense. The very expression of emotion is widely viewed as a feminine weakness that would interfere with effective business processes (McGregor, 1967, p. 23).

The value of such unmitigated agency is questionable (Chapter 16), but in many occupations, both in the business world and in academia, "that's the way it is." Women are not expected to be tough enough to succeed in a man's world (O'Leary, 1974). They are expected to be deferent to those who are.

But Would You Want Your Brother to Work for One? Basic to racism and sexism is the belief that people in certain ascribed status categories—like blacks and women—are inferior to those in other ascribed status categories—like whites and men—and therefore the inferior owe deference and respect to the superior. Some years ago, one frequently heard the comment that blacks "are all right in their place, but would you want your sister to marry one?" Today, women, too, are considered "all right in their place." Their "place" is to take orders from men, not to give orders to men.

Male executives in one study acknowledged that women in management had no appreciable negative effects on efficiency and production. However, one-third believed the women had a "bad" effect on employee morale, four-fifths did not agree that men feel comfortable with a female boss, and only about one-fourth indicated that they would feel comfortable working for a woman (Bowman, Wortney, & Geyser, 1965). Over half of these men considered women temperamentally unfit for management. Similarly, other male managers "justified" their rejection of women executives on the grounds of women's perceived lack of dependability because of "biological" characteristics (Bass, Krusell, & Alexander, 1971). The least favorable attitudes toward working women were expressed by male managers in superior positions to women. Clearly affirmative action is needed to help qualified women gain more high level positions where evidence of their competent performance can disconfirm men's negative stereotypes. But in terms of the myths previously reviewed, it won't be easy.

Toughness Norms. If she is to avoid being considered a nonentity in the work world, a woman must be assertive. She must participate actively in professional discussions, be willing to demand center-stage, be able to counter criticism, and appear insensitive to personal attacks. Toughness norms are not always well communicated to young women during graduate training, particularly if they are attractive as well as bright. A young woman who is nonassertive in seminar discussions might not become a faculty member's protégé; but if her work is good and if she is attractively ornamental, the male faculty generally will tolerate her continuation in graduate school. Many men in this culture still focus on women's qualifications as sex objects rather than on more relevant criteria. However, a nonassertive woman colleague—even an attractive one—tends to be considered a liability who has nothing important to contribute.

The male toughness norm is particularly reinforced in modes of expressing emotion. During doctoral oral examinations—the *defense* of the thesis—male faculty are annoyed if a woman breaks down into tears, but they remain unconcerned if a man grinds his fingertips into the chair arms. This norm also was exemplified when a faculty committee learned that a proposal requiring interminable hours had been subverted. A male colleague turned to the one woman in the group and said, "But for God's sake, don't cry." He then excused himself to go take one of his hypertension pills.

The Stag Effect. General discomfort with women professionals is reflected in men professionals' cliquish tendencies. Colleagueship is a unique relationship yet to be well investigated. It involves loyalty plus competition ("keeping up with the boys"). Perhaps men's exclusive professional cliques stem from their fear of being beaten by a woman. It is interesting that the sexes *can* work closely in male-dominant hierarchical rela-

tions—as boss–secretary or as research director and research assistant.

Colleague relations between women and men may also be hampered by wives' jealousy, which involves additional considerations beyond those about husbands' relations with secretaries. Often the wives who are following traditional patterns resent their husbands' devotion to professional interests that they cannot share, but that the woman colleague can.

People who work closely together and discover similarity in their interests, competencies, and values may well develop sexual attraction to be dealt with. Taboos about homosexuality and the kind of tough competitiveness of men's work groups often prevent men's recognizing the sexual aspect of their mutual attraction (Chapter 12). But **mores** prohibiting nonmarital or extramarital heterosexual relationships have less restrictive force now than previously. Thus people are more likely to be aware of heterosexual attractions and their implications. Some men, therefore, perpetuate stag groups to avoid the possibility of "getting involved." This is particularly likely among those who believe sex is such an overpowering drive that feelings are inevitably linked with actions. On the other hand, people who are comfortable with their sexuality can acknowledge sexual attraction and then choose whether or not to act on the feelings. Being able to communicate about sexual feelings and to decide jointly what to do about them could contribute to a more meaningful, honest relationship, be it platonic or sexual. Unfortunately, sexual scripts often interfere with such personal awareness and open communication (Chapter 12).

Whatever the reasons for it, the stag effect can hurt a woman professional's performance. Recognition from respected peers and opportunities for challenging interaction and collaboration help develop an inner sense of role competence and enhance one's work. Much professional information not yet published is shared at informal social gatherings where women tend to be excluded (see Simon, Clark, & Galway, 1967). Perhaps as more women are employed, the stag effect may diminish. The combination of only one woman in a group with several men may seem awkward; but two or three women might seem to "fit in" better, and they also could reinforce one another's participation.

To Succeed You Really Need a Wife. The top strata in many fields tend to be relatively exclusive men's clubs, and the structuring of administrative roles tends to exclude women. The typical managerial model incorporates the expectation that the manager will have a traditional marriage relationship. Most major administrative jobs require collateral duties in the form of entertainment; and it is assumed that the incumbent's accommodating wife will handle these obligations in addition to doing double parent duty because his job has first priority. The large-scale exploitation of women at the sides of their husbands is a fact of corporation life and is illustrated by the First Lady, who is required to give constant attention to protocol while receiving no salary for her contributions (Epstein, 1971). The structuring of executive roles thus encourages wives' vicarious achievement (Chapter 11). It also puts women and single men at a recruitment and role performance disadvantage, since these individuals do not have the free assistance provided by wives. They cannot offer "two for the price of one."

MARITAL INVOLVEMENT

Although women professionals do not *have* wives, slightly over half of them *are* wives, a relatively low figure compared to the 95 percent for men doctorates and the 90 percent for women of comparable ages in the general population (Simon, Clark, & Galway, 1967; Astin, 1969). The lower marriage rate may reflect some of the reality in some young women's concerns that intellectual achievement will make them less popular (Chapter 11). Indeed, many men seem to agree, "Women professionals are all right in their place, but *I* wouldn't want to marry one (or work for one)." In a recent survey of college men, the majority agreed that women should have opportunity to pursue careers at all levels, and they expressed higher respect for employed women than for housewives. Nevertheless, most of these men also were adamant in personally preferring "traditional wives" whose major concerns centered around the needs of husband and family (Komarovsky, 1973).

Apparent liberal ideology thus does not necessarily mean that a man will give up the *help*mate in favor of a more egalitarian relationship. The concern some men express—"But who will take care of the children?"—often seems really a projection of their own dependency needs—"But who will take care of me?" Many women professionals do not want to marry a man who needs a servant to promote his career; so their lessened "marriageability" stems not from their being less desirable, but from their finding fewer men desirable.

PROFESSIONAL AND PERSONAL IDENTITY

Since women typically are defined according to their relationships, especially to their husbands, others often try to allay their confusion about status inconsistent women professionals by reminding themselves and others about marital status. Thus, the single woman professional has certain stereotypes to contend with (Chapter 14), and the married woman professional sometimes finds herself introduced as "Mrs.," while her male colleagues are referred to as "Professor" or "Doctor." Sometimes at professional meetings I am appropriately introduced, but with the addition, ". . . and Dr. Gullahorn's husband is a sociologist, and she has three children." Comparable information is not provided about male colleagues, suggesting a need for a comfortable reassurance of a woman's but not a man's "normalcy" in having a family. Similarly a woman but not a man is asked, "But how do you manage a family and a career?" Since many consider children the sole responsibility of a mother, they fail to understand the response, "The children have a father, too." Women's roles as professional, spouse, and parent are assumed to be in conflict for them, whereas no conflict in these roles is assumed for men.

In American society work is defined in masculine ways and is considered vitally important only for men. In fact, masculine family roles are also defined in terms of work so that being a good husband and a good father is almost synonymous with being a good provider (Prather, 1971). The focus on the occupational role pressures a man to develop an occupational identity that becomes almost his whole identity. In Jungian terms (Chapter 2), the occupational **persona,** or mask, becomes glued to the ego so that other aspects of the self often go unexpressed or unrecognized. The equation of occupation with self is exemplified in the appellation, "Doctor." The male physician typically is not called "Bob" or "Dr. Jones" or even *the* doctor," but simply "Doctor," as in, "Doctor says you must. . . ." Women physicians are not referred to this way since women generally are defined by family relationships rather than occupational roles.

DUAL CAREER MARRIAGES

What types of men do women professionals marry? Among the married women doctorates in a study by Helen Astin (1969), 51 percent reported that their husbands also were Ph.D.s and an additional 12 percent were married to men with other professional degrees (such as M.D., D.D.S., and L.L.B.). Generally the women doctorates married men whose fields were the same as or related to their own.

Priority or Equality. Cooperating in the development of two careers requires genuine mutual respect, good communication, willingness to violate social norms regarding the priority of the husband's professional advancement, and maybe just plain good luck. Couples deviating from traditional patterns have few models for guidance. Perhaps inadvertently, therefore, they often fall into traditional nonegalitarian patterns modeled in the culture at large. Even though both careers are considered important by the partners, frequently both partners regard the man's career as more important (Poloma & Garland, 1971; Holmstrom, 1972). In one study of microbiologists, for example, 83 percent of the married men doctorates answered that they would move to a better position whether or not their professional wives had satisfactory employment prospects. In contrast, 93 percent of the women doctorates indicated that they would move *only* if their husbands obtained a satisfactory position before moving (Kashket, Robbins, Leive, & Huang, 1974).

Apparently such differences in occupational priority are not unusual, since one-fourth of the married women doctorates in another study (Astin, 1969) considered their husbands' job mobility a hindrance to their own careers. In some cases, limited opportunities in the new locale or antinepotism rules caused the wife to terminate her career temporarily. Antinepotism rules in organizations prohibit the employment of relatives. They developed during the Great Depression of the 1930s when it was considered inequitable to allow more than one breadwinner per family. Technically the regulations could apply to either spouse, but they almost always have been used against women. Recently antinepotism rules have been successfully challenged as discriminatory. This change might help reduce divorce.

Divorce Rates. The fact that women professionals tend to have higher divorce rates than women in the general population may indicate particular stresses on their marriages. It also may be that women professionals have relatively high standards for interpersonal relationships, or that they are more likely and able to get out of an unsatisfactory marriage because of the satisfactions and economic rewards of their work. According to Astin's survey of women doctorates (1969), the natural scientists had the most stable marriages: 54 percent were married and only 6 percent were separated or divorced. Women psychologists, on the other hand, had the highest marriage and divorce rates—62 percent were married and 14 percent were separated or divorced.

PARENTHOOD

Anticipated problems in managing two careers probably contribute to some professional couples' decision against having children. Compared with similarly aged married women in the general population, twice as many married women doc-

torates in one study (28 percent) were childfree; and those who had children had smaller families—two children on the average, compared with three in the general population (Astin, 1969). Many of these women, moreover, postponed motherhood until they were established professionally: 49 percent had preschool children at the time of the survey, about 10 years after their doctorates. Only 19 percent of comparably aged women in the general population had preschool children.

Sharing Child-Care Satisfactions and Responsibilities. At present this culture lacks a social policy facilitating couples' sharing work and family involvements (Chapter 16). Thus couples must make their own arrangements and seek outside assistance if both partners are to pursue full-time careers. Managing practical details requires energy, organization skill, confidence in the validity of their goals, genuine partnership, and a willingness to trust others and to share their children's love with them.

Although infant daycare centers still are relatively rare, high quality facilities for 2½- to 5-year-olds are available in many areas. Many parents are particularly enthusiastic about participating in community-controlled daycare centers that are staffed by both women and men trained as child-care specialists. Compared to their homebound peers, children in the centers often have the advantages of increased opportunities for social and emotional development as well as for enriched physical play with the diverse equipment and materials.

For parents who prefer child-care help at home, there are problems in locating suitable caregivers—especially since we have yet to create a specific role of child-care specialist that denotes and acknowledges the many competencies needed for that work (Chapter 7). The population of available domestic help presently tends to be overrepresented by destitute elderly widows or by immature high school dropouts who really cannot cope with child-care responsibilities. But there are middle-aged women with demonstrated competencies as mothers who are seeking personally satisfying work outside their homes after their own children are grown. These women are attracted by the opportunity to become involved again with children, particularly if the salary offered is competitive with other employment possibilities—as it should be. Thus, even now dual-career families have several options for sharing child-care responsibilities. Hopefully the options will become more widely available.

Part-Time Career Opportunities. Some professional couples manage part-time careers so that each can share child-care responsibilities. Such opportunities still are rare, but they may become increasingly available (Chapter 16). Unfortunately, most currently available part-time professional jobs are at a low skill level and tend to be temporary, dead-end commitments that do not count toward seniority or tenure. In many universities women with advanced degrees work as nontenured lecturers, usually in introductory courses, or as research associates whose contracts are renegotiated each year, with no guarantees of future employment. Although they reap some of the rewards of professional involvement, these individuals often miss the professional enhancement that comes from regular employment.

Interrupted Professional Involvement. Some women temporarily drop out of professional work when their children are young. The woman's family then may develop a life-style dependent on her homemaking contributions. Thus her return to work may be more disruptive for all than when her work role has been part of the family pattern from the beginning. A possibly more permanent adverse effect involves the consequences of an interrupted career for professional advancement (Bernard, 1971). It is hard to keep up with one's field when not really involved in professional work. And it is even harder to "tool up" after dropping out. Thus one can be at a disadvantage compared to a newly trained professional. Furthermore, given all the myths about working women, a potential employer might predict that the woman who has dropped out or settled for second-rate work will do so again. There is much

unexamined prejudice against women with unorthodox career lines—that is, careers that differ from the uninterrupted, full-time, male pattern.

Age and Achievement. The temporary dropout or part-time employment pattern may further disadvantage the woman who hopes to make a substantial contribution. At least among outstanding men professionals, the quality (though not the quantity) of their output seems related to age (Lehman, 1953). Generally what experts in their fields judge to be the peak of men's creative work tends to occur early—from the late twenties to the early thirties for men in the sciences, to the late thirties for those in music and philosophy. These are the very years when many women professionals are having babies and are involved, to a greater or lesser extent, in child care.

This caution is not intended to be another "anatomy is destiny" type of discouragement to women's achievement. Among even "great" men there are exceptions, like Verdi, to the age–achievement relationship. Furthermore, this apparent relationship might really reflect the fact that most original work is done when one first gets immersed in a field, before one fully accepts the set modes of thinking in that profession (Rossi, 1965). If that were the case, then the temporary dropout would have less to be concerned about—*if* the social environment were as supportive for women as it is for men.

The Mystique of Motherhood. Aside from the logistics, which actually constitute a rather interesting organizational challenge, the major problem besetting the woman professional who is also à mother involves social pressure. There is a cultural mystique of the "necessity" of full-time motherhood that influences even the prescriptions of child-care "experts." The labels some psychologists select indicate the cultural bias. For example, research about maternal absence is called "maternal deprivation." While the comparable research regarding fathers can be labeled "paternal deprivation," as in Chapter 8, it usually is more benignly termed "father absence" by professional (male) psychologists. Thus, because child care generally is considered the *mother's* prime responsibility, and because some claim her children will be deprived unless *she* is home full-time, it is difficult indeed for some working mothers to avoid guilt feelings.

Supermoms. Some women professionals seem to need extra social and personal support to assuage guilt feelings about possibly letting their families down. Their strategy in eliciting support and reducing guilt sometimes involves attempting to perform all of the functions of the traditional domestic role in addition to those of their career (Hall, 1972). These women cook gourmet meals, schedule diverse activities with their children, entertain lavishly, and still work. Thus they are called supermoms, and they must get terribly tired. A more realistic strategy chosen by many other women involves restructuring commitments or schedules to facilitate accomplishing a variety of objectives in different roles (Hall, 1972). For example, some women (and men) physicians engage in group practice with colleagues so that they work set hours and are assured of genuinely free time.

Impact of Maternal Employment. Despite the doomsday predictions of purveyors of the myth that mothers should be full-time housewives, there is considerable research evidence regarding the *positive* effect on her family of a mother's employment (Hoffman & Nye, 1974). Fathers in such families generally take more responsibility for child care, with benefits for all; and the children grow up with less stereotypic views of sex roles, with obvious positive effects for daughters particularly (Chapters 8 and 11).

The employed mother and her family also benefit from the fact that she tends to have more favorable attitudes about relationships with her children than do nonemployed mothers. This finding is not surprising since satisfaction with interpersonal relationships is contingent to a great extent on satisfaction with the self. A recent study compared a group of mothers who were faculty members of a large university with a comparably aged group of mothers who had graduated from college with honors but had pursued neither further education nor a career. Compared with the women faculty, the unemployed mothers had lower self-esteem and lower sense of competence, even about child-care skills (Birnbaum, 1975). The predominant answer from the faculty women about what they felt was missing from their lives was *"time,"* but for the housewives it was "challenge and creative involvement."

PROFESSIONAL PERFORMANCE

As this chapter documents, a woman professional experiences a career of many struggles with conflicting social pressures and pervasive sex discrimination. How does she perform with so many factors working against her? Admirably!

PRODUCTIVITY

In universities the widely used measure of productivity involves number of publications. This may reflect the agentic "masculine" nature of professions, where less importance is accorded equally legitimate communal criteria involving production in service to others—for example, production of student-scholars, production of worthwhile courses, and production of valuable and necessary committee work. "Publish or perish" still holds sway.

Some early studies reported that women publish less than men. Part of the reason for this is that women are more likely to be employed at colleges than at universities—and both women and men in colleges publish less than people in universities. When controls for academic affiliation and length of career are made, there is *not* a true difference in productivity between women and men professionals (Bernard, 1964; Guyer & Fidell, 1973; Simon, Clark, & Galway, 1967). In fact, contrary to expectations, married women Ph.D.s who are employed full-time publish slightly more articles and books than do men Ph.D.s. This is interesting because the average married woman professional spends about four hours per day on household and child-care tasks in addition to her full-time employment (Astin, 1969). Perhaps there has been a natural selection of high energy women who undertake involvement in two demanding jobs; furthermore, the demands for good organization might have a facilitative effect on their productivity. Husbands of working women do share home responsibilities, but their time contribution tends to be considerably less than that of their wives (Walker & Gauger, 1973).

COPING WITH
STATUS INCONSISTENCY

Despite the evidence regarding women's work commitment and performance, persistent sexist views devaluing the female ascribed status still make the woman professional a "deviant."

Developing Autonomy. A first step in dealing with this situation involves recognizing the state of affairs—which is not the same as condoning it. This requires carrying on in the face of repeated, painful rebuffs and frequent, negative feedback from the social environment (Anderson, 1974). To do this one must learn to function in an emotionally autonomous way. That is, one must keep faith in oneself and in the validity of one's goals and thus provide oneself with positive feedback when the environment is indifferent or oppositional.

Emotional autonomy is particularly important when a woman professional encounters situations like the stag effect that deny her some of the informal signs of belonging and recognition. Perhaps the relative aloofness of some women professionals stems from the necessity to be highly autonomous in nonsupportive environments. Autonomy is crucial also for successful women business executives in the male managerial world (Hennig, 1970).

Benefiting from Supporters. Becoming autonomous does not necessitate becoming "an island unto oneself." Increasingly, women colleagues are supporting each other, and there is more male support based on actual experience with competent women professionals. Most successful women acknowledge the continuing contributions of their parents in encouraging their achievement and in many instances providing

models of professional competence (Kundsin, 1974). In spite of the priority strains in some dual-career families, almost all of the husbands respected their wives' professional involvement (Holmstrom, 1972). Most of these couples also reported that they did not experience a sense of competition with each other. They valued both their own and their partner's goals.

With personal autonomy and support from significant others, a woman professional can work effectively in spite of the numerous pressures still against her. She then also can strive for social change by opposing everyday instances of sexism and working for affirmative action.

WORKING FOR
SOCIAL STRUCTURAL CHANGE

Sometimes employed women can individually negotiate a redefinition of aspects of the role structure to accomplish their goals. Given the pervasiveness of sexism, however, group action also is necessary.

Challenging Gresham's Law of Occupations. Some male occupational gatekeepers contend that "letting" more women into professions will somehow devalue the professions. As "evidence" for this prediction they cite the case of Russia where some 75 percent of the physicians are women, but medical practice has a lower status than in the United States. This argument is a Gresham's law of occupations. In economics, Gresham's law states that "bad drives out good." When two coins are equal in debt-paying value but unequal in intrinsic value (like copper vs. gold), the one having lesser intrinsic value tends to remain in circulation while the other is driven out (e.g., exported as bullion).

Sexist or racist views regarding "intrinsic" human worth are the basis of the application of Gresham's law to occupations. For example, some years ago, before the 1964 Civil Rights Act, my husband and I were consultants for a major airline. Our recommendation that black stewardesses be recruited was flatly rejected because airline officials feared that blacks would devalue the job, thereby diminishing the supply of desirable (white) applicants. Obviously for women, as for blacks, group action and legal protection are necessary to combat discriminatory practices.

With increasing numbers of people advocating an androgynous combination of agentic achievement and communal concern within professions, there may be an upward revaluation rather than a Gresham-like devaluation of occupations. What would professions now be like had women and third world people always been fully represented? Would women's natural functions have been considered so problematic as to warrant two medical specialties—obstetrics and gynecology? There is no comparable specialty of andrology (diseases of men). And would research priorities have differed so that now we would have really safe contraception and effective treatment of sickle-cell anemia?

Participating in the Women's Movement.
Increased proportions of women in an organization produce what Rossi (1973) terms a "social density" factor that facilitates political activity. For example, being one of 40 women on a faculty provides a woman with a very different perspective from being one of only three. Among a group of 40 women there is greater potential for mutual support that can generate confidence in combating sex discrimination, especially at the local level. Within professional organizations the social density in the late 1960s fostered the development of women's caucuses that have challenged previously unquestioned sexist assumptions and policies (Rossi & Calderwood, 1973).

Of course, the solidarity of the ranks is upset by the few women who "made it on their own" in the tough male environment and can't see why other women should have it easier (Staines, Tavris, & Jayaratne, 1973). Nevertheless, women's groups have demonstrated the value and power of cooperative effort in challenging salary inequities and pressing for affirmative action programs. Benefits of group support are illustrated by the almost 50 percent decrease in dropouts among women graduate students following the formation of a women's caucus in Berkeley's sociology department.

Thus there has been important progress, but much remains to be done in challenging sexist ideology and changing social practices so that eventually the energy diverted in this struggle can be reinvested in achieving one's life goals. The struggle will be personally costly, and there will be casualties, but tremendous personal rewards await those who in viewing their life's pursuits can tell themselves, "Well done."

SUMMARY

More than half of the American women between 18 and 64 are in the labor force, but most are concentrated in low prestige, low-paying occupations. On the average, furthermore, women are paid $3458 less than men with equal qualifications. Among the small number of women in top managerial and professional occupations, most resemble their male colleagues in competencies, interests, and training experiences. The women differ from the men in their fields, however, in their higher average scores on intelligence measures and in their relatively more communal rather than competitive emphasis in personal ambition. There is some evidence that women in some different professions share a core pattern of characteristics, indicating that they are more intelligent, aggressive, adventuresome, imaginative, unconventional, and self-sufficient than are women in the general population. Younger women in some professions, however, seem to have more problems of self-definition and less self-confidence than do women in general or their male colleagues.

Some of the difficulties in self-definition stem from status inconsistency. Women professionals occupy a high achieved status but a low ascribed status because of sexist devaluations of women. These negative evaluations are expressed in myths regarding women's competency and work commitment, and these myths are used to justify unequal treatment. The male managerial model for administrative roles also tends to disadvantage women professionals.

About half of the women professions are married, usually to men professionals in similar fields. While dual career couples are relatively egalitarian, many still give priority to the male's professional advancement, reflecting the American fusion of personal and occupational identity for men. Women professionals who are mothers face tremendous social pressures, but they have developed a number of strategies for dealing with competing role demands. Available evidence indicates a positive effect of maternal employment on the woman's family and on her own self-esteem.

Despite sexist myths and pervasive discrimination, women's productivity equals that of similarly qualified men in their fields; in fact, one study found that married women doctorates who were employed full-time published more than their male colleagues. In order to perform well in what frequently is a masculinized environment that is indifferent or nonsupportive, women professionals must learn to cope with being reacted to as a deviant and keep faith in themselves and in the validity of their goals. Support from family and friends is beneficial. In addition, women's groups are increasingly available to provide social and emotional support and to challenge inequities and press for social change. The past has been stormy, the present is cloudy, but the future is clearing for the woman professional.

CHAPTER
16
EQUALITY AND SOCIAL STRUCTURE

In previous chapters we have examined some of the personal and social consequences of many beliefs about women—from the seemingly benign assumption that they are fragile and need protection to the blatant devaluation of women, except for sexual and reproductive purposes. Here, we shall elaborate on some of these effects in examining the consequences of the cleavage between domestic and occupational spheres and the pervasiveness of **sex-typing** even in language. We shall consider different models of equality between the sexes and sketch some components of a "hybrid" egalitarian model involving social structural changes to facilitate personal growth and fulfillment of women, men, and children.

THE QUEST FOR EQUALITY

There is much discontent with current **sex role** divisions in our society. While the new women's movement has focused particularly on women's dissatisfaction and anger at inequities, men's concerns are evident also. Some young men reject status-dominated life-styles, possibly after viewing the existential despair experienced by some middle-aged men in confronting the emptiness of their occupational "success." Prescriptions of cures for sex-role malaise vary with diagnoses of the focal problem.

REACTIONS TO CURRENT PROBLEMS

Blaming the Victim. Some critics of the women's movement blame women themselves for "their" dilemmas. These faultfinders fail to recognize that men, too, have problems and that the social structure is producing dissatisfaction for all. Essentially, these critics claim that women's attitudes are responsible for their predicament—a response comparable to blaming miners for contracting black lung. This type of argument often is applied to other victimized groups as well. For example, some critics claim that poor people suffer their fate because they have defeatist attitudes, are lazy, and cannot delay gratification. While some of the poor may indeed have these characteristics, this does not mean that their attitudes *produced* the poverty; in fact, the discouragement may well be a result of their situation (Ferber & Huber, 1975).

With respect to women, Horner's formulation about women's "motive to avoid success" (see Chapter 11) achieved almost instant popularity as an "explanation" for women's underrepresentation in prestige occupations. Blaming the underrepresentation on women's hang-ups makes it *their* problem rather than a problem of the social structure in which the problem developed.

Blaming Society. Other critics of the current situation denounce sexist ideology and the economically profitable discrimination such prejudice supports. The Women's Liberation Movement has developed a variety of strategies in dealing with *"women's* problems" as *social* problems. The movement actually is not a single, unitary group but rather a conglomerate of different groups with varying goals, memberships, and organizational styles. Accordingly, there are varying ways women within "the" movement seek social change.

Seeking Change Within the Institutional System. The older branch of the women's movement typically functions as reformist pressure groups within the traditional social structure. The most prominent core group of this branch is the National Organization for Women (NOW). Also included are a lobbyist group (the Women's Equity Action League), a legal foundation (Human Rights for Women), numerous caucuses in professional organizations, as well as separate organizations of women in the professions and other occupations (Freeman, 1975). These national groups use the tools for change currently provided by the political, legal, and media institutions of our country. In the last few years they have successfully influenced rulings of the Equal Employment Opportunity Commission; they have been instrumental in the filing of complaints and lawsuits charging sex discrimination by universities and businesses; they lobbied for Congressional passage of the Equal Rights Amendment and are pressuring for its ratification; and they are continuing a major assault on salary inequities. Largely through their efforts, information on feminism has appeared in virtually every news medium.

Concentrating on the Grassroots Level. In relative contrast, the younger branch of the women's movement has a profound distaste for leadership and hierarchy and instead espouses "structurelessness" (Freeman, 1975). People in this branch do not want to deal with traditional political institutions, partly because they believe the basic changes necessary for liberation cannot be realized within the existing system. Most of their activities, therefore, are at the local level, centering on consciousness raising and the development of new institutions. For example, they form rap groups, distribute educational literature, and run service projects such as women's centers, bookstores, and health centers.

Women in academia have markedly increased scholarly attention to women and have introduced women's studies programs in colleges and universities across the country. Although some of these women are active in national professional women's organizations, many confine their efforts to their local campuses. Thus as a group, academic women are intermediate on the broad spectrum of organizational styles encompassed by the woman's movement.

These branches of the women's movement are complementary in covering a social spectrum ranging from formal institutions to grassroots community groups. While their strategies differ, they share the goals of fighting sexism, trying to change social institutions (e.g., schools, occupations, and the health-care system), and seeking a new understanding of what it is to be a woman. Many of their ideas and visions about social change are encompassed within the assimilation, pluralist, and hybrid models of equality delineated by Alice Rossi (1969).

THE ASSIMILATION MODEL OF EQUALITY

The assimilation model of equality idealizes the melting pot "one from many" concept in which minority groups are advised to lose their distinc-

tive ethnic identity and become absorbed into the mainstream of society. This model accepts the social institutions formed by the dominant group and idealizes the status quo. The "America: love it or leave it" stance is an extreme national chauvinistic expression of the assimilation model.

Within the women's movement, an expression of this model appears in attempts to liberate women from an exclusive relegation to the domestic sphere and to integrate them into the occupational world. This goal actually often substitutes one form of oppression for another. Women are admonished that they *cannot* find fulfillment as homemakers; they *must* compete with men for career positions and *must* emulate men's styles in politics, civic life, sexual affairs, and even in clothing, grooming, and speech. The advice is sexist in assuming that women are "all alike" and need authorities—men—as models of the good life. Women are assumed to want to be like men, and men's life-styles are assumed to be worth emulating. Furthermore, even if the current structure were desirable, procedures for assimilating women are ineffective and in some cases nonexistent.

The Unfeasibility of Assimilation. Many Americans are uncomfortable with Marxist-sounding claims that women are exploited for economic profit. Yet, like many other noncommunist countries, our country treats women outside of the traditional (low-paid) women's clerical, textile, and service trades as a reserve work force that is called into the labor market when male labor is scarce and dismissed when it is plentiful. This "yo-yo" policy was classically illustrated in World War II when women were quickly trained for jobs they previously had been (and now are) considered unfit for—for example, in ship building, auto assembly, oil refining, and truck driving. Women still comprise most of the low-paid university staff who teach introductory courses on one-year appointments when enrollments demand extra faculty. As long as women are regarded as temporary reserves for the core (male) labor group, only token numbers of women are likely to be assimilated in many trades and professions.

Another problem for women in labor market policy is that the expected pattern for occupational progress involves an uninterrupted work life beginning at the end of schooling and ending with compulsory retirement. This pattern is not feasible for many married women, given expectations regarding mothers' child-care responsibilities along with the scarcity of alternative arrangements. Thus, by male standards many women are latecomers in the labor market and generally are not given (re)training or counseling, with the net effect that they cannot compete equally with men for high-paying positions. In fact, rather than invest in women's training, employers often fractionalize the content of more demanding jobs into simpler jobs that untrained people (women) can perform for "justifiably" lower pay. Meanwhile men move up to higher positions with higher salaries (Cook, 1975).

Even trained women may not be equally eligible for prestigious jobs as comparably trained men. Often people in higher positions need an unpaid wife to fulfill social obligations (Chapter 15). The organization expects "two for the price of one." Thus given our social structure and practices, the assimilation model of equality cannot be egalitarian for all people—especially women.

Implications for Black Women. Assimilation has been relatively successful for some groups. For example, Catholic and Jewish workers now have higher average incomes than Protestants, and academic leaders no longer are exclusively WASPS (white, Anglo-Saxon Protestants). But current assimilationist trends may prove detrimental in the black community. Many black men contend that they have been psychologically emasculated not only by white racism but also by black women, who frequently have been more employable than they and have headed black households. Policies of some black organizations seem to lower the status of the black woman, by taking as an ideal the traditional white middle-class pattern of a dominating male breadwinner coupled with a dependent childbearer and housekeeper. Some

black women reject this attempted assimilation as another form of oppression, insisting that both sexes must improve themselves and work to better the black community. Nevertheless, some black women seem—by white feminist standards—to be deferential to black men. Actually, it is a tribute to these black women that they do not consider themselves "better" than their men and are willing to help raise the men's self-esteem. There is no comparable dedication on the part of many white American men toward their women; instead many seem to favor pluralism.

THE PLURALIST MODEL OF EQUALITY

Instead of advocating one standard "stew" that diverse cultural ingredients get melted into, the pluralist model of equality offers a "smorgasbord" of distinctive tastes. Diversity is valued, and groups that differ from the so-called mainstream of society—such as, blacks from whites, Catholics from Protestants, women from men—are encouraged to develop and maintain their distinctiveness. "Black is beautiful" is an expression of this model. Many societies use a pluralist model for sex differences, asserting that "Women should be what they *are*." Thus they assume **bio-psychological equivalence** in claiming that biological differences necessitate role differences (Chapter 1). For example, woman's nuturance often is seen as "naturally" being best expressed in maternity; a man's aggression is considered appropriate for competitive occupational pursuits.

The pluralist "separate but equal" social policies actually proved discriminatory for blacks. Similarly, the pluralist separation of women in the domestic realm and men in the occupational world is unfair to many individuals in both sexes. And in this instance, the separate worlds usually are not considered "equally" prestigious—except, perhaps, on Mother's Day. When all members of one sex are assumed to have biologically determined social destinies that differ from the destinies of the other sex, then pluralism becomes an ideological justification for inequality. Increasing individual freedom of choice is one goal of the hybrid model of equality, which advocates **androgyny** at the social structural level.

THE HYBRID ANDROGYNOUS MODEL OF EQUALITY

The hybrid model of equality advocates changes in both the dominant and minority groups. It rejects the assimilation endorsement of the present social organization and the concomitant life-style of middle- and upper-class men. It also rejects the pluralist assumption that women and men are inherently so different that they ought to maintain distinct social roles. What the hybrid model proposes is a society in which women and men become more androgynous, leading relatively similar lives, but lives that differ in many ways from the ones either sex lives now.

In enacting the hybrid model, women no longer would be relegated to domestic roles and to a relatively exclusive **communal** orientation to others. Instead they would have opportunities to develop and apply **agentic** as well as communal competencies both in the public sphere and at home. Men would no longer be prodded to an intense preoccupation with agentic career advancement and agentic sexual exploitation of women, but would have opportunities to develop a communal sense of interdependence with family and others. This model thus retains some positive integrative elements of the assimilation model. Furthermore, since the similarity in people's lives would also involve similarity in the range of options open to individual members of each sex, this model also encourages diversity—but at an *individual* level rather than at the group level, as advocated by pluralism.

CONCOMITANTS AND COSTS OF THE CURRENT SYSTEM

In order to understand why the hybrid model advocates certain social changes, let us consider in more detail some implications of our current combination of pluralism and assimilation. Our pluralistic beliefs support the relegation of women and men to separate domestic vs. occupational worlds. However, women are allowed to be assimilated into parts of the occupational realm *if* they abide by the rules developed by and for men (Chapter 15). Our language itself reflects the cleavage in women's and men's expected worlds, and this division fosters extremes in the socialization of girls and boys (Chapters 8 and 9).

STATUS DISTINCTIONS IN LANGUAGE

Speech is part of human gender display (see Chapter 3), and is one way in which sex differences and associated inequalities are socially marked, emphasized, and perpetuated. Not only is there frequently more prestige in terms describing males than females (for example, we hear of "kingpins," not "queenpins"), but formerly neutral words for females, acquire derogatory and often obscene implications (like wench, harlot, and dame). In everyday speech American men more frequently interrupt others (especially women) and dispute rather than acknowledge or build upon others' comments. Women's speech generally is less assertive, with more hesitations, false starts, and qualifications than men's (Thorne & Henley, 1975).

The Generic "Man." Inequality between the sexes and the pervasive practice of disregarding women are expressed by the generic *man* and *he* referring to human beings generally, as in "all men are created equal." Scholarly defenders of the status quo suggest that the generic *he* for a sex-indefinite referent is an inherent part of our language traditions. Actually, it results from an arbitrary decision that indicates the greater importance of men than of women (Bodine, 1975). The eighteenth-century grammarians who influenced our current usage of *he* decreed that consistency in number was more important than accuracy of gender. Their choice of *he* assures gender accuracy for male but not female referents (Table 16-1).

The scholarly critics do correctly note that in Old English, *man* originally was the term for human being, but their contention that it should continue being so overlooks the way the term has

TABLE 16-1.
Evolving Third-Person Pronouns

"Proper" Usage	Degree of Accuracy
Pre-Eighteenth Century "Everyone should raise *their* hand."	Disagreement in number between plural pronoun (their) and singular sex-indefinite antecedent (everyone). No disagreement in gender.
Post-Eighteenth Century "Everyone should raise *his* hand."	No disagreement in number: pronoun (his) and antecedent (everyone) both singular. Possible disagreement in gender if "everyone" includes females.
Nonsexist Variations "Everyone should raise *his or her* hand." "All present should raise their hands."	No disagreement in number, and no disagreement in gender.

evolved in practice. Anglo Saxons referred to an adult male as *waep(n)man* (weaponed man) and to an adult female as *wifman*. However, since men have lost their weapons—linguistically, if not otherwise—the prominent meaning for *man* now is male human being. Thus, even when *man* is intended in a generic sense designating humanity, it nonetheless connotes males and prompts imagery appropriate primarily to men, thus filtering out a consideration of women.

For example, in selecting pictures to illustrate a sociology textbook (Schneider & Hacker, 1973), students given chapter titles with "man"-associated labels (e.g., "Urban Man," "Industrial Man") submitted significantly more pictures containing males only than did students given neutral chapter titles (e.g., "Urban Life," "Industrial Life"). When the researchers sent their findings to textbooks publishers, urging avoidance of the generic *man* when the reference was *people*, some editors responded that *man* was preferred for its convenient brevity, "dramatic impact," and "meretricious suggestion of dignity."

The Relational Woman. Some status distinctions in language reflect societal assumptions that people in occupational roles are men, and women belong mainly in relation to other people (Table 16-2). Occupational terms for women often denote a deviant status through the addition of suffixes (aviatrix, stewardess, hostess, poetess, and—as suggested in jest for the first woman state governor—governess). Words applied to women in unmodified form indicate the social orientation expected of women. A prominent example is the Old English word *wif*, which originally meant female human being. It now means with-a-man, specifically, *wife*. Similarly, the marital status of a man is not communicated by *Mr.*, while the titles *Miss* and *Mrs.* indicate the perceived necessity of specifying a woman's marital status. Although there are seven times as many men as women in children's schoolbooks, the words *mother* and *wife* occur far more frequently than *father* or *husband* (Graham, 1975). Thus in our language women are referred to mainly in terms of family relationships, whereas men are defined primarily in occupational terms.

SEPARATION OF DOMESTIC AND PUBLIC SPHERES

Language patterns reflect and reinforce current social practices associated with assimilation and

TABLE 16-2.
Sexist and Neutral Vocabulary

Sexist Terms	Neutral Alternatives
Businessman	Business executive, manager
Cameraman	Camera operator
Chairman	Chairperson, moderator, the chair
Fireman	Fire fighter
Foreman	Supervisor
Insurance man	Insurance agent
Mailman	Mail carrier
Man-hours	Work-hours
Manpower	Labor force; work force
Salesman	Salesperson
Statesman	Leader, public servant
Workman	Worker
Miss	Ms.
Mrs.	Ms.
Housewife	Homemaker (Sweden has added "Househusband" to designate a legitimate new role)

pluralist models of "equality" of the sexes. Despite dramatic exceptions such as the Tchambuli of New Guinea (Chapter 1), women throughout the world tend to lead remarkably similar lives in their roles as wives of herders, farmers, and executives (Rosaldo, 1974). Women's contributions outside of the immediate domestic sphere are rarely recognized explicitly or rewarded appropriately—even when they contribute substantially to the subsistence of their communities. "Behind every great man, there is a woman" acknowledges a woman's contribution but admits that she in the backseat in the prestige system.

Obviously there is a substantial biological foundation to the traditional division of labor between the sexes. The fact that women give birth and lactate makes it highly probable that they will be associated with child-rearing and home responsibilities, particularly in settings where there are no alternatives to breast feeding of infants. But the "obvious" connection between a woman's reproductive activities and an exclusive and life-long domestic role actually is a cultural elaboration subject to modification with changes in technology, population size, and ideological values.

Family Authority Relations. Segregation of the sexes affects family authority relations. In some cultures the prestigious occupational, political, and religious activities are exclusively male; men and women interact only briefly, in bed and when wives serve dinner. When men are separated from the intimate, emotionally involving, and demanding (woman's) world of the home, they more easily can maintain a "paternalistic" authority role. Their emotional and maybe physical distance from their families facilitates a cooly agentic and impersonal exercise of their power as "heads" of their households. Even in this culture the suburban isolation of the **nuclear family** often results in children's perceiving men as the important but remote decision makers who have minimal emotional input as fathers.

"Maternalistic" authority tends to be quite different, based more on emotional demands than on power vested in the role. Women cannot really maintain distance from people they interact with in the domestic sphere. Their commitment to their children is enduring, time-consuming, and emotionally compelling. The demands for their care and affection are too persistent and diffuse for women to enact a "paternalistic" authority role. Typically, therefore, a woman's domestic life is marked by neither privacy nor distance: psychologically and maybe literally she does not have a room of her own (Woolf, 1957).

Impact on Child Socialization. The sex segregation of domestic and occupational worlds and the associated differences in authority patterns have many adverse effects on children. Girls have more exposure to the "sex-appropriate" adult role and start learning that role early as they are integrated into the woman's world of domestic work. In following the ever-present model of senior female relatives, typically the mother, the girl develops social skills in becoming nurturant and responsively attuned to others' needs. Unfortunately, as noted in previous chapters, she may fail to develop an adequate sense of separateness and independence.

Particularly when their fathers are psychologically or physically distant, boys have relatively little personal knowledge of the adult male world, except perhaps as it is portrayed in the culture's folklore or mass media. Boys thus learn manhood as a set of relatively abstract rights and duties; furthermore, the attainment of manhood generally requires emotional rejection of the women's domestic world (Chodorow, 1974). Some cultures institutionalize this rejection in various puberty rites, especially if the young boy has been sheltered from men early in life (Whiting, Kluckhohn, & Anthony, 1958). Rejection of the domestic world is further facilitated by the fact that boys usually have fewer household responsibilities than girls and thus are freer to participate in peer groups where relationships often are more hierarchically achievement-based than they are within the kin group. Male peer groups very likely provide background experience for the formation of "old boy" stag networks within many occupations and professions (Chapter 15).

Males, therefore, are reinforced for almost exclusive agentic orientations by a socialization pattern involving rejection of early dependence on the mother, relative isolation from ongoing family concerns, and participation in relatively competitive peer groups. As a result of their early experi-

ences, many adult men seem to have a continuing need to demonstrate their superiority to women in order, perhaps, to prove they are no longer dependent children.

UNMITIGATED COMMUNION AND AGENCY

Both women and men often pay high costs for the relatively exclusive communal or agentic orientations encouraged in them. Many problems of the exaggerated concern with communal relatedness for women have been discussed throughout this book. Noting such "women's problems," some people urge women toward an exclusive agentic orientation. The value of this proposed assimilation is questionable. Specific "men's problems," with far-reaching social ramifications, help illustrate the dangers of proposing a social change program in which women are encouraged to assimilate to the male way.

Personal Costs. Extreme traditional femininity is not associated with good adjustment. Neither does strong masculinity seem to facilitate general psychological or social adjustment, except perhaps during adolescence. In one **longitudinal study,** 17- and 18-year old males were categorized as high or low on masculinity according to their responses to a self-report inventory (Mussen, 1961). While both groups reflected dominant socialization patterns in their motivations toward autonomy, achievement, and aggression, the low-masculine group was rated as more expressive. This combination of characteristics proved problematic for the low-masculine boys: they had a less positive self-concept and were less carefree, content, and relaxed in social functioning than the high-masculine group. Apparently, therefore, conforming to sex-typing pressures leads to social rewards, emotional security, and personal satisfaction—during adolescence. However, 20 years later the picture changed markedly: the high masculine group scored as less self-accepting, less self-assured, less sociable, and generally less well-adjusted than the low-masculine group (Mussen, 1962).

Cultural Models. Socialization of males toward the inadequacies of relatively exclusive agentic orientation is abetted by dominant cultural models. The cowboy is one ideal, representing the ruggedly cool, strong, and resourceful "he-man" who overcomes both natural catastrophes and bad guys. With "true grit" he expresses no weakness or "feminine" emotion in dealing with a loss of a horse or with the presence of a woman. John Wayne convincingly demonstrates that the cowboy qualities apply also to the soldier–hero (Balswick & Peek, 1971).

Another cultural model, the playboy, also is concerned with conquest. Unlike the inexpressive cowboy, the playboy can simulate tender feelings in pursuit of his target. Like the cowboy, the playboy emerges from a conquest (a "love" affair) without interpersonal enrichment. In fact, the playboy's relationship with women is a mockery of communal relatedness, representing a culmination of an unmitigated agentic, manipulative, and exploitative orientation. Although the cowboy and the playboy are caricatures, their enduring popularity says something about cultural (male) values.

Most men may only fantasize about being a cowboy, soldier–hero, or playboy rather than actively seek such a life. However, they are likely to pursue a career life in earnest. Cultural expectations for a "career man" are not notably different in psychological essence from those for the cowboy, soldier, or playboy in their exaggeration of agentic and exclusion of communal values.

Careers and Careerism. The high cost of the current definition of career pursuits is well described by Philip Slater (1970):

When we say "career" it connotes a demanding rigorous, preordinated life pattern, to whose goals everything else is ruthlessly subordinated—everything pleasurable, human, emotional, bodily, frivolous. . . . Thus when a man asks a woman if she wants a career, it is intimidating. He is saying, are you willing to suppress half of your being as I am, neglect your family as I do, exploit personal relationships as I do, renounce all personal spontaneity as I do? (p. 72).

Thus defined, a career is a pernicious activity for *any* person to be engaged in. Often, the striving

pattern of career "commitment" becomes an end itself so that men pursue not only careers but "careerism" (Holmstrom, 1972). Such men become "workaholics"—insatiable in their needs to work, compete, and beat deadlines—and incapable of relaxing or of expressing emotions beyond the limited range required or allowed by their work involvement.

Social Costs. Although this model of careers has been assumed to promote work effectiveness and "efficiency," it is doubtful that people who follow it really benefit society, even within the occupational realm. Exclusive agency is not sufficient for doing the jobs required. Each year literally millions of dollars are spent by government and industry in "sensitivity training" for agentic males who advanced to executive roles, but cannot cope with the interpersonal demands of their positions. The limited success of such programs is due not only to the difficulty of undoing a lifetime's socialization, but also to the fact that most bureaucracies and professions are based on agency, valuing "productivity," and low self-disclosure. Organizations as well as people need to become more androgynous.

Dominance versus Harmony. The economic and scientific "progress" resulting from agentic pursuits for the sake of societal (and personal) "achievement" warrants evaluation. Long-range human and ecological problems seem the result of agentic solutions to short-term challenges. Because paternalistic leaders allegedly know what is best for people with whom they are minimally involved, people have suffered wars designed to "free" them, adopted alien religions designed to "save" them, and more recently have accepted relocated urban housing designed to "upgrade" them (while disrupting their established community relations).

Many horrors as well as marvels of modern science also seem attributable to agentic "dedication." Agentic science and technology have created useful products such as plastics and asbestos. Agentic profiteering also has resisted prohibiting the carcinogenic production of such materials. More broadly, agentically based science, with its philosophy of "neutrality" of knowledge, has often ignored social and environmental consequences of accomplishments. Perhaps some of these consequences could have been more adequately assessed scientifically, before the fact, had communal concern been considered relevant.

Man against nature is a time-honored theme in societal and scientific development. Since women are considered closer to nature than men—after all, women give birth, feed, and dispose of feces!—the communal harmony with nature expected of women, but not of men, has been too little valued in manly, scientific pursuits. The policy has been that nature, like women, is to be subordinated, controlled, and manipulated in the service of the cultural advancements of the cowboy/soldier/playboy/scientist/entrepreneur.   We have played a game against nature and we are losing. What is needed now, in this postatomic age, as we cope with pollution and other consequences of our ingenuity in using the world's energy resources, is a new ethic of science. Instead of short-sightedly seeking an ultimately impossible agentic domination of nature, we need to pursue harmony with nature by combining communal concerns with agency. This goal seems more likely if a hybrid model of equality is sought.

TOWARD ANDROGYNOUS EQUALITY

The hybrid model of equality involves an androgynous union of agentic mastery striving along with a communal sense of interdependence and harmony. Research indicates that androgynous people appear more creative, more flexible in the range of activities they will undertake, and less restricted in personal expression than are sextyped individuals (Chapter 8; Bem & Lenney, 1976). What other characteristics might one expect if androgyny were the prevalent pattern?

POSSIBLE PSYCHOLOGICAL CONSEQUENCES

If we promoted androgyny by fostering agentic and communal qualities in both females and males, would people then lose their sex identities? Most likely not. **Sex identity** basically in-

volves an affirmation of one's body and oneself as female or male. It involves appreciating and valuing one's genitals and later one's secondary sex characteristics, and the kinds of potentialities these structures offer. Androgynous people would value their sex identity, and would learn that they have choices about how to use their bodies.

Aside from differences in sex identity, would there be other psychological sex differences? Yes, but the ultimate impact on people's lives might be different. To take a couple obvious sex differences, the menstrual experience undoubtedly would continue to have psychological significance, but with enlightened socialization shame and disgust should not be involved. The emotional symbiosis between a nursing mother and her infant would continue to be rewarding, but not a prelude necessarily to a long relegation to the housewife role. Beards and breasts, would continue to provide unique experiences and decisions for males and females (Chapter 4). People might choose either to deemphasize structural sex differences or to elaborate them in the interest of variety.

If we treated males and females alike, males very likely would continue to display higher levels of aggression because of hormonal differences (see Introduction, Part III; Maccoby & Jacklin, 1974). In the case of aggression, therefore, androgynous goals would be facilitated by differential treatment of each sex, probably involving greater reinforcement of gentleness in males. Humans are remarkably plastic. Our biological potential is expressed to a greater or lesser degree depending upon the cultural environment (Chapter 1). Promoting androgyny requires fundamental changes in major social institutions such as the family and occupations. Changes are necessary also in the micropolitical structure of language.

CHANGING DISCRIMINATORY LANGUAGE

There is a reciprocal relationship between language and society. Language reflects and codifies a particular community's experience. For example, Eskimos have many more words for *snow* than do Arabs; and Arabs, in turn, have about

6000 different terms for *camel.* Language also has a deterministic effect on users' perceptions and categorizations. If our language has no word for *orange,* we will not so easily identify that color on a spectrum. We perceive and use the distinctions provided by our language. Thus, calling women *Mrs.* or *Miss* instead of *Ms.* maintains the importance of women's relational roles. And using words like *chairman* and *he* for sex-indefinite antecedents tends to exclude women from consciousness.

Verbal communication patterns are not social accessories: they are at the very core of social interaction and thus establish, maintain, and transmit ideological (sexist or egalitarian) standards. Perhaps that is why some people resist language change with ridiculous and latently hostile arguments, using letters (*m, a, n*) instead of thoughts in their attempted cleverness. For example, a university vice chancellor suggested that substituting *chairperson* for *chairman* would necessitate introducing words like *personure* (for manure), *personeuver* (for maneuver), and *Personhattan* (for Manhattan). Furthermore, he "humorously" contended, women would not have *hysterectomies;* they would have *hersterectomies.*

THE NEED FOR OCCUPATIONAL AND DOMESTIC INTEGRATION

Hybrid equality requires a true integration of women in the occupational world along with a true integration of men in the domestic sphere. With few exceptions, however, most nations have focused only on changes facilitating women's occupational involvement.

Limitations of Current Labor Policies. Concern with labor scarcity and "women's rights" has fostered varying policies among modern nations (Cook, 1975). In most Western countries where freedom of individual choice is valued, mothers who "wish" to work are left on their own to solve all the problems of finding employment, providing child care, and maintaining their home at an acceptable standard. Because of their pressing need for labor to promote rapid industrialization

as well as their beliefs that all citizens have a "duty" to work, communist countries have generated social solutions to working mothers' problems, such as provision of child-care facilities. Partly as a result of such policies, Soviet women have a far greater representation in professions than women in Western society (Mandel, 1971). But Soviet women still are underrepresented in the top political and occupational strata, and at home they carry an unequal burden of energy-draining responsibilities because Soviet men generally do not share household tasks.

Status inequities are even more pervasive in the domestic realm. Even in the Israeli kibbutz, women participated in agricultural work and military defense, but men were not integrated in the domestic and child-care services. This policy probably contributed to the current sex-role differentiation that is contrary to the inhabitants' professed egalitarian ideology (Rabin, 1970). At present only 5 percent of the supervisors in kibbutz factories are women, and none of these women holds a top position (Tannenbaum, et al., 1974).

Consequences of Men's Domestic Involvement. When both women and men share domestic as well as subsistence endeavors, sex roles tend to be relatively egalitarian, as exemplified by the Philippine Ilongots (Rosaldo, 1974) and by two tribes described in Chapter 1—the nomadic African !Kung and the New Guinea Arapesh, where both men and women are said to "grow" their children. A man who is involved in child care, cooking, and household tasks cannot easily maintain an aura of formal "paternalistic" authority and psychological distance. He is more likely to become a person to his children, rather than a figurehead, and to appreciate domestic work. Thus he is liberated from pressures toward a relatively exclusive agentic career dedication and is encouraged to develop more of a sense of communal relatedness.

But increased self-realization opportunities for men, women, and children will occur only in token numbers if individual couples must continue to work out their own accommodations to assimilationist labor policies. The hybrid model of equality necessitates national policy dealing more explicitly than before with the "private" domestic sector.

THE SWEDISH MODEL

Sweden provides the only example to date of a comprehensive, long-range policy for increasing women's and men's active participation in both parenthood and gainful employment. This policy was set forth in a 1968 report to the United Nations (reprinted in Dahlstrom, 1971):

A decisive and ultimately durable improvement in the status of women cannot be attained by special measures aimed at women alone; it is equally necessary to abolish the conditions which tend to assign certain privileges, obligations or rights to men. No decisive change . . . can be achieved if the duties of the male in society are assumed a priori to be unaltered. . . . If women are to attain a position in society outside the home which corresponds to their proportional membership of the citizen body, it follows that men must assume a greater share of responsibility for the upbringing of children and the care of the home. . . . This aim can be realized only if the man is also educated and encouraged to take an active part in parenthood and is given the same rights and duties as the woman in his parental capacity (pp. 213–214).

Ideology and Economics. From their commitment to social equality and their diagnosis of the inequities resulting from traditional sex-role training, the Swedes have been developing nonsexist parent education, reforming textbooks, and changing school curricula. Both girls and boys have compulsory training in wood, metal, textile handicraft, domestic science, and child care. The educational reforms are concurrent with fundamental changes in labor market policy, tax reform, new marriage and divorce laws, and a projected expansion of child-care places from the 105,000 currently available to 300,000 by 1980 (Cook, 1975; Palme, 1972).

Economic factors in Sweden's policy stemmed from a decision that the reserve pool of married women constituted a better labor source than did imported foreign labor. To enact this decision Swedish policymakers had to modify the social structure for the full integration of women in the labor force: this was not another "yo-yo" policy. One attempt to combat the traditional sex-typing of some occupations was a system of incentives to employers. Some government grants and loans to industries in geographical areas requiring industrial development were contingent on at least 40 percent of the workforce being of the sex that was in the minority in the industry in question (Cook, 1975). Other policies have focused on individual workers.

Helping Women's Employment. A Swedish woman who reports to a labor office is immediately counted as unemployed and therefore eligible for an unemployment benefit until she finds work. Her abilities and experiences are evaluated, and she receives occupational counseling and any necessary training. She receives grants-in-aid for education or training along with supplementary aid for associated expenses, including child care costs. Travel money is provided for interviews with prospective employers; if her new job requires relocation, she is assisted with moving expenses and given help in finding housing and child care in her new locale.

Obviously, this comprehensive program is very expensive. But the Swedes estimate that within four years after receiving these benefits, a woman contributes not only to her own and her family's support, but also to the national economy by her productivity and taxable income. Thus within a relatively short time she more than repays the investment which enabled her to work (see Cook, 1975).

Helping Men's Domestic Involvement. Swedish policy helps both parents to assume child-care responsibilities and also makes provision for supplemental child care. Legislation makes it equally possible for men as well as for women to interrupt their work lives to care for children. Either father or mother may take child-care leave for six months after birth, may remain home to care for sick children or other family members with compensation of about 90 percent of pay, and may receive the child-care allowance paid to parents of children under 16. Assumptions about the patriarchal household have also been abolished from Swedish tax law. The Swedes have discontinued joint tax returns that gave married men a tax deduction for their wives along with lower rates than those assessed single taxpayers. Now each adult is considered economically independent and pays individual income tax.

POSSIBLE APPLICATIONS

Obviously, what works in the Swedish system might not be applicable here. And while the examples just cited appear to have good consequences from a number of personal and social viewpoints, their success does not mean that all is well with the total Swedish social system. High suicide rates, for example, continue to be a Scandinavian problem.

In piecemeal manner, some elements of a hybrid model of equality are being enacted in the United States. But a comprehensive national program involves many complexities (see discussion at the beginning of Part IV) and is unlikely unless policymakers are convinced that it will pay off. For a fair assessment we need better social indicators in addition to traditional economic indices.

Increasing Child-Care Options. To facilitate women's and men's participation in both parenthood and gainful employment, leaves of absence for infant care by either parent would be beneficial. Training Scientists of Child Rearing is especially important to provide supplemental high quality child care in either individual homes or day-care centers (see Chapter 7). Furthermore, encouraging men as well as women to become qualified child-care specialists will reinforce the hybrid model's recommended androgyny. With qualified personnel the "custodial" stereotype perhaps deservedly attached to many current day-care facilities will be negated by the advantages of more enriched social and physical environments than usually are possible in a home setting. Community controlled centers with active parental participation seem to achieve the best of both worlds.

For those who fear that increased day-care options will weaken family bonds, we may cite the case of China where the change in family life was far more radical than the modifications suggested for the United States. Yet, according to a psychiatric social worker with extensive international experience with child-care facilities, the Chinese day-care centers have not weakened family structure or parental involvement in their children; furthermore, the children appear happy, well-adjusted, and less in conflict with their parents than many homebound American children (Sidel, 1972).

Modifying Work Schedules. Increasing the flexibility of work schedules also will facilitate women's and men's dual participation in employment as well as in family or other involvements. Such flexibility involves options regarding both the specific hours at work and the total number of hours worked. The goal is to fit jobs to individuals rather than force a fit of individuals to jobs whose assumed necessary properties are based on largely untested assumptions. People such as professors, research scientists, farmers, and self-employed heads of businesses now generally have considerable freedom of choice in scheduling work activities—and their job satisfaction tends to be high.

In an effort to "humanize" work generally, Robert Kahn (1973) has proposed a work module system. A module is simply a time-task unit—for example, two hours at a given task. Kahn's proposal involves identifying the component modules of various jobs and then having the worker decide the allocation of her or his time among the modules. For example, for one day a supermarket stock clerk might choose two modules stamping prices, one module at the cash register, and another learning inventory control. Another day the clerk may choose a different mix or a different number of modules, so long as the weekly sum of modules equaled the total agreed upon. According to Kahn, sufficient details have been worked out to implement major field experiments of work modules. By adding the option that people can contract for less than, say, 20 modules per week, we could then realistically experiment with maximally flexible work schedules.

Varying Total Work Modules. Definitions of "full-time" employment have changed in different periods and in different occupations. Some people devote virtually all their waking hours to occupational pursuits. This is hardly a viable orientation for a substantial part of the occupational world. In many sectors we are overproducing and promoting unwanted products while we contend with the pollution from our productivity. Perhaps, indeed, it would be better if more people worked less than what we now consider full-time.

Many women and men now want a more varied life-style that permits a significant but not excessive commitment to work. They want their work to help satisfy a need for meaningful activity and growth, but do not want it to impair their capacity to perform other life roles—as a spouse, parent, citizen, or friend. Many parents for example, may wish to work less than 20 modules a week to allow more time with their children at home or among the volunteers at a day-care center. Other people may wish to be employed for varying numbers of modules at different periods of their lives to enable them to continue their education, engage in community activities, or pursue other interests.

Modularized jobs and flexibility in total modules contracted will complicate bookkeeping and payroll computations and will necessitate negotiations about time definitions for fringe benefits, seniority, tenure, and so on. But some of the modifications really are extensions rather than radical changes of existing practices. For example, many people work and go to school part-time. In some universities, over one-fourth of the full-time male faculty at senior ranks have joint appointments. If a university department can share a man with another department, perhaps it can as readily share a man or a woman faculty member with a family or other involvement (Holmstrom, 1972).

Experimenting with Social Policy. Obviously much experimentation is needed to implement social changes. Social structural support is essential if individuals are to have a variety of options so they can lead more diverse and satisfying lives. Will androgynous adults then also be more productive in their paid employment? The Swedish experience suggests that investments in hybrid equality yield an economic profit. But we should note that American industrial research data indicate only a modest relationship between worker satisfaction and productivity. Perhaps, however, current indices do not adequately assess the full productivity costs of low satisfaction and the full range of accountable benefits from high satisfaction (Likert, 1967). In any event, an experimental approach to social policy will help identify conditions that benefit the social system at personal, interpersonal, and economic levels.

Persuading policymakers to experiment with social structural changes will not be easy. Assumptions about sex-typed traits are so much a part of our cultural heritage, like barnacles on a travelworn vessel, that they cannot easily be removed—especially since they support some economically profitable discriminatory practices. But we do have an ethic of egalitarianism and fair play. Dissatisfaction with current life-styles for each sex also promotes proposals for change. The more we increase the freedom for individuals of both sexes, the more all people can become responsible agents for their own destiny. Through increased options to generate themselves they can be responsible for what they become in living deeply and meaningfully at work, at home, and at play.

SUMMARY

A society gets the kind of excellence it values. The assimilationist and pluralist models of equality in our society foster a division between domestic and public worlds, reflected in our everyday language, and reinforced in socialization practices that promote relatively exclusive communal orientations in females and agentic pursuits in males. At its worst our occupational structure seems to value competition over cooperation, short-term efficiency over participation, social formulas over self-expression, and striving over gratification. This is not the type of orientation into which women should be assimilated in an effort to be "equal" to men; rather it is one that men need liberation from.

While the focused, moderate-risk, short-term foresight of the agentic achiever has contributed to our technological progress, it also has left a legacy of social and ecological problems. What is needed now is a union of agentic mastery striving with communal concern for human interdependence. Androgyny is the goal of the hybrid model of equality, which advocates social structural changes to facilitate women's and men's participation in gainful employment as well as in parenthood or other personal involvements. So far Sweden has developed the only comprehensive national policy to promote hybrid equality, and we have sketched some potential applications of Swedish practices in our society. Planning and experimenting with such changes requires agentic competencies and communal sensitivities to anticipate and identify consequences. There is much to be done to meet the challenge of providing all persons opportunities for meaningful activities and involvements at work and at home, but the goal of androgynous fulfillment is well worth the effort.

GLOSSARY

Achieved status: Social status based on indicators such as education, income, and job classification that usually are not fixed at birth and that an individual can control to some extent. See **ascribed status** and **sex roles.** (254)

Achievement motivation: Conventionally, competition with a standard of excellence, with the desire to accomplish something difficult, to master objects, people, or ideas and to do so rapidly and independently. Usually used narrowly, centering on competitive academic and occupational endeavors. (170)

Actualization: A widely used term generally denoting full recognition and development of human characteristics, or personal fulfillment as an ideal goal. Used in varying forms by some personality theorists (e.g., Jung, Rogers, and Maslow). (25)

Affiliation motivation: To draw near and enjoy cooperation or reciprocation with another person. To please and win affection of a desired object. To adhere and remain loyal to a friend. (170)

Agency; agentic: An orientation to the world in which an organism is concerned with self-protection, self-assertion, and self-expansion. **Achievement motivation** and **competence,** as usually conceptualized, are aspects of an agentic orientation. Used in contrast with **communal,** though the ideal person is assumed to have both agentic and communal orientations well developed (e.g., **androgynous**). From David Bakan. (20)

Anaclitic (dependent) identification: **Identification** with an object whose positive characteristics are salient, such as one who is warm, nurturant, and loving—one on whom the individual is dependent for positive desired outcomes. Young girls' identification with mother in the phallic stage is often said to be the prototype of this kind of identification. Contrast with **defensive identification.** (23)

Androgyny, androgynous: Having both characteristics expected in females and those expected in males. In research, psychological androgyny is (1) having relatively equal scores on scales of femininity and masculinity or (2) having relatively equally high or well-developed characteristics of both the feminine and masculine roles (preferred approach of this text book). **Hermaphrodite** is more likely to be used than androgyny in referring to people who have distinctly *physical* characteristics of both sexes. (20)

Anima: In Jungian theory, the part of the soul (inner character) of a man that is feminine and complementary to the outer character. In contemporary Western society, the **communal** orientation of many men is an underdeveloped anima function. See also **animus.** (26)

Animus: In Jungian theory, the part of the soul (inner character) of a woman that is masculine and complementary to the outer character. In contemporary Western society, the **agentic** orientation of many women is an underdeveloped animus function. See also **anima.** (26)

Aphasia: From the Greek, meaning "speechlessness." Loss or impairment of speech functions, usually resulting from a brain lesion. See **lesion.** (85)

Appetitive or preconsummatory behavioral component: The stimuli and responses that are influenced by evolutionary and genetic conditions and constitute the preliminary activities, such as courting, for a consummatory activity, such as copulating. See **species-specific behavior.** (43)

Artificial insemination: A procedure for fertilizing the ovum, or egg, of the female by introducing the sperm of the male by mechanical means. (48)

Ascribed status: Social status based on indicators such as sex, race, and age that generally are fixed attributes beyond the control of the individual. See **achieved status** and **sex roles**. (254)

Attachment: Term used to describe the social-emotional bond that develops between infant and caregiver. Thought by Bowlby to serve the survival needs of the infant. (104)

Authoritarian: A personality style involving a set of beliefs, values, and behavioral preferences focusing on autocratic power relations, denial of feelings, and cynicism about people. Authoritarian parental behavior involves coercion without reasoning and sensitivity to the child's needs and capabilities. Contrast with **authoritative**. (176)

Authoritative: A style of parental behavior involving responsibility, clear communication of expectations, sensitivity to the child's needs and abilities, and use of reason with some punishment but without autocratic coerciveness. Contrast with **authoritarian**. (175)

Between-group variation: Differences between two or more groups of scores, usually a difference between means. See also **within-group variation**. (9)

Bimodal distribution: Having two modes, or two scores that are very frequent. In a normal distribution, the mean and the single mode (the most typical score) are the same. The **mean** of a bimodal distribution is misleading, because there are two large groups of subjects, neither of which is well described by the mean. (52)

Biopsychological equivalence: Psychological characteristics are said to be directly associated with and determined by biological characteristics. For example, behaviors considered feminine are erroneously said to be "just natural" for biological reasons. Not to be confused with **psychobiological**. (7)

Bipolarity: A dimension with opposites at each extreme. Femininity–masculinity has often been conceptualized erroneously as bipolar, meaning that a person cannot be both extremely masculine and extremely feminine. Contrast with the more defensible concept of **androgyny**. (7)

Bisexual: A person who is sexually oriented to and may have had sexual experience with members of both sexes. Also sometimes used to denote having characteristics of each sex, psychologically or physically; **androgyny** currently is preferred for psychological duality. (201)

Chromosomes: Small, rod-shaped bodies in the cell nucleus that contain the genes or hereditary factors. (50)

Circadian rhythms: Rhythms or cycles that are approximately 24 hours in length, for example, the adult human sleep–waking cycle. (63)

Classical conditioning: A learning procedure that requires the individual to associate two stimulus events, one (unconditional stimulus) that initially elicits a given response and one (conditional stimulus) that does not initially elicit the response. (109)

Communion; communal: An orientation to the world in which the organism is concerned with the community of others and feels at-one-with other organisms and the rest of the world. Affiliation and social sensitivity, as usually conceptualized, are aspects of a communal orientation. Used in contrast with **agentic,** though the ideal person is assumed to have both agentic and communal orientations well developed (e.g., **androgynous**). From David Bakan. (20)

Comparative psychology: A branch of psychology that deals with behaviors of all animals, emphasizing the diversities of such behaviors as well as the similarities in behavior organization. (38)

Competence motivation: A desire for a sense of competence in interacting with and having an impact on the world. Curiosity, activity, manipulation of objects, and exploration are usually cited as clearly defined aspects of competence motivation, but it may be expressed through many other activities and motives. See **effectance motivation**. (136)

Conditions of worth: In Rogerian theory, standards people feel they must meet if they are to like themselves ("I can accept myself only upon conditions"), typically derived from interaction with other people who have held or do hold conditional positive regard for the person. Defensiveness helps prevent awareness of violations of conditions of worth. Similar to the Freudian concept of **superego**. (28)

Consummatory behavioral component: The stimuli and responses that are strongly influenced by evolutionary and genetic conditions and constitute the culminating activities of a species or sex-specific behavior, such as copulating. See **species-specific behavior.** (43)

Content analysis: A technique for quantifying written or spoken language, by establishing categories of "themes" (thema) on which verbal productions are assessed and scored; such as content analysis of responses to a projective test (e.g., **TAT**) to measure achievement concerns. (73)

Corpus Callosum: A wide-arched band of white matter (white brain and spinal cord tissue, consisting mostly of nerve fibers) that connects the cerebral hemispheres at the base of the longitudinal fissure. (85)

Critical period: Period during the early life of an individual when the behavior of the individual is especially sensitive to particular kinds of stimulation and is then affected later in life by this stimulation. (47)

Dating persona: Persona relevant in dating rituals among United States adolescents particularly; prescribes pleasant and safe interactions but limits interpersonal intimacy. Also see **persona.** (161)

Defensive identification, or identification with the aggressor: Identification with an object whose negative characteristics are salient, such as one having dominance, power to hurt or to control the individual. Young boys' identification with father in the **phallic stage** is often said to be the prototype of this kind of identification, however, it has also been argued (Chapter 9) that it characterizes the conventional socialization of females. Contrast with **anaclitic identification.** (23, 141)

Descriptive statement: A statement that simply describes an existing state of affairs without explaining why the described condition occurs or maintaining that it must occur. Unfortunately, descriptive statements are often treated as if they were prescriptive statements, for example, that the condition must occur. Contrast with **prescriptive statement.** (9)

Developmental psychology: The study of behavior organization throughout the life span of the organism. Emphasizes human development but is not restricted to the human species. (106)

Dichotic listening: "Dicho" means two parts or the division into two parts. Dichotic listening refers to simultaneous listening to two different signals, one presented to each ear. In *monotic listening,* the same signal is presented to each ear. (85)

Dimorphism: The condition in which a species lives and reproduces by existing in two biological forms, such as female and male forms. (38)

Dogmatism: Close-mindedness in structure of beliefs (regardless of content of beliefs) often with opinionated insistence on the correctness of one's own opinions without sensitivity to others' views. (163)

Double standards: Principles that apply differently and more rigorously to members of one group than to another. Typically sexual double standards prescribe that "good" single women should be virgins, whereas single men may act on their presumably strong "sex drive." Similarly, extramarital sex is considered more blameworthy for women than for men. (192)

Effectance motivation: Robert White's term for what is usually called **competence motivation,** that is, having an effect on the world. (136)

Electra complex: See **Oedipal complex.** (22)

Empty nest syndrome: Restlessness, anxiety, and depression in middle-aged parents whose children have left home; formerly said to be due to a woman's menopause and loss of ability to bear children. Now recognized as relatively specific to people (usually women) who have defined themselves only through their children and feel "life is over" when children leave home. (149)

Eros: In Jungian theory, the passive and receptive life principle, involving seeing relatedness and pattern in parts of the whole separated by **Logos;** uses intuition and openness. Modern concepts of communal orientation and field dependence may be seen as specific indications of the Eros principle. Distinguished from Logos, but is balanced with Logos in a complete person. (26)

Ethogram: A detailed description of the behaviors of a species using verbal or pictorial representations of the many stimuli and responses that characterize the behavior of the species. (41)

Ethology (ethologist): Branch of zoology concerned with behavioral comparisons among species. Generally is a **psychobiological**–constructivist approach to the study of behavior but has tendencies to be **nativistic.** (106)

Exacerbation theory: Theory that premenstrual symptoms of a woman are exaggerations of personality traits and behaviors that occur also, to a lesser extent, throughout the menstrual cycle. Thus, there is continuity of behavior from one phase of the cycle to another and individual differences among women in their menstrual **symptoms.** (74)

Family of origin: The family group that includes one's parents and siblings; the family in which one is born and reared. Contrast with **family of procreation.** (215)

Family of procreation: The family group that includes the individual's spouse and offspring. Contrast with **family of origin.** (215)

Fear of failure: One component of **achievement motivation.** Fear about consequences of possible failure, which encourages attempted avoidance of situations in which failure would reflect on one's own abilities; can lead to unrealistically low or high **LOAs.** (171)

Fear of success: One component of **achievement motivation.** Fear about negative consequences expected for success in achievement situations, particularly competitive ones. Said by some (e.g., Horner) to imply a motive to avoid success and to be very strong in women, lest they lost their femininity; these claims have been critized by others. (172)

Field dependence–independence: Dependence is responsiveness to the stimulus field as a coherent whole, with judgments about the stimulus being influenced by, "dependent upon," the stimulus itself. In contrast, independence is responsiveness to only particular aspects selected out of the total stimulus, and judgments about the stimulus are relatively uninfluenced by, "independent of," the total stimulus field. (8)

Fixed response: A genetically organized response to a **sign stimulus** in a consummatory sequence of stimuli and responses, such as courting and mating. (41)

Genotype: The genetic structure of an individual or group of individuals. See **phenotype.** (50)

Hemispherectomy: Literally, the removal or excision, through surgery, of the cerebral hemisphere. (92)

Hermaphrodite: An organism having both male and female reproductive organs; an individual with a congenital condition in which the reproductive structures are ambiguous so that the individual's sex is not exclusively male or exclusively female. (39)

Homoeroticism: Engaging in heterosexual activities as a means of acquiring or maintaining status with same-sex peers rather than out of interest or concern for person of the other sex. Apparent in 14 to 16 year old girls but more marked and persistent among adolescent boys. Can occur in adults also. (161)

Hope of success: One component of **achievement motivation.** A person sees a situation as providing an opportunity for a meaningful success and thus achievement motivation is "aroused" or becomes relevant in the situation. (170)

Ideal self: A person's conscious view of what is wanted for oneself; varies in degree of consistency or congruence with the perceived actual self, the **self-concept.** Moderate discrepancy between actual and ideal self is assumed most indicative of psychological health; low discrepancy suggests defense against recognition of shortcomings; high discrepancy denotes discomfort. (122)

Identification: (1) Conventionally, the process(es) of incorporating features of another person into one's own personality, particularly with respect to major cultural conventions, such as obedience to sex role and moral standards. Although the phallic stage has been assumed a critical time, identification is also seen as (2) a lifelong process of relatedness to other people, and roughly equivalent to social responsiveness. Also see **phallic stage, Oedipal complex, anaclitic identification, defensive identification.** (23, 141)

Imaginary audience: The tendency, especially of adolescents, to feel that they are the focus of everyone's attention; good friendships may help to overcome it (Elkind). (159)

Implicit personality theory: A theory people have about human beings, usually without recognizing it (it is implicit rather than explicit). Although implicit, it affects our perceptions and inferences and gives a feeling of comforting order; we "see" ourselves and others through the "template" of our theories. Theories differ in their accuracy, usefulness, flexibility, and complexity. (18)

Imprinting: The development of responses to a stimulus during a **critical period** early in the life of an animal—as when young ducks learn to follow a moving object, usually the mother. (42)

Individuation: The developing sense of oneself as a unique individual—an integral part of identity formation. (224)

Lesion: Most generally, a wound or injury. In the case of the brain, a circumscribed pathological alteration of tissue. (85)

Level of aspiration, LOA or LA: Level of accomplishment a person attempts or aspires to attain, rather than what they expect to attain. Generally, actual achievement is facilitated by an LOA that is realistically high rather than unreasonably low or high. (171)

Logos: In Jungian theory, the active and forming life principle involving compartmentalization and analysis of separable parts of a whole. Modern concepts of agency and field independence may be seen as specific indicants of Logos. Distinguished from **Eros,** but is balanced with Eros in a complete person. (26)

Longitudinal study: A study of the same individuals over time. Generally preferable to simultaneous observation of several groups of subjects varying in age at time of the observation (cross-sectional study). (274)

Mean: The arithmetic average of a group of scores often used to describe the group as a whole. However, there is likely to be within-group variation because many people of the group are not average. See **within-** and **between-group variation.** (9)

Misogynist: A person who hates women. (50)

Mores: Culturally prescribed customs. Patterns of group behavior that perpetuate cultural traditions or assert group membership. (225)

Nativistic (nativism): Theory stating that there are innate ideas. "Explanations" refer to "built-in" properties of the mind that are not constructed through interaction with the environment. (103)

Neuroanatomy: The science of the shape and structure of the nervous system. (84)

Neuropsychology: A field combining the disciplines of psychology and neurology. The *neurologist* is a medical specialist with an M.D. degree, who is typically concerned with the diagnosis and treatment of diseases of the nervous system. The *neuropsychologist* is a psychologist with the Ph.D. degree, who uses the research tools of psychology to evaluate the psychological functions of neurological structures. (84)

Nuclear family: Family group consisting only of two parents and their offspring. Contrasted with the *extended* family, which includes other relatives and often three generations. (226)

Oedipal complex: In Freudian theory, feelings of love for parent of the same sex and concomitant fear of retaliation by and aggression toward parent of the other sex along with fear of loss of love by that parent. For the girl, feelings of castration lead to the Oedipal situation (also called **Electra complex**). For the boy, the Oedipal situation leads to fears of castration by father. See also **phallic stage** and **identification.** (22)

Operant conditioning: A learning procedure that requires the individual to change a given behavior as a result of the reinforcement that follows a previous occurrence of the behavior. (108)

Persona: In Jungian theory, the "mask" we wear in interacting with other people (similar to concept of roles). Part of the "outer character." Human qualities not developed as part of the outer character are present in the "inner character" (soul). See **anima, animus,** and **dating persona.** (26)

Phallic stage: A Freudian stage of psychosexual development, around ages 4 to 6 years, during which children are assumed to identify with parents, especially the same-sex parent; thus, **superego** development begins. Psychologists recognize the importance of this age for **sex-role** learning, while not necessarily agreeing with the explanatory mechanisms Freud postulated. See also **Oedipal complex** and **identification.** (21)

Phenotype: The detectable expression of the interaction of genotype and environment, constituting the visible characteristics of a particular organism. See **genotype.** (50)

Pheromone: Secretion of a bodily substance by one individual of a species that acts as a stimulus for the response of other members of the species. (62)

Phoneme: The basic, different, and distinct speech sounds out of which mature language is built. Linguists regard phonemes as the basic unit of sound by which "morphemes" (the minimal grammatical units of a language), words, and sentences are represented. (80)

Polymorphism: The condition of a species that lives and reproduces by existing in two or more forms, such as the several forms of the jellyfish and some social insects, such as bees. (38)

Postconsummatory behavioral component: The stimuli and responses that are influenced by evolutionary and genetic conditions and constitute the species- or sex-specific activities that follow a consummatory component. See **species-specific behavior.** (44)

Premenstrual syndrome: A collection of **symptoms** (therefore, a syndrome) said to occur in women premenstrually. The existence of a single syndrome across large groups of women is challenged by evidence. (73)

Prescriptive statement: A statement that a state of affairs must necessarily exist; often **descriptive statements** about sex differences are treated as if they were prescriptive ones, typically on the claimed basis of biological or moral reasons. (9)

Proactive: A model or view of human beings as "origins," whose behavior is internally rather than externally controlled, that is, people initiate action (pro-act) to affect the environment rather than simply react to it. Also used as a mode of functioning; a person may function proactively either habitually or only temporarily, or in only some areas of behavior. From Allport and deCharms; similar to Rotter's concept of internal control. Contrast with **reactive.** (19)

Projective techniques: Methods of psychological measurement in which the subject is presented relatively ambiguous stimuli (e.g., **TAT** pictures, inkblots, **verbal leads**) onto which personal meaning is "projected." For research purposes, results are often **content analyzed.** (8)

Psychobiology (psychobiological): A point of view concerning the organization of behavior which stresses the inherent biological and psychological unity of the individual, and the reciprocity of organism–environment interaction. (106)

Queen Bee: A derogatory term applied to occupationally successful women who show little concern or support for younger women working toward similar goals. Ironically, a bee who is "queen" of a colony is one who serves the rest of the hive in complete interdependence with the workers in maintaining the hive. (165)

Reactive: A model or view of human beings as "pawns" or victims, whose behavior is controlled by the external world, that is, they react to the current environment (often on the basis of past experiences) rather than initiate action (pro-act). Also used as a mode of functioning; a person may function reactively either habitually or only temporarily, or in only some areas of behavior. From Allport and deCharms; similar to Rotter's concept of external control. Contrast with **proactive.** (19)

Regression: A return to an historically earlier or developmentally more primitive mode of adaptation. Often occurs under stress or frustration, when more mature behavior patterns become disorganized or prove ineffective. (220)

Rhythm method: A technique of birth control based on the fact that there are typically only about 5 to 6 days during each menstrual cycle when conception can occur. However, the technique has minimal effectiveness because of difficulties of predicting when these days will occur. (71)

Role(s): The socially defined pattern of behavior expected of an individual occupying a given position in a group; for example, behaviors expected of a mother in a family, and those expected of a professor in a university. (6)

Role strain: Discomfort with a role caused by such factors as ambiguity of role content; incongruence of role demands with one's predispositions, skills, and preferences; inconsistency in the application of role expectations; or conflict between two or more roles. (144)

Self-concept: In Rogerian theory, a person's conscious views of self and of things related to self (I, me, mine). Most contemporary research definitions are also of conscious views of self, though the term sometimes refers to unconscious aspects as well. (28)

Self-disclosure: Willingness to show oneself to other people, especially by explicit communication of some relatively personal information not likely to be known other than through personal revelation and not likely to be given to many other people (Jourard). Also used in a general sense to refer to free display of feelings nonverbally as well as verbally. (163)

Sex assignment: Newborn is labeled as female or male; the decision is sometimes difficult when physical criteria of sex are inconsistent with each other. (124)

Sex-role adoption: Display of **sex-role** behavior; adopted behaviors vary in consistency with preferences and with **sex-role identity.** One's own view of degree of role consistency of behavior may or may not match with judgments made by others. (122)

Sex-role identity: The extent to which an individual feels feminine or masculine by criteria of **sex roles.** Occurs on conscious and unconscious levels; identities at different levels may be consistent or inconsistent with each other or with physical sex. Often carelessly used as equivalent for **sexual identity.** (121)

Sex-role preference: A preference for or a desire to adopt behavior of a given **sex role,** part of **ideal self.** A person may prefer all or only some behaviors perceived relevant to the sex role; sex-role preference often includes some behaviors considered feminine and some considered masculine. (122)

Sex roles: Expectations for behavior held for a person

on the basis of sex; thus, sex roles are based on ascribed characteristics (the individual has no choice) rather than on achieved status indicators (for which the individual strives). See also **achieved** and **ascribed status.** (6)

Sex-typed: Generally the sex differences in characteristics or experiences. (1) Behavior in which males and females do differ or are expected to differ. (2) The extent to which an individual matches stereotypes in **sex-role identity, preference,** or **adoption.** (124)

Sexual identity: A person's definition of self as female or male, in reference to the incorporation of aspects of the physical body into self-perceptions. Often carelessly used as an equivalent to **sex-role identity.** (121)

Shock theory of marriage: View that conventional marriage introduces emotional health hazards into the life of a woman, while it has beneficial effects for a man (Jessie Bernard). Generally supported by mental health data. (149)

Sign stimulus: A stimulus, such as the color of the female animal, that provides the appropriate stimulus for a fixed response in a consummatory sequence, such as mating. See **fixed response.** (41)

Socialization: An all-inclusive term that refers to the sum total of factors that affect the development of attitudes, beliefs, values, and behaviors of the child. (103)

Sociometric: Measurement technique by which people rate a single person or, more typically, every person in a group on dimensions, or name group members who fit varying descriptions, such as "the group leader," "the most popular person," "the one you most want on your team." (135)

Species-specific behavior: Patterns or sequences of responses of individuals of a species to stimuli where the stimulus and associated responses are determined at least in part by the evolution and genetics of the individual. (43)

Superego: One of three major structures of personality (along with id and ego) in Freudian theory, consisting of an ego-ideal that rewards with pride and a conscience that punishes with guilt for behaviors thought appropriate or inappropriate according to the cultural standards as perceived and internalized by the person. See **phallic stage** and **identification.** (23)

Symbiosis: Mutual interdependence that is necessary to the welfare and survival of both partners. Applied to humans (in a psychological sense) by analogy from types of organisms biologically dependent on each other for suvival. (220)

Symptom: Behavioral or physical manifestations or indicants of a condition, usually but not necessarily a pathological condition. Symptoms that frequently occur together constitute a syndrome. (60, 150)

TAT, Thematic Apperception Test: A projective technique in which the subject is asked to tell a story about relatively ambiguous pictures. Frequently used to measure motives such as achievement, as well as in clinical assessment and diagnosis. May be scored by **content analysis.** (170)

Transexual: A person who is convinced that she or he is really a member of the other sex and desires to have the appearance, body, and social interaction typical of the other sex. (35)

Unidimensionality: One dimension rather than more than one (multidimensionality). Femininity–masculinity has been assumed unidimensional when actually many dimensions or concepts or kinds of behaviors are implied. (6)

Vaginal smears: Sample of vaginal tissue whose physiological characteristics vary with menstrual cycle phases. (71)

Vasocongestion: The filling of the blood vessels with fluid. Vasocongestion associated with sexual excitement causes the genital structures to swell. (194)

Verbal lead: Verbal stimuli, such as a sentence description of a situation, used as a **projective technique,** patterned after the use of **TAT** pictorial stimuli. (173)

Vicarious achievement: An attempt to gratify achievement strivings through the accomplishments of others (usually family members) rather than through one's own direct goal striving. (180)

Within-group variation: Differences *within* any one group of scores; also called variation around the **mean.** For many measures, female and male groups have mean differences (**between-group variation**) but also large within-group differences when many females and males differ greatly from what is average for their group; often, many females and males score the same. (9)

REFERENCES

Abel, T., & Joffe, N. Cultural backgrounds of female puberty. *American Journal of Psychotherapy,* 1950, *4,* 90–113.

Abt, I. A., Adler, M. A., & Bartelme, P. The relationship between the onset of speech and intelligence. *Journal of the American Medical Association,* 1929, *93,* 1351–1355.

Adams, M. The single woman in today's society: A reappraisal. *American Journal of Orthopsychiatry,* 1971, *41,* 776–786.

Ahammer, I. M. Social-learning theory as a framework for the study of adult personality development. In P. B. Baltes & K. W. Schaie (Eds.), *Life-span developmental psychology, personality and socialization.* New York: Academic Press, 1973.

Ainsworth, M. D. S. *Infancy in Uganda.* Baltimore: Johns Hopkins Press, 1967.

Ainsworth, M. D. S., Bell, S. M., & Stayton, D. J. Individual differences in the development of some attachment behaviors. *Merrill-Palmer Quarterly,* 1972, *18,* 123–143.

Akamatsu, T. J., & Thelen, M. H. A review of the literature on observer characteristics and imitation. *Developmental Psychology,* 1974, *10,* 38–47.

Alger, W. R. *Friendships of women.* Boston: Roberts Brothers, 1879.

Allen, F. R., Jr., & Diamond, L. K. Prevention of Kernicterus: Management of erythroblastosis fetalis according to current knowledge. *Journal of the American Medical Association,* 1954, *155,* 1209–1213.

Allport, G. *Becoming: Basic considerations for a psychology of personality.* New Haven: Yale University Press, 1955.

Allport, G. *Pattern and growth in personality.* New York: Holt, Rinehart, & Winston, 1961.

Almquist, E. M., & Angrist, S. M. Career salience and atypicality of occupational choice among college women. *Journal of Marriage and the Family,* 1970, *32,* 242–249.

Altman, M., Knowles, E., & Bull, H. A psychosomatic study of the sex cycle in women. *Psychosomatic Medicine,* 1941, *3,* 199–225.

Anderson, J. V. Psychological determinants. In R. B. Kundsin (Ed.), *Women and success.* New York: William Morrow, 1974.

Anthony, E. J., & Benedek, T. (Eds.). *Parenthood: Its psychology and psychopathology.* Boston: Little, Brown, 1970.

Aronoff, J., & Crano, W. D. A re-examination of the cross-cultural principles of task segregation and sex role differentiation in the family. *American Sociological Review,* 1975, *40,* 12–20.

Astin, H. S. Career development of girls during the high school years. *Journal of Counseling Psychology,* 1968, *15,* 536–540.

Astin, H. S. *The woman doctorate in America.* New York: Russell Sage Foundation, 1969.

Astin, H. S. Career profiles of women doctorates. In A. S. Rossi & A. Calderwood (Eds.), *Academic women on the move.* New York: Russell Sage Foundation, 1973.

Astin, H. S., Suniewick, N. & Dweck, S. *Women: A bibliography on their education and careers.* Washington: Human Services Press, 1971.

Atkin, C. K., & Miller, M. M. *Experimental effects of television advertising on children.* Paper presented at the meeting of the International Communication Association, Chicago, April, 1975.

Atkinson, J. W. (Ed.). *Motives in fantasy, action, and society.* Princeton, N.J.: Van Nostrand, 1958.

Bachtold, L. M., & Werner, E. E. Personality profiles of gifted women psychologists. *American Psychologist*, 1970, *25*, 234–243.

Bachtold, L. M., & Werner, E. E. Personality profiles of women psychologists: Three generations. *Developmental Psychology*, 1971, 5, 273–278.

Bachtold, L. M., & Werner, E. E. Personality characteristics of creative women. *Perceptual and Motor Skills*, 1973, *36*, 311–319.

Bakan, D. *The duality of human existence: An essay on psychology and religion*. Chicago: Rand McNally, 1966.

Balint, A. Identification. In S. Lorand (Ed.), *The yearbook of psychoanalysis* (Vol. 1). New York: International University Press, 1945.

Balswick, J. O., & Peek, C. W. The inexpressive male: A tragedy of American society. *The Family Coordinator*, 1971, *20*, 363–368.

Bandura, A. Influence of models' reinforcement contingencies on the acquisition of imitative responses. *Journal of Personality and Social Psychology*, 1965, *1*, 589–595.

Bandura, A., Ross, D., & Ross, S. A. A comparative test of the status envy, social power, and secondary reinforcement theories of identificatory learning. *Journal of Abnormal and Social Psychology*, 1963, *66*, 3–11.

Bardwick, J. M. *Psychology of women: A study of biocultural conflicts*. New York: Harper & Row, 1971.

Barry, H., III, Child, I. L., & Bacon, M. K. Relation of child training to subsistence economy. *American Anthropologist*, 1959, *61*, 51–63.

Barry, W. A. Marriage research and conflict: An integrative review. *Psychological Bulletin*, 1970, *73*, 41–54.

Bart, P. B. Depression in middle-aged women. In V. Gornick & B. K. Moran (Eds.), *Woman in sexist society: A study in power and powerlessness*. New York: Signet, 1972.

Baruch, G. K. Maternal influences upon college women's attitudes toward women and work. *Developmental Psychology*, 1972, *6*, 32–37.

Bass, B. M., Krusell, J., & Alexander, R. H. Male managers' attitudes toward working women. *American Behavioral Scientist*, 1971, *15*, 77–83.

Baumrind, D. Current patterns of parental authority. *Developmental Psychology Monograph*, 1971, *4* (1, Pt. 2).

Baxter, J. C., Lerner, M. J., & Miller, J. S. Identification as a function of the reinforcing quality of the model and the socialization background of the sub-ject. *Journal of Personality and Social Psychology*, 1965, *2*, 692–697.

Bayley, N. Growth curves of height and weight by age for boys and girls, scaled according to physical maturity. *Journal of Pediatrics*, 1956, *48*, 187–194.

Becker, W. C. Consequences of different kinds of parental discipline. In M. L. Hoffman & L. W. Hoffman (Eds.), *Review of child development research* (Vol. 1). New York: Russell Sage Foundation, 1964.

Bell, R. Q. A reinterpretation of the direction of effects in studies of socialization. *Psychological Review*, 1968, *75*, 81–95.

Bell, R. Q., Weller, G. M., & Waldrop, M. F. Newborn and preschooler: Organization of behavior and relations between periods. *Monographs of the Society for Research in Child Development*, 1971, *36* (1–2, Serial No. 142).

Bell, S. M., & Ainsworth, M. D. S. Infant crying and maternal responsiveness. *Child Development*, 1972, *43*, 1171–1190.

Bem, S. L. The measurement of psychological androgyny. *Journal of Consulting and Clinical Psychology*, 1974, *42*, 155–162.

Bem, S. L. Sex role adaptability: One consequence of psychological androgyny. *Journal of Personality and Social Psychology*, 1975, *31*, 634–643.

Bem, S. L., & Bem, D. J. Case study of a nonconscious ideology: Training the woman to know her place. In D. J. Bem (Ed.), *Beliefs, attitudes and human affairs*. Belmont, Cal.: Brooks/Cole, 1970.

Bem, S. L., & Lenney, E. Sex typing and the avoidance of cross-sex behavior. *Journal of Personality and Social Psychology*, 1976, *33*, 48–54.

Benedek, T., & Rubenstein, B. The correlations between ovarian activity and psychodynamic processes: 1. The ovulative phase. *Psychosomatic Medicine*, 1939a, *1*, 245–270.

Benedek, T., & Rubenstein, B. The correlations between ovarian activity and psychodynamic processes: 2. The menstrual phase. *Psychosomatic Medicine*, 1939b, *1*, 461–485.

Bengis, I. *Combat in the erogenous zone*. New York: Knopf, 1972.

Bennett, C. C. *An inquiry into the genesis of poor reading*. New York: Teachers College, Columbia University, Contributions to Education, 1938, No. 755.

Bennett, G. K., Seashore, H. G., & Wesman, A. G. *Differential aptitude tests* (3rd Ed.). New York: The Psychological Corporation, 1959.

Bennett, G. K., Seashore, H. G., & Wesman, A. G. *Differential aptitude tests* (4th Ed.). New York: The Psychological Corporation, 1966.

Bentzen, F. Sex ratios in learning and behavior disorders. *American Journal of Orthopsychiatry*, 1963, *33*, 92–98.

Berenda, R. W. *The influence of the group on the judgments of children.* New York: King's Crown Press, 1950.

Bernard, J. *American family behavior.* New York: Harper, 1942.

Bernard, J. *Academic women.* University Park: Pennsylvania University Press, 1964.

Bernard, J. *Women and the public interest.* New York: Aldine–Atherton, 1971.

Bernard, J. The paradox of the happy marriage. In V. Gornick & B. K. Moran (Eds.), *Woman in sexist society: Studies in power and powerlessness.* New York: Signet, 1972.

Bernard, J. *The future of marriage.* New York: Bantam Books, 1973.

Bernstein, A. W. *Fear of failure in college women.* Unpublished doctoral dissertation, Michigan State University, 1975.

Berzins, J. *New perspectives on sex-roles and personality dimensions.* Paper presented at the meeting of the American Psychological Association, Chicago, August, 1975.

Best, C. T., & Glanville, B. B. A cardiac measure of cerebral asymmetries in infants' perception of speech and nonspeech. Paper presented at the meeting of the Midwestern Psychological Association, Chicago, May, 1976.

Bettelheim, B. *Symbolic wounds.* New York: Collier Books, 1962.

Biller, H. B. Father absence, maternal encouragement, and sex role development in kindergarten-age boys. *Child Development*, 1969, *40*, 539–546.

Biller, H. B. *Father, child and sex role.* Lexington, Mass.: Lexington Books, 1971.

Birk, J. M., Barbanel, L., Brooks, L., Herman, M. H., Juhasz, J. B., Seltzer, R. A., & Tangri, S. S. A content analysis of sexual bias in commonly used psychology textbooks. JSAS *Catalog of Selected Documents in Psychology*, 1974, *4*, 107. (Ms. No. 733)

Birnbaum, J. A. Life patterns and self-esteem in gifted family oriented and career committed women. In M. T. S. Mednick, S. S. Tangri, & L. W. Hoffman (Eds.), *Women and achievement.* Washington: Hemisphere Publishing Corporation, 1975.

Block, J. H. Conceptions of sex role: Some cross cul-

tural and longitudinal perspectives. *American Psychologist*, 1973, *28*, 512–526.

Block, J., von der Lippe, A., & Block, J. H. Sex-role and socialization patterns: Some personality concomitants and environmental antecedents. *Journal of Consulting and Clinical Psychology*, 1973, *41*, 321–341.

Blum, J. E., Fosshage, J. L., & Jarvik, L. F. Intellectual changes and sex differences in octogenarians: A twenty-year longitudinal study of aging. *Developmental Psychology*, 1972, *7*, 178–187.

Bodine, A. Androcentrism in prescriptive grammar. *Language in Society*, 4, 1975, 129–146.

Bolsche, W. *Love life in nature: The story of evolution of love.* London: J. Cape, 1931.

Bonhoeffer D. [*Life together*] (J. W. Doberstein, trans.). London: SCM Press, Billing & Sons, 1954. (Translation from 5th ed., originally published, 1949).

Bonner, H. *On being mindful of man: Essay toward a proactive psychology.* Boston: Houghton Mifflin, 1965.

Boszormenyi-Nagy, I., & Framo, J. L. *Intensive family therapy.* New York: Harper & Row, 1965.

Boucher, S. In, Living without them. *Ms.*, October 1975, pp. 68–71.

Boutourline-Young, H., & Ferguson, L. R. *Puberty to manhood: A cross-cultural study of adolescent development.* In preparation.

Bowlby, J. *Attachment, Volume I: Attachment and loss.* New York: Basic Books, 1969.

Bowlby, J. *Attachment, Volume II: Separation, anxiety, and anger.* New York: Basic Books, 1973.

Bowman, G., Wortney, B. N., & Geyser, S. H. Are women executives people? *Harvard Business Review*, 1965, *43*, 14–28; 164–178.

Brackbill, Y. The cumulative effects of continuous stimulation on arousal level in infants. *Child Development*, 1970, *42*, 17–26.

Braine, M. D. S., Heimer, C. B., Wortis, H., & Freedman, A. M. Factors associated with impairment of the early development of prematures. *Monographs of the Society for Research in Child Development.* 1966, 31(4, Serial No. 106).

Brazelton, T. B., & Young, G. An example of imitative behavior in a nine-week-old infant. *Journal of Child Psychiatry*, 1964, *3*, 53–58.

Brenton, M. *Friendship.* New York: Stein and Day, 1974.

Brewer, J. I., & DeCosta, E. J. *Textbook of gynecology.* Baltimore: Williams and Wilkins, 1967.

Briffault, R. *The mothers.* New York: Macmillan, 1927.

Broca, P. Remarques sur le siège de la faculté du langage articulé, suivés d'une observation d'aphemie. *Bulletin Société Anatomie*, Paris, 1861, *6*, 330–357.

Bronfenbrenner, U. Socialization and social class through time and space. In E. E. Maccoby, T. M. Newcomb, & E. L. Hartley (Eds.), *Readings in social psychology* (3rd ed.). New York: Holt, 1958.

Bronfenbrenner, U. Some familial antecedents of responsibility and leadership in adolescents. In L. Petrullo & B. M. Bass (Eds.), *Leadership and interpersonal behavior*. New York: Holt, 1961a.

Bronfenbrenner, U. The changing American child—a speculative analysis. *Journal of Social Issues*, 1961b, *17*, 6–18.

Bronson, G. W. Fear of the unfamiliar in human infants. In H. R. Schaffer (Ed.), *The origins of human social relations*. New York: Academic Press, 1971.

Bronson, W. C. Central orientations: A study of behavior organization from childhood to adolescence. *Child Development*, 1966, 37, 125–155.

Brooks, L. Interactive effects of sex and status on self-disclosure. *Journal of Counseling Psychology*, 1974, *21*, 469–472.

Broverman, I. K., Broverman, D. M., Clarkson, F. E., Rosenkrantz, P. S., & Vogel, S. R. Sex-role stereotypes and clinical judgments of mental health. *Journal of Consulting and Clinical Psychology*, 1970, *34*, 1–7.

Broverman, I. K., Vogel, S. R., Broverman, D. M., Clarkson, F. E., & Rosenkrantz, P. S. Sex-role stereotypes: A current appraisal. *Journal of Social Issues*, 1972, *28*, 2, 59–78.

Brownmiller, S. *Against our will*. New York: Simon & Schuster, 1975.

Broyard, A. Lifting the female curse. A review of Delaney, J., Lupton, M. J., & Toth, E., *The curse: A cultural history of menstruation*, Dulton, 1976. New York Times, September 21, 1976.

Bryden, M. P., Allard, F., & Scarpino, F. The development of language lateralization and speech perception. Unpublished manuscript, University of Waterloo, 1973.

Buck, R. Nonverbal communication of affect in children. *Journal of Personality and Social Psychology*, 1975, *31*, 644–653.

Buck, R., Miller, R. E., & Caul, W. F. Sex, personality, and physiological variables in the communication of affect via facial expression. *Journal of Personality and Social Psychology*, 1974, *30*, 587–596.

Burns, G. W. *The science of genetics: An introduction to heredity*. New York: Macmillan, 1972.

Byrne, D. *An introduction to personality, research, theory, and applications* (2nd ed.). Englewood Cliffs, N.J.: Prentice-Hall, 1974.

Byrne, D., & Lamberth, J. The effect of erotic stimuli on sex arousal, evaluative responses, and subsequent behavior. In *Technical report of the Commission on Obscenity and Pornography* (Vol. VIII). Washington, D.C.: U.S. Government Printing Office, 1971, 41–67.

Cameron, J., Livson, N., & Bayley, N. Infant vocalizations and their relationship to mature intelligence. *Science*, 1967, *157*, 331–333.

Campbell, A. The American way of mating: Marriage sí, children only maybe. *Psychology Today*, May 1975, pp. 37–40; 42–43.

Campbell, J. (Ed.). *The portable Jung*. New York: Viking, 1971.

Canady, H. G. Sex differences in intelligence among Negro college freshmen. *Journal of Applied Psychology*, 1938, *22*, 437–439.

Caplan, G. Psychological aspects of maternity care. *American Journal of Public Health*, 1957, *47*, 25.

Carlson, J. S., Cook, S. W., & Stromberg, E. L. Sex differences in conversation. *Journal of Applied Psychology*, 1936, *20*, 727–735.

Carlson, R. Stability and change in the adolescent's self-image. *Child Development*, 1965, *36*, 659–666.

Carlson, R. Where is the person in personality research? *Psychological Bulletin*, 1971a, 75, 203–219.

Carlson, R. Sex differences in ego functioning. *Journal of Consulting and Clinical Psychology*, 1971b, 37, 267–277.

Carnegie Commission on Higher Education. *Opportunities for women in higher education*. New York: McGraw-Hill, 1973.

Carter, C. O. *Human heredity*. Baltimore: Penguin Books, 1962.

Certner, B. C. Exchange of self-disclosures in same-sexed groups of strangers. *Journal of Consulting and Clinical Psychology*, 1973, *40*, 292–297.

Chadwick, M. The psychological effects of menstruation. *Nervous and Mental Disease Monograph Series*, No. 56. New York: Nervous and Mental Disease Publishing Company, 1932.

Chaikin, A. I., & Derlega, V. J. Variables affecting the appropriateness of self-disclosure. *Journal of Consulting and Clinical Psychology*, 1974, *42*, 588–593.

Chesler, P. *Women & madness*. New York: Avon, 1972.

Child, I., Potter, E., & Levine, E. Children's textbooks and personality development. An explanation in *The Social Psychology of Education Psychology Monographs*, 1946, *60*, 1–54.

Chodorow, N. Being and doing: A cross-cultural examination of the socialization of males and females. In V. Gornick & B. K. Moran (Eds.), *Woman in sexist society: Studies in power and powerlessness*. New York: Signet, 1972.

Chodorow, N. Family structure and feminine personality. In M. Z. Rosaldo & L. Lamphere (Eds.), *Woman, culture, and society*. Stanford, Cal.: Stanford University Press, 1974.

Coates, B., Anderson, E. P., & Hartup, W. W. The stability of attachment behaviors in the human infant. *Developmental Psychology*, 1972, *6*, 231–237.

Cohen, L. B., & Gelber, E. R. Infant visual memory. In L. B. Cohen & P. Salapatek (Eds.), *Infant perception: From sensation to cognition*, Vol. I: *Basic Visual Processes*. New York: Academic Press, 1975.

Cohen, L. J., & Campos, J. J. Father, mother, and stranger as elicitors of attachment behaviors in infancy. *Developmental Psychology*, 1974, *10*, 146–154.

Collard, E. D. *Achievement motive in the four-year-old child and its relationship to achievement expectancies of the mother*. Unpublished doctoral dissertation, University of Michigan, 1964.

Colley, T. The nature and origins of psychological sexual identity. *Psychological Review*, 1959, *66*, 165–177.

Conger, J. J. *Adolescence and youth: Psychological development in a changing world*. New York: Harper & Row, 1973.

Coniglio, L. P., Paup, D. C., & Clemens, L. G. Hormonal factors controlling the development of sexual behaviors in the male golden hamster. *Physiology and Behavior*, 1973, *10*, 1087–1094.

Constantinople, A. An Eriksonian measure of personality development in college students. *Developmental Psychology*, 1969, *1*, 357–372.

Constantinople, A. Masculinity-femininity: An exception to a famous dictum? *Psychological Bulletin*, 1973, *80*, 389–407.

Cook, A. H. *The working mother: A survey of problems and programs in nine countries*. Ithaca, N.Y.: New York State School of Industrial and Labor Relations, 1975.

Cooke, W. *American Journal of Obstetrics and Gynecology*, 1945, *49*, 457.

Coppen, A., & Kessel, N. Menstruation and personality. *British Journal of Psychiatry*, 1963, *109*, 711–721.

Corkin, S. Tactually-guided maze learning in man: Effects of unilateral cortical excisions and bilateral hippocampal lesions. *Neuropsychologia*, 1965, *3*, 339–351.

Cosentino, F., & Heilbrun, A. B. Anxiety correlates of sex-role identity in college students. *Psychological Reports*, 1964, *14*, 729–730.

Cozby, P. C. Self-disclosure: A literature review. *Psychological Bulletin*, 1973, 79, 73–91.

Crandall, V. C., & Battle, E. S. The antecedents and adult correlates of academic and intellectual achievement effort. In J. P. Hill (Ed.), *Minnesota Symposia on Child Psychology* (Vol. 4). Minneapolis: University of Minnesota Press, 1970.

Critchley, M. *Developmental dyslexia*. London: Heinemann, 1964.

Cross, K. P. College women: A research description. *Journal of the National Association of Women Deans and Counselors*, 1968, *31*, 12–21.

Crowley, J. E., Levitin, T. E., & Quinn, R. P. Seven deadly half truths about women. *Psychology Today*, March 1973, pp. 94–96.

Dahlstrom, E. (Ed.). *The changing roles of men and women*. Boston: Beacon Press, 1971.

Dalton, K. *The premenstrual syndrome*. Springfield, Ill.: Charles C. Thomas, 1964.

Dalton, K. The influence of mother's menstruation on her child. *Proceedings of the Royal Society of Medicine*, 1966, *59*, 1014.

Davidson, N. L. *Pacification in infants as a function of the agent and preference for tactile stimulation*. Unpublished doctoral dissertation, Michigan State University, 1973.

Davis, J. A. *Great aspirations*. Chicago: Aldine Press, 1964.

Davis, J. A. *Undergraduate career decisions*. Chicago: Aldine Press, 1965.

Deaux, K., & Emswiller, T. Explanations of successful performance on sex-linked tasks: What's skill for the male is luck for the female. *Journal of Personality and Social Psychology*, 1974, 29, 80–85.

Deaux, K., White, L., & Farris, E. Skill versus luck: Field and laboratory studies of male and female preferences. *Journal of Personality and Social Psychology*, 1975, 32, 629–636.

de Charms, R. *Personal causation: The internal affective determinants of behavior*. New York: Academic Press, 1968.

Deckard, B. S. *The women's movement: Political, socio-*

economic, and psychological issues. New York: Harper & Row, 1975.

Dellas, M., & Gaier, E. L. Identification of creativity: The individual. *Psychological Bulletin,* 1970, *73,* 55–73.

Denny, M. R., & Ratner, S. C. *Comparative psychology* (Rev. ed.). Homewood, Ill.: Dorsey, 1970.

DeRopp, R. S. *Sex energy.* New York: Delacorte Press, 1969.

Devereux, G. Institutionalized homosexuality of the Mohave Indians. *Human Biology,* 1937, *9,* 498–527.

Dion, K. K. Children's physical attractiveness and sex as determinants of adult punitiveness. *Developmental Psychology,* 1974, *10,* 772–778.

Donelson, E. *Personality: A scientific approach.* New York: Appleton-Century-Crofts & Goodyear Publishing Co., 1973.

Donelson, E. *Sex differences in developmental perspective.* Programmed learning aid. Homewood, Ill.: Learning Systems Company, 1975.

Doran, E. W. A study of vocabularies. *Pedagogical Seminary,* 1907, *14,* 401–438.

Douvan, E. New sources of conflict in females at adolescence and early adulthood. In J. M. Bardwick, E. Douvan, M. S. Horner, & D. Gutmann. *Feminine personality and conflict.* Belmont, Cal.: Brooks/Cole, 1970.

Douvan, E., & Adelson, J. *The adolescent experience.* New York: Wiley, 1966.

Douvan, E., & Gold, M. Modal patterns in American adolescence. In L. W. Hoffman and M. W. Hoffman (Eds.), *Review of child development research* (Vol. 2). New York: Russell Sage Foundation, 1966.

Duvall, E. M. Implications for education through the family life cycle. *Marriage and Family Living,* 1958, *20,* 334–342.

Dweck, C. S., & Gilliard, D. Expectancy statements as determinants of reactions to failure: Sex differences in persistence and expectancy change. *Journal of Personality and Social Psychology,* 1975, *32,* 1077–1084.

Dweck, C. S., & Reppucci, N. D. Learned helplessness and reinforcement responsibility in children. *Journal of Personality and Social Psychology,* 1973, *25,* 109–116.

Dymond, R. F., Hughes, A. S., & Raabe, V. L. Measureable changes in empathy with age. *Journal of Consulting Psychology,* 1952, *16,* 202–206.

Eagleson, H. Periodic changes in blood pressure, muscular coordination, and mental efficiency in women. *Comparative Psychology Monographs,* 1927, *4,* 1–65.

Eagly, A. H., & Whitehead, G. I. Effect of choice on receptivity to favorable and unfavorable evaluations of oneself. *Journal of Personality and Social Psychology,* 1972, *22,* 223–230.

Ehrhardt, A. A., & Baker, S. Fetal androgens, human central nervous system differentiation, and behavior sex differences. In R. Friedman, R. Richart, & R. Wiele (Eds.), *Sex differences in behavior.* New York: Wiley, 1974.

Ehrhardt, A. A., & Money, J. Progestin-induced hermaphroditism: IQ and psychosexual identity in a study of ten girls. *Journal of Sex Research,* 1967, *3,* 83–100.

Eibl-Eibesfeldt, I., [*Ethology: The biology of behavior*] (E. Klinghammer, trans.). New York: Holt, Rinehart & Winston, 1970.

Eisenberg, L. The epidemiology of reading retardation and a program for preventative intervention. In J. Money (Ed.), *The disabled reader: Education of the dyslexic child.* Baltimore: Johns Hopkins Press, 1966, 3–20.

Eisenberg, L., Berlin, C. I., Dill, A., & Frank, S. Class and race effects on the intelligibility of monosyllables. *Child Development,* 1968, *39,* 1077–1089.

Elkind, D. *Children and adolescents: Interpretive essays on Jean Piaget.* New York: Oxford University Press, 1970.

Emerson, R. W. *Friendship.* Boston: Houghton Mifflin, 1925.

Emmerich, W. Variations in the parent role as a function of the parent's sex and the child's sex and age. *Merrill-Palmer Quarterly,* 1962, *8,* 3–11.

Emmerich, W. Socialization and sex-role development. In P. B. Baltes & K. W. Schaie (Eds.), *Life-span developmental psychology: Personality and socialization.* New York: Academic Press, 1973.

Entus, A. K. Hemispheric asymmetry in processing of dichotically presented speech and nonspeech sounds by infants. In L. J. Harris (Chair), *Functional specialization of the cerebral hemispheres in infants and children: New experimental and clinical evidence.* Symposium presented at the meeting of the Society for Research in Child Development, Denver, April, 1975.

Epstein, C. F. *Woman's place.* Berkeley and Los Angeles: University of California Press, 1971.

Erikson, E. H. *Childhood and society* (2nd ed.). New York: Norton, 1963.

Etaugh, C., & Brown, B. Perceiving the causes of success and failure of male and female performers. *Developmental Psychology*, 1975, *11*, 103.

Etaugh, C., Collins, G., & Gerson, A. Reinforcement of sex-typed behaviors of two-year-old children in a nursery school setting. *Developmental Psychology*, 1975, *11*, 255.

Fabre, J. H. *Social life in the insect world*. New York: Century, 1914.

Fagot, B. I. Sex-related stereotyping of toddlers' behaviors. *Developmental Psychology*, 1973, *9*, 429.

Fagot, B. I. Sex differences in toddlers' behavior and parental reaction. *Developmental Psychology*, 1974, *10*, 554–558.

Fallaci, O. Why I never married. *Ms.*, December 1974, pp. 56–57.

Farberow, N. L., & Reynolds, D. K. Dyadic crisis suicides in mental hospital patients. *Journal of Abnormal Psychology*, 1971, *78*, 77–85.

Feather, N. T. Attribution of responsibility and valence of success and failure in relation to initial confidence and task performance. *Journal of Personality and Social Psychology*, 1969, *13*, 129–144.

Feather, N. T. Positive and negative reactions to male and female success and failure in relation to the perceived status and sex-typed appropriateness of occupations. *Journal of Personality and Social Psychology*, 1975, *31*, 536–548.

Fein, G., Johnson, D., Kosson, N., Stork, L., & Wasserman, L. Sex stereotypes and preferences in the toy choices of 20-month-old boys and girls. *Developmental Psychology*, 1975, *11*, 527–528.

Ferber, M. A., & Huber, J. A. Sex of student and instructor: A study of student bias. *American Journal of Sociology*, 1975, *80*, 949–963.

Ferguson, L. R. *Personality development*. Belmont, Cal.: Brooks/Cole, 1970.

Fidell, L. S. Empirical verification of sex discrimination in hiring practices in psychology. *American Psychologist*, 1970, *25*, 1094–1097.

Fiebert, M. S., & Fiebert, P. S. A conceptual guide to friendship formation. *Perceptual and Motor Skills*, 1969, *28*, 383–390.

Firestone, S. *The dialectic of sex: The case for feminist revolution*. New York: Bantam, 1971.

Fisher, M. S. Language patterns of preschool children. *Child Development Monographs*, 1934, No. 15.

Fisichelli, V. C., & Karelitz, S. The cry latencies of normal infants and those with brain damage. *Journal of Pediatrics*, 1963, *62*, 724–734.

Fitzgerald, H. E., & Brackbill, Y. Classical conditioning during infancy: Development and constraints. *Psychological Bulletin*, 1976, *83*, 353–376.

Fitzgerald, H. E., McKinney, J. P., & Strommen, E. *Developmental psychology: The infant and young child*. Homewood, Ill.: The Dorsey Press, in press.

Flavell, J. H., Botkin, P. T., Fry, C. L., Loright, J. W., & Jarvis, P. E. *The development of role-taking and communication skills in children*. New York: Wiley, 1968.

Flory, C. D. Sex differences in skeletal development. *Child Development*, 1935, *6*, 205–212.

Fogarty, M. P., Rapoport, R., & Rapoport, R. N. *Sex, career, and family*. Beverly Hills, Cal.: Sage Publications, 1971.

Folger, J. K., Astin, H. S., & Bayer, A. E. *Human resources and higher education*. New York: Russell Sage Foundation, 1969.

Ford, C. S. *A comparative study of human reproduction*. New Haven: Yale University Press, 1945.

Ford, C. S., & Beach, F. A. *Patterns of sexual behavior*. New York: Harper, 1951; and (2nd ed.) 1970.

Franks, V., & Burtle, V. (Eds.). *Women in therapy: New psychotherapies for a changing society*. New York: Brunner/Mazel, 1974.

Freed, S. The treatment of premenstrual distress with special consideration of the androgens. *Journal of the American Medical Association*, 1945, *127*, 377.

Freedman, M. Homosexuals may be healthier than straights. *Psychology Today*, March 1975, pp. 28–32.

Freeman, J. *The politics of women's liberation: A case study of an emerging social movement and its relation to the policy process*. New York: McKay, 1975.

Freud, S. [*An outline of psychoanalysis*] (J. Strachey, Ed. and trans.). New York: Norton, 1963. (Originally published, 1940.)

Freud, S. [*New introductory lectures in psychoanalysis*] (J. Strachey, Ed. and trans.). New York: Norton, 1965. (Originally published, 1933.)

Freud, S. [Some psychological consequences of the anatomical distinction between the sexes] (J. Strachey, trans.). In P. Rieff (Ed.), *Sexuality and the psychology of love*. New York: Collier, 1972a. (Originally published, 1925.)

Freud, S. [Female sexuality] (J. Riviere, trans.). In P. Rieff (Ed.), *Sexuality and the psychology of love*. New York: Collier, 1972b. (Originally published, 1931.)

Friedenberg, E. *The vanishing adolescent*. New York: Dell, 1959.

Frisch, R. E., & McArthur, J. W. Menstrual cycles: Fatness as a determinant of minimum weight for height necessary for their maintenance or onset. *Science*, 1974, *185*, 949–951.

Fromm, E. *The art of loving, an enquiry into the nature of love.* New York: Harper, 1956.

Fromm-Reichmann, F. On loneliness. In D. M. Bullard (Ed.), *Psychoanalysis and psychotherapy, Selected papers.* University of Chicago Press, 1959.

Frueh, T., & McGhee, P. E. Traditional sex role development and amount of time spent watching television. *Developmental Psychology*, 1975, *11*, 109.

Gagnon, J., & Simon, W. *Sexual conduct: The social sources of human sexuality.* Chicago: Aldine, 1973.

Gall, M. D. The relationship between masculinity-femininity and manifest anxiety. *Journal of Clinical Psychology*, 1969, *25*, 294–295.

Garai, J. E. Sex differences in mental health. *Genetic Psychology Monographs*, 1970, *81*, 123–142.

Garai, J. E., & Scheinfeld, A. Sex differences in mental and behavioral traits. *Genetic Psychology Monographs*, 1968, *77*, 169–299.

Gardner, J., & Gardner, H. A note on selective imitation by a six-week-old infant. *Child Development*, 1970, *41*, 1209–1213.

Gates, A. I. Sex differences in reading ability. *Elementary School Journal*, 1961, *61*, 431–434.

Gatewood, M. C., & Weiss, A. P. Race and sex differences in newborn infants. *Journal of Genetic Psychology*, 1930, *38*, 31–49.

Gergen, K. J. *The concept of self.* New York: Holt, Rinehart & Winston, 1971.

Geschwind, N., & Levitsky, W. The organization of language and the brain. *Science*, 1970, *170*, 940–944.

Giattino, J.; & Hogan, J. G. Analysis of a father's speech to his language-learning child. *Journal of Speech and Hearing Research*, 1975, *40*, 524–537.

Giele, J. Z. Changes in the modern family: Their impact on sex roles. *American Journal of Orthopsychiatry*, 1971, *41*, 757–766.

Ginzberg, E., Berg, I. E., Brown, C. A., Herman, J. L., Yohalem, A. M., & Gorelick, S. *Life styles of educated women.* New York: Columbia University Press, 1966.

Goldberg, P. A. Are women prejudiced against women? *Transaction*, 1968, *5*, 28–30.

Goldberg, S., & Lewis, M. Play behavior in the year-old infant: Early sex differences. *Child Development*, 1969, *40*, 21–32.

Goodenough, F. L. Inter-relationships in the behavior of young children. *Child Development*, 1930, *1*, 29–47.

Gornick, V. Consciousness and raising. New York: *The New York Times Magazine*, January 10, 1971, 22–23; 77–84.

Gottschalk, L., Kaplan, S., Gleser, G., & Winget, C. Variations in magnitude of emotion: A method applied to anxiety and hostility during phases of the menstrual cycle. *Psychosomatic Medicine*, 1962, *24*, 300–311.

Gough, H. G. An interpreter's syllabus for the California Psychological Inventory. In P. McReynolds (Ed.), *Advances in psychological assessment.* Palo Alto, Cal.: Science and Behavior Books, 1968.

Graham, A. The making of a nonsexist dictionary. In B. Thorne & N. Henley (Eds.), *Language and sex: Difference and dominance.* Rowley, Mass.: Newbury House, 1975.

Gray, S. W. Masculinity-femininity in relation to anxiety and social acceptance. *Child Development*, 1957, *28*, 203–214.

Greenberg, M., & Morris, N. Engrossment: The newborn's impact upon the father. *American Journal of Orthopsychiatry*, 1974, *44*, 520–531.

Greene, R., & Dalton, K. The premenstrual syndrome. *British Medical Journal*, 1953, *1*, 1007.

Gregory, A. The menstrual cycle and its disorders in psychiatric patients. 1. *Journal of Psychosomatic Research*, 1957a, *2*, 61–79.

Gregory, A. The menstrual cycle and its disorders in psychiatric patients. 2. *Journal of Psychosomatic Research*, 1957b, *2*, 199–224.

Grossman, S. P. *A textbook of physiological psychology.* New York: Wiley, 1967.

Grusec, J. E., & Brinker, D. B., Jr. Reinforcement for imitation as a social learning determinant with implications for sex-role development. *Journal of Personality and Social Psychology*, 1972, *21*, 149–158.

Guilford, J. P. *The nature of human intelligence.* New York: McGraw-Hill, 1967.

Gullahorn, J. T., & Gullahorn, J. E. Visiting Fulbright professors as agents of cross-cultural communication. *Sociology and Social Research*, 1962, *46*, 282–293.

Gump, J. P. Sex-role attitudes and psychological well-being. *The Journal of Social Issues*, 1972, *28*, 2, 79–92.

Gurwitz, S. B., & Dodge, K. A. Adults' evaluations of a child as a function of sex of adult and sex of child. *Journal of Personality and Social Psychology*, 1975, *32*, 822–828.

Guyer, L. & Fidell, L. Publications of men and women psychologists. *American Psychologist*, 1973, *28*, 157–160.

Haan, N., Smith, M. B., & Block, J. Moral reasoning of young adults: Political-social behavior, family background, and personality correlates. *Journal of Personality and Social Psychology*, 1968, *10*, 183–201.

Hall, C. S., & Lindzey, G. *Theories of personality* (2nd ed.). New York: Wiley, 1970.

Hall, D. T. A model for coping with role conflict: The role behavior of college educated women. *Administrative Science Quarterly*, 1972, *17*, 471–486.

Halverson, L. F., Jr., & Shore, R. F. Self-disclosure and interpersonal functioning. *Journal of Consulting and Clinical Psychology*, 1969, *38*, 213–217.

Halverson, C. F., & Waldrop, M. F. Maternal behavior toward own and other preschool children: The problem of "ownness." *Child Development*, 1970, *41*, 839–845.

Hamburg, D. A., & Lunde, D. T. Sex hormones in the development of sex differences in human behavior. In E. E. Maccoby (Ed.), *The development of sex differences*. Stanford, Cal.: Stanford University Press, 1966.

Handel, G. Psychological study of whole families. *Psychological Bulletin*, 1965, *63*, 19–41.

Harford, T. C., Willis, C. H., & Deabler, H. L. Personality correlates of masculinity-femininity. *Psychological Reports*, 1967, *21*, 881–884.

Hariton, E. B. The sexual fantasies of women. In C. Tavris (Ed.), *The female experience*. Del Mar, Cal.: *Psychology Today*, 1973.

Harlow, H. Love in infant monkeys. *Scientific American*, 1959, *200*, 68–74.

Harlow, H. The heterosexual affectional system in monkeys. *American Psychologist*, 1962, *17*, 1–9.

Harms, I., & Spiker, C. Factors associated with the performance of young children on intelligence scales and tests of speech development. *The Journal of Genetic Psychology*, 1959, *94*, 3–22.

Harris, A. S. The second sex in academe. *American Association of University Professors Bulletin*, 1970, *56*, 283–295.

Harris, L. J. Neurophysiological factors in the development of spatial skills. In J. Eliot & N. J. Salkind (Eds.), *Children's spatial development*. Springfield, Ill.: Charles C. Thomas, 1975.

Harris, L. J. Sex differences in spatial ability: Possible environmental, genetic, and neurological factors. In M. Kinsbourne (Ed.), *Hemispheric asymmetries of function*. Cambridge: Cambridge University Press, in press.

Hartup, W. W. Peer interaction and social organization. In P. Mussen (Ed.), *Carmichael's manual of child psychology* (Vol. 2). New York: Wiley, 1970.

Hartup, W. W. & Coates, B. Imitation of peers as a function of reinforcement from the peer group and rewardingness of the model. *Child Development*, 1967, *38*, 1003–1016.

Hartup, W. W., Moore, S. G., & Sager, G. Avoidance of inappropriate sex-typing by young children. *Journal of Consulting Psychology*, 1963, *27*, 467–473.

Haugen, G. M. & McIntire, R. W. Comparisons of vocal imitation, tactile stimulation, and food as reinforcers for infant vocalizations. *Developmental Psychology*, 1972, *6*, 201–209.

Hawley, P. What women think men think. *Journal of Counseling Psychology*, 1971, *3*, 193–199.

Havighurst, R. J. & Breese, F. F. Relation between ability and social status in a midwestern community: III. Primary Mental Abilities. *Journal of Educational Psychology*, 1947, *38*, 241–247.

Hays, H. R. *The dangerous sex: The myth of feminine evil.* New York: Paperback Books, 1966.

Hefner, R., Rebecca, M., & Oleshansky, B. The development of sex-role transcendence. *Human Development*, 1975, *18*, 143–158.

Heilbrun, A. B., Jr. Sex role, instrumental-expressive behavior, and psychopathology in females. *Journal of Abnormal Psychology*, 1968, *73*, 131–136.

Heilbrun, A. B., Jr. & Fromme, D. K. Parental identification of late adolescents and level of adjustment: The importance of parent-model attributes, ordinal position, and sex of the child. *Journal of Genetic Psychology*, 1965, *107*, 49–59.

Heiman, J. R. The physiology of erotica: Women's sexual arousal. *Psychology Today*, April 1975, pp. 90–94.

Heiman, M. Discussion of Sherfey's paper on female sexuality. *American Psychoanalytic Association Journal*, 1968, *16*, 405–416.

Helper, M. M. Learning theory and the self-concept. *Journal of Abnormal and Social Psychology*, 1955, *51*, 184–194.

Hennig, M. *Career development for women executives.* Unpublished doctor of business administration dissertation, Harvard University, 1970.

Hermans, H. J. M., ter Laak, J. J. F., & Maes, P. C. J. M. Achievement motivation and fear of failure in family and school. *Developmental Psychology*, 1972, *6*, 520–528.

Herzberg, F., & Lapkin, M. A. A study of sex differences on the Primary Mental Abilities Test. *Educational & Psychological Measurement*, 1954, *14*, 687–689.

Hetherington, E. M. A developmental study of the effects of sex of the dominant parent on sex-role performance, identification, and imitation in children. *Journal of Personality and Social Psychology*, 1965, *2*, 188–194.

Hetherington, E. M. The effects of familial variables on sex role typing, parent-child similarity and imitation in children. In J. P. Hill (Ed.), *Minnesota symposium on child development* (Vol. 1), Minneapolis: University of Minnesota Press, 1967.

Hetherington, E. M. Effects of father absence on personality development in adolescent daughters. *Developmental Psychology*, 1972, *7*, 313–326.

Hetherington, E. M. Girls without fathers. *Psychology Today*, February 1973, pp. 46–52.

Hetherington, E. M., & Frankie, G. Effects of parental dominance, warmth, and conflict on imitation in children. *Journal of Personality and Social Psychology*, 1967, *6*, 119–125.

Hill, R., & Aldous, J. Socialization for marriage and parenthood. In Goslin, D. A. (Ed.), *Handbook of socialization theory and research*. Chicago: Rand McNally, 1969.

Hodges, L. A., & Byrne, D. Verbal dogmatism as a potentiator of intolerance. *Journal of Personality and Social Psychology*, 1972, *21*, 312–317.

Hoffman, L. W. Early childhood experiences and women's achievement motives. *Journal of Social Issues*, 1972, *28*, 2, 129–155.

Hoffman, L. W. Effects of maternal employment on the child—a review of the research. *Developmental Psychology*, 1974a, *10*, 204–228.

Hoffman, L. W. Fear of success in males and females: 1965 and 1971. *Journal of Consulting and Clinical Psychology*, 1974b, *42*, 353–358.

Hoffman, L. W., & Nye, F. I. *Working mothers*. San Francisco: Jossey-Bass, 1974.

Hoffman, M. L. Sex differences in moral internalization and values. *Journal of Personality and Social Psychology*, 1975, *32*, 720–729.

Holmes, D. S., & Jorgensen, B. W. Do personality and social psychologists study men more than women? *Representative Research in Social Psychology*, 1971, *2*, 71–76.

Holmstrom, L. L. *The two-career family*. Cambridge, Mass.: Schenkman, 1972.

Horgan, D. Sex differences in language development. Paper presented at the meeting of the Midwestern Psychological Association, Chicago, May, 1976.

Horner, M. S. Toward an understanding of achievement-related conflicts in women. *Journal of Social Issues*, 1972, *28*, 2, 157–176.

Horney, K. The flight from womanhood. *International Journal of Psychoanalysis*, 1926, *7*, 324–339.

Hoyt, D., & Kennedy, C. Interest and personality correlates of career-motivated and homemaking-motivated college women. *Journal of Counseling Psychology*, 1958, *5*, 44–48.

Hoyt, M. F. & Raven, B. H. Birth order and the 1971 Los Angeles earthquake. *Journal of Personality and Social Psychology*, 1973, *28*, 123–128.

Hubert, M. A. G. & Britton, J. H. Attitudes and practices of mothers rearing their children from birth to the age of two years. *Journal of Home Economics*, 1957, *49*, 208–223.

Hunt, M. *Sexual behavior in the 1970s*. Chicago: Playboy Press, 1974.

Hutt, C. *Males & females*. Baltimore: Penguin Books, 1972.

Hyde, J. S., Rosenberg, B. G., & Behrman, J. Tomboyism: Implications for theories of female development. Paper presented at the meeting of the Western Psychological Association, April, 1974.

Institute for Social Research. The University of Michigan. *Newsletter*, Summer 1974, pp. 3–6; 8.

Irwin, O. C., & Chen, H. P. Development of speech during infancy: Curve of phonemic types. *Journal of Experimental Psychology*, 1946, *36*, 431–436.

Iscoe, I., Williams, M., & Harvey, J. Modification of children's judgments by a simulated group technique: A normative development study. *Child Development*, 1963, *34*, 963–978.

Iscoe, I., Williams, M., & Harvey, J. Age, intelligence, and sex as variables in the conformity behavior of Negro and white children. *Child Development*, 1964, *35*, 451–460.

Israel, S. Premenstrual tension. *Journal of the American Medical Association*, 1938, *110*, 1721.

Ivey, M., & Bardwick, J. Patterns of affective fluctuations in the menstrual cycle. *Psychosomatic Medicine*, 1968, *30*, 336–345.

Jacobi, J. [*The Psychology of C. G. Jung*] (R. Manheim, trans.). New Haven: Yale University Press, 1968. (Originally published, 1942).

Jacobs, T., & Charles, E. Correlation of psychiatric symptomatology and the menstrual cycle in an outpatient population. *American Journal of Psychiatry*, 1970, *126*, 1504–1508.

Janiger, O., Riffenburgh, R., & Kersh, R. Cross cultural study of premenstrual symptoms. *Psychosomatics*, 1972, *13*, 226–235.

Janofsky, A. I. Affective self-disclosure in telephone versus face to face interviews. *Journal of Humanistic Psychology*, 1971, *11*, 93–103.

Johnson, D. D. Sex differences in reading across cultures. *Reading Research Quarterly*, 1973–74, *9*, 67–86.

Johnson, M. M. Sex role learning in the nuclear family. *Child Development*, 1963, *34*, 319–334.

Jones, S. J., & Moss, H. A. Age, state, and maternal behavior associated with infant vocalizations. *Child Development*, 1971, *42*, 1039–1051.

Jong, E. *Fear of flying*. New York: Signet, 1973.

Joreen. "Trashing"—The dark side of sisterhood. *Ms.*, April 1976, pp. 49–51; 92–98.

Jourard, S. *The transparent self*. Cincinnati: D. Van Nostrand and Reinhold, 1971.

Jung, C. G. [*Two essays on analytical psychology*] (R. F. C. Hull, trans.). Cleveland: World Publishing Co., 1956. (Originally published, 1943, 1945.)

Kagan, J. Acquisition and significance of sex-typing and sex-role identity. In M. L. Hoffman & L. W. Hoffman (Eds.), *Review of child development research* (Vol. 1). New York: Russell Sage Foundation, 1964.

Kagan, J., & Lewis, M. Studies of attention in the human infant. *Merrill-Palmer Quarterly*, 1965, *11*, 95–127.

Kagan, J., & Moss, H. A. *Birth to maturity*. New York: Wiley, 1962.

Kahn, R. L. The work module—a tonic for lunchpail lassitude. *Psychology Today*, February 1973, pp. 35–39; 94–95.

Kashket, E. V., Robbins, M. L., Leive, L., & Huang, A. S. Status of women microbiologists. *Science*, 1974, *183*, 488–494.

Katz, B. J. The IUD: Out of sight, out of mind? *Ms.*, July 1975, pp. 108–115.

Kilham, W., & Mann, L. Level of destructive obedience as a function of transmitter and executant roles in the Milgram obedience paradigm. *Journal of Personality and Social Psychology*, 1974, *29*, 696–702.

Kimmel, H., & Kimmel, E. Sex differences in adaptation of the GSR under repeated applications of a visual stimulus. *Journal of Experimental Psychology*, 1965, *70*, 536–537.

Kimura, D. Cerebral dominance and the perception of verbal stimuli. *Canadian Journal of Psychology*, 1961, *15*, 156–165.

Kimura, D. Speech lateralization in young children as determined by an auditory test. *Journal of Comparative and Physiological Psychology*, 1963, *56*, 899–902.

Kimura, D. Functional asymmetry of the brain in dichotic listening. *Cortex*, 1967, *3*, 163–178.

Kinsey, A. C., Pomeroy, W. B., Martin, C. E., & Gebhard, P. H. *Sexual behavior in the human female*. Philadelphia: Saunders, 1953.

Kirkpatrick, J. J. *Political women*. New York: Basic Books, 1975.

Klinger, E., & McNelly, F. W., Jr. Fantasy need achievement and performance. *Psychological Review*, 1969, *76*, 574–591.

Kluckhohn, C., & Murray, H. A. Personality formation: The determinants. In C. Kluckhohn & H. A. Murray, with the collaboration of D. M. Schneider (Eds.), *Personality in nature, society, and culture* (2nd ed.). New York: Knopf, 1964.

Koeske, R. K. Physiological, social, and situational factors in the premenstrual syndrome. Unpublished paper, 1973. Available from Dr. Randi K. Koeske, Department of Psychology, Carnegie-Mellon University, Pittsburgh, Pa. 15213.

Koeske, R. K., & Koeske, G. F. An attributional approach to moods and the menstrual cycle. *Journal of Personality and Social Psychology*, 1975, *31*, 473–478.

Kogan, N. Creativity and cognitive style: A life-span perspective. In P. B. Baltes, and K. W. Schaie (Eds.) *Life-span developmental psychology: Personality and socialization*. New York: Academic Press, 1973.

Kohlberg, L. A cognitive developmental analysis of children's sex-role concepts and attitudes. In E. E. Maccoby (Ed.), *The development of sex differences*. Stanford, Cal.: Stanford University Press, 1966.

Kolata, G. B. !Kung hunter-gatherers: Feminism, diet, and birth control. *Science*, 1974, *185*, 932–934.

Komarovsky, M. Cultural contradictions and sex roles: The masculine case. *American Journal of Sociology*, 1973, *78*, 873–884.

Komisar, L. The image of woman in advertising. In V. Gornick & B. K. Moran (Eds.), *Woman in sexist society: Studies in power and powerlessness*. New York: Signet Books, 1972.

Korner, A. F. The effect of the infants' state, level of arousal, sex, and ontogenetic stage on the caregiver. In M. Lewis & L. A. Rosenblum (Eds.), *The effect of the infant on its caregiver*. New York: Wiley-Interscience, 1974.

Kovach, J. K., & Hess, E. H. Imprinting effects of painful stimulation upon the following response. *Journal of Comparative and Physiological Psychology,* 1963, *56,* 461–464.

Kramer, Y., & Rosenblum, L. A. Responses to "frustration" in one-year-old infants. *Psychosomatic Medicine,* 1970, *32,* 243–257.

Krekorian, C. O., & Dunham, D. W. Parental egg care in the spraying characid, *Copeina arnoldi Regan:* Role of the spawning surface. *Animal Behaviour,* 1972, *20,* 356–360.

Kundsin, R. B. *Women and success.* New York: William Morrow & Co., 1974.

Kwitney, Z. In, Living without them. *Ms.,* October 1975, pp. 68–71.

Landers, A. *A longitudinal investigation of clinical concomitants of the menstrual cycle.* Unpublished doctoral dissertation, Michigan State University, 1972.

Landis, M. H., & Burtt, H. E. A study of conversations. *Journal of Comparative Psychology,* 1924, *4,* 81–89.

Landy, F., Rosenberg, B. G., & Sutton-Smith, B. The effects of limited father absence on cognitive development. *Child Development,* 1969, *40,* 941–944.

Lansdell, H. The use of factor scores from the Wechsler-Bellevue Scale of Intelligence in assessing patients with temporal lobe removals. *Cortex,* 1968a, *4,* 257–268.

Lansdell, H. Effect of extent of temporal lobe ablations on two lateralized deficits. *Physiology and Behavior,* 1968b, *3,* 271–273.

L'Armand, K., & Pepitone, A. Helping to reward another person: A cross-cultural analysis. *Journal of Personality and Social Psychology,* 1975, *31,* 189–198.

Lehman, H. C. *Age and achievement.* Princeton, N.J.: Princeton University Press, 1953.

Leonard, C. V. Depression and suicidality. *Journal of Consulting and Clinical Psychology,* 1974, *42,* 98–104.

Lepp. I. *The ways of friendship: A psychological exploration of man's most valuable relationship.* New York: Macmillan, 1966.

Lerner, L., & Weiss, R. L. Role of value of reward and model affective response in vicarious reinforcement. *Journal of Personality and Social Psychology,* 1972, *21,* 93–100.

Levine, A., & Crumrine, J. Women and the fear of success: A problem in replication. *American Journal of Sociology,* 1975, *80,* 964–974.

Levine, J., Fishman, C., & Kagan, J. *Sex of child and social class as determinants of maternal behavior.* Paper presented at the meeting of the Society for Research in Child Development, New York, March 1967.

Levitin, T. E., Quinn, R. P., & Staines, G. L. A woman is 58% of a man. *Psychology Today,* March 1973, pp. 89–92.

Levy, D. M., & Tulchin, S. H. The resistant behavior of infants and children. II. *Journal of Experimental Psychology,* 1925, *8,* 209–224.

Levy-Agresti, J., & Sperry, R. W. Differential perceptual capacities in major and minor hemispheres. *Proceedings of the National Academy of Science,* 1968, *61,* 1151.

Lewis, C. S. *The four loves.* New York: Harcourt, Brace & Jovanovich, 1960.

Lewis, M. Infants' responses to facial stimuli during the first year of life. *Developmental Psychology,* 1969, *1,* 75–86.

Lewis, M. State as an infant-environment interaction: An analysis of mother-infant interaction as a function of sex. *Merrill-Palmer Quarterly,* 1972, *18,* 95–121.

Likert, R. *The human organization: Its management and value.* New York: McGraw-Hill, 1967.

Linton, S. Woman the gatherer: Male bias in anthropology. In S. E. Jacobs (Ed.), *Women in perspective: A guide for cross-cultural studies.* Urbana: University of Illinois, Department of Urban and Regional Planning, 1973.

Lipman-Blumen, J. How ideology shapes women's lives. *Scientific American,* 1972, *226,* 34–42.

Lipsitt, P. D., & Strodtbeck, F. L. Defensiveness in decision making as a function of sex-role identification. *Journal of Personality and Social Psychology,* 1967, *6,* 10–15.

Littlefield, R. P. Self-disclosure among some Negro, white, and Mexican-American adolescents. *Journal of Counseling Psychology,* 1974, *21,* 133–136.

Livesay, T. M. Sex differences in performance on the American Council Psychological Examination. *Journal of Educational Psychology,* 1937, *28,* 694–702.

Lockheed, M. E. Female motive to avoid success: A psychological barrier or a response to deviancy? *Sex Roles,* 1975, *1,* 41–50.

Lopate, C. *Women in medicine.* Baltimore: Johns Hopkins Press, 1968.

Lorenz, K. *King Solomon's ring.* New York: Cromwell, 1952.

Lott, A. J., & Lott, B. E. Group cohesiveness as interpersonal attraction: A review of relationships with antecedent and consequent variables. *Psychological Bulletin*, 1965, *64*, 259–309.

Luce, G. G. *Biological rhythms in human and animal physiology*. New York: Dover, 1971.

Lynd, H. M. *On shame and the search for identity*. New York: Science Editions, 1961.

Lynn, D. B. Sex differences in masculine and feminine identification. *Psychological Review*, 1959, *66*, 126–135.

Lynn, D. B. *The father: His role in child development*. Monterey, Cal.: Brooks/Cole, 1974.

Maccoby, E. E. Sex differences in intellectual functioning. In E. E. Maccoby (Ed.), *The development of sex differences*. Stanford, Cal.: Stanford University Press, 1966.

Maccoby, E. E., & Feldman, S. S. Mother attachment and stranger reactions in the third year of life. *Monographs of the Society for Research in Child Development*, 1971, 37 (1, Serial No. 146).

Maccoby, E. E., & Jacklin, C. N. *Sex differences and their implications for sex roles*. Paper presented at the meetings of the American Psychological Association, Washington, D. C., August, 1971.

Maccoby, E. E., & Jacklin, C. N. *The psychology of sex differences*. Stanford, Cal.: Stanford University Press, 1974.

Maccoby, E. E., & Masters, J. C. Attachment and dependency. In P. H. Mussen (Ed.), *Carmichael's manual of child psychology* (Vol. 2). New York: Wiley, 1970.

Maccoby, E. E., & Wilson, W. C. Identification and observational learning from films. *Journal of Abnormal and Social Psychology*, 1957, *55*, 76–87.

MacCracken, H. N. *Hickory limb*. New York: Scribner's, 1950.

Mandel, W. M. Soviet women in the work force and professions. *American Behavioral Scientist*, 1971, *15*, 255–280.

Margolin, G., & Patterson, G. R. Differential consequences provided by mothers and fathers for their sons and daughters. *Developmental Psychology*, 1975, *11*, 537–538.

Masters, W. H., & Johnson, V. G. *Human sexual response*. Boston: Little, Brown, 1966.

Matheny, A. P., Jr. *Heredity and environmental components of competency of children's articulation*. Paper presented at the meeting of the Society for Research in Child Development, Philadelphia, 1973.

Matthews, E., & Tiedeman, D. V. Attitudes toward career and marriage and the development of life style in young women. *Journal of Counseling Psychology*, 1964, *11*, 375–383.

Mausner, J. S., & Steppacher, R. C. Suicide in professionals: A study of male and female psychologists. *American Journal of Epidemiology*, 1973, *98*, 436–445.

McCance, R., Luff, M., & Widdowson, E. Physical and emotional periodicity in women. *Journal of Hygiene*, 1937, *37*, 571.

McCandless, B. R. *Children, behavior and development* (2nd ed.). New York: Holt, Rinehart & Winston, 1967.

McCandless, B. R. *Adolescents: Behavior and development*. Hinsdale, Ill.: Dryden Press, 1970.

McCarthy, D. The language development of the preschool child. *Institute of Child Welfare Monograph Series No. 4*. Minneapolis: University of Minnesota Press, 1930.

McCarthy, J. J., & Kirk, S. A. *The construction, standardization, and statistical characteristics of the Illinois Test of Psycholinguistic Abilities*. Urbana: University of Illinois Press, 1963.

McCary, J. L. *Human sexuality*. Princeton, N. J.: Van Nostrand, 1967.

McClelland, D. C., Atkinson, J. W., Clark, R. A., & Lowell, E. L. *The achievement motive*. New York: Appleton-Century-Crofts, 1953.

McClintock, M. K. Menstrual synchrony and suppression. *Nature*, 1971, *229*, 244–245.

McGinnis, M. *Single: The woman's view*. Old Tappan, N. J.: Fleming H. Revell Co., 1974.

McGlone, J., & Kertesz, A. Sex differences in cerebral processing of visuospatial tasks. *Cortex*, 1973, *9*, 313–320.

McGregor, D. *The professional manager*. New York: McGraw-Hill, 1967.

McGrew, W. C. *An ethological study of children's behavior*. New York: Academic Press, 1972.

McGuire, W. J. The nature of attitudes and attitude change. In G. Lindzey & E. Aronson (Eds.), *The handbook of social psychology* (2nd ed., Vol. 3). Reading, Mass.: Addison-Wesley, 1969.

McKee, J. P., & Sherriffs, A. C. The differential evaluation of males and females. *Journal of Personality*, 1957, *25*, 356–371.

McKee, J. P., & Sherriffs, A. C. Men's and women's beliefs, ideals, and self-concepts. *American Journal of Sociology*, 1959, *64*, 356–363.

McKinney, J. P. The development of choice stability in children and adolescents. *Journal of Genetic Psychology*, 1968, *113*, 79–83.

Mead, C. D. The age of walking and talking in relation to general intelligence. *Pedagogical Seminary*, 1913, *20*, 460–484.

Mead, M. *Sex and temperament in three primitive societies.* New York: Dell, 1963. (Originally published, 1935.)

Mead, M. *Blackberry winter: My earlier years.* New York: Simon & Schuster, 1972.

Messer, S. B., & Lewis, M. Social class and sex differences in the attachment and play behavior of the year-old infant. *Merrill-Palmer Quarterly*, 1972, *18*, 295–306.

Michelson, K., Vuorenkoski, V., Partanen, T., Vallane, E., & Wasz-Hoeckert, O. [*Identification of the baby's preverbal communication*] (Trans. Division of Research Science, NIMH). *Finsk Lakaresellsk Handl*, 1965, *10S*, 43–47.

Miller, A. D., Margolin, J. B., & Yolles, S. F. Epidemiology of reading disabilities. *American Journal of Public Health and the Nation's Health*, 1957, *47*, 1250–1256.

Miller, M. M. Television and sex-typing in children: A review of theory and research. Unpublished paper, 1976. Available from M. M. Miller, Department of Communication, Michigan State University, East Lansing, Mich. 48824.

Miller, M. M., & Reeves, B. *Children's occupational sex role stereotypes: The linkage between television content and perception.* Paper presented at the meeting of the International Communication Association, Chicago, March, 1975.

Miller, S. M. Effects of maternal employment on sex role perception, interests, and self-esteem in kindergarten girls. *Developmental Psychology*, 1975, *11*, 405–406.

Millett, K. *Sexual politics.* New York: Doubleday, 1970.

Milner, B. Visually-guided maze learning in man: Effects of bilateral hippocampal, bilateral frontal, and unilateral cerebral lesions. *Neuropsychologia*, 1965, *3*, 317–338.

Minuchin, P., Biber, B., Shapiro, E., & Zimiles, H. *The psychological impact of school experience: A comparative study of nine-year-old children in contrasting schools.* New York: Basic Books, 1969.

Mischel, W. Sex-typing and socialization. In P. Mussen (Ed.), *Carmichael's manual of child psychology* (Vol. 2). New York: Wiley, 1970.

Mitchell, E. Interest profiles of university students. *The Vocational Guidance Quarterly*, 1957, *5*, 95–100.

Mitchell, J. *Woman's estate.* New York: Vintage Books, 1973.

Mitchell, J. *Psychoanalysis and feminism: Freud, Reich, Laing and women.* New York: Vintage, 1975.

Molfese, D. L. *Cerebral asymmetry in infants, children, and adults: Auditory evoked responses to speech and noise stimuli.* Unpublished doctoral dissertation, Pennsylvania State University, 1973.

Monahan, L., Kuhn, D., & Shaver, P. Intrapsychic versus cultural explanations of the "fear of success" motive. *Journal of Personality and Social Psychology*, 1974, *29*, 60–64.

Money, J. Components of eroticism in man: The hormones in relation to sexual morphology and sexual desire. *Journal of Nervous and Mental Disease*, 1961, *132*, 239–248.

Money, J. Sex reassignment as related to hermaphroditism and transsexualism. In R. Green & J. Money (Eds.), *Transsexualism and sex reassignment.* Baltimore: Johns Hopkins Press, 1969.

Money, J. Prenatal hormones and postnatal socialization in gender identity differentiation. In J. K. Cole & R. Dienstbier (Eds.), *Nebraska symposium on motivation* (Vol. 21). Lincoln: University of Nebraska Press, 1973.

Money, J., & Ehrhardt, A. A. *Man & woman, boy & girl.* Baltimore: Johns Hopkins Press, 1972.

Monge, R. H. Developmental trends in factors of adolescent self-concept. *Developmental Psychology*, 1973, *8*, 382–393.

Montagu, J. Habituation of the psychogalvanic reflex during serial tests. *Journal of Psychosomatic Research*, 1963, *7*, 199–214.

Montaigne, Michel E. de. [*Complete Essays*] (D. M. Frame, trans.). Stanford, Cal.: Stanford University Press, 1960. (Originally published, 1580, 1588.)

Mooney, J. D. Attrition among Ph.D. candidates: An analysis of a cohort of recent Woodrow Wilson fellows. *The Journal of Human Resources*, 1968, *3*, 47–62.

Moore, T. Language and intelligence: A longitudinal study of the first eight years. Part I: Patterns of development in boys and girls. *Human Development*, 1967, *10*, 88–106.

Moos, R. The development of a menstrual distress questionnaire. *Psychosomatic Medicine*, 1968a, *19*, 87–94.

Moos, R. Psychological aspects of oral contraceptives.

Archives of General Psychiatry. 1968b, *19*, 87–94.

Moos, R. Typology of mentrual cycle symptoms. *American Journal of Obstetrics and Gynecology*, 1969a, *103*, 390–402.

Moos, R. *Preliminary manual for the menstrual distress questionnaire.* Stanford, Cal.: Department of Psychiatry, Stanford University School of Medicine, 1969b.

Moos, R., Kopell, B., Melges, F., Yalom, I., Lunde, D., Clayton, R., & Hamburg, D. Variations in symptoms and mood during the menstrual cycle. *Journal of Psychosomatic Research*, 1969, *13*, 37–44.

Morley, M. E. *The development and disorders of speech in childhood.* London: Livingstone, 1957.

Morris, J. *Conundrum.* New York: Harcourt, Brace & Jovanovich, 1974.

Morton, J. H., Additon, H., Addison, R. G., Hunt, L., Sullivan, J. J. A clinical study of premenstrual tension. *American Journal of Obstetrics and Gynecology*, 1953, *65*, 1182–1191.

Moss, H. A. Sex, age, and state as determinants of mother–infant interaction. *Merrill-Palmer Quarterly*, 1967, *13*, 19–36.

Moss, H. A., & Robson, K. Maternal influences in early social visual behavior. *Child Development*, 1968, *39*, 401–408.

Mowatt, F. *Never cry wolf.* Boston: Little, Brown, 1963.

Mueller, W. J. Need structure and the projection of traits onto parents. *Journal of Personality and Social Psychology*, 1966, *3*, 63–72.

Murphy, L. B. Later outcomes of early infant and mother relationships. In L. J. Stone, H. T. Smith, & L. B. Murphy (Eds.), *The competent infant.* New York: Basic Books, 1973.

Murray, H. A. *Explorations in personality.* New York: Oxford, 1938.

Mussen, P. H. Some antecedents and consequents of masculine sex-typing in adolescent boys. *Psychological Monographs*, 1961, *75* (2, Whole No. 506).

Mussen, P. H. Long-term consequences of masculinity of interests in adolescence. *Journal of Consulting Psychology*, 1962, *26*, 435–440.

Mussen, P. H. Early sex-role development. In A. A. Goslin (Ed.), *Handbook of socialization theory and research.* Chicago: Rand McNally, 1969.

Mussen, P. H., & Rutherford, E. Parent-child relations and parental personality in relation to young children's sex-role preferences. *Child Development*, 1963, *34*, 589–607.

Nadelman, L. Sex identity in American children: Memory, knowledge, and preference tests. *Developmental Psychology*, 1974, *10*, 413–417.

National Center for Health Statistics: *Selected symptoms of psychological distress.* Washington, D. C.: U. S. Department of Health, Education and Welfare, 1970.

National Center for Health Statistics: Data from the National Health Survey. *Parent ratings of behavioral patterns of children, United States. Vital and Health Statistics.* Washington, D. C.: U. S. Department of Health, Education and Welfare Publications, 1971.

National Organization for Women, Task Force of the Central New Jersey Chapter. *Dick and Jane as victims: Sex stereotyping in children's readers.* Princeton, N. J., 1972.

National Research Council, Commission on Human Resources. *Doctoral scientists and engineers in the United States, 1973 profile.* Washington, D. C., April 1974.

Nelson, K. Structure and strategy in learning to talk. *Monographs of the Society for Research in Child Development*, 1973, *38* (2, Serial No. 149).

Nesbitt, M. *Friendship, love, and values.* ONR Technical Report, ONR Research Contract Nonr 1858 (15), Project Designation N R 150-088, and National Science Foundation Grant G-642, 1959.

Neugarten, B. L., & Gutmann, D. L. Age-sex roles and personality in middle-age: A thematic apperception study. In B. L. Neugarten (Ed.), *Middle age and aging: A reader in social psychology.* Chicago: University of Chicago Press, 1968.

Nevill, D. Experimental manipulation of dependency motivation and its effects on eye contact and measures of field dependency. *Journal of Personality and Social Psychology*, 1974, *29*, 72–79.

Newcomb, T. M. *The acquaintance process.* New York: Holt, Rinehart, & Winston, 1961.

Newton, N. Psychologic differences between breast and bottle feeding. *American Journal of Clinical Nutrition*, 1971, *29*, 993–1004.

Newton, N. Trebly sensuous woman. In C. Tavris (Ed.), *The female experience.* Del Mar, Cal.: Psychology Today, 1973.

Nicholls, J. G. Causal attributions and other achievement-related cognitions: Effects of task outcome, attainment value, and sex. *Journal of Personality and Social Psychology*, 1975, *31*, 379–389.

Nicolson, A. B., & Hanley, C. Indices of physiological maturity: Derivation and interrelationships. *Child Development*, 1953, *24*, 3–38.

Nourse, A. E. *The body*. New York: Time-Life Books, 1968.

Nowlis, V. Research with the Mood Adjective Check List. In S. Tomkins & C. Izard (Eds.), *Affect, cognition, and personality*. New York: Springer, 1965.

Oetzel, R. M. Annotated bibliography. In E. E. Maccoby (Ed.), *The development of sex differences*. Stanford, Cal.: Stanford University Press, 1966.

O'Leary, V. E. Some attitudinal barriers to occupational aspirations in women. *Psychological Bulletin*, 1974, *81*, 809–826.

Olley, G. *Mother-infant interaction during feeding*. Paper presented at the meeting of the Society for Research in Child Development, Philadelphia, March 1973.

Olson, W. C., & Koetzle, V. S. Amount and rate of talking of young children. *Journal of Experimental Education*, 1936, 5, 175–179.

Oppenheimer, V. K. The sex-labeling of jobs. In M. T. S. Mednick, S. S. Tangri, & L. W. Hoffman (Eds.), *Women and achievement*. Washington: Hemisphere Publishing Corporation, 1975.

Orcutt, F. S. Effects of oestrogen on the differentiation of some reproductive behaviours in male pigeons (*Columbia livia*). *Animal Behaviour*, 1971, *19*, 277–286.

Orne, M. T. On the social psychology of the psychological experiment. *American Psychologist*, 1962, *17*, 776–783.

Packard, V. *The sexual wilderness*. New York: McKay, 1968.

Paige, K. E. Women learn to sign the menstrual blues. *Psychology Today*, September 1973, pp. 41–46.

Palme, O. The emancipation of man. *The Journal of Social Issues*, 1972, *28*, 2, 237–246.

Parke, R. D. Family interaction in the newborn period: Some findings, some observations, and some unresolved issues. In K. Riegel & J. Meacham (Eds.), *Proceedings of the international society for the study of behavioral development*. New York: Academic Press, 1974.

Parke, R. D., O'Leary, S. E., & West, S. Mother–father–newborn interaction: Effects of maternal medication, labor, and sex of infant. *Proceedings of the 80th Annual Convention of the American Psychological Association*, 1972, 7, 85–86 (Summary).

Parkes, C. M. *Bereavement: Studies of grief in adult life*. New York: International Universities Press, 1972.

Parlee, M. B. The premenstrual syndrome. *Psychological Bulletin*, 1973, *80*, 454–465.

Pennington, V. Meprobate (Miltown) in premenstrual tension. *Journal of the American Medical Association*, 1957, *164*, 638.

Perry, D. G., & Perry, L. C. Observational learning in children: Effects of sex of model and subject's sex role behavior. *Journal of Personality and Social Psychology*, 1975, *31*, 1083–1088.

Pheterson, G. I., Kiesler, S. B., & Goldberg, P. A. Evaluation of the performance of women as a function of their sex, achievement, and personal history. *Journal of Personality and Social Psychology*, 1971, *19*, 114–118.

Piaget, J. *Play, dreams, and imitation*. New York: Norton, 1963. (Originally published, 1945.)

Pizzamiglio, L., & Cecchini, M. Development of the hemispheric dominance in children from 5 to 10 years of age and their relations with the development of cognitive processes. *Brain Research*, 1971, *31*, 363–364.

Poloma, M. M., & Garland, T. N. The myth of the egalitarian family: Familial roles and the professionally employed wife. In A. Theodore (Ed.), *The professional woman*. Cambridge, Mass.: Schenkman, 1971.

Poole, I. Genetic development of articulation of consonant sounds in speech. *Elementary English Review*, 1934, *11*, 159–161.

Prather, J. Why can't women be more like men: A summary of the sociopsychological factors hindering women's advancement in the professions. *American Behavioral Scientist*, 1971, *15*, 39–47.

Puryear, G. R., & Mednick, M. S. Black militancy, affective attachment, and the fear of success in black college women. *Journal of Consulting and Clinical Psychology*, 1974, *42*, 263–266.

Putney, S., and Putney, G. J. *The adjusted American: Normal neuroses in the individual and society*. New York: Harper & Row, 1966.

Pyle, S. I., Stuart, H. C., Cornoni, J., & Reed, R. B. Onsets, completions, and spans of the osseous stage of development in representative bone growth centers of the extremities. *Monographs of the Society for Research in Child Development*, 1961, *26* (1, Serial No. 79).

Rabin, A. I. Motivation for parenthood. *Journal of Projective Techniques and Personality Assessment*, 1965, *29*, 405–411.

Rabin, A. I. The sexes: Ideology and reality in the Israeli kibbutz. In G. H. Seward & R. C. Williamson (Eds.), *Sex roles in changing society.* New York: Random House, 1970.

Rand, L. Masculinity or femininity? Differentiating career-oriented and home-making-oriented college freshmen women. *Journal of Counseling Psychology,* 1968, *15,* 444–450.

Raush, H. L., Barry, W. A., Hertel, R. K., & Swain, M. A. *Communication, conflict and marriage,* San Francisco: Jossey-Bass, 1974.

Rebelsky, F. G., & Hanks, C. Fathers' verbal interaction with infants in the first three months of life. *Child Development,* 1971, *42,* 63–68.

Rees, L. Psychosomatic aspects of the premenstrual tension syndrome. *Journal of Mental Science,* 1953, *99,* 62.

Reuben, D. *Everything you always wanted to know about sex.* New York: McKay, 1969.

Rheingold, H. To rear a child. *American Psychologist,* 1973, *28,* 42–46.

Rheingold, H. L., & Eckerman, C. O. Fear of the stranger: A critical examination. In H. W. Reese (Ed.), *Advances in child development and behavior,* Vol. 8. New York: Academic Press, 1973.

Rheingold, H. L., Gewirtz, J. L., & Ross, H. Social conditioning of vocalization in the infant. *Journal of Comparative and Physiological Psychology,* 1959, *52,* 68–73.

Rheingold, H. L., & Keene, G. C. Transport of the human young. In B. M. Foss (Ed.), *Determinants of infant behavior III.* London: Methuen, 1965.

Rhodes, P. Sex of fetus in antepartum hemorrhage. *Lancet,* 1965, *2,* 718–719.

Richardson, H. M. Community of values as a factor in friendships of college and adult women. *Journal of Social Psychology,* 1940, *11,* 303–312.

Ricketts, A. F. A study of the behavior of young children in anger. *University of Iowa Studies in Child Welfare,* 1934, *9,* No. 5.

Robson, K. S. The role of eye-to-eye contact in maternal–infant attachment. *Journal of Child Psychology and Psychiatry,* 1968, *8,* 13–27.

Rogers, C. R. A theory of therapy, personality, and interpersonal relationships, as developed in the client-centered framework. In S. Koch (Ed.), *Psychology: A study of a science* (Vol. 3). New York: McGraw-Hill, 1959.

Rogers, C. R. *On becoming a person: A therapist's view of psychotherapy.* Boston: Houghton Mifflin, 1961.

Rogers, C. R. The actualizing tendency in relation to "motives" and to consciousness. In M. R. Jones (Ed.), *Nebraska symposium on motivation* (Vol. 11). Lincoln: University of Nebraska Press, 1963.

Rosaldo, M. Z. Woman, culture, and society: A theoretical overview. In M. Z. Rosaldo & L. Lamphere (Eds.), *Woman, culture, and society.* Stanford, Cal.: Stanford University Press, 1974.

Rosen, B. C., & D'Andrade, R. The psychosocial origins of achievement motivations. *Sociometry,* 1959, *22,* 185–218.

Rosenberg, B. G., & Sutton-Smith, B. Sibling age spacing effects on cognition. *Developmental Psychology,* 1969, *1,* 661–668.

Rosenberg, F. R., & Simmons, R. G. Sex differences in the self-concept in adolescence. *Sex Roles,* 1975, *1,* 147–159.

Rosenfeld, H. M., & Jackson, J. Temporal mediation of the similarity-attraction hypothesis. *Journal of Personality,* 1965, *33,* 649–656.

Rosenfeld, H. M., & Nauman, D. J. Effects of dogmatism on the development of informal relations among women. *Journal of Personality,* 1969, *37,* 497–511.

Rosenkrantz, P., Vogel, S., Bee, H., Broverman, I., & Broverman, D. M. Sex-role stereotypes and self-concepts in college students. *Journal of Consulting and Clinical Psychology,* 1968, *32,* 287–295.

Rosenthal, R., Archer, D., DiMatteo, M. R., Koivumaki, J. H., & Rogers, P. L. Body talk and tone of voice: The language without words. *Psychology Today,* September 1974, pp. 64–68.

Ross, D. R. *The story of the top 1% of the women at Michigan State University.* East Lansing: Michigan State University Counseling Center, 1963.

Rossi, A. S. Equality between the sexes: An immodest proposal. In R. J. Lifton (Ed.), *The woman in America.* Boston: Beacon Press, 1964.

Rossi, A. S. Barriers to the career choice of engineering, medicine, or science among American women. In J. A. Mattfeld & C. G. Van Aken (Eds.), *Women and the scientific professions.* Cambridge, Mass.: The MIT Press, 1965.

Rossi, A. S. Transition to parenthood. *Journal of Marriage and the Family,* 1968, *30,* 26–39.

Rossi, A. S. Sex equality: The beginnings of ideology. *The Humanist,* 1969, *29,* 3–6; 16.

Rossi, A. S. *Changing sex roles and family development.* Paper presented at the meeting of the American Psychological Association, Washington, D. C., September, 1971.

Rossi, A. S. Summary and prospects. In A. S. Rossi &

A. Calderwood (Eds.), *Academic women on the move*. New York: Russell Sage Foundation, 1973.

Rossi, A. S., & Calderwood, A. (Eds.). *Academic women on the move*. New York: Russell Sage Foundation, 1973.

Rothbart, M., & Maccoby, E. E. Parents' differential reactions to sons and daughters. *Journal of Personality and Social Psychology*, 1966, *4*, 237–243.

Routh, D. K. Conditioning of vocal response differentiation in infants. *Developmental Psychology*, 1969, *1*, 219–226.

Russo, N. F. Eye contact, interpersonal distance, and the equilibrium theory. *Journal of Personality and Social Psychology*, 1975, *31*, 497–502.

Salk, L. The role of the heartbeat in the relations between mother and infant. *Scientific American*, 1973, *228*, 24–29.

Sampson, E. E. The study of ordinal position: Antecedents and outcomes. In B. A. Maher (Ed.), *Progress in experimental personality research* (Vol. 2). New York: Academic Press, 1965.

Sarnoff, I. Identification with the aggressor: Some personality correlates of anti-Semitism among Jews. *Journal of Personality*, 1951, *20*, 199–218.

Saylor, H. D. The effect of maturation upon defective articulation in grades seven through twelve. *Journal of Speech and Hearing Disorders*, 1949, *14*, 202–207.

Schachter, S. *The psychology of affiliation: Experimental studies of the source of gregariousness*. Stanford, Cal.: Stanford University Press, 1959.

Schachter, S., & Singer, J. E. Cognitive, social and physiological determinants of emotional state. *Psychological Review*, 1962, *69*, 379–399.

Schaefer, E. S. A circumplex model for maternal behavior. *Journal of Abnormal and Social Psychology*, 1959, *59*, 226–235.

Schaffer, H. R., & Emerson, P. E. Patterns of response to physical contact in early human development. *Journal of Child Psychology and Psychiatry*, 1964, *5*, 1–13.

Schaller, G. B. *The year of the gorilla*. New York: Ballantine Books, 1965.

Scheinfeld, A. *Your heredity and environment*. Philadelphia: Lippincott, 1965.

Schmale, A. H., Jr. Relationship of separation and depression to disease: A report on a hospitalized medical population. *Psychosomatic Medicine*, 1958, *20*, 259–277.

Schmidt, G., Sigusch, V., & Schafer, S. Responses to reading erotic stories: Male-female differences. *Archives of Sexual Behavior*, 1973, *2*, 181–199.

Schneider, J. W., & Hacker, S. L. Sex role imagery and use of the generic "man" in introductory texts: A case in the sociology of sociology. *The American Sociologist*, 1973, *8*, 12–18.

Schnell, H. Sex differences in relation to stuttering: Part I. *Journal of Speech Disorders*, 1946, *11*, 277–298.

Schnell, H. Sex differences in relation to stuttering: Part II. *Journal of Speech Disorders*, 1947, *12*, 23–38.

Schopenhauer, A. [*On women*] (T. B. Saunders, trans.). *Essays from the Pararga and Paralpomena*. London: Allen & Unwin, 1951. (Originally published, 1851.)

Seaman, B. *Free and female*. Greenwich, Conn.: Fawcett Publications, 1972.

Seaman, B. The new pill scare. *Ms.*, June 1975, pp. 61–64; 98–102.

Sears, P. S. *The effects of classroom conditions on the strength of achievement motive and work output of elementary school children*. Washington, D. C.: U. S. Office of Education, Cooperative Research Project No. 873, 1963.

Sears, R. R. Relation of early socialization experiences to self-concepts and gender role in middle childhood. *Child Development*, 1970, *41*, 267–289.

Sears, R. R., Maccoby, E. E., & Levin, H. *Patterns of child rearing*. Evanston, Ill: Row, Peterson, 1957.

Sears, R. R., Rau, L., & Alpert, R. *Identification and child rearing*. Stanford, Cal.: Stanford University Press, 1965.

Selig, E. B. In, Living without them. *Ms.*, October 1975, pp. 68–71.

Seligman, M. E. P. On the generality of the laws of learning. *Psychological Review*, 1970, *77*, 406–418.

Sermat, V., & Smyth, M. Content analysis of verbal communication in the development of a relationship: Conditions influencing self-disclosure. *Journal of Personality and Social Psychology*, 1973, *26*, 332–346.

Seward, J., & Seward, G. The effect of repetition on reactions to electric shock: With special reference to the menstrual cycle. *Archives of Psychology*, 1934, No. 168.

Shainess, N. A reevaluation of some aspects of femininity through a study of menstruation: A preliminary report. *Comparative Psychiatry*, 1961, *2*, 20–25.

Shaw, M. C., & McCuen, J. R. The onset of academic underachievement in bright children. *Journal of Educational Psychology*, 1960, *51*, 103–108.

Sherfey, M. J. *The nature and evolution of female sexuality.* New York: Vintage, 1973. (Originally published in 1966 and 1972.)

Sherman, J. A. *On the psychology of women: A survey of empirical studies.* Springfield, Ill.: Charles C. Thomas, 1971.

Shipman, V. C. Disadvantaged children and their first school experiences. Educational Testing Service Head Start Longitudinal Study, 1971. (Cited in E. E. Maccoby & C. N. Jacklin, *The psychology of sex differences.* Stanford, Cal.: Stanford University Press, 1974.)

Should you be single? *New Woman,* September–October 1975, pp. 77–78; 80.

Sidel, R. *Women and child care in China: A firsthand report.* New York: Hill & Wang, 1972.

Silverman, J. Attention styles and the study of sex differences. In D. I. Mostofsky (Ed.), *Attention: Contemporary theory and analysis.* New York: Appleton-Century-Crofts, 1970.

Simon, R. J., Clark, S. M., & Galway, K. The woman Ph. D.: A recent profile. *Social Problems,* 1967, *15,* 221–236.

Sister Edna Mary. *The religious life.* Baltimore: Penguin Books, 1968.

Sistrunk F., & McDavid, J. W. Sex variable in conforming behavior. *Journal of Personality and Social Psychology,* 1971, *17,* 200–207.

Slater, P. E. *The pursuit of loneliness: American culture at the breaking point.* Boston: Beacon Press, 1970.

Smith, E. A. *American youth culture.* Glencoe, Ill.: Free Press, 1962.

Smith, P. K., & Connolly, K. Patterns of play and social interaction in pre-school children. In N. B. Jones (Ed.), *Ethological studies of child behavior.* London: Cambridge, 1972.

Soares, A. T., & Soares, L. M. Self-perceptions of culturally disadvantaged children. *American Educational Research Journal,* 1969, *6,* 31–45.

Sommer, A. T. The effect of group training upon the correction of articulatory defects in preschool children. *Child Development,* 1932, *3,* 91–103.

Sorenson, R. C. *Adolescent sexuality in contemporary America. Personal values and sexual behavior ages 13–19.* New York: World Publishing, 1973.

Spelke, E., Zelazo, P., Kagan, J., & Kotelchuck, M. Father interaction and separation protest. *Developmental Psychology,* 1973, *9,* 83–90.

Spence, J. T. The Thematic Apperception Test and attitudes toward achievement in women: A new look at the motive to avoid success and a new method of measurement. *Journal of Consulting and Clinical Psychology,* 1974, *42,* 427–437.

Spence, J. T., Helmreich, R., & Stapp, J. Ratings of self and peers on sex role attributes and their relation to self-esteem and conceptions of masculinity and femininity. *Journal of Personality and Social Psychology,* 1975, *32,* 29–39.

Spitz, R. A. Authority and masturbation: Some remarks on a bibliographical investigation. *The Psychoanalytic Quarterly,* 1952, *21,* 490–527.

Staines, G., Tavris, C., & Jayaratne, T. E. The queen bee syndrome. *Psychology Today,* January 1974, pp. 55–60.

Stanford Research Institute. Follow-through pupil tests, parent interviews, and teacher questionnaires. Appendix C, 1972. (Cited in E. E. Maccoby & C. N. Jacklin, *The psychology of sex differences.* Stanford, Cal.: Stanford University Press, 1974.)

Stanley, J. P. *Paradigmatic woman: The prostitute.* Paper presented at the meeting of the Linguistic Society of America, San Diego, 1973.

Stein, A. H., & Bailey, M. M. The socialization of achievement orientation in females. *Psychological Bulletin,* 1973, *80,* 345–366.

Steininger, M., & Lesser, H. Sex and generation differences and similarities in social attitudes. *Journal of Counseling Psychology,* 1974, *21,* 459–460.

Steinmann, A., & Fox, D. J. Male-female perceptions of the female role in the United States. *The Journal of Psychology,* 1966, *64,* 265–276.

Stern, A. B., *The relationship between fulfillment of interpersonal needs and orgasm in women.* Unpublished master's thesis, Michigan State University, 1975.

Stern, D. N. Mother and infant at play: The dyadic interaction involving facial, vocal, and gaze behaviors. In M. Lewis & L. A. Rosenblum (Eds.), *The effect of the infant on its caregiver.* New York: Wiley-Interscience, 1974.

Stern, W. [*Psychology of early childhood up to the sixth year of age*] (A. Barwell, trans.) London: Allen & Unwin, 1924.

Sternglanz, S. H., & Serbin, L. A. Sex role stereotyping in children's television programs. *Developmental Psychology,* 1974, *10,* 710–715.

Stevens, W. A cross-cultural study of menstrual taboos. *Genetic Psychology Monographs,* 1961, *64,* 385–416.

Stevenson, H. W. Social reinforcement of children's behavior. In L. P. Lipsitt & C. C. Spiker (Eds.),

Advances in child development and behavior (Vol. 2). New York: Academic Press, 1965.

Stoke, S. M., & West, E. D. Sex differences in conversational interests. *Journal of Social Psychology,* 1931, *2,* 120–126.

Stone, M. Olfaction. *Life Sciences Research Reports,* Stanford Research Institute, 1970, *2.*

Storr, A. *Human aggression.* New York: Atheneum, 1968.

Strainchamps, E. Our sexist language. In V. Gornick & B. K. Moran (Eds.), *Woman in sexist society: Studies in power and powerlessness.* New York: Signet, 1972.

Stuart, H. C., Pyle, S. I., Cornoni, J., & Reed, R. B. Onsets, completions, and spans of ossification in the 29 bone-growth centers of the hand and wrist. *Pediatrics,* 1962, *29,* 237–249.

Sullivan, H. S. The interpersonal theory of psychiatry. Chapters 16 and 17 in *The collected works of Harry Stack Sullivan,* M.D. New York: Norton, 1953.

Sutherland, H., & Stewart, I. A critical analysis of the premenstrual syndrome. *Lancet,* 1965, *1,* 1180–1183.

Sutton-Smith, B., & Rosenberg, B. G. *The sibling.* New York: Holt, Rinehart & Winston, 1970.

Sweeney, J. Menstrual edema: Preliminary report. *Journal of the American Medical Association,* 1934, *103,* 234.

Szalai, A. (Ed.). *The use of time.* The Hague, The Netherlands: Mouton, 1973.

Tangri, S. S. Determinants of occupational role innovation among college women. *Journal of Social Issues,* 1972, *2, 28,* 177–199.

Tannenbaum, A., Kavacic, B., Rosner, M., Vianello, M., & Wieser, G. *Hierarchy in organizations: An international comparison.* San Francisco: Jossey-Bass, 1974.

Tavris, C. Who likes women's liberation—and why: The case of the unliberated liberals. *The Journal of Social Issues,* 1973, *29, 4,* 175–198.

Taylor, M. A. Sex ratios of newborns associated with prepartum and postpartum schizophrenia. *Science,* 1969, *164,* 723–724.

Taynor, J., & Deaux, K. When women are more deserving than men: Equity, attribution, and perceived sex differences. *Journal of Personality and Social Psychology,* 1973, *28,* 360–367.

Taynor, J., & Deaux, K. Equity and perceived sex differences: Role behavior as defined by the task, the mode, and the actor. *Journal of Personality and Social Psychology,* 1975, *32,* 381–390.

Teevan, R. C., & McGhee, P. E. Childhood development of fear of failure motivation. *Journal of Personality and Social Psychology,* 1972, *21,* 345–348.

Templin, M. C. Norms on a screening test of articulation for ages three through eight. *Journal of Speech and Hearing Disorders,* 1953, *18,* 323–331.

Templin, M. C. Certain language skills in children. *Institute of Child Welfare Monograph, No. 26.* Minneapolis: University of Minnesota Press, 1957.

Terman, L. M., & associates. *Genetic studies of genius: Vol. 1.* Mental and physical traits of 1000 gifted children. Stanford, Cal.: Stanford University Press, 1925.

Thoman, E. B., Leiderman, P. H., & Olson, J. P. Neonate-mother interaction during breast-feeding. *Developmental Psychology,* 1972, *6,* 110–118.

Thomas, A., Chess, S., Birch, H. G., Herzig, M. E., & Korn, S. *Behavioral individuality in early childhood.* New York: University Press, 1963.

Thompson, C. M. *On Women: [Selected from Interpersonal Psychoanalysis]* M. R. Green (Ed.). New York: Mentor, 1971. (Originally published, 1964.)

Thompson, N. L., McCandless, B. R., & Strickland, B. B. Personal adjustment of male and female homosexuals and heterosexuals. *Journal of Abnormal Psychology,* 1971, *78,* 237–240.

Thorne, B., & Henley, N. Difference and dominance: An overview of language, gender, and society. In B. Thorne & N. Henley (Eds.), *Language and sex: Difference and dominance.* Rowley, Mass.: Newbury House, 1975.

Tiger, L. *Men in groups.* New York: Random House, 1969.

Tinbergen, N. *Social behaviour in animals.* London: Methuen, 1953.

Tomlinson-Keasey, C. Role variables: Their influence on female motivational constructs. *Journal of Counseling Psychology,* 1974, *21,* 232–237.

Torok, M. The significance of penis envy in women. In Chassequet–Smirgel, J. (Ed.), *Female sexuality: New psychoanalytic views.* Ann Arbor: University of Michigan Press, 1970.

Touhey, J. C. Effects of additional women professionals on ratings of occupational prestige and desirability. *Journal of Personality and Social Psychology,* 1974, *29,* 86–89.

Tuddenham, R. D., Brooks, J., & Milkovich, L. Mothers' reports of behavior of ten-year-olds: Relationships with sex, ethnicity, and mother's education. *Developmental Psychology,* 1974, *10,* 959–995.

Tuddenham, R. D., & Snyder, M. M. Physical growth

of California boys and girls from birth to 18 years. *University of California Publications in Child Development*, 1954, *1*, No. 2.

Turner, C. D., & Bagnara, J. T. *General endocrinology*. Philadelphia: Saunders, 1971.

Turner, R. Role theory—a series of propositions. *Encyclopedia of the Social Sciences*. New York: Macmillan and the Free Press, 1968.

Turner, R. H. Some aspects of women's ambition. *American Journal of Sociology*, 1964, *70*, 271–285.

Tyler, L. E. The development of career interests in girls. *Genetic Psychology Monograph*, 1964, *70*, 203–212.

Tyler, L. E. *The psychology of human differences*. New York: Appleton-Century-Crofts, 1965.

U'Ren, M. B. The image of woman in textbooks. In V. Gornick & B. K. Moran (Eds.), *Woman in sexist society: Studies in power and powerlessness*. New York: Signet, 1972.

U. S. Census Bureau. *1970 Census of population. Employment status and work experience.*

U. S. Census Bureau. *1970 Census of population. Occupational characteristics.*

U. S. Department of Labor, Wage and Labor Standards Administration, Women's Bureau. *Fact sheet on the earnings gap*. Washington, D. C., 1971.

U. S. Department of Labor, Wage and Labor Standards Administration, Women's Bureau. *The myth and the reality*. Washington D. C.: U. S. Government Printing Office, 1974.

Useem, R. H., & Useem, J. The job: Stresses and resources of Americans at work in The Third Culture. Paper presented at the meeting of the Society for Applied Anthropology, Albany, May 1963.

Uzgiris, I. C. Patterns of vocal and gestural imitation in infants. In F. Monks & W. Hartup (Eds.), *Proceedings of the symposium on genetic and social influences on psychological development: Methodological approaches and research results*. Basel: Karger, 1972.

Valentine, C. W. The psychology of imitation with special reference to early childhood. *British Journal of Psychology*, 1930, *21*, 105–132.

Van den Berge, H. Nuclear sexing in a population of Congolese metropolitan newborns. *Science*, 1970, *169*, 1318–1320.

Van der Lee, S., & Boot, L. M. Spontaneous pseudopregnancy in mice. *Acta Physiologica et Pharmacologica Neerlandica*, 1955, *4*, 442–444.

Van der Lee, S., & Boot, L. M. Spontaneous pseudopregnancy in mice: II. *Acta Physiologica et Pharmacologica Neerlandica*, 1956, *5*, 213–215.

van Dusen, R. A., & Sheldon, E. B. The changing status of American women: A life cycle perspective. *American Psychologist*, 1976, *31*, 106–116.

Veroff, J. Theoretical background for studying the origins of human motivational dispositions. *Merrill-Palmer Quarterly*, 1965, *11*, 1–18.

Vogel, S. R., Broverman, I. K., Broverman, D. M., Clarkson, F. E., & Rosenkrantz, P. S. Maternal employment and perception of sex roles among college students. *Developmental Psychology*, 1970, *3*, 383–391.

Vonnegut, K., Jr., *Slaughterhouse five*. New York: Dell, 1969.

Vroegh, K. Masculinity and femininity in the elementary and junior high school years. *Developmental Psychology*, 1971, *4*, 254–261.

Wada, J. A., Clark, R., & Hamm, A. Cerebral hemispheric asymmetry in humans: Cortical speech zones in 100 adult and 100 infant brains. *Archives of Neurology*, 1975, *32*, 239–246.

Walker, K., & Gauger, W. H. *The dollar value of household work*. Social sciences, consumer economics and public policy no. 5, information bulletin 60. Ithaca, N.Y.: New York State College of Human Ecology, Cornell University, June, 1973.

Walraven, M. *Mother and infant cardiac responses during breast and bottle feeding*. Unpublished doctoral dissertation, Michigan State University, 1974.

Warren, J. R. Birth order and social behavior. *Psychological Bulletin*, 1966, *65*, 38–49.

Watley, D. J. Career or marriage? A longitudinal study of able young women. National Merit Scholarship Corporation *Research Reports*, 1969, *5*, 1–16.

Watson, J. S. Operant conditioning of visual fixation in infants under visual and auditory reinforcement. *Developmental Psychology*, 1969, *1*, 508–516.

Waxler, C. Z., & Yarrow, M. R. An observational study of maternal models. *Developmental Psychology*, 1975, *11*, 485–494.

Webb, A. P. Sex-role preferences and adjustment in early adolescents. *Child Development*, 1963, *34*, 609–618.

Webster, H. Personality development during the college years: Some quantitative results. *Journal of Social Issues*, 1956, *12*, 29–43.

Weideger, P. Diaphragms: A new look at the old standby. *Ms.*, August 1975, pp. 101–104.

Weiss, E., & English, O. *Psychosomatic medicine* (3rd ed.). Philadelphia: Saunders, 1957.

Weiss, R. S. The fund of sociability. *Transaction*, 1969, *6*, 36–43.

Weizmann, F., Cohen, L. B., & Pratt, J. Novelty, familiarity and the development of infant attention. *Developmental Psychology*, 1971, *4*, 149–154.

Wendt, H. *The sex life of the animals*. New York: Simon & Schuster, 1965.

Wernicke, C. *Der aphasische Symptomencomplex*. Breslau, 1874.

Wetter, R. *Levels of self-esteem associated with four sex-role categories*. Paper presented at the meeting of the American Psychological Association, Chicago, August 1975.

White, B. L., & Watts, J. C. and associates. *Experience and environment* (Vol. 1). Englewood Cliffs, N. J.: Prentice-Hall, 1973.

White, R. W. Competence and the psychosexual stages of development. In M. R. Jones (Ed.), *Nebraska symposium on motivation* (Vol. 8). Lincoln: University of Nebraska Press, 1960.

Whiting, J. W. M., Kluckhohn, R., & Anthony, A. The function of male initiation ceremonies at puberty. In E. E. Maccoby, T. Newcomb, & E. Hartley (Eds.), *Readings in social psychology* (3rd ed.). New York: Holt, Rinehart & Winston, 1958.

Whitten, W. K. Modification of the oestrus cycle of the mouse by external stimuli associated with the male. *Journal of Endocrinology*, 1956, *13*, 399.

Whitten, W. K., Bronson, F. H., & Greenstein, J. A. Estrus-inducing pheromone of male mice: Transport by movement of air. *Science*, 1968, *161*, 584–585.

Wickler, W. [*The sexual code: The social behavior of animals and men*] (F. Garvie, trans.). Garden City, New York: Doubleday, 1972. (Originally published 1969.)

Wiggins, N., & Wiggins, J. S. A typological analysis of male preferences for female body types. *Multivariate Behavioral Research*, 1969, *4*, 89–102.

Williams, M. *Brain damage and the mind*. Harmondsworth, Middlesex: Penguin Books, 1970.

Wills, T. A., Weiss, R. L., & Patterson, G. R. A behavioral analysis of the determinants of marital satisfaction. *Journal of Consulting and Clinical Psychology*, 1974, *42*, 802–811.

Winder, C. L., & Rau, L. Parental attitudes associated with social deviance in pre-adolescent boys. *Journal of Abnormal and Social Psychology*, 1962, *64*, 418–424.

Wineman, E. Autonomic balance changes during the human menstrual cycle. *Psychophysiology*, 1971, *8*, 1–6.

Witelson, S. F., & Pallie, W. Left hemisphere specialization for language in the newborn: Neuroanatomical evidence of asymmetry. *Brain*, 1973, *96*, 641–646.

Wolff, P. H. Observations on the early development of smiling. In B. M. Foss (Ed.), *Determinants of infant behavior II*. New York: Wiley, 1963.

Wolff, P. H. The natural history of crying and other vocalizations in early infancy. In B. M. Foss (Ed.) *Determinants of infant behavior* IV. London: Methuen, 1969.

Woodruff, D. S., & Birren, J. E. Age changes and cohort differences in personality. *Developmental Psychology*, 1972, *6*, 252–259.

Woolf, V. *A room of one's own*. New York: Harcourt, Brace, 1957.

Worby, C. M. The family life cycle: An orienting concept for the family practice specialist. *Journal of Medical Education*, 1971, *46*, 198–203.

Wyer, R. S., Jr. Self-acceptance, discrepancy between parents' perceptions of their children, and goal-seeking effectiveness. *Journal of Personality and Social Psychology*, 1965, *2*, 311–316.

Wylie, R. C. The present status of self theory. In E. F. Borgatta & W. W. Lambert (Eds.), *Handbook of personality theory and research*. Chicago: Rand McNally, 1968.

Yalom, I. D. *The theory and practice of group psychotherapy*. New York: Basic Books, 1970.

Yarrow, L. J. Maternal deprivation: Toward an empirical and conceptual re-evaluation. *Psychological Bulletin*, 1961, *58*, 459–490.

Yarrow, M. R., Waxler, C. Z., & Scott, P. M. Child effects on adult behavior. *Developmental Psychology*, 1971, *5*, 300–311.

Yedinack, J. G. A study of the linguistic functioning of children with articulation and reading disabilities. *Journal of Genetic Psychology*, 1949, *74*, 23–59.

Young, F. M. An analysis of certain variables in a developmental study of language. *Genetic Psychology Monographs*, 1941, *23*, 3–141.

Young, M. L. Age and sex differences in problem solving. *Journal of Gerontology*, 1971, *26*, 330–336.

Young, W. C., Goy, R. W., & Phoenix, C. H. Hormones and sexual behavior. In J. Money (Ed.), *Sex research: New developments*. New York: Holt, Rinehart & Winston, 1965.

Zazzo, R. Le probleme de l'imitation chez le nouveau-né. *Enfance*, 1957, *10*, 135–142.

Zelnick, M., & Kantner, J. Sexuality, contraception, and pregnancy among young unwed females in the

United States. In U. S. Commission on Population Growth and the American Future, *Demographic and Social Aspects of Population Growth*, 1972.

Zigler, E., & Phillips, L. Social effectiveness of symptomatic behaviors. *Journal of Abnormal and Social Psychology*, 1960, *61*, 231–238.

Zucker, R. A., Manosevitz, M., & Lanyon, R. I. Birth order, anxiety, and affiliation during a crisis. *Journal of Personality and Social Psychology*, 1968, *8*, 354–359.

Zuckerman, M. Scales for sex experience for males and females. *Journal of Consulting and Clinical Psychology*, 1973, *41*, 27–29.

Zuckerman, M., Lipets, M. S., Koivumaki, J. H., & Rosenthal, R. Encoding and decoding nonverbal cues of emotion. *Journal of Personality and Social Psychology*, 1975, *32*, 1068–1076.

PHOTO CREDITS

AUTHOR INDEX

SUBJECT INDEX